AF669623

BEST Solution
Guaranteed •••

NCERT EXEMPLAR
Problems - Solutions

Biology 12th

Author
Nidhi Sehgal

arihant
SUCCESS AND NOTHING LESS

arihant
SUCCESS AND NOTHING LESS

ARIHANT PRAKASHAN (Series), MEERUT

All Rights Reserved

© Publisher

No part of this publication may be re-produced, stored in a retrieval system or by any means, electronic, mechanical, photocopying, recording, scanning, web or otherwise without the written permission of the publisher. Arihant has obtained all the information in this book from the sources believed to be reliable and true. However, Arihant or its editors or authors or illustrators don't take any responsibility for the absolute accuracy of any information published and the damage or loss suffered thereupon.

All disputes subject to Meerut (UP) jurisdiction only.

Administrative & Production Offices

Regd. Office

'Ramchhaya' 4577/15, Agarwal Road, Darya Ganj, New Delhi -110002
Tele: 011- 47630600, 43518550

Head Office

Kalindi, TP Nagar, Meerut (UP) - 250002
Tel: 0121-7156203, 7156204

Sales & Support Offices

Agra, Ahmedabad, Bengaluru, Bareilly, Chennai, Delhi, Guwahati, Hyderabad, Jaipur, Jhansi, Kolkata, Lucknow, Nagpur & Pune.

PRICE ₹225.00

PO No : TXT-59-T070483-4-26

Published by Arihant Publications (India) Ltd.

For further information about the books published by Arihant, log on to www.arihantbooks.com or e-mail at info@arihantbooks.com

Follow us on

PREFACE

NCERT Exemplar Problems, published by the NCERT, are designed to provide students with a diverse range of quality questions in formats such as Multiple Choice Questions, Very Short Answer Type Questions, Short Answer Type Questions, and Long Answer Type Questions, catering to varying levels of difficulty.

These problems are essential for success in school and board exams, as well as competitive exams like engineering and medical entrances. Regular practice with these problems prepares students to tackle challenging questions effectively.

This book, **NCERT Exemplar Problems-Solutions Biology 12th**, offers precise and detailed solutions to all the questions in the NCERT Exemplar Biology textbook. Each solution is complemented by explanatory notes and authentic explanations, enabling students to deepen their conceptual understanding and enhance their analytical skills.

Key features

- **Thinking Process** Provides simple steps to approach and solve the question, clearing up any confusion.
- **Concept Insight** Explains the main ideas and concepts needed to answer the questions correctly.
- **Mistake Alert!** Points out common mistakes students might make and helps them avoid these errors.

I hope this book proves to be a valuable resource, aiding students in their academic journey and leading them to great success.

Author

CONTENTS

***Note(*)** These Chapters have been deleted from latest NCERT.*

Chapter

01

Reproduction in Organisms*

Multiple Choice Questions (MCQs)

Q.1 A few statements describing certain features of reproduction are given below

I. gametic fusion takes place.
II. transfer of genetic material takes place.
III. reduction division takes place.
IV. progeny have some resemblance with parents.

Select the options that are true for both asexual and sexual reproduction from the options given below

(a) I and II (b) II and III (c) II and IV (d) I and III

Thinking Process Reproduction is a biological process in which an organism gives rise to young ones (offspring) similar to itself. It enables the continuity of the species, generation after generation.

Ans. *(c)* Statement (II) and (IV) are correct as in both types of reproduction (asexual and sexual) genetic material is transferred from the parents to their offspring, resulting in some resemblance between the offspring and their parents.

Statements (I) and (III) are incorrect because

Reduction division (meiosis) occur when a diploid body has to produce haploid gametes which is in case of sexual reproduction only.

Gametic fusion The formation of male and female gametes and their fusion to form the zygote also takes place only in the sexual reproduction.

Q.2 The term 'clone' cannot be applied to offspring formed by sexual reproduction because

(a) offspring do not possess exact copies of parental DNA
(b) DNA of only one parent is copied and passed on to the offspring
(c) offspring are formed at different times
(d) DNA of parent and offspring are completely different

Ans. *(a)* In sexual reproduction, DNA of both parents, (*i.e.*, male and female gametes) is copied and passed on to the offspring after the fusion of gametes. The offspring, thus formed do not possess exact copies of parental DNA.

Note (*) *This Chapter has been deleted from latest NCERT.*

Q.3 Asexual method of reproduction by binary fission is common to which of the following?

I. Some eukaryotes
II. All eukaryotes
III. Some prokaryotes
IV. All prokaryotes

Choose the correct options from the following.

(a) I and II
(b) II and III
(c) I and III
(d) III and IV

Ans. ***(c)*** Binary fission is common in some eukaryotes and prokaryotes. It is not universal for all eukaryotes and all prokaryotes because eukaryotes include many multicellular organisms that reproduce sexually, and not all prokaryotes reproduce by binary fission.

Q.4 A few statements with regard to sexual reproduction are given below

I. Sexual reproduction does not always require two individuals.
II. Sexual reproduction generally involves gametic fusion.
III. Meiosis never occurs during sexual reproduction.
IV. External fertilisation is a rule during sexual reproduction.

Choose the correct statements from the options below.

(a) I and IV
(b) I and II
(c) II and III
(d) I and IV

Ans. ***(b)*** Statements (I) and (II) are correct as sexual reproduction involves formation of the male and female gametes either in the same individual (*e.g., Taenia*) or by different individuals of the opposite sex (*e.g.*, rabbit).

These gametes fuse to form the zygote which develops to form the new organism. Statements (III) and (IV) are incorrect and can be corrected as Meiosis (reduction division) occurs only during sexual reproduction to produce haploid gametes. Only internal fertilisation occurs during sexual reproduction. In this type of fertilisation egg is formed inside the female body where they fuse with the male gamete.

Q.5 A multicellular, filamentous alga exhibits a type of sexual life cycle in which the meiotic division occurs after the formation of zygote. The adult filament of this alga has

(a) haploid vegetative cells and diploid gametangia
(b) diploid vegetative cells and diploid gametangia
(c) diploid vegetative cells and haploid gametangia
(d) haploid vegetative cells and haploid gametangia

Thinking Process The literary meaning of alternation of generation is one in which one generation follows the other in alternating and repeating manner.

Ans. ***(d)*** A multicellular gametophyte (gametangia), which is haploid (n) alternates with a multicellular sporophyte, which is diploid ($2n$). A mature sporophyte produces spores (haploid cells) by meiosis, a process which reduces the number of chromosomes to half, from $2n$ to n.

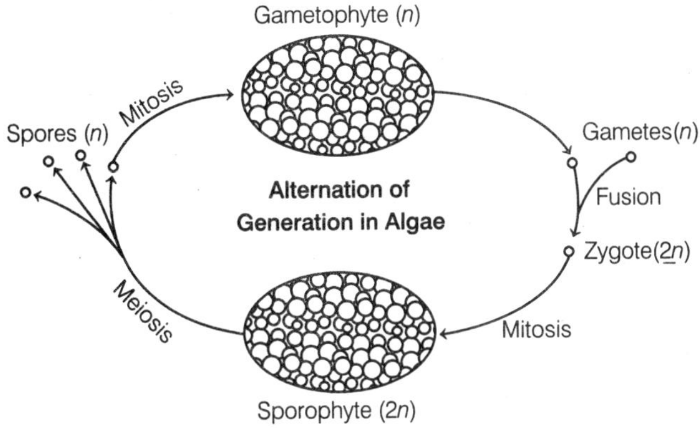

Q.6 The male gametes of rice plant have 12 chromosomes in their nucleus. The chromosome number in the female gamete, zygote and the cells of the seedling will be, respectively

(a) 12, 24, 12 (b) 24, 12, 12 (c) 12, 24, 24 (d) 24, 12, 24

- **Concept Insight** Gametes are formed from the meiotic division of meiocytes. In each gamete only one set of chromosomes gets incorporated.

Ans. ***(c)*** In female gamete the chromosome number will be same as that of the male gamete (12). A zygote is a fertilised egg or seed which means gametes from the parents have been combined (diploid) and thus, the chromosome number will be 24 ($2n$). A seedling is a young plant sporophyte developing out of a plant embryo from a seed. So, the chromosome number in the cells of the seedlings will be 24 ($2n$), which will further give rise to new diploid individual.

Q.7 Given below are a few statements related to external fertilisation.

I. The male and female gametes are formed and released simultaneously.

II. Only a few gametes are released into the medium.

III. Water is the medium in a majority of organisms exhibiting external fertilisation.

IV. Offspring formed as a result of external fertilisation have better chances of survival than those formed inside an organism.

Choose the correct statements.

(a) III and IV (b) I and III (c) II and IV (d) I and IV

Ans. ***(b)*** Statements (I) and (III) are correct as the male and female gametes are formed and released simultanously in the medium to increase chances of fertilisation. External fertilisation occurs outside the body of the organism. It takes place in most aquatic organisms, such as a majority of algae, fishes as well as amphibians. Organisms exhibiting external fertilisation release a large number of gametes in the surrounding medium. (*e.g.*, water) in order to enhance the chances of syngamy.

Statements (II) and (IV) are incorrect and can be corrected as

A large member of gametes are released into the medium to increase chances of fertilisation. The chances of survival in external fertilisation are less as they face risks from predators and other harsh conditions.

Q.8 The statements given below describe certain features that are observed in the pistil of flowers.

I. Pistil may produce more than one seed.
II. Each carpel may have more than one ovule.
III Each carpel has only one ovule.
IV. Pistil have only one carpel.

Choose the statements that are true from the options below.

(a) I and II (b) I and III
(c) II and IV (d) III and IV

Thinking Process The gynoecium represents the female reproductive part of the flower. The pistil is the free unit of gynoecium. Each pistil is constructed of one to many enrolled leaf-like structures or carpels.

Ans. ***(a)*** Statement (I) and (II) are correct as a pistil may produce more than one seed because its ovary can contain multiple ovules and each ovule can develop into a seed after fertilisation. The swollen part of the pistil is ovary which contains an angiospermic, and whitish structure called ovule. Inside the ovary the ovule is attached to a parenchymatous cushion called placenta, either singly or in cluster. Hence, ovary may have more than one ovule.

Statements (III) and (IV) are incorrect and can be corrected as

Some carpels have only one ovule but many others have multiple ovules.

The pistil may consist of one or more carpels, depending on the flower species.

Q.9 Which of the following situations correctly describe the similarity between an angiospermic egg and a human egg?

I. Eggs of both are formed only once in a lifetime.
II. Both the angiosperm egg and human egg are stationary.
III. Both the angiosperm egg and human egg are motile transported.
IV. Syngamy in both results in the formation of zygote.

Choose the correct answer from the options given below.

(a) II and IV (b) only IV
(c) III and IV (d) I and IV

Ans. ***(b)*** Statement (IV) is correct as in case of many terrestrial organisms including both angiosperms and humans which exhibit internal fertilisation, syngamy occurs inside the body of the organism to form zygote.

Statements (I), (II) and (III) are incorrect ans can be corrected as

Eggs of both angiosperms and humans are produced throughout the course of their reproductive life. In humans the eggs are immobile in the ovary until released into the fallopian tube. While in angiosperms, egg is immobile whithin the ovule.

Q.10 Appearance of vegetative propagules from the nodes of plants such as sugarcane and ginger is mainly because

(a) nodes are shorter than internodes
(b) nodes have meristematic cells
(c) nodes are located near the soil
(d) nodes have non-photosynthetic cells

Ans. ***(b)*** Appearance of vegetative propagules from the nodes of plants such as sugarcane and ginger is mainly because of the nodes having meristematic cells.

These cells are responsible to control the growth and development of tissues and organs in plants. Nodes (present in the modified stems) when come in contact with damp soil or water, they produce roots and gives rise to new plants.

Q.11 Which of the following statements, support the view that elaborate sexual reproductive process appeared much later in the organic evolution.

I. Lower groups of organisms have simpler body design.
II. Asexual reproduction is common in lower groups.
III. Asexual reproduction is common in higher groups of organisms.
IV. The high incidence of sexual reproduction in angiosperms and vertebrates.

Choose the correct answer from the options given below.

(a) II and III
(b) III and IV
(c) I, II and IV
(d) III and IV

- **Concept Insight** All living things are identified and categorised on the basis of their body design (structuce and function). When we connect this idea of classification to evolution we will find some organisms which have ancient body designs and have not changed much, while the other groups have acquired their particular body designs relatively recently.

  Those in the first group are referred to as primitive or lower organisms, while those in the second group are called advanced or higher organisms.

Ans. ***(c)*** Statements, (I) (II) and (IV) are correct as

Asexual reproduction (budding) has been found in most primitive animals like *Hydra*, but over the evolutionary time as the higher or advanced organisms came into existence, they resorted sexual reproduction as it ensures the genetic recombination that results in variation. Due to these reasons there is high incidence of sexual reproduction in angiosperms and vertebrates.

Statements (III) is incorrect and can be corrected as

Sexual reproduction is common in higher group of organisms.

Q.12 Offspring formed by sexual reproduction exhibit more variation than those formed by asexual reproduction because

(a) sexual reproduction is a lengthy process
(b) gametes of parents have qualitatively different genetic composition
(c) genetic material comes from parents of two different species
(d) greater amount of DNA is involved in sexual reproduction

Ans. ***(b)*** In sexual reproduction genetic variation is created and inherited. In this type of reproduction, two parents (opposite sex) having different genetic composition participate in the reproductive process and also involve the fusion of male and female gametes, which gives rise to the new individual having genetic composition of both.

Q.13 Choose the correct statement from amongst the following.

(a) Dioecious (hermaphrodite) organisms are seen only in animals.
(b) Dioecious organisms are seen only in plants.
(c) Dioecious organisms are seen in both plants and animals.
(d) Dioecious organisms are seen only in vertebrates.

Thinking Process Hermaphrodite is an organism that has reproductive organs normally associated with both male and female sexes. It is a bisexual condition found in both plants (*e.g.*, rose) and animals (*e.g.*, snail).

Ans. *(c)* Dioecious is the term used to describe unisexual condition. Dioecious organisms are seen in both plants and animals.
Example of dioecious plant- *Marchantia*
Example of dioecious animal-Cockroach (invertebrate).

Q.14 There is no natural death in single celled organisms like *Amoeba* and bacteria because

(a) they can'not reproduce sexually
(b) they reproduce by binary fission
(c) parental body is distributed among the offspring
(d) they are microscopic

Ans. *(c)* There is no natural death in single celled organisms like *Amoeba* and bacteria because parental body is distributed among the offspring. In such organisms, reproduction occurs by cell division where a cell (parent) divides by mitosis into two halves and each half rapidly grows into an adult (offspring).

Q.15 There are various types of reproduction. The type of reproduction adopted by an organism depends on

(a) the habitat and morphology of the organism
(b) morphology of the organism
(c) morphology and physiology of the organism
(d) the organism's habitat, physiology and genetic makeup

Ans. *(d)* The type of reproduction adopted by an organism depends on the organism's habitat, its internal physiology and several other factors. There is a large diversity in the biological world and each organism has evolved its own mechanism to multiply and produce offspring.
This is because the habitat physiology and genetic variation determines weather the organism undergoes sexual reproduction.

Q.16 Identify the incorrect statement.

(a) In asexual reproduction, the offspring produced are morphologically and genetically identical to the parent.
(b) Zoospores are sexual reproductive structures.
(c) In asexual reproduction, a single parent produces offspring with or without the formation of gametes.
(d) Conidia are asexual structures in *Penicillium*.

Thinking Process In asexual reproduction, a single individual (parent) is capable of producing offspring. As a result, the offsprings produced are identical to one another and their parent, both genetically and morphologically.

Ans. ***(b)*** Statement (b) is incorrect and can be corrected as zoospores are asexual reproductive structure in certain fungi and algae. They are produced by a single parent without involvement of gametes. The three statements are corrects as asexual reproduction occurs usually in unicellular organisms by various ways like binary fission, budding, sporulation, etc. In this method, a single parent produces offspring with or without the involvement of gametes.

Members of the kingdom fungi and simple plants reproduce through special asexual reproductive structures like conidia (*Penicillium*) buds (*Hydra*) etc. The most common of these structures are zoospores that are microscopic motile structures.

All other options are correct.

Q.17 Which of the following is a post-fertilisation event in flowering plants?

(a) Transfer of pollen grains
(b) Embryo development
(c) Formation of flower
(d) Formation of pollen grains

Ans. ***(b)*** Embryo development takes place after the fertilisation, *i.e.,* fusion of male and female gametes (n) results in the formation of zygote ($2n$). Thus, it is a post fertilisalion event.

The other three events *i.e* transfer of pollen grain, formation of pollen grain and formation of flowers takes place before the occurrrence of fertilisation, hence are pre- fertilisation events.

Q.18 The number of chromosomes in the shoot tip cells of a maize plant is 20. The number of chromosomes in the microspore mother cells of the same plant shall be

(a) 20
(b) 10
(c) 40
(d) 15

Ans. ***(a)*** The whole plant body of maize plant including shoot tip cells remains in diploid ($2n$) condition. As the microspore mother cell is a part of reproductive organ, the chromosome number in these cells will remain same as the individual. *i.e.,* $2n=20$.

Very Short Answer Type Questions

Q.1 Mention two inherent characteristics of *Amoeba* and yeast that enable them to reproduce asexually.

Ans. The characteristics that enable Amoeba and yeast to reproduce asexually, are as follows

(i) Unicellular condition
(ii) Simple body organisation
(iii) Uniparental condition (Any two)

Q.2 **Why do we refer to offspring formed by asexual method of reproduction as clones?**

Ans. The reproduction is called **asexual**, when offsprings are produced by a single parent without the involvement of gamete formation.

As a result, the offspring that are produced are not only similar to one another, but are also exact copies of their parent. Such a group of morphologically and genetically similar individuals is called **clone.**

Q.3 **Although potato tuber is an underground part, it is considered as a stem. Give two reasons.**

Ans. Potato tuber is considered as a stem because of the following reasons

(i) The tuber has nodes and internodes. (ii) Leafy shoots appear from the nodes.

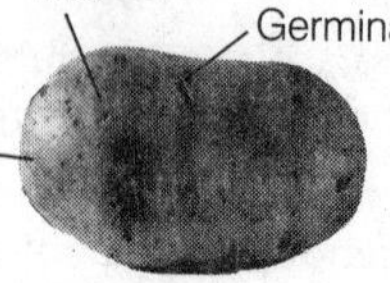

Q.4 **Between an annual and a perennial plant, which one has a shorter juvenile phase? Give one reason.**

Ans. In a lifespan, plant or an organism has to grow and develop (the juvenile phase). After which it mature sexually and enters into the reproductive phase, before it undergoes senescence followed by death.

As, the entire life cycle of an annual plant is shorter and has to be completed in one growing season, its juvenile phase is shorter than that of a perennial plant.

Q.5 **Rearrange the following events of sexual reproduction in the sequence in which they occur in a flowering plant embryogenesis, fertilisation, gametogenesis, pollination.**

Ans. The correct sequence of events of sexual reproduction in a flowering plant are as follows gametogenesis, pollination, fertilisation, embryogenesis.

The gametes are formed first, followed by, pollination which ensures their transfer, so that fertilisation can take place. Fertilised zygote divides and differentiates during embryogenesis.

Q.6 **The probability of fruit set in a self-pollinated bisexual flower of a plant is far greater than a dioecious plant. Explain.**

Ans. The probability of fruit set in a self-pollinated bisexual flower of a plant is far greater than a dioecious plant because in self-pollinated bisexual plants transfer of pollen to stigma of flowers is easier than the dioecious plants. As both anther and stigma lie close to each other and pollination is not effected even in the absence of pollinator. But in dioecious plants, the presence of pollinator is necessary to bring about effective pollination as the anther and stigma lie away from each other.

Q.7 Is the presence of large number of chromosomes in an organism a hindrance to sexual reproduction? Justify your answer by giving suitable reasons.

Ans. No, presence of large number of chromosomes in an organism is not a hindrance to sexual reproduction. *Ophioglossum* (a fern) has a chromosome number of 1260, still it can reproduce sexually.

In higher organisms, the chromosomes are enclosed in the nucleus, within the cell. Whether the number is small or large, the chromosomes are duplicated and then segregated inside the nucleous, during cell division.

Q.8 Is there a relationship between the size of an organism and its life span? Give two examples in support of your answer.

Ans. There is no relationship between the size and life span of an organism. Few example are given below,

(i) The mango tree has a shorter life span as compared to a peepal tree though both are of the same size.

(ii) The size of crow and parrot is almost same but the life span is 15 years and 150 years respectively.

Q.9 In the figure given below the plant bears two different types of flowers marked 'A' and 'B'. Identify the types of flowers and state the type of pollination that will occur in them.

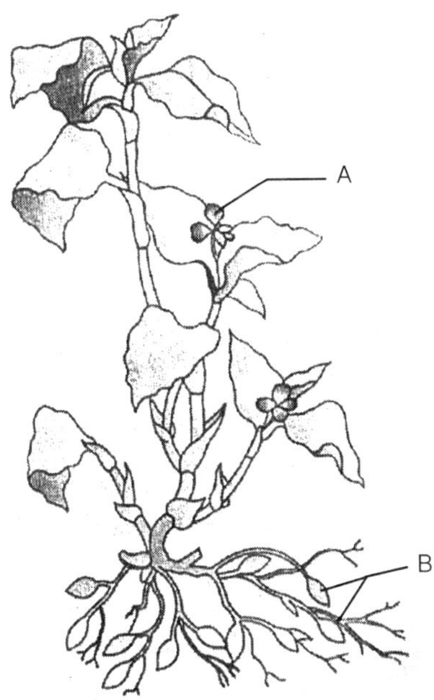

Ans. In the figure given below the plant bears folllowing two types of flowers

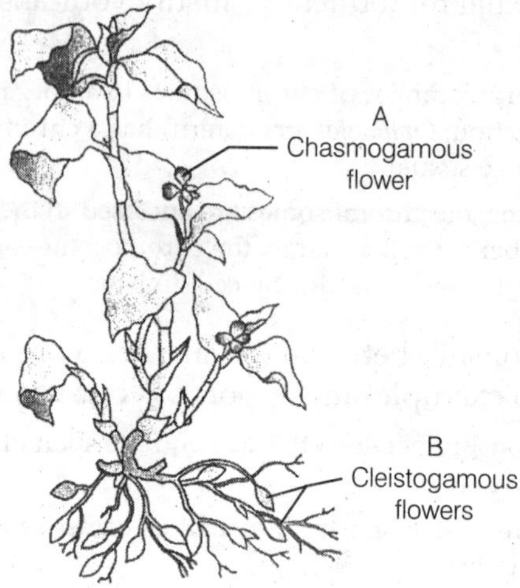

In—chasmogamous flower are the flowers that remain open, exposing anthers and stigmas. Whereas—cleistogamous flowers are the flowers that remain closed, so that anthers and stigmas are never exposed.

In chasmogamous flowers, the flowers may undergo self-pollination or cross-pollination, while in cleistogamous flowers, the flowers undergo only self-pollination.

Q.10 Give reasons as to why cell division cannot be a type of reproduction in multicellular organisms.

Ans. In unicellular animals, cell division is the means of reproduction to increase their number. While, in case of multicellular organisms, they have well developed reproductive organs which help in reproduction and their whole body does not participate in reproduction like unicellular organisms. Hence, cell division cannot be a type of reproduction in multicelluar organisms.

Q.11 In the figure given below, mark the ovule and pericarp.

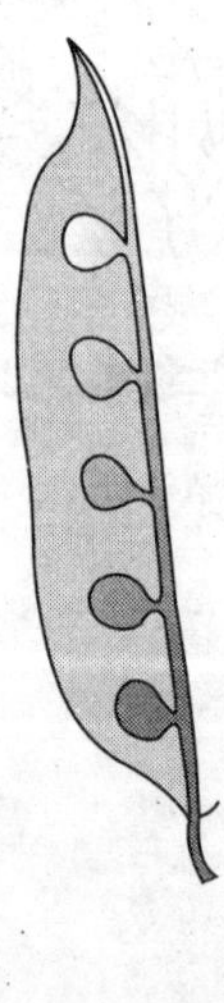

Ans.

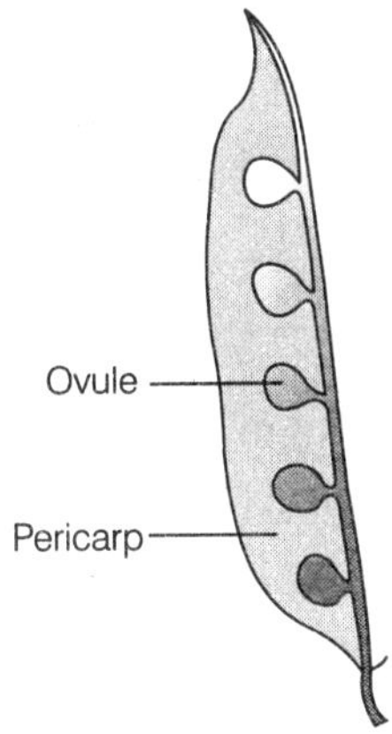

Q.12 Why do gametes produced in large numbers in organisms exhibit external fertilisation?

Thinking Process In most aquatic organisms, such as a majority of algae and fishes as well as amphibians, syngamy (fusion of gametes in sexual reproduction) occurs in the external medium (water) , *i.e.,* outside the body of the organism. This type of genetic fusion is called **external fertilisation.**

Ans. Organisms that take part in proceses like external fertillisation produce large number of gametes because

(i) In external fertilisation, there is a great chance that the sperm and the eggs released by the organisms can be affected by factors present in the environment like dessication, predators, etc. So, to make up for the high fatality rate of the gametes, the organism produces a lot of gametes.

(ii) Producing large number of gametes increase the chance for some eggs and sperms to meet in the environment ensuring that atleast a stable number of offspring are able to survive and pasive.

Q.13 Which of the following are monoecious and dioecious organisms?

(a) Earthworm .... (b) *Chara* ....

(c) *Marchantia* .... (d) Cockroach ....

- **Concept Insight** In several fungi and plants, terms such as **homothallic** and **monoecious** are used to denote the **bisexual condition** (male and female reproductive structures in the same plant) and **heterothallic and dioecious** are the terms used to describe **unisexual condition** (male and female reproductive structures on different plants). But in animals, individuals are either male or female (unisexual) or possess both the reproductive organs (bisexual).

Ans. (a) Earthworm- Monoecious animal

(b) *Chara*- Monoecious plant

(c) *Marchantia*-Dioecious plant

(d) Cockroach- Dioecious animal

Q.14 Match the organisms given in column I with the vegetative propagules given in column II.

Column I	Column II
A. *Bryophyllum*	1. Offset
B. *Agave*	2. Eyes
C. Potato	3. Leaf buds
D. Water hyacinth	4. Bulbils

Ans. The correct matching is as follows

A - 3, B - 4, C - 2, D - 1,

Leafbuds, bubils, eyes and offset are the vegetative propagules if Bryophyllom, Agave, Potato and water hyacinth respectively.

Q.15 What do the following parts of a flower develop into after fertilisation?

(a) Ovary .... (b) Ovules ......

Ans. (a) Fruit (b) Seed

Short Answer Type Questions

Q.1 In haploid organisms that undergo sexual reproduction, name the stage in the life cycle when meiosis occurs. Give reasons for your answer.

Thinking Process The requirement of meiosis is to reduce the number of chromosomes by half to maintain the ploidy. As the organism is haploid meiosis cannot occur during gametogenesis.

Ans. In haploid organisms that undergo sexual reproduction gametes are formed by mitosis. Meiosis can take place only in a diploid stage (post-zygotic stage) because the zygote is the only diploid cell in the life cycle of organism which undergo sexual reproduction . Thus, meiosis in case of haploid organisms will occur after zygote formation.

Q.2 The number of taxa exhibiting asexual reproduction is drastically reduced in higher plants (angiosperms) and higher animals (vertebrates) as compared with lower groups of plants and animals. Analyse the possible reasons for this situation.

Ans. Higher plants (angiosperms) and higher animals (vertebrates) have a more complex structural organisation as compared to the lower groups of plants and animals. They have evolved form a very efficient mechanism of sexual reproduction. These groups have resorted to reproduction by the sexual method for the following reasons

(i) To ensure healthy progeny

(ii) To produce genetically varied offsprings that adapt to changes in environment and survival in all climatic conditions.

(iii) It ensures the genetic recombination that results in variation which gives rise to evolution.

Q.3 Honeybees produce their young ones only by sexual reproduction. Inspite of this, in a colony of bees we find both haploid and diploid individuals. Name the haploid and diploid individuals in the colony and analyse the reasons behind their formation.

Ans. The haploid and diploid individuals in a honeybee colony are as follows

(i) Sterile diploid females as workers

(ii) One fertile diploid female as queen

(iii) Fertile haploid males as drones.

In case of honeybees, both haploid and diploid individuals formed as a result of both sexual reproduction and parthenogenesis. Fertilised eggs (zygote) give rise to queen and workers (both are females) by the process of sexual reproduction and unfertilised eggs (ova) develop into drones (males) by the process of parthenogenesis.

Q.4 With which type of reproduction do we associate the reduction division? Analyse the reasons for it.

Ans. Reduction division (meiosis) is associated with sexual reproduction due to following reasons.

(i) Since, sexual reproduction involves the fusion of two types of gametes male and female), they must have haploid number of chromosomes.

(ii) The cell (meiocyte) which gives rise to gametes often has diploid number of chromosomes and it is only by reducing the number by half that haploid gametes are produced.

(iii) Reduction division also ensures maintenance of constancy of chromosome number from generation to generation.

Q.5 Is it possible to consider vegetative propagation observed in certain plants like *Bryophyllum*, water hyacinth, ginger, etc., as a type of asexual reproduction? Give two/three reasons.

Ans. The formation of new plants from vegetative units (vegetative propagules) such as buds, tubers, rhizomes. etc., is called vegetative propagation (vegetative reproduction). It can be considered as a type of asexual reproduction as it involves the production of new individuals

(i) by a single parent

(ii) without the formation and fusion of gametes

(iii) without resulting in any genetic or morphological variations.

Q.6 'Fertilisation is not an obligatory event for fruit production in certain plants'. Explain the statement.

Ans. Fertilisation is not an obligatory event for fruit production in certain plants. Some fruits are developed from unfertilised ovary called parthenocarpic fruits.

These are seedless fruits, such as banana, pineapple, grapes, etc. Flowers of these plants are sprayed by a growth hormone that induces fruit development even though fertilisation has not occurred. The ovules of such fruits, however, fail to develop into seeds.

Q.7 In a developing embryo, analyse the consequences if cell divisions are not followed by cell differentiation.

Thinking Process The process of development of embryo from the zygote is referred as embryogenesis. During embryogenesis, zygote undergoes cell division (mitosis) and cell differentiation.

Ans. Cell divisions increase the number of cells in the developing embryo, while cell differentiation helps group of cells to undergo certain modifications to form specialised tissues and organs to form an organism.

At any stages of embryogenesis, if cell differentiation does not occur, the embryo cannot develop into a new organism. It will only remain as a mass of cells.

Q.8 List the changes observed in an angiosperm flower subsequent to pollination and fertilisation.

Ans. In an angiosperm flower, the post-fertilisation changes occur as follows

Sepal	Fall off
Petal	Fall off
Stamen	Fall off
Zygote	Embryo
Central cell	Endosperm (3n)
Synergid	Disintegrate
Antipodals	Disintegrate
Ovary	Fruit
Ovule	Seed
Ovary wall	Pericarp (epicarp+mesocarp + endocarp)
Integument	Seed coat (testa+tegmen)
Funicle of the ovule	Stalk of the seed
Micropyle	Seed pore

Mistake Alert ! *Student should pay attention while, learning about the changes that are subsequent to pollination and fertilisation under post-fertilisation changes (events).*

Q.9 Suggest a possible explanation why the seeds in a pea pod are arranged in a row, whereas those in tomato are scattered in the juicy pulp.

Ans. The arrangement of seeds in a pea pod and tomato reflects differences in their fruit structure and dispersal strategies. In pea pods, a **legume**, seeds are arranged in a single row along the inner wall, ensuring efficient development and orderly dispersal when the pod splits open. In contrast, a tomato, a **berry**, has seeds scattered in the juicy pulp within locules. This arrangement helps attract animals, which eat the fruit and disperse the seeds, ensuring wider propagation. These adaptations suit their respective modes of seed dispersal—mechanical for peas and animal-mediated for tomatoes.

Q.10 Draw the sketches of a zoospore and a conidium. Mention two dissimilarities between them and atleast one feature common to both structures.

Ans. The common feature of zoospores and conidia is that they are the asexual reproductive structures, which facilitate the process of reproduction in asexually reproducing organisms.

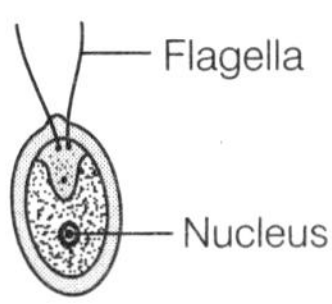

(a) Zoospore of *Chlamydomonas*

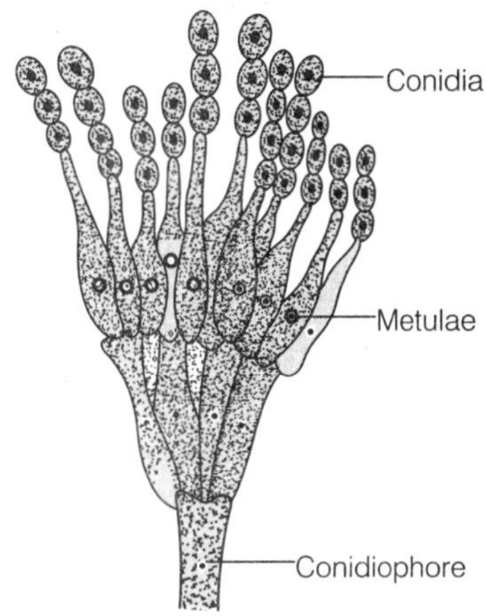

(b) Conidium of *Penicillium*

The two dissimilarities between zoospore and conidium are as follows

Zoospore (Found usually in Algae)	**Conidium** (Found usually in Fungi)
Flagellated	Non-flagellated
Formed inside a sporangium (endogenously)	Formed at the tip of conidiophores (exogenously)

Q.11 Justify the statement 'vegetative reproduction is also a type of asexual reproduction'.

Ans. In flowering plants, the units of vegetative reproduction such as runners, stolons, suckers, offsets, rhizome, tuber, etc., are capable of giving rise to new offsprings. These structures are called vegetative propagules.

In all these plants the formation of vegetative structures does not involve two parents, therefore the process involved is asexual. So, it can be said that vegetative reproduction is also a type of asexual reproduction.

Long Answer Type Questions

Q.1 Enumerate the differences between asexual and sexual reproduction. Describe the types of asexual reproduction exhibited by unicellular organisms.

Ans. The differences between asexual and sexual reproduction are mentioned below

Asexual Reproduction	Sexual Reproduction
Uniparental	Biparental
Somatic cells are involved.	Germ cells are involved.
It involves the production of asexual spores	It involves the formation and fusion of gametes.
Offsprings are genetically similar to parents.	Offsprings are genetically dissimilar to parents.
The rate of reproduction is faster.	The rate of reproduction is slower.

Asexual reproduction usually occurs in unicellular organisms, such as monerans, protists and in certain plants and animals.

It takes place in the following ways

(i) Binary Fission In this type of asexual reproduction, the parent organism divides into two halves, each half forming an independent daughter organism.

For example., Amoeba, Euglena, Paramecium.

(ii) Budding In this type of asexual reproduction, a daughter individual is formed from a small projection, a bud, arising from the parent body.

*For example.,*yeast, *Hydra.*

(iii) Fragmentation In this type of asexual reproduction, the parent body breaks into two or more fragments. Each fragment develops into an organism.

For example., sponges, *Selaginella.*

(iv) Gemmule In this type of asexual reproduction, internal buds, called gemmules are involved. Gemmules are asexually reproduced mass of cells, that is capable of developing into a new organism.

For example., sponges.

(v) Sporulation In this type of asexual reproduction, dispersive structures called spores are released from the parent body that germinate under favourable conditions form new individuals.

(a) Motile spores are called zoospores and are found in aquatic animals. *For example., Albugo, Chlamydomonas.*

(b) Non-motile spores are named as sporangiospores (*e.g., Rhizopus, Mucor*) and conidia *For example., Penicillium.*

Q.2 Do all the gametes formed from a parent organism have the same genetic composition (identical DNA copies of the parental genome)? Analyse the situation with the background of gametogenesis and provide or give suitable explanation.

Ans. *No*, all the gametes formed from a parent organism do not have the same genetic composition. It can be better understood with the help of the explanation given below. Sexual reproduction in organisms involves the fusion of gametes from two different individuals. These gametes are formed by the process of gametogenesis. In the heterogametic species, gametes are of two types namely male and female. Gametes always are haploid, though the parent body from which they arise may be either haploid or diploid.

(a) A haploid parent like Monera, fungi, algae and bryophytes produce gametes by mitotic division. The number of chromosomes, *i.e.*, the genetic composition remain same after such type of division.

(b) The diploid parent like pteridophytes, gymnosperms, angiosperms and most of the animals including human beings produces gametes by meiosis. In such organisms (diploid), specialised cells called meiocytes (gamete mother cell) undergo meiosis. At the end of meiosis only one set of chromosomes gets incorporated into each gamete. It means that the gametes formed contain a haploid number of chromosomes in contrast to the number of chromosomes in mother cells.

Q.3 Although sexual reproduction is a long drawn, energy-intensive complex form of reproduction, many groups of organisms in kingdom–Animalia and Plantae prefer this mode of reproduction. Give atleast three reasons for this.

Ans. Following are the three reasons for the occurence mode of sexual reproduction in higher group of organisms

(i) The sexual mode of reproduction ensures creation of new variants.

(ii) Genetically varied offsprings that are produced quickly adapt to changes in environment and survive in all climatic conditions.

(iii) Sexual reproduction ensures the genetic recombination that results in variation which gives rise to evolution.

Q.4 Differentiate between (a) oestrus and menstrual cycles; (b) ovipary and vivipary. Give an example for each type.

Ans. The differences between oestrus and menstrual cycle are as follows

(a)

Oestrus cycle	Menstrual cycle
• The cyclic changes in the activities of ovaries and accessory ducts as well as hormones during the reproductive phase of non-primate mammals is called oestrus cycle.	The cyclic changes in the activities of ovaries and accessory ducts as well as hormones during the reproductive phase of primate mammals is called menstrual cycle.
• There is estrus/heat production at the time of ovulation and copulation occurs only in that period.	There is no heat period and copulation occurs during any time of the cycle.
• The shedding of endometrium and bleeding do not occur. *e.g.*, cows, sheep, rats, deers, dogs and tigers etc.	The shedding of endometrium and bleeding occurs. *e.g.*, monkeys, apes and humans.

(b) The differences between ovipary and vivipary are as follows

Ovipary	Vivipary
• In ovipary, animals lay eggs.	In vivipary, animals give birth to young ones.
• The eggs are covered by hard calcareous shell.	Ovum are not covered by calcareous shell.
• The development of zygote takes place outside the female's body.	The development of zygote takes place inside the female's body.
• Females lay eggs in a safe place in the environment, but the chances of survival are less	Females deliver young ones and the chances of survival are more.
For example, all birds, most of reptiles, egg laying mammals.	*For example.,* mammals except monotremes egg laying mammals.

Q.5 Rose plants produce large, attractive bisexual flowers, but they seldom produce fruits. On the other hand a tomato plant produces plenty of fruits though they have small flowers. Analyse the reasons for failure of fruit formation in rose. Both these plants rose and tomato both selected by human beings for different characteristics, the rose for its flower and tomato for its fruit. Roses, being vegetatively propagated do not need to produce seeds.

Ans. Rose plants produce large, attractive bisexual flowers, but they seldom produce fruits. The reasons for failure of fruit formation in rose are as follows

(i) Rose plants may not produce viable pollens, hence, no fertilisation can take place.

(ii) Rose plants may not have functional eggs.

(iii) Rose plants may have defective and non-functional ovule ,which produces the female gametophyte.

(iv) There may be self-incompatibility.

(v) There may be internal barriers for pollen tube growth or fertilisation.

(vi) As rose plants are hybrids and reproduce vegetatively, there are chances for them to be sterile.

Chapter

02

Sexual Reproduction in Flowering Plants

Multiple Choice Questions (MCQs)

Q.1 Among the terms listed below, those that of are not technically correct names for a floral whorl are

(i) androecium (ii) carpel
(iii) corolla (iv) sepal

(a) (i) and (iv) (b) (iii) and (iv) (c) (ii) and (iv) (d) (i) and (ii)

Ans. ***(c)*** Carpel and sepal are not technically correct names of flower whorl. The technically correct terms for the floral whorls (from outermost to innermost) are calyx, corolla, androecium and gynoecium formed by the sepals, petals, stamens and carpels respectively.

Q.2 Embryo sac is to ovule as .... is to an anther.

(a) stamen (b) filament (c) pollen grain (d) androecium

Thinking Process Within an ovule a single Megaspore Mother Cell (MMC) differentiates into four megaspores. Out of these, only one megaspore, i.e., functional, develops into an **embryo sac** (female gametophyte) and the other three degenerate.

Ans. ***(c)*** As embryo sac represents female gametophyte in ovule. Similarly the pollen grains represent the male gametophytes. As the anthers mature and dehydrate, the microspores dissociate from each other and develop into pollen grains.

So, **embryo sac** is to **ovule** as **pollen grains** is to an **anther**.

Q.3 In a typical complete, bisexual and hypogynous flower the arrangement of floral whorls on the thalamus from the outermost to the innermost is

(a) calyx, corolla, androecium and gynoecium
(b) calyx, corolla, gynoecium and androecium
(c) gynoecium, androecium, corolla and calyx
(d) androecium, gynoecium, corolla and calyx

Ans. ***(a)*** In a typical complete, bisexual and hypogynous flower the arrangement of floral whorls on the thalamus from the outermost to the innermost is

(i) The calyx, a whorl of sepals (outermost).
(ii) The corolla, a whorl of petals (inside the calyx).
(iii) The androecium, a whorl of stamens (inside the corolla).
(iv) The gynoecium, a whorl of pistils (in the centre of the flower forming inner most whorl).

Q.4 A dicotyledonous plant bears flowers, but never produces fruits and seeds. The most probable cause for the above situation is

(a) plant is dioecious and bears only pistillate flowers
(b) plant is dioecious and bears both pistillate and staminate flowers
(c) plant is monoecious
(d) plant is dioecious and bears only staminate flowers

Thinking Process Fertilisation of male and female gametes is essential for the formation of fruit and seed. Usually, the male gamete constitute the motile structure while female gamete is large and non-motile.

Ans. *(d)* For the production of fruits and seeds, fertilisation must take place, which is possible only in the presence of both male and female flowers.

In dioecious plants, the unisexual male flower is staminate, i.e., bearing stamens only, while the female is pistillate or bearing pistils only.

When the plant is dioecious, it will give rise to the following situations

(i) If the plant is dioecious and bears only pistillate flowers, fertilisation can take place with the help of pollinators.

(ii) If the plant is dioecious and bears only staminate flowers, fertilisation can't take place, because female gamete is non-motile which can't reach the male gamete in order to fuse with it.

When the plant is monoecious (*i.e.*, carrying both stamen and pistill together, it may lead to self-fertilisation and production of seed.

Q.5 The outermost and innermost wall layers of microsporangium in an anther are respectively.

(a) Endothecium and tapetum
(b) Epidermis and endodermis
(c) Epidermis and middle layer
(d) Epidermis and tapetum

Ans. *(d)* A typical microsporangium is generally surrounded by four-wall layers, *i.e.*, the epidermis, (outermost protective layer), endothecium, (middle fibrous layers) middle layer and the tapetum (innermost nutritive layer). Therefore epidermis is the outermost and tapetum is the inner most layer in an anther.

Mistake Alert! *Many times students get confused between the layers of anther from outer to inner layers. So, learn about them carefully.*

Q.6 During microsporogenesis, meiosis occurs in

(a) endothecium
(b) microspore mother cells
(c) microspore tetrads
(d) pollen grains

Ans. *(b)* During microsporogenesis, meiosis occurs in microspore mothercell. As the anther develops, the microspore mother cells of the sporogenous tissue undergoes meiotic divisions to form microspore tetrads. The microspore tetrad after dehydration is separated into pollen grains. Endothecium is the layer present between epidermis and middle layer, it is formed by columna cells.

Q.7 From among the sets of terms given below, identify those that are associated with the gynoecium.

(a) Stigma, ovule, embryo sac, placenta
(b) Thalamus, pistil, style, ovule
(c) Ovule, ovary, embryo sac, tapetum
(d) Ovule, stamen, ovary, embryo sac

Ans. *(a)* The gynoecium represents the female reproductive part of the flower and consists of pistil. Each pistil has three parts, *i.e.*, stigma, style and ovary. Inside the ovarian cavity, the placenta is located.

Arising from the placenta there are the megasporangia, commonly called ovules. The functional megaspore undergoing the meiotic division develops into the female gametophyte or embryo sac.

Q.8 Starting from the innermost part, the correct sequence of parts in an ovule are

(a) egg, nucellus, embryo sac, integument
(b) egg, embryo sac, nucellus, integument
(c) embryo sac, nucellus, integument, egg
(d) egg, integument, embryo sac, nucellus

Ans. *(b)* Starting from the innermost part, the correct sequence of parts in an ovule is egg, embryo sac, nucellus, integument. *This sequence can be seen in following diagram.*

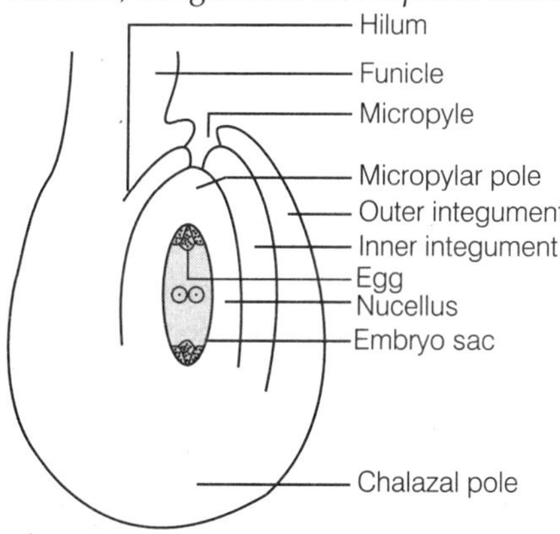

A diagrammatic view of an ovule

Mistake Alert! *Students should carefully learn all the labellings and functions of an anatropous ovule.*

Q.9 From the statements given below choose the option that are true for a typical female gametophyte of a flowering plant.

(i) It is eight-nucleate and seven-celled at maturity.
(ii) It is free-nuclear during the development.
(iii) It is situated inside the integument, but outside the nucellus.
(iv) It has an egg apparatus situated at the chalazal end.

(a) (i) and (iv) (b) (ii) and (iii) (c) (i) and (ii) (d) (ii) and (iv)

Ans. *(c)* Statements (i) and (ii) are true for a female gametophyte as.

In a majority of flowering plants, one of the megaspore is functional while the other three degenerate. Three repeated mitotic divisions of the functional megaspore results in the formation of seven-celled or **eight-nucleate** embryo sac.

Six of the eight nuclei are organised at the two poles. Three cells grouped at micropylar end froms **egg-apparatus** and 3 at the **chalazal end** forms **antipodal cells**. The large central cell at the centre has two polar nuclei.

Statements (iii) and (iv) are incorrect and can be corrected as

The female gametophyte or embroyo sac is located inside the nucellus enclosed within the integuments.

The meiotic divisions in the formation of embryo sac are strictly free nuclear, that is nuclear divisions are not followed immediately by cell-well formation. Gametophyte is situated at micropylar end at chalazal end.

Q.10 Autogamy can occur in a chasmogamous flower if

(a) pollen matures before maturity of ovule
(b) ovules mature before maturity of pollen
(c) both pollen and ovules mature simultaneously
(d) both anther and stigma are of equal lengths

Ans. *(c)* Autogamy is a method of self-pollination in which the stigma of a flower receive pollens from the anther of same flower. For autogamy both sex organs of a chasmogamous flower should mature at the same time. As chasmogamous flowers open at maturity, pollen release and stigma receptivity should be synchronised for the process of autogamy.

Q.11 Choose the correct statement from the following.

(a) Cleistogamous flowers always exhibit autogamy.
(b) Chasmogamous flowers always exhibit geitonogamy.
(c) Cleistogamous flowers exhibit both autogamy and geitonogamy.
(d) Chasmogamous flowers never exhibit autogamy.

Thinking Process Chasmogamous flowers are flowers with exposed anthers and stigma and cleistogamous flowers are flowers, which do not open at all.

Ans. *(a)* Statement (a) is correct about cleistogamous flowers (flower that don't open) as they always exhibit autogamy.

The pollination that occurs in opened flowers is called chasmogamy. It is the most common type of pollination in all types of flowers. Chasmogamy is of two types *i.e.*, self-pollination (autogamy) and cross-pollination. Cross-pollination is of two types *i.e.*, **geitonogamy** and **xenogamy.**

So, we can say that chasmogamous flowers exhibit both autogamy (self-pollination) and allogamy (cross-pollination). While, in cleistogamous flower, the anthers and stigma lie close to each other with in the closed flowers.

When anthers dehisces in the flower buds, pollen grains come in contact with the stigma for effective pollination. Thus, these flowers are invariably autogamous as there is no chance of cross-pollen landing on the stigma.

Q.12 A particular species of plant produces light, non-sticky pollen in large numbers and its stigmas are long and feathery. These modifications facilitate pollination by

(a) insects (b) water (c) wind (d) animals

Ans. *(c)* Wind pollination requires light and non-sticky pollen grains so that, they can be transported in wind currents. They often possess well-exposed stamens (so that the pollens are easily dispersed by wind currents) and large often-feathery stigma to easily trap air-borne pollen grains. Wind pollination is common in grasses.

Q.13 From among the situations given below, choose the one that prevents both autogamy and geitonogamy.

(a) Monoecious plant bearing unisexual flowers.
(b) Dioecious plant bearing only male or female flowers.
(c) Monoecious plant with bisexual flowers.
(d) Dioecious plant with bisexual flowers.

Ans. *(b)* Dioecious (unisexual) plants bearing only one or male flowers will not show autogamy or geitonogamy hence, only xenogamy is possible. Monoecious plant (bisexual) bearing either bisexual or unisexual flowers can exhibit both autogamy as well as geitonogamy.

Q.14 In a fertilised embryo sac, the haploid, diploid and triploid structure are

(a) synergid, zygote and primary endosperm nucleus
(b) synergid, antipodal and polar nuclei
(c) antipodal, synergid and primary endosperm nucleus
(d) synergid, polar nuclei and zygote

Ans. *(a)* Since, all these cells three cells (synergid, polar nuclei and antipodals) are formed by mitosis from the functional megaspore, they are haploid (n). Egg cell fertilises with the male gamete to form a diploid zygote.

Diploid secondary nucleus fertilises with a haploid male gamete to form a triploid Primary Endosperm Nucleus (PEN).

Q.15 In an embryo sac, the cells that degenerate after fertilisation are

(a) synergids and primary endosperm cell
(b) synergids and antipodals
(c) antipodals and primary endosperm cell
(d) egg and antipodals

Ans. *(b)* In unfertilised embryo sac, the antipodals and synergids are distinctly present at chalazal end and micropylar end respectively While, in fertilised embryo sac antipodals and synergids gradually degenerate after the formation of zygote.

Q.16 While planning for an artificial hybridisation programme involving dioecious plants, which of the following steps would not be relevant?

(a) Bagging of female flower
(b) Dusting of pollen on stigma
(c) Emasculation
(d) Collection of pollen

Thinking Process Artificial hybridisation is human peformed crossing of two different plants having complementary good traits in order to obtain an overall superior variety. Two precautionary measures in artificial hybridisatian are emasculation and bagging.

Ans. *(c)* If the female parent produces unisexual flowers, there is no need for emasculation. The female flower buds are bagged before the flowers open.

When the stigma becomes receptive, pollination is carried out using the desired pollen and the flowers are rebagged. This protects them from contamination by unwanted pollen grains.

Note If the female parent bears bisexual flowers, removal of anthers from the flower bud before the anther dehisces is necessary. This is called emasculation.

Q.17 In the embryos of a typical dicot and a grass, true homologous structures are

(a) coleorrhiza and coleoptile
(b) coleoptile and scutellum
(c) cotyledons and scutellum
(d) hypocotyl and radicle

Ans. *(c)* A typical dicotyledonous embryo consists of two cotyledons.

While, embryos of monocotyledons possess only one cotyledon and it is called **scutellum** (in grass) .

Q.18 The phenomenon observed in some plants where in parts of the sexual apparatus is used for forming embryos without fertilisation is called

(a) parthenocarpy
(b) apomixis
(c) vegetative propagation
(d) sexual reproduction

Ans. *(b)* Apomixis is the term given to the phenomenon that leads to the formation of embryo during which parts of the sexual apparatus are used, but without fertilisation. An example of apomixis is citrus. Fertilisation is also absent in vegetative propagation, but parts of sexual apparatus are not involved.

Q.19 In a flower, if the megaspore mother cell forms megaspores without undergoing meiosis and if one of the megaspores develops into an embryo sac, its nuclei would be

(a) haploid
(b) diploid
(c) a few haploid and a few diploid
(d) with varying ploidy

- **Concept Insight** Replacement of the normal sexual reproduction without fertilisation is called apomixis. It does not involve meiosis.

Ans. *(b)* In some species, the diploid egg cell is formed without reduction division and develops into an embryo without fertilisation.

Apomixis is an asexual reproduction which occurs in the absence of pollinators or in extreme environments. In some species like citrus plants, nucellar cells surrounding the embryo sac start dividing and develops into embryos.

It occurs in the megaspore mother cell without undergoing meiosis, and produces diploid embryo sac through mitotic divisions. It helps in the preservation of desirable characters for indefinite period.

Q.20 The phenomenon wherein, the ovary develops into a fruit without fertilisation is called

(a) parthenocarpy
(b) apomixis
(c) asexual reproduction
(d) sexual reproduction

Ans. *(a)* Parthenocarpy is the formation of seed less fruits without fertilisation. The fruits developed from unfertilised ovary are called parthenocarpic fruits.

Very Short Answer Type Questions

Q.1 Name the component cells of the 'egg-apparatus' in an embryo sac.

Ans. The component cells of the 'egg-apparatus' in an embryo sac include, two synergids, one egg cell and the filiform apparatus.

Q.2 Name the part of gynoecium that determines the compatible nature of pollen grain.

Ans. Stigma is that part of gynoecium that determines the compatible nature of pollen grains.

Q.3 Name the common function that cotyledons and nucellus perform.

Ans. The common functions that cotyledons and nucellus perform are as follows

(i) Storage of reserve food material.

(ii) Cotyledons nourishes the embryo after fertilisation and nucellus nourishes the embryo sac before fertilisation.

Q.4 Complete the following flow chart

Pollen mother cell → Pollen tetrad → Pollen grain ⟨ Vegetative cell / ....

Ans. Pollen mother cell → Pollen tetrad → Pollen grain ⟨ (i) Vegetative cell / (ii) Generative cell

Q.5 Indicate the stages where meiosis and mitosis occur (1, 2 or 3) in the flow chart.

Megaspore mother cell $\xrightarrow{1}$ Megaspores $\xrightarrow{2}$ Embryo sac $\xrightarrow{3}$ Egg

Ans. Megaspore mother cell ($2n$) $\xrightarrow{\text{Meiosis}}$ Megaspores $\xrightarrow{\text{Mitosis}}$ Embryo sac (n) $\xrightarrow{\text{Mitosis}}$ Egg.

Q.6 In the diagram given below, show the path of a pollen tube from the pollen on the stigma into the embryo sac. Name the components of egg apparatus.

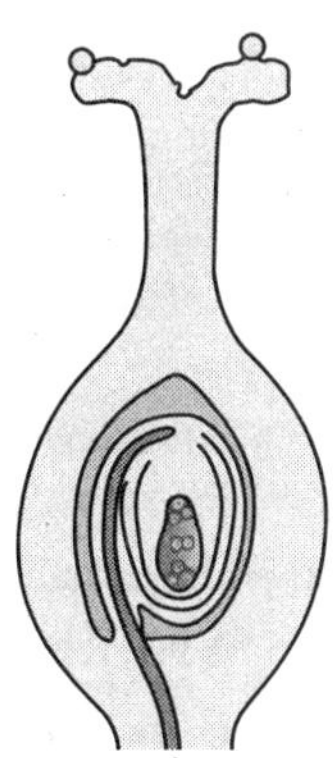

Ans. Following compatible pollination, the pollen grain germinates on the stigma to produce a pollen tube through one of the germ pores. The contents of the pollen grain (2 Polar nuclei) move into the pollen tube. Pollen tube grows through the tissues of the stigma and reaches the ovary.

Egg apparatus consists of two synergids and one egg cell.

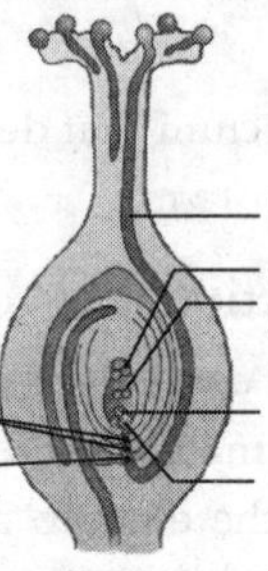

Longitudinal section of a flower showing path of pollen tube growth

Q.7 Name the parts of pistil which develop into fruit and seeds.

Ans. Pistil is the female reproductive organ that receives pollen to fertilise the egg located in ovary. A pistil has three parts, *i.e.*, **stigma** (receives pollen), which grows down through **style** to **ovary.** Ovary contains ovules, which contains egg. The ovary develops into the fruit and ovule develops into a seeds.

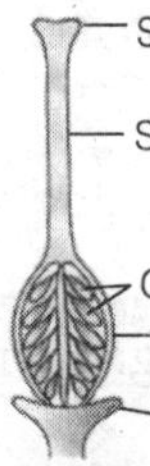

Parts of a pistil

Q.8 In case of polyembryony, if an embryo develops from the synergid and another from the nucellus which is haploid and which is diploid?

Thinking Process Presence of more than one embryo in a seed is called **polyembryony.** *e.g.*, lemon, groundnut, etc.

Ans. Embryo developed from the synergid is haploid as the ploidy of the synergid is haploid. Embryo developed from the nucellus is diploid as the ploidy of the nucellus is diploid.

Q.9 Can an unfertilised, apomictic embryo sac give rise to a diploid embryo? If yes, then how?

- **Concept Insight** Apomixis is a form of asexual reproduction to produce seeds without fertilisation.

Ans. Yes, if megaspore develops into embryo sac without meiotic division, the egg will be diploid. This, diploid egg develops into an embryo by mitotic divisions.

Q.10 Which are the three cells found in a pollen grain when it is shed at the three celled stage?

Ans. When a pollen grain is shed at three celled stage, it contains two male gametes and one vegetative cell.

The generative cell divides mitotically into two male gametes.

Q.11 What is self-incompatibility?

Ans. It is a genetic mechanism which prevents pollens from self fertilising the ovules by inhibiting pollen germination or pollen tube growth in the pistil when the pollen comes from the same plant.

Q.12 Name the type of pollination in self-incompatible plants.

- **Concept Insight** Self-incompatibility is a genetic mechanism which prevents pollens from self-fertilising the ovules by inhibiting pollen germination or pollen tube growth in the pistil.

Ans. In self-incompatible plants, (while self-pollination is incompatible) cross-pollination occurs.

Q.13 Draw the diagram of a mature embryo sac and show its eight-nucleate, seven-celled nature. Show the following parts-antipodals, synergids, egg, central cell, polar nuclei.

Ans.

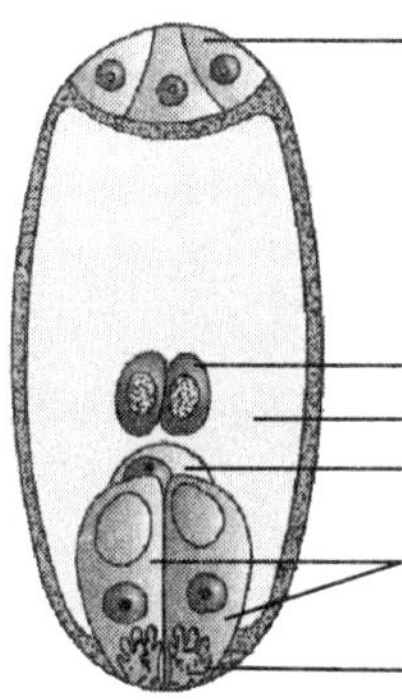

A diagrammatic representation of a mature embryo sac (seven celled with eight nucleated structure)

Q.14 Which is the triploid tissue in a fertilised ovule? How is the triploid condition achieved?

Ans. Endosperm is the triploid tissue ($3n$) in a fertilised ovule. It results from triple fusion involving union of one male gamete and two haploid polar nuclei.

Q.15 Are pollination and fertilisation necessary in apomixis? }
Give reasons.

Thinking Process The phenomenon of asexual reproduction that mimics sexual reproduction by formation of seed without fertilisation is called apomixis.

Ans. Pollination and fertilisation are not necessary for apomixis. The reasons in support of this are given below

(i) Embryo sac can develop from megaspore without reduction division where the egg is diploid and develops into embryo.

(ii) Embryo sac can also develop from diploid nucellus cells that develop into embryo parthogenetically.

Q.16 Identify the type of carpel with the help of diagrams given below

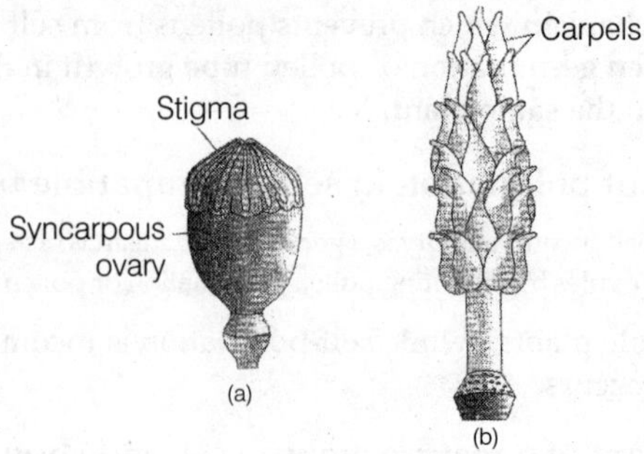

Thinking Process The gynoecium represents the female reproductive part of the flower and may consist of a single pistil (monocarpellary) or many pistils (multicarpellary).

Ans. (a) If a gynoecium has multiple carpels fused into a single structure, it is syncarpous. In this given diagram, the type of carpel is syncarpous (*e.g.*,poppy).

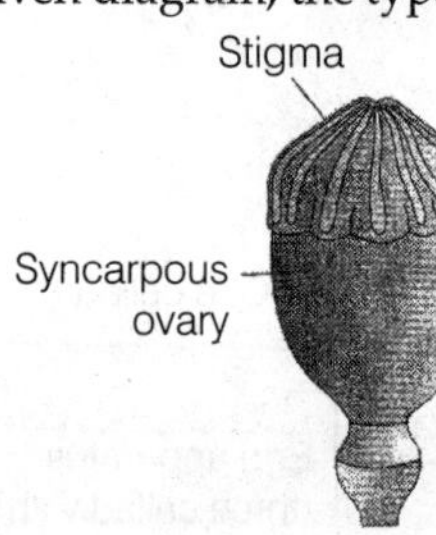

Multicarpellary, syncarpous pistil of *Papaver*

(b) If a gynoecium has multiple carpels in free form, it is apocarpous. In this given diagram, the type of carpel is apocarpous. (*e.g., Michelia*)

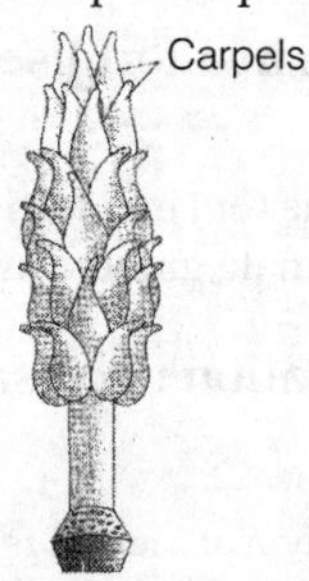

A multicarpellary, apocarpous gynoecium of *Michelia*

Q.17 How is pollination carried out in water plants?

Ans. Pollination in water plants takes place *via* certain methods. They are

(a) In many aquatic plants with emergent flowers, pollination occurs by wind and insects.

(b) If pollination occurs below the surface of water it is known as hypohydrophilly, *e.g., Ceratophyllum.*

(c) If pollination takes place above the surface of water is known as epihydrophily, *e.g., Vallisneria spiralis.*

Q.18 What is the function of the two male gametes produced by each pollen grain in angiosperms.

Thinking Process Mature pollen grain contains two cells, the vegetative cell and generative cell. Generative cell is the generation cell that divides mitotically to give rise to the two male gametes .

Ans. The function of two male gametes produced by each pollen grain in the angiosperms are as follows :

(i) One male gamete fuses with egg forming zygote ($2n$).This process is called fertilisation or syngamy.

(ii) Second male gamete fuses with two polar nuclei diploid secondary nucleus to form primary endosperm nucleus ($3n$). This process is called triple fusion.

Short Answer Type Questions

Q.1 List three strategies that a bisexual chasmogamous flower can evolve to prevent self-pollination (autogamy).

Thinking Process Majority of flowering plants produce hermaphrodite flowers and pollen grains are likely to come in contact with the stigma of the same flower. This self-pollination result in inbreeding depression. Flowering plants have evolved many devices to discourage self- pollination.

Ans. A bisexual chasmogamous flower can evolve the following (three) strategies to prevent self-pollination (autogamy).

(a) **Dichogamy** In this mechanism, pollen release and stigma receptivity are not synchronised. In sunflower, the pollen is released before the stigma becomes receptive (protandry). In *Datura, Solanum*, the stigma becomes receptive much before the release of pollen (protogyny) leads to cross-pollination.

(b) **Herkogamy** The male and female sex organs are placed at different positions in the same plant is called Herkogamy. In these plants, the pollen does not come in contact with the stigma of the same flower. It undergoes cross pollination, *e.g., Hibiscus, Gloriosa*.

(c) **Self-incompatibility** It is a genetic mechanism which prevents the self-pollen from fertilising the ovules by inhibiting pollen germination or pollen tube growth in the pistil, *e.g.*, Abutilon.

Q.2 Given below are the events that are observed in an artificial hybridisation programme. Arrange them in the correct sequential order in which they are followed in the hybridisation programme (a) Re-bagging (b) Selection of parents (c) Bagging (d) Dusting the pollen on stigma (e) Emasculation (f) Collection of pollen from male parent.

Thinking Process One of the major approaches of crop improvement programme is 'Artificial hybridisation'. In such crossing experiments it is important to make sure that only the desired pollen grains are used for pollination and the stigma is protected from contamination (from unwanted pollen).

Ans. The correct sequential order of artificial hybridisatian is as following

(a) Selection of parents.

(b) Emasculation (removal of anthers from the flower bud before the anther dehisces).

(c) Bagging (process to cover the emasculated flower with a bag made up of butter paper).

(d) Collection of pollen from other male plant.

(e) Dusting of pollen on stigma.

(f) Re-bagging

Note If the female parent produces unisexual flowers, there is no need of emasculation.

Q.3 Vivipary automatically limits the number of offsprings in a litter. How?

Ans. Vivipary is the form of reproduction in animals in which the development of embryo takes place within the mother's/female parent's body. The embryo obtains its nourishment directly from mother via placenta or by other means and subsequently mother gives birth to the full term young ones. It is common in most mammals. Viviparity limits the number of offsprings a little due to following reason

(i) As the number of eggs released during ovulation are limited during oestrous or menstrual cycle so the number of eggs fertilised during reproductive cycle of female are also limited.

(ii) As the entire period of development called gestation is passed within the mother's or female parent's body. It restricts the number of embryo that can develop together at one tissue.

(iii) During gestation no ova or egg are released.

Q.4 Does self-incompatibility impose any restrictions on autogamy? Give reasons and suggest the method of pollination in such plants.

Ans. Self-incompatibility imposes restrictions on autogamy. The reason for this may be that majority of flowering plants produce hermaphrodite flowers. When pollen grains come in contact with the stigma of the same flower to continue self-pollination.

Such type of continued self-pollination result in inbreeding depression. That's why flowering plants have developed many devices to discourage self-pollination and to encourage cross-pollination. One of the major way to prevent self-pollination is self-sterility.

Self-incompatibility in some bisexual flowers occurs, if the pollen grains fall on the stigma of the same flower, germination does not occur. But the same pollen grain will germinates when they fall on the stigma of other flowers of the same species. It is a genetic mechanism to prevent self pollination.

Q.5 In the given diagram, write the names of parts shown with lines.

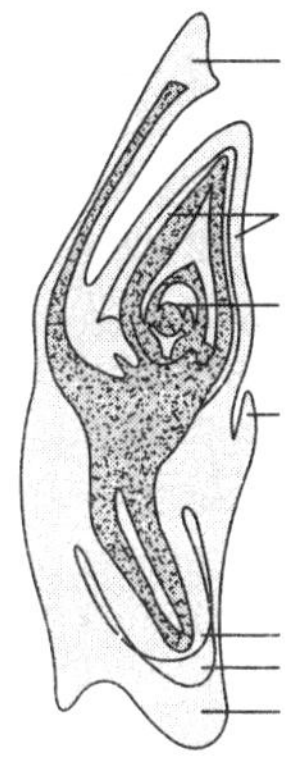

Ans. Embryos of monocotyledons possess only one cotyledon. In the grass family the cotyledon is called **scutellum** that is situated towards one side (lateral) of the embryonal axis.

At its lower end, the embryonal axis has the **radical** and **root cap** enclosed in an undifferentiated sheat called **coleorrhiza**. The portion of the embryonal axis above the level of attachment of scutellum is the **epicotyl**.

Epicotyl has a shoot apex and a few leaf primordia enclosed in a hollow foliar structure, the **coleoptile**.

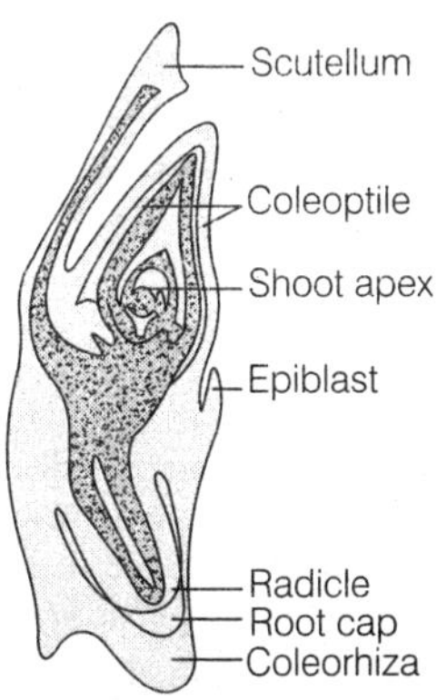

LS of a monocot embryo of grass

Q.6 What is polyembryony and how can it be commercially exploited?

Ans. Polyembryony is the occurrence of more than one embryo in a seed. In many citrus and mango varieties, some of the nucellar cells surrounding the embryo sac starts dividing, protrude into the embryo sac and develop into embryos. In such species, each ovule contains many embryos.

Polyembryony plays a main role in plant breeding and horticulture. The plantlets obtained from these embryos are virus free and has more vigour. Hybrid varieties of several food and vegetable crops are being extensively cultivated and these hybrid cultivars possess high productiviy. Commercially, polyembryony can be exploited for the production of uniform rootstocks and virus-free varieties, which can help in the mass propagation of high-quality plants.

Q.7 Are parthenocarpy and apomixis different phenomena? Discuss their benefits.

Ans. *Yes,* parthenocarpy and apomixis are different phenomenon.

Benefits of Parthenocarpy

(i) It produces fruits which do not contains seeds.

(ii) Processing of fruits by food industry requires the removal of seeds which is quite difficult. Therefore, seedless fruits are preferred by food industry.

(iii) Fruits can be developed inside green houses.

Benefits of Apomixis

(i) During apomixis, chromosomal segregation and recombination does not occur. So, characters are stable for several generations.

(ii) It simplifies commercial hybridised production because it eliminates the need for repeated hybridisation and isolation to produce F_1 or maintain parental generation.

(iii) Adventive embryony is being used in the production of uniform root-stock and virus free varieties.

Q.8 Why does the zygote begin to divide only after the division of Primary Endosperm Cell (PEC)?

Thinking Process The zygote needs nourishment to develop.

Ans. After fertilisation, zygote begins to divide only after the division of Primary Endosperm Cell (PEC). The primary endosperm cell divides repeatedly and forms a triploid endosperm tissue. The cells of this tissue are filled with reserve food materials and are used to nourish the developing embryo.

Q.9 The generative cell of a two celled pollen divides in the pollen tube, but not in a three-celled pollen. Give reasons.

Thinking Process Pollen grains at maturity, divides and produce two unequal cells. The large cell is vegetative cells, has abundant food reserve and contains a large irregular nucleus. The smaller cell is generative cell and floats in the cytoplasm of vegetative cell, which is spindle shaped with dense cytoplasm and a nucleus.

Ans. In over 60 % of angiosperms, pollen grains are shed at this 2-celled stage. In the remaining species, the generative cell divides mitotically to give rise to the two male gametes before pollen grains are shed, forming 3-celled stage.

In 3 celled stage, the pollen grains further germinate on the stigma to produce pollen tube through one of the germ pores. The contents of the pollen grains move into the pollen tube and grows through the tissues of the stigma and style and reaches to ovary.

In plants, when pollen grain are shed at 2 celled stage the generative cell divides and form two male gametes during the growth of the pollen tube in the stigma. Thus, the generative cell of a two celled pollen divides in the pollen tube, but not in a three-celled pollen.

Q.10 In the figure given below label the following parts-male gametes, egg cell, polar nuclei, synergid and pollen tube

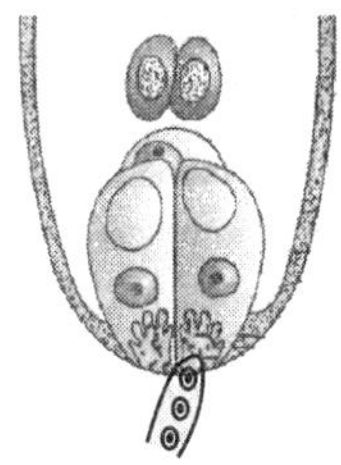

Ans. The following are the parts of this figure

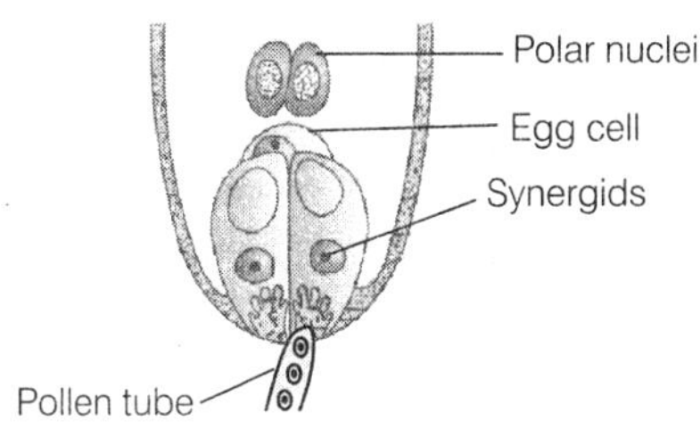

Long Answer Type Questions

Q.1 Starting with the zygote, draw the diagrams of the different stages of embryo development in a dicot.

Thinking Process The zygote gives rise to the proembryo and subsequently to the globular, heart-shaped and mature embryo

Ans.

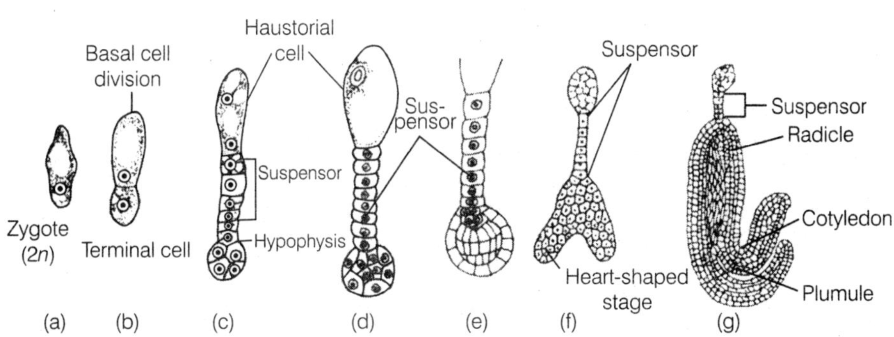

Stage in the developemnt of a dicot embryo

Note The early stages of embryogeny (embryo development) in both monocotyledons and dicotyledons are similar. In case of monocotyledonous embryo a single cotyledon is present.

Q.2 What are the possible types of pollinations in chasmogamous flowers. Give reasons.

Thinking Process The pollination that occurs in open flowers is called **chasmogamy.** It is the most common type of pollination in all types of flowers.

Ans. There are two types of pollinations (chasmogamy) in chasmogamous flowers, *i.e.*, self-pollination and cross-pollination.

(a) **Self-pollination**(Autogamy) The transfer of pollen grains from anther to stigma of the same flower is called **self-pollination.** It is found in both cleistogamous and chasmogamous flowers.

(b) **Cross-pollination** (Allogamy) The transfer of pollen grains from anther to stigma of another flower is called a **cross-pollination.** It is of two types

(i) **Geitonogamy** It is the transfer of pollen grains from anther to the stigma of another flower of the same plant. It is functionally a type of cross-pollination involving a pollinating agent, genetically. It is similar to autogamy.

(ii) **Xenogamy** The transfer of pollen grains from the flower of one plant to the stigma of another plant. This is the only type of pollination, which brings genetically different types of pollen grains to the stigma.

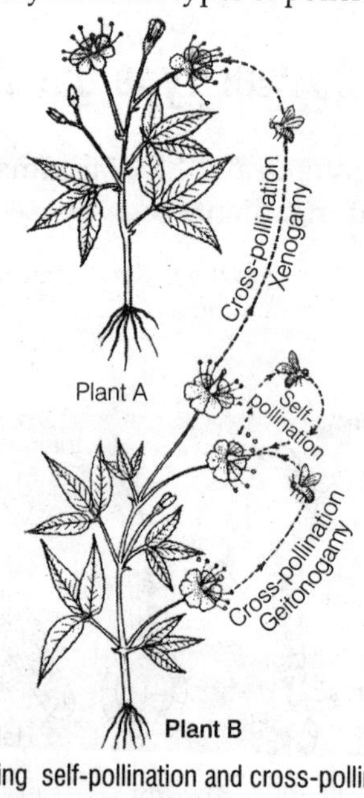

Showing self-pollination and cross-pollination

Q.3 With a neat, labelled diagram, describe the parts of a mature angiosperm embryo sac. Mention the role of synergids.

Thinking Process Megaspore is the mother cell for the development of female gametophyte (embryo sac). The nucleus of the functional megaspore divides mitotically to form two nuclei, which moves to the opposite poles forming two nucleus embryo sacs. Two more mitotic nuclear divisions occur in two nuclei, resulting in the formation of eight-nucleate 7-celled embryo sac.

Ans. After the 8-nucleate stage, cell walls are laid down leading to the organisation of the typical female gametophyte or embryo sac.

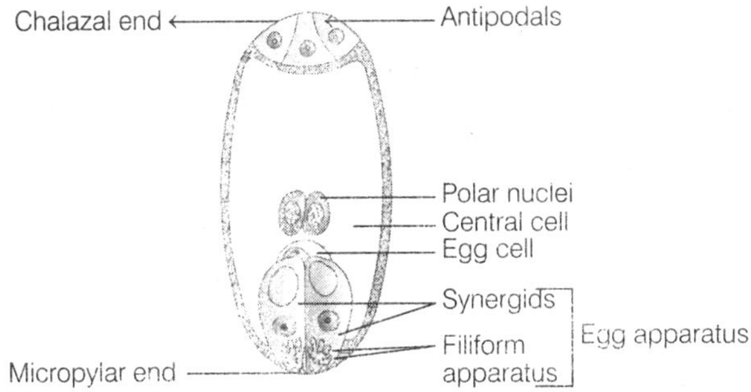

A mature embryo sac of angiosperm

Six of the eight nuclei are surrounded by cell walls and organised into cells. Three cells present towards the micropylar end grouped together, constitute the egg apparatus. The egg apparatus, in turn consists of two synergids and one egg cell. Three cells of the chalazal end are called the antipodals. The large central cell is formed by the fusion of 2-polar nuclei. Thus, a typical angiospermic embryo sac, at maturity consists of eight nuclei and seven cells. This embryo sac is formed from, the single megaspore, so it is called 'monosporic embryo sac.

Role of Synergids The synergids have special cellular thickenings at the micropylar tip called filiform apparatus, which play an important role in guiding the pollen tubes into the synergid.

Q.4 Draw the diagram of a microsporangium and label its wall layers. Write briefly about the wall layers?

- **Concept Insight** A typical angiospermic anther is bilobed with each lobe having two theca. The anther is a four sided structure consisting of four microsporangia located at the corners, two in each lobe.

Ans. The diagram representation of a microsporangium is shown below

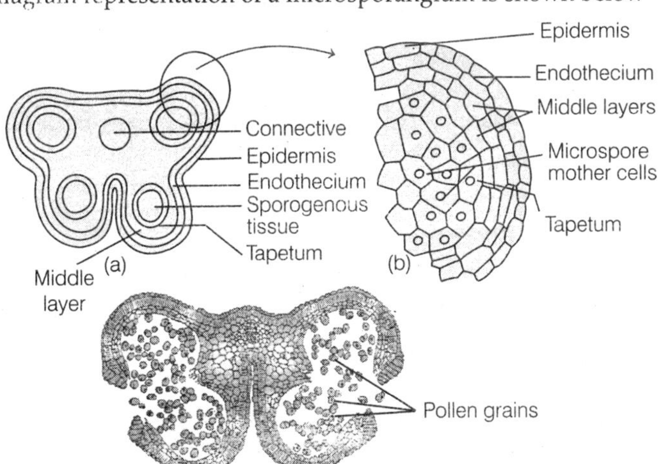

(a) Transverse section of a mature anther (b) Enlarged view of one microsporangium showing wall layers (c) Mature dehisced anther showing

In a transverse section, a typical microsporangium is circular in outline and is surrounded by four wall layers.

(a) **Epidermis** The epidermis is the outermost protective layer. It is composed of tangentially flattened cells. The cells are closely fitted and have thick walls which is helpful in the dehiscence of anther.

(b) **Endothecium** It is present below the epidermis and expands radically with fibrous thickenings, at maturity these cells loose water and help in dehiscence of pollen sac.

(c) **Middle Layers** It is present between well marked endothecium and tapetum. These are thin walled layers, arranged in one to five layers, which also help in dehiscence of anther.

(d) **Tapetum** It is the innermost wall layer with large cells, thin cell walls, abundant cytoplasm and have more than one nuclei. Tapetum is a nutritive tissue which nourishes the developing pollen grains.

The centre of the microsporangium consists of sporogenous tissue, which undergoes meiotic divisions to form microspore tetrads. This process is known as microsporogenesis.

Q.5 Embryo sacs of some apomictic species appear normal, but contain diploid cells. Suggest a suitable explanation for the condition.

Ans. Apomixis is the devlopment of an embryo without fertilisation from the diploid cells of the ovule thus producing seeds without sexual reproduction.

Apomictically produced offsprings are genetically identical to the parent plant. In flowering plants, apomixis is used in a restricted sense to mean angiosperm, *i.e.*, asexual reproduction through seeds.

In some plant species *e.g.*, Asteraceae, Poaceae the diploid egg cell is formed without reduction division and develops into embryo without fertilisation. It is an asexual reproduction in the absence of pollinators such as in extreme environments.

In other species like citrus, some of the nucellar cells surrounding the embryo sac start dividing and develop into embryo. It occurs if the megaspore mother cell does not undergo meiosis, thus produces diploid embryo sac through mitotic divisions.

As a result the embryo sacs of some apomictic species appear normal, but produce diploid cells.

Chapter

03

Human Reproduction

Multiple Choice Questions (MCQs)

Q.1 Choose the incorrect statement from the following

(a) In birds and mammals internal fertilisation takes place
(b) Colostrum contains antibodies and nutrients
(c) Polyspermy is prevented by the chemical changes in the egg surface
(d) In the human female implantation occurs almost seven days after fertilisation

Ans. *(c)* Statement (c) is incorect and can be corrected as polyspermy describes as a condition in which an egg has been fertilised by more than one sperm. In humans, only one sperm nucleus actually fuses with the egg nucleus. Due to acrosomal secretions, sperm digest zona pellucida, allowing it to reach the egg's plasma membrane the plasma membrane blocks the entry of additional sperms. Thus ensuring only one sperm can fertilise the ovum.

Q.2 Identify the correct statement from the following.

(a) High levels of oestrogen triggers the ovulatory surge.
(b) Oogonial cells start to proliferate and give rise to functional ova in regular cycles from puberty onwards.
(c) Sperms released from seminiferous tubules are highly motile.
(d) Progesterone level is high during the post ovulatory phase of menstrual cycle.

Ans. *(d)* Statement (d) is correct as progesterone level is high during post ovulatory phase of menstrual cycle. Progesterone prepares the endometrium for potential implantation of the fertilised egg.

Statements (a), (b) and (c) are incorrect and can be corrected as.

Ovulation is triggered by high levels of Luteinising hormone (LH), not oestrogen. Oogenesis begins before birth in females. The primary oocytes are formed during fetal development and remain dormant unit puberty. After puberty they resume development. Sperms released from seminiferous tubules are not highly motile. They gain motility lates during their passage through the epididymis, where they undergo maturation.

Q.3 Spot the odd one out from the following structures with reference to the male reproductive system

(a) rete testis (b) epididymis (c) vasa efferentia (d) isthmus

Ans. *(d)* Isthmus is the part of female reproductive system. Isthmus has a narrow lumen and it joins the uterus.

Q.4 Seminal plasma, the fluid part of semen, is contributed by

I. Seminal vesicle II. Prostate
III. Urethra IV. Bulbourethral gland

(a) I and II (b) I, II and IV
(c) II, III and IV (d) I an IV

Ans. *(b)* Seminal plasma is contributed by seminal vesicle, prostate and bulb ourethral gland. They are the male accessory glands. Secretions of these glands constitute the seminal plasma which is rich in fructose, calcium and certain enzymes. The secretions of bulbourethral glands also helps in the lubrication of the penis.

Q.5 Spermiation is the process of the release of sperms from

(a) seminiferous tubules (b) vas deferens
(c) epididymis (d) prostate gland

Thinking Process The fully developed sperms become free in the cavity of seminiferous tubules.

Ans. *(a)* The process of release of spermatozoa from Sertoli cells into the cavity of the seminiferous tubules is called spermiation. From here, sperms pass *via* vasa efferentia, then to the epididymis where maturation of the sperm occurs.

Q.6 Mature Graafian follicle is generally present in the ovary of a healthy human female around

(a) 5-8 day of menstrual cycle (b) 11-17 day of menstrual cycle
(c) 18-23 day of menstrual cycle (d) 24-28 day of menstrual cycle

Concept Insight The menstrual cycle can be divided into the following phases, *i.e.*, menstrual phase, follicular (proliferating) phase, ovulatory phase and luteal phase.

Ans. *(b)* In human females, the menstrual cycle lasts for about 28/29 days. It is the follicular phase in which the primary follicles in the ovary grow to become a fully mature graafian follicle (due to FSH stimulation). This phase (follicular) lasts for about 11-17 days of menstrual cycle.

Q.7 Acrosomal reaction of the sperm occurs due to

(a) its contact with zona pellucida of the ova
(b) reactions within the uterine environment of the female
(c) reactions within the epididymal environment of the male
(d) androgens produced in the uterus

Thinking Process The secondary oocyte reaching the Fallopian tube is surrounded by zona pellucida and corona radiata. A capacitated sperm passes through the corona radiata to reach the zona pellucida.

Ans. *(a)* When head of sperm comes in contact with zona pellucida of ovum the acrosome release its contents by exocytosis. This is called acrosomal reaction. It helps the sperm to reach the plasma membrane of ovum, by dissolving corona radiata and zona pellucida.

Q.8 Which one of the following is not a male accessory gland?

(a) Seminal vesicle (b) Ampulla
(c) Prostate (d) Bulbourethral gland

Thinking Process The male accessory glands include paired seminal vesicles, a prostate and paired bulbourethral glands.

Ans. *(b)* Ampulla is one of the three region of Fallopian tubes and not a part of male accessory gland. The oviducts (Fallopian tubes), uterus and vagina constitute the female accessory ducts. Each Fallopian tube is about 10-12 cm long that extends from the periphery of each ovary to the uterus.

The Fallopian tube has three mains regions, *i.e.*, infundibulum, ampulla and isthmus. Ampulla region is the long, wide, thin walled part found next to the infundibulum.

Q.9 The immature male germ cell undergo division to produce sperms by the process of spermatogenesis. Choose the correct one with reference to above.

(a) Spermatogonia have 46 chromosomes and always undergo meiotic cell division
(b) Primary spermatocytes divide by mitotic cell division
(c) Secondary spermatocytes have 23 chromosomes and undergo second meiotic division
(d) Spermatozoa are transformed into spermatids

Ans. *(c)* Statement (c) is correct as secondary spermatocytes have 23 chromsomes and undergo second meiotic division. Statements (a), (b) and (d) are incorrect and can be corrected as in testis, the immature male germ cells (spermatogonia) produce sperms by spermatogenesis. The spermatogonia present on the inside wall of seminiferous tubules multiply by mitotic division and increase in numbers.

Each spermatogonia is diploid and contains 46 chromosomes. ($2n$) Some of the spermatogonia called primary spermatocytes periodically undergo meiosis. A primary spermatocyte completes the first meiotic division (reduction division) leading to formation of two equal, haploid cells called secondary spermatocytes, which have only 23 chromosomes each (n).

The secondary spermatocytes undergo the second phage of meiotic division to produce four equal, haploid spermatids. The spermatids are transformed into spermatozoa (sperms) by the process called spermiogenesis.

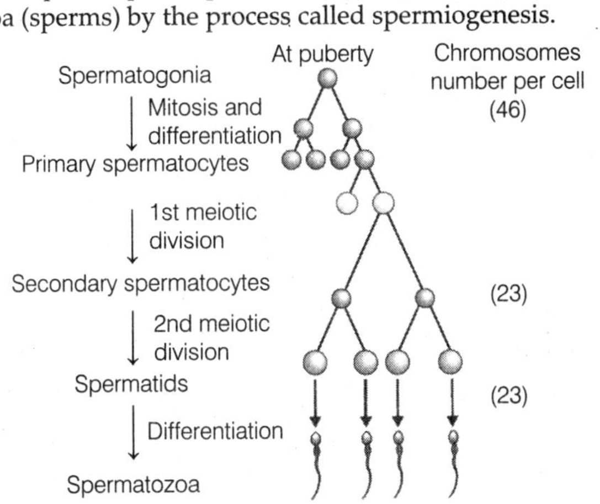

Schematic representation of spermatogenesis in human male

Q.10 Match between the following representing parts of the sperm and their functions and choose the correct option.

Column I	Column II
A. Head	1. Enzymes
B. Middle piece	2. Sperm motility
C. Acrosome	3. Energy
D. Tail	4. Genetic material

Codes

	A	B	C	D		A	B	C	D
(a)	2	4	1	3	(b)	4	3	1	2
(c)	4	1	2	3	(d)	2	1	3	4

Ans. ***(b)***

Column I	Column II
A. Head	4. Genetic material
B. Middle piece	3. Energy
C. Acrosome	1. Enzymes
D. Tail	2. Sperm motility

Q.11 Which among the following has 23 chromosomes?

(a) Spermatogonia (b) Zygote
(c) Secondary oocyte (d) Oogonia

Ans. ***(c)*** Secondary oocyte has 23 chromosomes as it is a product of meiotic division of primary oocyte during oogenesis in the ovary. Spermatogonia are the cells found on the innerwall of the seminiferous tubules and consists of 46 chromosomes. Oognia are the diploid cell found in foetal ovary. Zygote is also a diploid and fertilised ovum.

Mistake Alert ! *Students make mistakes while learning the process of spermatogenesis especially the number of chromosomes involved at each step and in type of division.*

Q.12 Match the following and choose the correct options.

Column I	Column II
A. Trophoblast	1. Embedding of blastocyst in the endometrium
B. Cleavage	2. Group of cells that would differentiate as embryo
C. Inner cell mass	3. Outer layer of blastocyst attached to the endometrium
D. Implantation	4. Mitotic division of zygote

Codes

	A	B	C	D		A	B	C	D
(a)	2	1	3	4	(b)	3	4	2	1
(c)	3	1	2	4	(d)	2	4	3	1

Ans. *(b)*

	Column I	Column II
A.	Trophoblast	3. Outer layer of blastocyst attached to the endometrium
B.	Cleavage	4. Mitotic division of zygote
C.	Inner cell mass	2. Group of cell that would differentiate as embryo
D.	Implantation	1. Embedding of blastocyst in the endometrium

Q.13 Which of the following hormones is not secreted by human placenta?

(a) hCG (b) Estrogens
(c) Progesterone (d) LH

Ans. *(d)* LH or Luteizing Hormone is produced by anterior pituitary gland and not by placenta. The placenta is an organ that connects the developing embryo (foetus) and maternal body (uterine wall) to allow nutrient uptake, waste elimination and gas exchange *via* the mother's blood supply.

Placenta also acts as an endocrine tissue and produces several hormones like **Human chorionic gonadotropin** (hCG), Human Placental Lactogen (hPL), **oestrogens, progesterone, etc.**

Q.14 The vas deferens receives duct from the seminal vesicle and opens into urethra as

(a) epididymis (b) ejaculatory duct
(c) efferent ductule (d) ureter

Thinking Process The male sex accessory ducts include rete testis, vasa efferentia, epididymis and vas deferens.

Ans. *(b)* The vas deferens is a continuation of the epididymis. It is about 40 cm long and slightly coiled at first but becomes straight as it enters the abdominal cavity through the inguinal canal.

Here, it passes over the urinary bladder, curves around the ureter, joins a duct from seminal vesicle and opens into urethra as the ejaculatory duct. These ducts store and transport the sperms from the to the outside through urethra.

Q.15 Urethral meatus refers to the

(a) urinogenital duct
(b) opening of vas deferens into urethra
(c) external opening of the urinogenital duct
(d) muscles surrounding the urinogenital duct

Ans. *(c)* The urethra originates from the urinary bladder and extends through the penis to its external opening called urethral meatus. The vas deferens along with a duct of seminal vesicle open into urethra as the ejaculatory duct.

Q.16 Morula is a developmental stage

(a) between the zygote and blastocyst
(b) between the blastocyst and gastrula
(c) after the implantation
(d) between implantation and parturition

Ans. *(a)* The embryo with 8 -16 blastomeres is called morula. This morula continues to divide and transform into blastocyst. It moves further to get embedded in the endometrium of the uterus. This is called implantation.

Q.17 The membranous cover of the ovum at ovulation is

(a) corona radiata (b) zona radiata (c) zona pellucida (d) chorion

Ans. *(a)* The ovum is enclosed by the inner thin, transparent, non-cellular coat, zona pellucida and outer thick coat, corona radiata. During fertilisation sperm first comes in contact with the corona radiata and zona pellucida to reach the plasma membrane of the egg (ovum).

Q.18 Identify the odd one from the following

(a) labia minora (b) fimbriae (c) infundibulum (d) isthmus

Ans. *(a)* Labia minora is the part of female external genitalia. The female accessory ducts constitute the oviducts (Fallopian tubes), uterus and vagina. Each Fallopian tube extends from the periphery of each ovary to the uterus. The part closer to the ovary is the funnel-shaped infundibulum.

The edges of the infundibulum possess finger-like projections called fimbriae. The infundibulum leads to a wider part of the oviduct called ampulla. The last part of the oviduct is isthmus.

Very Short Answer Type Questions

Q.1 Given below are the events in human reproduction. Write them in correct sequential order.

Insemination / gemetogenesis / fertilisation, parturition / gestation / Implanation.

Ans. The reproductive events in humans include

Gametogenesis → Insemination → Fertilisation → Implantation → Gestation → Parturition

Q.2 The path of sperm transport is given below. Provide the missing steps in blank boxes.

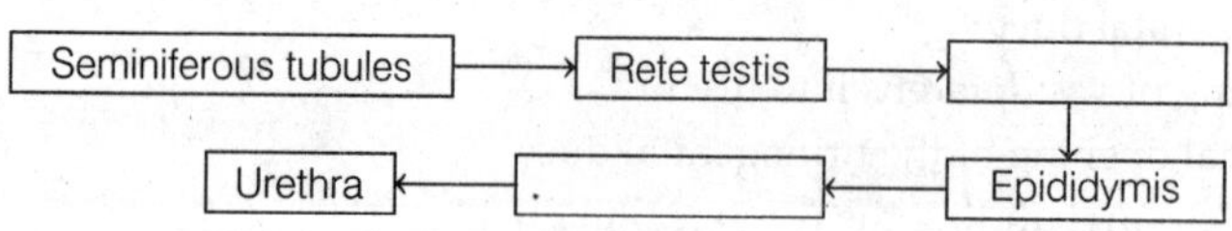

Ans.

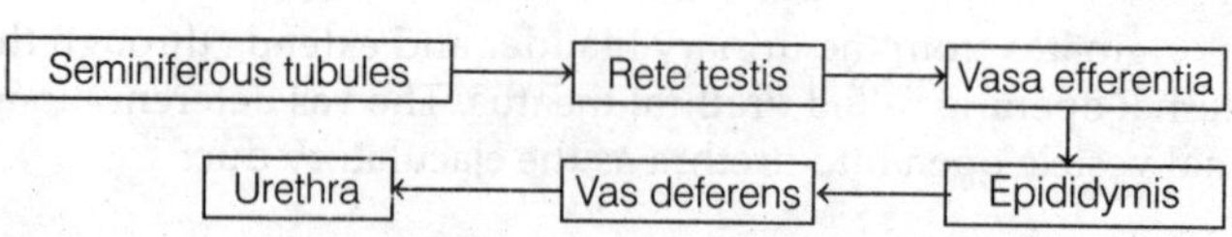

Q.3 What is the role of cervix in the human female reproductive system?

Ans. Role of cervix in human female reproductive system are as follows.

(i) Cervical canal i.e., the cavity of cervix and vagina together forms the birth canal to facilitate parturition.

(ii) It regulates the passage of sperms into the uterus.

Q.4 Why are menstrual cycles absent during pregnancy?

- **Concept Insight** Lack of menstruation may be indicative of pregnancy. However, it may also be caused due to some other underlying causes like stress, poor health, etc.

Ans. The menstrual flow results due to breakdown of endometrial lining of the uterus and its blood vessels which forms a liquid that comes out through vagina. Menstruation only occurs if the released ovum is not fertillised.

During pregnancy, all events of the menstrual cycle stop. The corpus luteum secretes large amounts of progesterone which is essential for the maintenance of the endometrium. These changes lead to no menstruation, during pregnancy.

Q.5 Female reproductive organs and associated functions are given below in column I and II. Fill the blank blanks.

Column I	Column II
Ovaries	Ovulation
Oviduct	A
B	Pregnancy
Vagina	Birth

Ans.

Column I	Column II
Ovaries	Ovulation
Oviduct	Fertilisation
Uterus	Pregnancy
Vagina	Birth

Q.6 From where the parturition signals arise-mother or foetus? Mention the main hormone involved in parturition.

Ans. Parturition is induced by a complex neuro-endocrine mechanism. The signals for parturition originate from the fully developed foetus and the placenta which induce mild uterine contractions called foetal-ejection reflex.

The hormone involved in parturition is oxytocin that acts on the uterine muscle and causes stronger uterine contractions. This leads to the expulsion of the baby out of the uterus through the birth canal.

Q.7 What is the significance of epididymis in male fertility?

Ans. The epididymis helps the sperm in attaining maturity, acquiring increased motility and fertilising capacity. It also stores sperms for a short period before entering the vas deferens. The epididymis shows peristaltic and segmenting contractions at intervals to push the sperm away from the testis.

Q.8 Give the names and functions of the hormones involved in the process of spermatogenesis. Write the names of the endocrine glands from where they are released.

Ans. Hormones involved in spermatogenesis are

Hormone	Function	Gland
1. Gonadotrophin releasing hormone (GnRH)	Acts on pituitary to secrete LH and FSH.	Hypothalamus
2. Luteinizing Hormone (LH)	Acts on Leydig cells and stimulates synthesis and secretion of androgens	Pituitary
3. Androgens	Stimulate process of spermatogenesis	Testis
4. Follicle Stimulating Hormone (FSH)	Acts ons sertoli cell and stimulates secretion of some factors that help in process of spermiogenesis	Pituitary

Q.9 The mother germ cells are transformed into a mature follicle through series of steps. Provide the missing steps in the blank boxes.

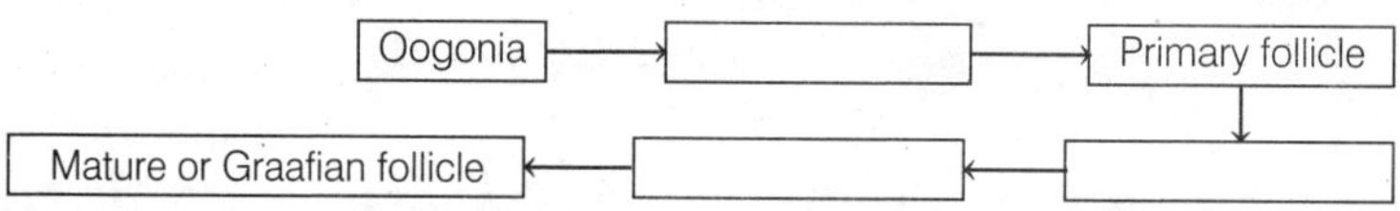

Ans.

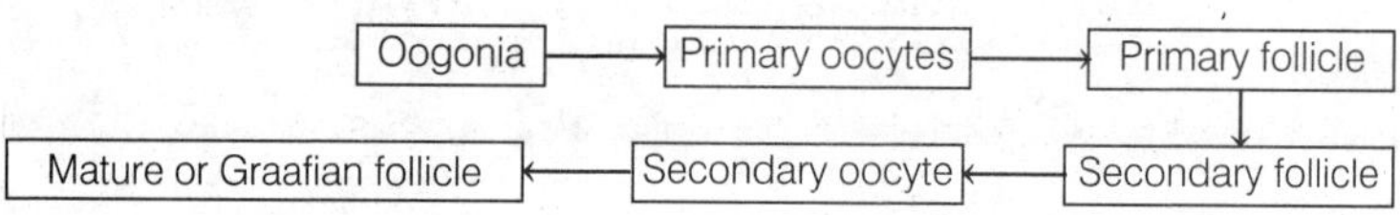

Q.10 During reproduction, the chromosome number ($2n$) reduces to half (n) in the gametes and again the original number ($2n$) is restored in the offspring. What are the processes through which these events take place?

Thinking Process Gametes are haploid while zygotes are diploid.

Ans. The processes involved are meiosis and fertilisation. The meiotic cell division reduces the chromosome number to half during gametogenesis and diploid (2n) number of chromosome is restored by the union of male and female gamete as a result of fertilisation.

Q.11 What is the difference between a primary oocyte and a secondary oocyte?

Ans. The difference between primary oocyte and secondary oocyte are as follows

	Primary oocyte	Secondary oocyte
(i)	These are formed at fetal, stage	These are formed at onset of puberty
(ii)	Surrounded by follicular cells	Surrounded by follicular cells along with zona pellucida and corona radiata.
(iii)	Chromosome numbers is 46	Chromosome number is 23

Q.12 What is the significance of ampullary-isthmic junction in the female reproductive tract?

- **Concept Insight** Fertilisation can only occur if the ovum and sperms are transported simultaneously to the ampullary - isthmic junction. All copulations do not lead to fertilisation and pregnancy.

Ans. The act of fertilisation takes place in the female genital tract that is at the junction of the isthmus and ampulla (ampullary - isthmic junction) of the Fallopian tube.

Q.13 How does zona pellucida of ovum help in preventing polyspermy?

Ans. When a sperm penetrates ovum, it induces changes in the membrane that make the zona pellucida layer impenetrable to additional sperms. Thus, it ensures that only one sperm can fertilise an ovum at one time thus, stopping polyspermy.

Q.14 Mention the importance of LH surge during menstrual cycle.

Ans. Rapid secretion of LH leading to its maximum level during the mid menstrual cycle (14th day) is called LH surge. It induces the rupture of Graafian follicle and thereby the release of ovum (ovulation).

Q.15 Which type of cell division forms spermatids from the secondary spermatocytes?

Thinking Process Secondary spermatocytes are produced, when the primary spermatocytes undergo the first meiotic division (reduction division).

Ans. The secondary spermatocytes undergoes the second meiotic division to produce four equal, haploid spermatids.

Short Answer Type Questions

Q.1 A human female experiences two major changes, menarche and menopause during her life. Mention the significance of both the events.

Ans. In human beings, initiation of menstruation at puberty (between age 9-15 years) is called menarche. While, menstrual cycles ceases around 50 years of age, that is termed as menopause. Menarche signifies the maturation and preparedness of the female reproductive system for child bearing.

It marks the capability of the ovaries to produce mature oocyte (female gamete) that can now be fertilised by the sperm and also that the uterus is capable of supporting the foetal growth and development.

Menopause signifies the end of child bearing age. At this age supply of healthy eggs is very low, the levels of the hormones secreted by the ovaries decline and the menstruation stops. The uterus no longer remains conducive for foetal growth.

Q.2 (a) How many spermatozoa are formed from one secondary spermatocyte?

(b) Where does the first cleavage division of zygote take place?

Thinking Process In testis, the spermatogonia (immature germ cells) present in the form of germinal layer on the inner wall of seminiferous tubules multiply by mitotic division and increase in numbers. Each spermatogonium is diploid and contains 46 chromosomes. Some of them periodically undergo meiosis and are called primary spermatocytes.

Ans. (a) A primary spermatocyte completes the first meiotic division (reduction division) leading to formation of two equal, haploid cells called secondary spermatocytes ($n = 23$ chromosomes each). The secondary spermatocytes undergo the second meiotic division to produce four equal, haploid spermatids (n) each spermatid produces spermatazoa.

(b) The mitotic division called cleavage starts 30 h after fertilisation and take place in ampulla of fallopian tube. This happens when the zygote moves through the isthmus of the Fallopian tube (oviduct) towards the uterus and forms blastomeres.

Q.3 Corpus luteum in pregnancy has a long life. However, if fertilisation does not take place, it remains active only for 10-12 days. Explain.

Ans. The ruptured Graafian follicle transform into the corpus luteum and secretes large amounts of progesterone which is essential for the maintenance of the endometrium. Such an endometrium is required for the implantation of fertilised ovum (blastocyst) and other events of pregnancy.

This is the reason why corpus luteum in pregnancy has a long life. But in the absence of fertilisation, maintenance of endometrium is not required. Therefore, corpus luteum degenerates with in 10-12 days.

Q.4 What is foetal-ejection reflex? Explain how it leads to parturition?

Ans. Foetal-ejection reflex encompasses the mild uterine contractions in response to the signals that originate from the fully developed foetus and the placenta. This triggers release of hormone oxytocin from maternal pituitary. Oxytocin acts on the uterine muscle and causes stronger contractions, which in turn stimulates further secretion of oxytocin.

The stimulatory reflex between the uterine contraction and oxytocin secretion continues resulting in stronger and stronger contractions leading to the expulsion of baby out of uterus through birth canal.

Q.5 Except endocrine function, what are the other functions of placenta.

Ans. Placenta is structural and functional unit between developing embryo (foetus) and maternal body.

Placenta act's as an endocrine tissue and produces several hormones like human Chorionic Gonadotropin (hCG), human Placental Lactogen (hPL), estrogens, progesterones, etc.

Other than the endocrine function, placenta also facilitates the supply of oxygen and nutrients to the embryo and removes carbon dioxide and excretory waste materials produced by the developing faetus.

Q.6 Why doctors recommend breast feeding during initial period of infant growth?

Ans. The milk produced during the initial few days of lactation is called **colostrum.** It contains several antibodies (especially IgA) essential to develop resistance, in the new-born babies, against diseases. Breast feeding during the initial period of infant growth is recommended by doctors for bringing up a healthy baby.

Q.7 What are the events that take place in the ovary and uterus during follicular phase of the menstrual cycle.

Ans. The major events of the menstrual cycle are **menstrual phase**, **follicular phase**, **ovulatory phase** and **luteal phase**.

The follicular phase follows the menstrual phase. During this phase, the primary follicles in the ovary grow to become a fully mature Graafian follicle. Simultaneously the endometrial layer of uterus regenerates through proliferation. These changes in the ovary and the uterus are induced by changes in the levels of pituitary and ovarian hormones.

The secretion of gonadotropins (LH and FSH) increases gradually during the follicular phase and stimulates follicular development as well as secretion of oestrogens by the growing follicles.

Both LH and FSH attain a peak level in the middle of cycle (about 14th day). This rapid secretion of LH leading to its maximum level induces rupture of Graafian follicle to release ovum.

Q.8 Given below is a flow chart showing ovarian changes during menstrual cycle. Fill in the spaces giving the name of the hormones responsible for the events shown.

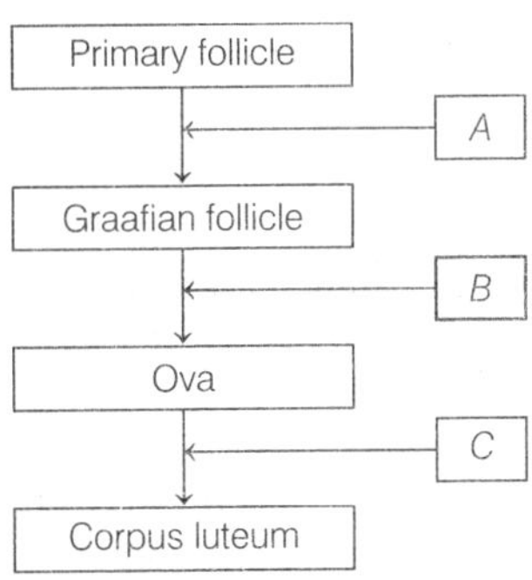

Ans. The secretion of gonadotropins (LH and FSH) increases gradually during the follicular phase and stimulates follicular development as well as secretion of estrogens. Rapid secretion of LH leading to its maximum level during the midcycle (14th day) which induces rupture of Graafian follicle to release ovum. The remaining parts of the Graafian follicle transform into the corpus luteum. The corpus luteum secretes large amounts of progesterone which is essential for maintenance of the endometrium during pregnancy.

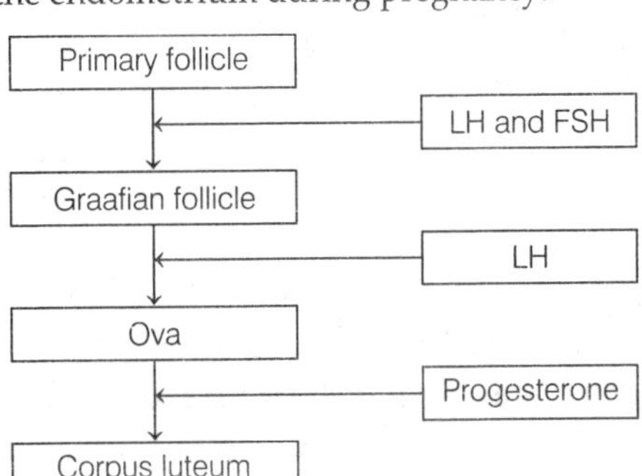

Q.9 Give a schematic labelled diagram to represent oogenesis (without descriptions).

Ans.

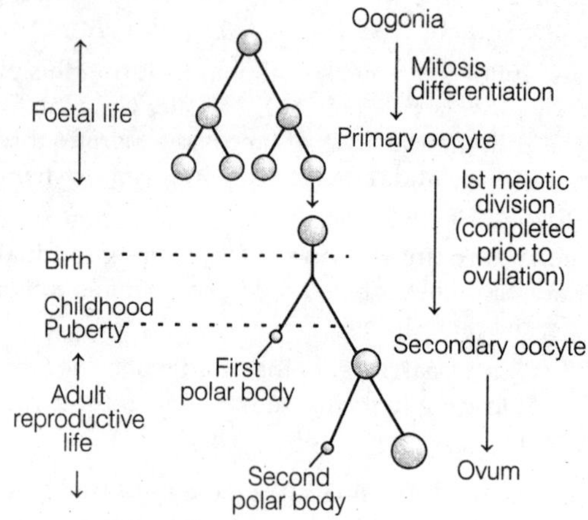

Schematic representation of oogenesis

Q.10 What are the changes in the oogonia during the transition of a primary follicle to Graafian follicle?

Ans. The germinal epithelial cells divide repeatedly until many diploid oogonia are formed. The oogonia grow to form primary oocytes. Each primary oocyte then gets surrounded by a layer of granulosa cells and then called the primary follicle. The primary follicles get surrounded by more layers of granulosa cells and called secondary follicles.

The secondary follicle soon transforms into a tertiary follicle which is characterised by a fluid filled cavity called **antrum**. The primary oocyte within the tertiary follicle undergoes meiotic division to become a secondary oocyte and a first polar body (haploid).

The tertiary follicle further changes into the mature follicle or Graafian follicle that ruptures to release the secondary oocyte (ovum) from the ovary by the process called ovulation.

Long Answer Type Questions

Q.1 What role does pituitary gonadotropins play during follicular and ovulatory phases of menstrual cycle? Explain the shifts in steroidal secretions.

Thinking Process The major events of the menstrual cycle include menstrual phase, follicular phase, ovulatory phase and luteal phase.

Ans. Hormonal Control during Follicular Phase are as follows

(i) FSH from pituitary transforms the primary follicle into Graafian Follicle.

(ii) FSH also stimulates Graafian folliclular cells to secrete oestrogen.

(iii) Oestrogen causes proliferation of endometrium of the uterine wall.

Hormonal Control during Ovulatory Phase

(i) Pituitary glands are stimulated by oestrogen to release LH.

(ii) LH surge (maximum level of LH) cause ovulation from the ovary on the 14th day of menstrual cycle. LH also induces the transformation of Graafian follicle into corpus luteum, which secrete progestrone to help implantation, placenta formation and maintenance of pregnancy.

(iii) In menstrual phase, there is reduction in secretion of progestrone and oestrogen.

(iv) Gonadotropin releasing hormine (GnRH) stimulates the release of FSH and LH. FSH stimulates the ovarian follicles to produce oestrogen during proleferative phase. LH stimulates the ovulation in ovulatory phase.

The shift in steroidal during different of menstruation is given below.

(i) **Menstrual Phase** (1-5 days) Endrometrium breaks down. The cells of endometrium and unfertilised ovum constitute menstrual flow. Progesterone production is reduced

(ii) **Follicular Phase** (6-13 days) Endometrium regenerates FSH and oestrogen secretion is increased.

(iii) **Ovulatory Phase** (14-16 days) Both LH and FSH attain peak level. It leads to ovulation. Oestrogen level is also high.

(iv) **Luteal Phase** (16-28 days). The secretion of progesterone increases as it maintain the endometrium lining.

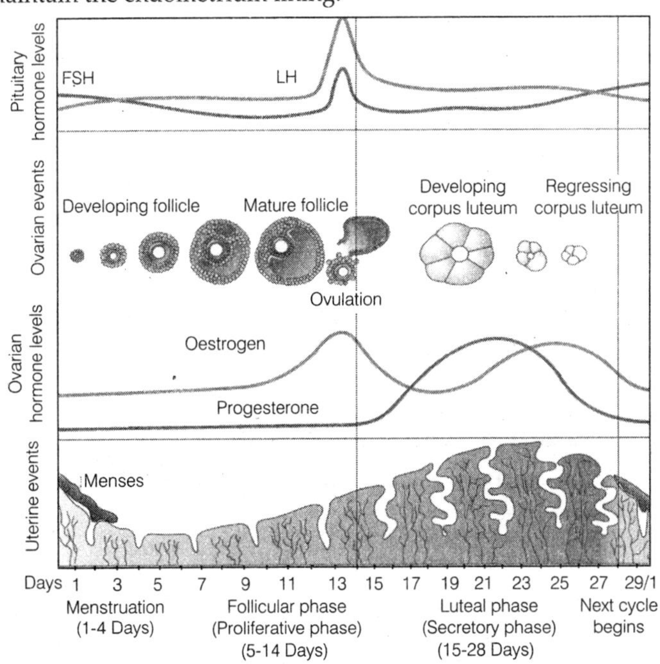

Diagrammatic presentation of various events during a mentrual cycle

Q.2 Meiotic division during oogenesis is different from that in spermatogenesis. Explain how and why?

Ans. Oogenesis is different from that of spermatogenesis in the following aspects

Spermatogenesis	Oogenesis
Sperm generation starts at puberty.	Oocytes generation occurs before birth.
Many Millions sperms generated at a time.	Only one egg matures at a time, every month.
After two complete meiotic divisions, four equal sized cells are produced.	Meiosis-I get arrested at prophase-I and when completed at later stage, one big cell with almost all the cytoplasm and one very small sized polar body is produced.
They mature into flagellated and motile cell.	Mature ovum is non-flagellated and non-motile.

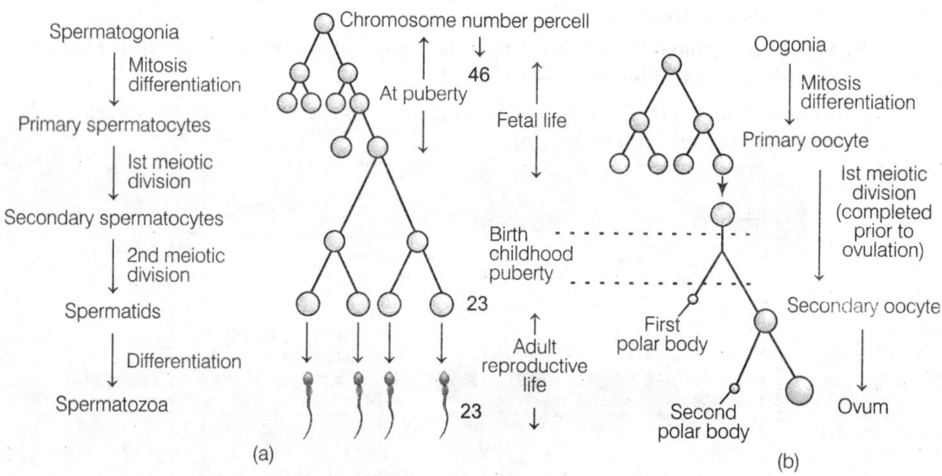

Schematic representation of (a) Spermatogenesis (b) Oogenesis

Reasons

(i) Unequal cell division makes the ovum much larger than the other two polar bodies. This is because ovum has more cytoplasm and organelles, therefore it has a better chance of surviving.

(ii) The male produce millions of tiny sperms while, the female makes only one egg per month that also waits for second meiotic division, just before fertilisation. This is a way of conserving energy.

(iii) Sperm is smaller and motile as it has to move out of male system to female reproductive system. Larger egg has abundant reserve food so that embryo starts developing right after fertilisation.

Q.3 The zygote passes through several developmental stages till implantation. Describe each stage briefly with suitable diagrams.

Thinking Process The zygote undergoes mitotic division (cleavage) as it moves through isthmus of oviduct towards uterus and forms 2, 4, 8, 16 daughter cells called blastomeres.

Ans. The zygote passes through the following stages till implantations

(i) The single called zygote undergoes rapid mitotic division to form embryo

(ii) The embryo with 8-16 blastomeres is called a morula.

(iii) The morula continues to divide and transforms into blastocyst as it moves further into uterus.

(iv) The blastomeres in the blastocyst are arranged into a surface layer called trophoblast and a cluster of interior cells attached to trophoblast are called the inner cell mass.

(v) The trophoblast layer then gets attached to the endometrium and inner mass cells get differentiated as embryo.

(vi) After attachment, the uterine cells divide rapidly to cover the blastocyst.

(vii) The blastocyst becomes embedded in the uterine endometrium. This is called implantation.

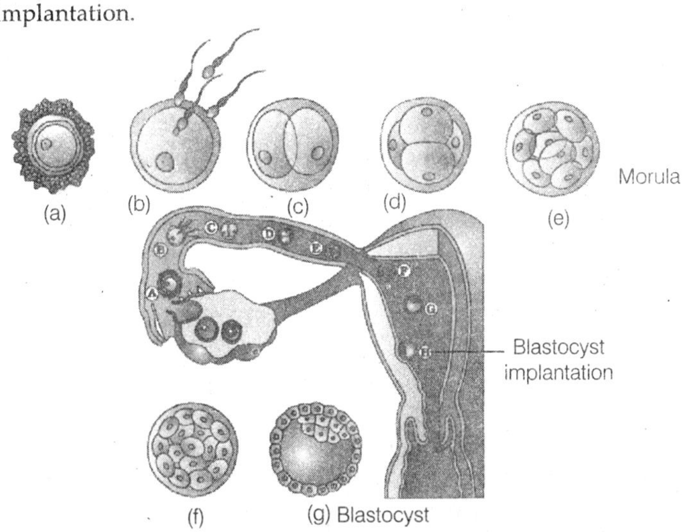

Transport of ovum, fertilisation and passage of growing embryo through Fallopian tube

Q.4 Draw a neat diagram of the female reproductive system and label the parts associated with the following (a) production of gamete, (b) site of fertilisation (c) site of implantation and (d) birth canal.

Ans. The female reproductive system consists of a pair of ovaries and oviducts along with a uterus, cervix, vagina and the external genitalia located in the pelvic region.

These parts are integrated structurally and functionally to support the processes of ovulation, fertilisation, pregnancy and child birth.

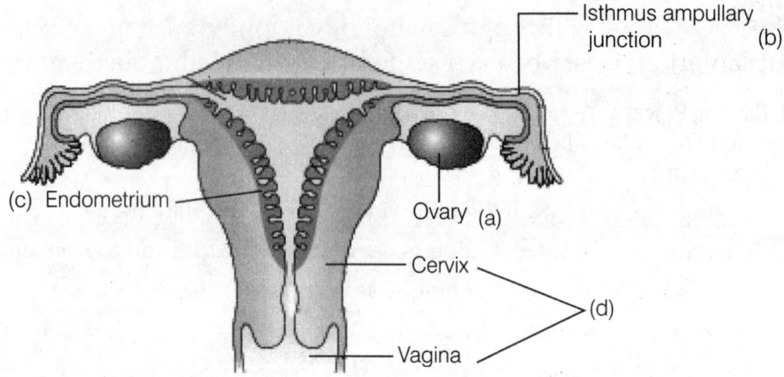

Diagrammatic sectional view of the female reproductive system

Labels

(a) Ovary (production of gamete)
(b) Isthmus-ampullary junction(site of fertilisation)
(c) Uterine endometrium (site of implantation)
(d) Cervix and vagina (birth canal)

Q.5 With a suitable diagram, describe the organisation of mammary gland.

Ans. The description of mammary gland is as follows

(i) The mammary glands are paired structures (breasts) that contain adipose tissue (fat containing cells) and undeveloped duct system

(ii) During pregnancy, in response to oestrogen and progesterone, mammary glands develops for milk production.

(iii) Glandular tissue of each breast is divided into mammary lobes containing clusters of cells called alveoli.

(iv) The cells of alveoli secrete milk, which is stored in the cavities (lumens) of alveoli

(v) The alveoli open into mammary tubules. The tubules of each lobe join to form a mammary duct.

(vi) Several mammary ducts join to form a wider mammary ampulla which is connected to lactiferous duct through which milk is sucked out by the baby.

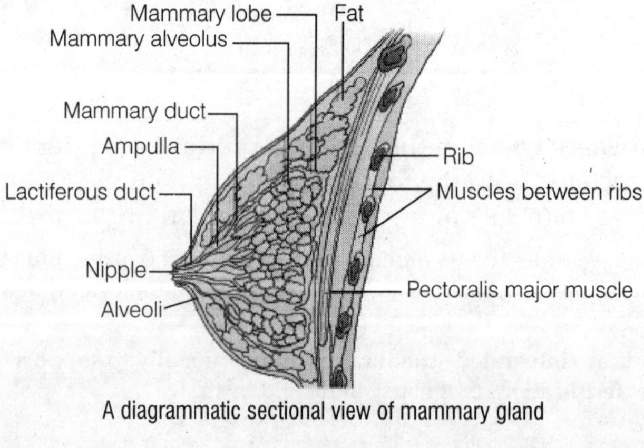

A diagrammatic sectional view of mammary gland

Chapter

04 Reproductive Health

Multiple Choice Questions (MCQs)

Q.1 The method of directly injecting a sperm into ovum in Assisted reproductive technology is called

(a) GIFT (b) ZIFT (c) ICSI (d) ET

Ans. *(c)* ICSI or Intra Cytoplasmic Sperm Injection is a specialised procedure of assisted reproductive technology (ART) that helps the couples to overcome their infertility. In this technique, a sperm is directly injected into the ovum placed in a nutrient broth in the laboratory to form a zygote. This zygote is then impanted through ZIFT into woman.

Q.2 Increased IMR and decreased MMR in a population will

(a) cause rapid increase in growth rate
(b) result in decline in growth rate
(c) not cause significant change in growth rate
(d) result in an explosive population/exp

Ans. *(c)* **IMR** (Infant Mortility Rate) and **MMR** (Maternal Mortility Rate) both are responsible for affecting the growth rate inversely. It means decline in IMR as well as MMR will result in high population growth and *vice-versa.*

Here, if IMR has been increased then it will result in decline in growth rate. While, decreased MMR will cause rapid increase in growth rate.

Therefore, in the above situation, if IMR has been increased and MMR has been decreased in a population, it will not cause any significant change in growth rate.

Q.3 Intensely lactating mothers do not generally conceive due to the

(a) suppression of gonadotropins
(b) hypersecretion of gonadotropins
(c) suppression of gametic transport
(d) suppression of fertilisation

Thinking Process The natural methods of birth control work on the principle of avoiding the meeting of ovum and sperm. One of these methods is lactational amenorrhea, that is based on the principle that during the period of lactation after parturition, ovulation does not occur.

Ans. *(a)* Breastfeeding is one of the natural contraceptive methods. It reduces fecundity by affecting the production of certain reproductive hormones. It is known to suppress the production of **Gonadotropin-Releasing Hormone** (GnRH) and **Follicle Stimulating Hormone** (FSH).

The release of these hormones triggers ovulation. Breastfeeding also leads to increased level of prolactin, a hormone that inhibits ovulation. So, even when a woman ovulates, her likelihood of conceiving is low if she is breast-feeding.

Q.4 Sterilisation techniques are generally full proof methods of contraception with least side effects. Yet, this is the last option for the couples because

I. it is almost irreversible.

II. of the misconception that it will reduce sexual urge/drive.

III. it is a surgical procedure.

IV. of lack of sufficient facilities in many parts of the country.

Choose the correct option

(a) I and III (b) II and III

(c) II and IV (d) I, II, III and IV

Ans. *(d)* All the above statements are true as surgical methods or sterilisation techniques are generally opted by the male or female partner as a terminal method to prevent any more pregnancies. This method blocks gamete transport and thereby prevent conception.

In males, this is called vasectomy, while in females, this is called tubectomy. It is a surgical and permanent contraceptive method.

Even though it is very effective yet it is often used as a last option by most couples. One, because it is almost irreversible and second because of few misconceptions such as the absence of ejaculation and lowering of sexual urge. Third, because it is a surgical procedure, there are certain risk of infection. Last but not least, there are lack of sufficient facilities in many parts of developing countries (*e.g.*, lack of hygiene, lack of qualified personnel etc.)

Q.5 A national level approach to build up a reproductively healthy society was taken up in our country in

(a) 1950s (b) 1960s

(c) 1980s (d) 1990s

Ans. *(a)* India was amongst the first countries in the world to initiate action plans and programmes at a national level to attain total reproductive health as a social goal. These programmes called 'family planning' were initiated in 1951 and were periodically assessed over the past decades.

Creating awareness among people about various reproduction related aspects and providing facilities and support for building up a reproductively healthy society are the major tasks under these programmes.

Q.6 Emergency contraceptives are effective if used within 72 hrs of

(a) coitus
(b) ovulation
(c) menstruation
(d) implantation

Thinking Process Progestogens alone or in combination with estrogen can also be used as contraceptive method by females in the form of tablets (pills).

Ans. *(a)* Administration of higher doses progestogens or progestogen-oestrogen combinations within 72 hrs of coitus have been found to be very effective as emergency contraceptives. They could be used to avoid possible pregnancy due to rape or casual unprotected intercourse. These drugs delay or disrupt the ovulation and fertilisation.

Q.7 Choose the right one among the statements given below.

(a) IUDs are generally inserted by the user herself.
(b) IUDs increase phagocytosis reaction in the uterus.
(c) IUDs suppress gametogenesis.
(d) IUDs once inserted need not be replaced.

Ans. *(b)* Statement (b) is true as IUDs increase phogocytosis reaction in uterus. Non-mediated IUDs increase phagocytosis of sperms within the uterus and the Cu ions released suppress sperm motility and the fertilising capacity of sperms. Hormone releasing IUDs make the uterus unsuitable for implantation and the cervix hostile to sperms, *e.g.*, progestasert, LNG-20.

Intra Uterine Devices (IUDs) are used as one of the effective and popular contraceptive method. These devices are inserted by doctors or expert nurses in the uterus through vagina. IUDs are presently available as the non-mediated IUDs (*e.g.*, Lipens loop), copper releasing IUDs (Cu-T, Cu-7, Multiload 375) and the hormone releasing IUDs (Progestasert, LNG-20).

IUDs do not suppress gametogenesis as gametogenesis (oogenesis) takes place in the ovary, while IUDs are inserted in the uterus (through vagina) with the help of an doctor or an expert personnel.

Q.8 Following statements are given regarding MTP. Choose the correct options given below.

I. MTPs are generally advised during first trimester.
II. MTPs are used as a contraceptive method.
III. MTPs are always surgical.
IV. MTPs require the assistance of qualified medical personnel.

(a) II and III
(b) II and III
(c) I and IV
(d) I and II

Thinking Process MTP (Medical Termination of Pregnancy) is intentional or voluntary termination of pregnancy before full term. It is also known as induced abortion.

Ans. *(c)* Statements (I) and (IV) are correct regarding MTP as MTPs is considered relatively safe during the first trimester, i.e. upto 12 weeks of pregnancy. Second trimester abortions are much more riskier. MTPs require the assistance of qualified medical professional.

Statements (II) and (III) are incorrect and can be corrected as MTPs is done to get rid of unwanted pregnancies either due to casual unprotected intercourse or failure of the contraceptive used during coitus or rapes. MTPs are also essential in certain cases where continuation of the pregnancy could be harmful or even fatal either to the mother or to the foetus or both.

MTPs are not always surgical. Certain pills also act as abortants. They function by inducing menstruation, which checks the implantation of the zygote or detaches the implanted foetus.

Q.9 From the sexually transmitted diseases mentioned below, identify the one which does not specifically affect the sex organs?

(a) Syphilis (b) AIDS (c) Gonorrhoea (d) Genital warts

Ans. ***(b)*** AIDS (Acquired Immuno Deficiency Syndrome) is a set of symptoms caused by HIV virus in humans. It is transmitted through sexual contacts from infected to healthy person. The HIV virus does not directly affect sex organs as such but produce other set of symptoms in the body of infected person. Where as syphilis, gonorrhoea and genital warts are STD caused by *Treponema pallidum, Neisseria gonorrhoeae* and human papilloma virus respectively. These pathogens directly infect and damage sex organs causing ichting, fluid discharge, slight pain and swelling of genitalia.

Q.10 Condoms are one of the most popular contraceptives because of the following reasons

(a) these are effective barriers for insemination
(b) they do not interfere with coital act
(c) these help in reducing the risk of STDs
(d) All of the above

Ans. ***(d)*** Condoms are barriers made of thin rubber/latex sheath used to cover the penis in the male or vagina and cervix in females. It prevents the deposition of ejaculated semen into the vagina of the female.

Condom should be discarded after a single use. It also safe guards against transmission of AIDS and other Sexually Transmitted Diseases (STDs).

Condom should be used regularly and put on before starting coital activity, otherwise sperm containing lubricating fluid may be left in the vagina. Condoms do not interfere with coital act.

Q.11 Choose the correct statement regarding the ZIFT procedure.

(a) Ova collected from a female donor are transferred to the fallopian tube to facilitate zygote formation.
(b) Zygote is collected from a female donor and transferred to the fallopian tube
(c) Zygote is collected from a female donor and transferred to the uterus
(d) Ova collected from a female donor and transferred to the uterus

Ans. *(b)* Statement (b) is correct regarding ZIFT as

The zygote or early embryo with upto 8 blastomeres is collected from a female donor and transferred into the Fallopian tube, this process is called Zygote Intra Fallopian Transfer or ZIFT.

Embryo more than 8 blastomeres is transferred into the uterus by the process called Intra Uterine Transfer or IUT.

When ovum is collected from donor and transferred to Fallopian tube of other female who cannot produce ovum. This is known as Gamete Intra Fallopian Transfer (GIFT)

Q.12 The correct surgical procedure as a contraceptive method is

(a) ovariectomy (b) hysterectomy
(c) vasectomy (d) castration

Ans. *(c)* Surgical methods, also called sterilisation are terminal and permanent methods which block the transport of gametes, thereby preventing conception. In males, this is called vasectomy, in which a small part of vas deferens is removed or tied up through a small cut on scrotum.

Q.13 Diaphragms are contraceptive devices used by the females. Choose the correct option from the statements given below

I. They are introduced into the uterus.
II. They are placed to cover the cervical region.
III. They act as physical barriers for sperm entry.
IV. They act as spermicidal agents.

(a) I and II (b) I and III
(c) II and III (d) III and IV

Ans. *(c)* Statements (II) and (III) are correct about diaphragms as diaphragms are soft, hemispherical rubber caps that are inserted into the female reproductive tract to cover the cervix during coitus. They prevent the entry of sperms through cervix when combined with the use of spermicidal agents like creams, jellies and foams are used along with these barriers to increase their contraceptive efficiency.

Statements (I) and (IV) are incorrect and can be corrected as Diaphragms are introduced into the cevix during coitus. They do not act as spermicidal agents but these agents can be used along with diaphragms.

Very Short Answer Type Questions

Q.1 Reproductive health refers only to healthy reproductive functions. Comment.

Ans. According to the World Health Organisation (WHO), reproductive health means a total well-being in all aspects of reproduction, *i.e.*, physical emotional, behavioural and social.

Therefore, a society with people having physically and functionally normal reproductive organs and normal emotional and behavioural interactions among them in all sex-related aspects might be called reproductively healthy.

Q.2 Comment on the Reproductive and Child Health Care programme of the government to improve the reproductive health of the people.

Ans. India was amongst the first countries in the world to initiate action plans and programmes at a national level to attain total reproductive health as a social goal.

These programmes called 'family planning' were initiated in 1951 and were periodically assessed over the past decades. Improved programmes covering wider reproduction-related areas are currently in operation under the popular name 'Reproductive and Child Healthcare (RCH) programmes'.

Creating awareness among people about various reproduction related aspects and providing facilities and support for building up a reproductively healthy society are the major tasks under these programmes.

Q.3 The present population growth rate in India is alarming. Suggest ways to check it.

Ans. The present population growth rate in India is alarming. Such an alarming growth rate could lead to an absolute scarcity of even the basic requirements, *i.e.,* food, shelter and clothing, in spite of significant progress made in those areas.

Following are some important ways to overcome this problem

(i) By raising marriageable age of the female from 18 years and that of males from 21 years.

(ii) By promoting use of birth control measures to motivate smaller families.

(iii) By providing incentives to couples with small families.

(iv) By educating people about consequences of uncontrolled population growth.

Q.4 STDs can be considered as self-invited diseases. Comment.

Ans. Diseases or infections which are transmitted through sexual intercourse are collectively called Sexually Transmitted Diseases (STDs) or Venereal Diseases (VD) or Reproductive Tract Infections (RTIs).

Though all People are vulnerable to these infections, these incidences are very high among people in the age group of 15-24 years. STDs can be considered as self-invited diseases because one could be free of these infections by following the simple principles given below

(i) Avoid sex with unknown partners or multiple partners.

(ii) Always use condoms during coitus.

(iii) In case of doubt, one should go to a qualified doctor for early detection and get complete treatment if diagnosed with disease.

Q.5 Suggest the reproduction-related aspects in which counselling should be provided at the school level.

Ans. In following aspects counselling should be provided at the school level

(i) Introduction of sex education in schools that helps in eradicating myths and misconceptions regarding sex-related aspects.

(ii) Proper information about reproductive organs, safe and hygienic sexual practices and Sexually Transmitted Diseases (STDs).

(iii) Awareness of problems due to uncontrolled population growth, social evils like sexual abuse and sex-related crimes, etc.

(iv) Educating people about available birth control options, care of pregnant mothers, post-natal care of mother and child, importance of breast-feeding, equal opportunities for the male and female child.

Q.6 Mention the primary aim of the 'Assisted Reproductive Technology' (ART) programme.

Ans. 'Assisted Reproductive Technology' (ART) is the collection of certain special techniques to assit couples with no children. The primary aim of the ART programme is to assist infertile couples to have children through certain special techniques (like ZIFT, IUT, GIFT, ICSI, AI, etc.) when corrective treatment is not possible.

Q.7 What is the significance of progesterone-estrogen combination as a contraceptive measure?

Ans. Progestogens or progestogen-estrogen combinations plays an important role in contraception. They are used in the form of tablets or pills. They inhibit ovulation and hence prevent implantation.

They are also used by females as injections or implants under the skin. Their mode of action is similar to that of pills but their effective periods are longer. Example of some oral pills are Mala-D and Mala-N.

Q.8 Strict conditions are to be followed in Medical Termination of Pregnancy (MTP) procedures. Mention two reasons.

Ans. Strict conditions are to be followed in Medical Termination of Pregnancy (MTP) procedures due to following two reasons

(i) It is being misused to abort even the normal female foetus leading to female foeticide.

(ii) MTP performed after first trimister *i.e.*, 12 weeks of pregnancy become riskier as foetus becomes more deeply associated with the uterine tissue of the mother.

Q.9 Males in whom testes fail to descend to the scrotum are generally infertile. Why?

Ans. The testes are very sensitive to temperature and also sperms need slightly lower temperature than normal body temperature for its formation which is provided by scrotal sac. Thus, if they do not descend into the scrotum prior to adolescence, then they will stop producing sperms that will lead to infertility in males.

Q.10 Mention two advantages of lactational amenorrhea as a contraceptive method.

Ans. The two advantages of lactational amenorrhea as a contraceptive method are mentioned as below

(i) If the mother is breast feeding, completely she would not ovulate, therefore chances of conception would be low.

(ii) She would not need to use any pill or devices for birth control. So, there will be no side effects.

Short Answer Type Questions

Q.1 Suggest some important steps that you would recommend to be taken to improve the reproductive health standards in India.

Thinking Process Reproductive health means total well being in all aspects of reproduction, *i.e.*, physical, emotional, behavioural and social.

Ans. Following measures are needed to be taken to improve the reproductive health standards in India

(i) Providing infrastructural facilities and professional expertise to attain reproductive health.

(ii) Educating people about birth control methods, care of pregnant mothers, importance of breast feeding, safe and hygienic sexual practices and safeguard against STDs.

(iii) Introduction of sex education in schools to give proper information to the young minds about sex-related aspects.

(iv) Help of audio-visual and print media to create awareness among people about reproduction related aspects.

(v) Awareness of problems due to population explosion, social evils like sexual abuse and sex-related crimes.

(vi) Statutory ban on amniocentesis to legally check female foeticides.

Q.2 The procedure of GIFT involves the transfer of female gamete to the Fallopian tube. Can gametes be transferred to the uterus to achieve the same result? Explain.

Ans. The procedure of GIFT involves the transfer of female gamete to the Fallopian tube. Gametes cannot be transferred to the uterus to achieve the same result because microenvironment of Fallopian tube is ideal for fertilisation and early development of an embryo. Hence, the anatomy and physiology of Fallopian tube plays an important role in egg transport and fertilisation. Whereas, the uterine environment is not congenial for the survival of the gamete. Hence, if the female gamete is directly transferred to the uterus they will undergo degeneration or could be phagocytosed and, viable zygote would not be formed.

Q.3 Copper ions-releasing IUDs are more efficient than non-medicated methods. Why?

Ans. Intra Uterine Devices (IUDs) are inserted in the uterus through vagina and are presently available as the non-medicated IUDs,copper releasing IUDs (Cu-T, Cu-7) and hormone releasing IUDs

Cu ions-releasing IUDs are more efficient methods because

(i) Cu ions released suppress sperm motility and fertilising capacity of sperms.

(ii) It increases phagocytosis of sperms within the uterus.

(iii) It is one of the safest, most effective, convenient and least expensive reversible contraceptives available.

(iv) It has no systemic effects and can be safely used by breast-feeding women.

Q.4 What are the probable factors that contributed to population explosion in India?

Ans. Following are some factors that have probably contributed to population explosion in India

(i) Ignorance and complete lack of awareness about the ill effects of increasing population especially in rural regions.

(ii) Poverty and illiteracy

(iii) Social stigmas about girl child and desire to have boy child.

(iv) Decline in death rate.

(v) Decline in maternal and infant mortality rate.

(vi) Increase in the young, reproductive age population.

Q.5 Briefly explain IVF and ET What are the conditions in which these methods are advised?

Ans. The IVF (In Vitro Fertilisation) takes place outside the body of female in similar conditions as that in the body followed by E.T. (Embryo Transfer). It is performed as follows :

(i) Ova from the wife or donor female and sperms from husband or donor male are collected in a hygienic manner.

(ii) Both ova and sperms are then kept in the culture medium under aseptic conditions.

(iii) Gametes are induced to fuse and form zygote under simulated conditions.

In ET (embryo transfer) technique, developing embryo is transferred from culture medium to female reproductive tract. It is performed as follows :

(i) Zygote is induced in culture medium to develop.

(ii) Endometrium is stimulated to be prepared for implantation.

(iii) Embryo is transferred to fallopian tube is 8-celled conditions or transferred to uterus when it is at 16-32 celled stage.

When in a woman normal conception is not possible because of blocked oviducts or spermicidal secretions in the vagina or when a woman cannot produce ova or man cannot produce sperms. In such conditions these method are advised.

Q.6 What are the advantages of natural methods of contraception over artificial methods?

Thinking Process Natural methods of contraception work on the principle of avoiding chances of ovum and sperm meeting.

Ans. Natural methods of contraception include rhythm method, coitus interrupts and lactational amenorrhea.

These methods does not involve the use of any contraceptive or any chemical or surgery. On the other hand, artificial methods of contraception which includes IUDs, oral pills, etc. have certain drawbacks. IUDs may cause occassional haemorrhage or infections. Combined oral pills generally have side effects such as nausea, breast tenderness, weight gain, breakthrough bleeding, melasma, etc.

Q.7 What are the conditions in which medical termination of pregnancy is advised?

Ans. Medical termination of pregnancy (MTP) is carried out to get rid of unwanted pregnancies. It is also essential when the foetus is suffering from an incurable disease or when continuation of the pregnancy could be harmful or even fatal to the mother and or foetus. It is advised in the following conditions.

(i) To get rid of unwanted pregnancy either due to unprotected intercourse or failure of the contraceptive used or rape.

(ii) If baby's suffering from an incurable and congenital developmental defect.

(iii) If continuation of pregnancy is harmful for either mother or foetus or even both.

Q.8 Comment on the essential features required for an ideal contraceptive.

Ans. An ideal contraceptive should

(i) be user-friendly

(ii) effective and reversible with least or no side effects

(iii) no interference with the sexual drive or desire or the sexual act of the user

(iv) Is easily available

Q.9 All reproductive tract infections RTIs are STDs, but all STDs are not RTIs. Justify with example.

Ans. Among the common STDs, hepatitis-B and AIDS are not infections of the reproductive organs at though their mode of transmission could be through sexual contact. All other diseases like gonorrhoea, syphilis, genital herpes, chlamydia are transmitted through sexual contact and are also cause infections of the reproductive tract so, they both are STDs and RTI. Whereas, AIDS and hepatitis are STDs but not RTI.

Long Answer Type Questions

Q.1 What are the Assisted Reproductive Techniques practised to help infertile couples? Describe any three techniques.

Thinking Process The infertile couples could be assisted to have children through certain special techniques called Assisted Reproductive Technologies (ART).

Ans. Assisted Reproductive Technologies (ART) are used to help infertile couples conceive. Some common.

ART techniques are described as follows

(i) **Test-tube Baby Programmes** In this method, ova from the wife or donor (female) and the sperms from the husband or donor (male) are collected and are induced to form zygote under simulated conditions in the laboratory. This process is called *In Vitro* Fertilisation (IVF).

The zygote or early embryo with upto 8 blastomeres is transferred into the Fallopian tube (process is called Zygote Intra Fallopian Transfer or ZIFT) and embryo with more than 8 blastomeres is transferred into the uterus (process is called Intra Uterine Transfer or IUT).

In females who cannot conceive, embryos formed by fusion of gametes within the female (called *in vivo* fertilisation) are transferred.

(ii) **Gamete Intra Fallopian Transfer (GIFT)** It is the transfer of an ovum collected from a donor into the Fallopian tube of another female who cannot produce one, but can provide suitable environment for fertilisation and further development of the embryo.

(iii) **Artificial Insemination** (AI) In this method, the semen collected either from the husband or a healthy donor is artificially introduced into the vagina or into the uterus (Intra Uterine Insemination or IUI). This technique is used in cases where the male is unable to inseminate healthy sperms in the female reproductive tract or due to very low sperm counts in the ejaculation.

Q.2 Discuss the mode of action and advantages/disadvantages of hormonal contraceptives.

Thinking Process Intra Uterine Devices (IUDs) are effective and popular method of contraception.

Ans. Intra Uterine Devices are presently available as

(a) Non-medicated IUDs (*e.g.*, Lippes loop).

(b) Copper releasing IUDs (*e.g.*, Cu-T, Cu-7, Multiload 375).

(c) Hormone releasing IUDs (*e.g.*, Progestasert, LNG-20).

Mode of Action of Hormonal Contraceptives The hormones releasing IUDs, make the uterus unsuitable for implantation and the cervix hostile to the sperms. Progesterone can also be used as injections and implants (slow release of hormones) to inhibit ovulation.

Advantages of Hormonal Contraceptives Administration of progestogens or progestogen-oestrogen combinations or IUDs within 72 hrs of intercourse have been found to be effective as emergency contraceptives as they could be used to avoid possible pregnancy due to rape or causal unprotected intercourse.

Disadvantages of Hormonal Contraceptives

(i) IUDs are suggested as ideal contraceptives for the females but they can have serious side effects.

(ii) Can cause allergic reaction.

(iii) If displaced, can cause tissue damage and profuse bleeding.

(iv) IUDs can damage the normal hormonal balance and later even if desired, pregnancy may not be achieved.

(v) Artificial hormone intake can disrupt normal hormonal interactions in the body system.

Q.3 STDs are a threat to reproductive health. Describe any two such diseases and suggest preventive measures.

Ans. Diseases or infections which are transmitted through sexual intercourse are collectively called Sexually Transmitted Diseases (STDs) or Venereal Diseases (VD) or Reproductive Tract Infections (RTI).

Though all people are vulnerable to these infections, these incidences are high among persons in the age group of 15-24 years. STDs can be considered as self-invited diseases.

STDs include gonorrhoea, syphilis, genital herpes, chlamydias, genital warts, trichomoniasis, hepatitis-B, HIV. These diseases may cause some complications like Pelvic Inflammatory Diseases (PID), abortions, still births, ectopic pregnancies, infertility, or even cancer of the reproductive tract.

Hepatitis-B and HIV are such diseases that get transmitted by the following ways besides sexual contacts

(i) Sharing of injection needles or surgical instruments with infected persons.

(ii) Transfusion of infected blood.

(iii) Transfer from infected mother to the foetus through placenta.

Preventive Measures

By following simple principles, STDs can be prevented

(i) Avoid sex with unknown or multiple partners.

(ii) Always use condoms during coitus.

(iii) Contact a qualified doctor for any doubt in early stage of infection.

Q.4 Do you justify the statutory ban on amniocentesis in our country? Give reasons.

Ans. *Yes*, the ban is necessary because amniocentesis is misused now-a-days. It is used to determine the sex of the foetus and in many cases it led to female foeticide. It has become so serious that it disturbed the male female ratio that can lead to a negative impact on society.

The test is actually meant to determine the genetic defects or metabolic disorders in foetus by doing a chromosomal analysis. In such extreme cases that would be incurable, a decision to abort the foetus could be taken.

Q.5 Enumerate and describe any five reasons for introducing sex education to school-going children.

Ans. The reasons for introducing sex education to school-going children are as follows

(i) At school level, children from age group 12 and above should be counselled for reproductive system, processes and practices and importance of safe and responsible sex.

(ii) Sex related issues and problems like adolescence changes, menstrual cycle, menstrual problems, unwanted pregnancy, unsafe abortion, reproductive tract infections (RTIs) and cancers.

(iii) They should know about body changes during their age and taught about healthy habits including personal cleanliness and hygiene.

(iv) Students should become part of such education, so that they overcome hesitation and gain confidence to discuss any query with their teacher or parents.

(v) Counselling and awareness regarding reproductive organs, safe and hygienic sexual practices will play an important role to make people reproductively healthy.

Chapter 05

Principle of Inheritance and Variation

Multiple Choice Questions (MCQs)

Q.1 All genes located on the same chromosome

(a) form different groups depending upon their relative distance
(b) form one linkage group
(c) will not from any linkage group
(d) form interactive groups that affect the phenotype

Ans. *(b)* All the genes, present on a particular chromosome form a linkage group.

A linkage group is a group of linked gene on the same chromosome and corresponds to the genome of organism. It is not simply just the number of chromosomes in haploid set.

e.g., in human male = 22 pairs of autosomes + 1X-chromosome + 1Y-choromosme *i.e.,* 24 linkage groups and in female = 22 pairs autosomes + 2X-chromosomes *i.e.,* 23 linkage groups.

Q.2 Conditions of a karyotype $2n \pm 1$ and $2n \pm 2$ are called

(a) aneuploidy (b) polyploidy (c) allopolyploidy (d) monosomy

Thinking Process Numerical changes in chromosome number are referred to as changes in ploidy.

Ans. *(a)* Aneuploidy involves changes in chromosome number by additions or deletions of less than a whole set. An organism gains or loses one or more chromosomes but not a complete set as chromatids failed to segregate during cell division. Polyploidy is defined as the addition of entire set of chromosome. The polyploidy can be triploidy ($3n$), tetraploidy ($4n$), pentaploidy ($5n$), etc.

Allopolyploidy is the polyploidy in which chromosome sets are non-homologous. In other words we can say that the allopolyploids are derived from a stock which is heterozygous. Monosomy is the process in which one chromosome is removed from diploid set of chromosome ($2n$-1).

Q.3 Distance between the genes and percentage of recombination shows

(a) a direct relationship (b) an inverse relationship
(c) a parallel relationship (d) no relationship

Thinking Process Crossing over (recombination) is the mutual exchange of the corresponding segments of the adjacent paternal and maternal chromatids of the synapsed homologous chromosomes producing new combinations of genes.

Ans. *(a)* Crossing over separates genes away from each other. So, the distance between the genes and percentage of recombination shows an direct relationship, *i.e.,* when genes are close together they have high linkage and exhibit low recombination frequencies.

Q.4 If a genetic disease is transferred from a phenotypically normal but carrier female to only some of the male progeny, the disease is

(a) autosomal dominant
(b) autosomal recessive
(c) sex-linked dominant
(d) sex-linked recessive

Thinking Process Sex-linked disorders are those genetic diseases where the defective genes are carried on either the X or Y-chromosomes.

Ans. *(d)* Most sex-linked (X-linked) conditions are recessive. This means that in a person with two X-chromosomes (females), both copies of a gene (*i.e.,* one on each X-chromosome), must have a change or mutation.

Whereas in a person with one X-chromosomes (males), only one copy of a gene must have a mutation.

A female with a mutation in one copy of a gene on the X-chromosome is said to be a 'carrier' for an X-linked condition. e.g., Haemophilia, colour blindness.

For X-linked recessive disorders, an unaffected carrier mother who has a mutation in a gene on the X-chromosome can transmit either the X-chromosome with this mutation or a normal X-chromosome to her children.

Autosomal dominant inheritance refers to the pattern of inheritance of a condition directly or indirectly due to a dominant faulty gene located on autosome.

Autosomal recessive inheritance is the condition caused directly or indirectly due to a recessive faulty gene copy on autosome.

Sex-linked dominant is a rare trait that is caused by a single abnormal gene on the X-chromosome.

Q.5 In sickle-cell anaemia glutamic acid is replaced by valine. Which one of the following triplet codes for valine?

(a) G G G
(b) A A G
(c) G A A
(d) G U G

Ans. *(d)* Sickle-cell anaemia is an autosome linked recessive trait. This disease is controlled by a single pair of allele Hb^A and Hb^S, only the homozygous individuals for Hb^S, *i.e.,* $Hb^S\ Hb^S$ shows the diseased phenotype. The heterozygous individuals are carriers ($Hb^A\ Hb^S$).

Due to point mutation, glutamic acid (Glu) is replaced by valine (Val) at sixth position of β-chain of haemoglobin molecule. This substitution occurs due to the single base substitution of the beta globin gene from GAG (Glu) to GUG (Val).

Whereas, the other codes GGG, AAG, GAA do not codes for valine.

Q.6 Person having genotype $I^A\ I^B$ would show the blood group as AB. This is because of

(a) pleiotropy
(b) codominance
(c) segregation
(d) incomplete dominance

Thinking Process The alleles which are able to express themselves independently when present together are called codominant alleles. This biological phenomenon of expressing together is called codominance.

Ans. ***(b)*** ABO blood grouping in humans is an example of codominance. ABO blood groups are controlled by gene I. Gene I has three alleles I^A, I^B and i· I^A and I^B are the dominant alleles. When I^A and I^B are present together, both express equally and produce the surface antigens A and B, whereas i is the recessive allele and does not produce any antigen.

Pleiotropy refers to the genetic effect of a single gene on multiple phenotypic traits.

Incomplete dominance refers to the genetic effect in which one allele does not completely dominate another allele.

Segregation is the separation of allele during the process of gametogenesis. This is the basis of reappearance of recessive character in F_2-generation.

Q.7 ZZ/ZW type of sex determination is seen in

(a) platypus (b) snails
(c) cockroach (d) peacock

Thinking Process In birds the ZZ/ZW type of sex determination is seen.

Ans. ***(d)*** In ZZ/ZW case, the female has heteromorphic (ZW) sex chromosomes and the male has homomorphic (ZZ) sex chromosomes. Thus, birds (*e.g.,*) peacock shows ZZ/ZW sex determination type.

In platypus the sex determination is of XX-XY type. The male has XY and female has XX.

In snails the sex determination is environmentally induced. In cockroaches it is of XX-XO types. In this type Y-chromosome is completely lacking and the presence of unpaired X-chromosomes determines the masculine sex.

Q.8 A across between two tall plants resulted in offspring having few dwarf plants. What would be the genotypes of both the parents?

(a) TT and Tt (b) Tt and Tt
(c) TT and TT (d) Tt and tt

Thinking Process On the basis of monohybrid cross (a cross involving only one trait) Mendel formulated the law of segregation.

Ans. ***(b)*** In Tt and Tt the genotype of parents was heterozygous. Both the parents had "Tt" type of genotype leading to formation of few dwarf offsprings.

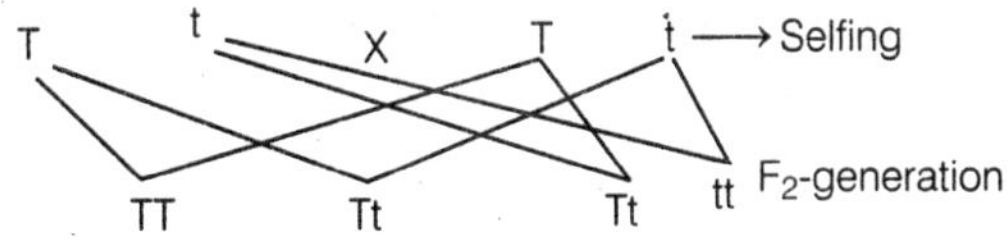

Phenotypic ratio : Tall : Dwarf
3 : 1

Genotypic ratio : Pure tall : Hybrid : Pure dwarf
1 : 2 : 1

Thus, the tall parents plants having heterozygous alleles, results in offsprings which comprises of both tall and dwarf plants.

Q.9 In a dihybrid cross, if you get 9 : 3 : 3 : 1 ratio it denotes that

(a) the alleles of two genes are interacting with each other
(b) it is a multigenic inheritance
(c) it is a case of multiple allelism
(d) the alleles of two genes are segregating independently

Thinking Process A cross that involves the analysis of two independent traits is termed a dihybrid cross. The law of independent assortment was deduced from Mendel's experiment with dihybrid cross.

Ans. *(d)* Alleles of two genes are segregating independently. It can be explained as, suppose crosses are made between a pea plant with round and yellow seeds with wrinkled and green ones. All F_1 hybrids give yellow and round seeds. Since yellow colour is dominant over the green and the round shape is dominant over the wrinkled. When the F_1-hybrid plants are crossed to each other or allowed to self fertilise, an F_2-generation form as represented in the following figure

P-generation: YYRR (Yellow-Round Seed) X yyrr (Green-Wrinkled Seed)

Gametes: YR, yr

F_1-generation: YyRr — Yellow-round seed (dominant character)

The F_1 hybrid plants are allowed to self fertilise

YyRr X YyRr

Gametes: $\frac{1}{4}$ YR $\frac{1}{4}$ Yr $\frac{1}{4}$ yR $\frac{1}{4}$ yr | $\frac{1}{4}$ YR $\frac{1}{4}$ Yr $\frac{1}{4}$ yR $\frac{1}{4}$ yr

F_2-generation

♀ \ ♂	YR	Yr	yR	yr
YR	YYRR	YYRr	YyRR	YyRr
Yr	YYRr	YYrr	YyRr	Yyrr
yR	YyRR	YyRr	yyRR	yyRr
yr	YyRr	Yyrr	yyRr	yyrr

Phenotypic ratio – 9 : 3 : 3 : 1

The outcome of the dihybrid cross makes it very clear that segregation of the seed colour is independent of the seed shape and both the parental and new combinations of the characters appear in the F_2 offspring, *i.e.*, assortment of genes of one pair is independent of the other pair.

Q.10 Which of the following will not result in variations among siblings?

(a) Independent assortment of genes
(b) Crossing over
(c) Linkage
(d) Mutation

Ans. *(c)* Linkage will not result in variations among siblings as it refers to the physical association of genes on chromosome. Independent assortment of genes means that allele pair separate during the formation of gametes independently. It means that traits are transmitted to offspring independently of one another. Crossing over is the exchange of genetic material between homologous chromosomes. It is one of the final phases of genetic recombination. Mutation is the alteration of DNA sequences resulting to changes in the genotype and phenotype of an organism.

Q.11 Mendel's law of independent assortment holds good for genes situated on the

(a) non-homologous chromosomes
(b) homologous chromosomes
(c) extra nuclear genetic element
(d) same chromosome

Ans. *(a)* The law of independent assortment holds true as long as two different genes are on separate chromosomes. When the genes are on separate chromosome the two alleles of one gene (A and a) will segregate into gametes independently of the two alleles of the other gene
(B and b).

Equal numbers of four different gametes will form AB, aB, Ab,ab. But if the two genes are on the same chromosome, then they will be linked and will segregate together during meiosis, producing only two kinds of gametes.

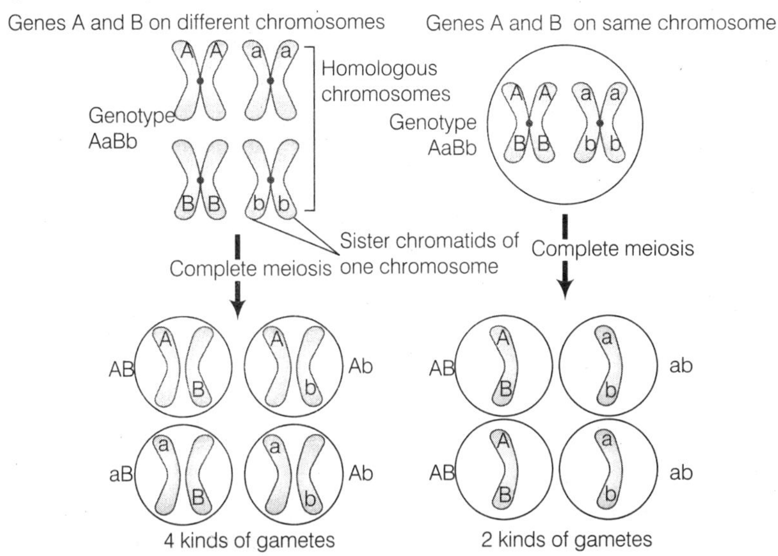

Homologous chromosomes are similar but not identical. Each carries the same gene in same order but the alleles for each trait may not be the same.

Q.12 Occasionally, a single gene may express more than one effect. The phenomenon is called

(a) multiple allelism
(b) mosaicism
(c) pleiotropy
(d) polygeny

Ans. *(c)* Occasionally, a single gene may express more than one trait. This phenomenon is called pleiotropy. Sometimes, one trait will be very evident and others will be less evident, *e.g.*, a gene for white eye in *Drosophila* also affect the shape of organs in male responsible for sperm storage as well as other structures.

Similarly, sickle-cell anaemic individuals suffer from a number of problems, all of which are pleiotropic effects of the sickle-cell alleles.

Multiple allelism is when a gene has three or more alternative or allelic forms, but only two of which can exist in any normal diploid individual, *e.g.*, genes of blood groups in humans.

Mosaicism describes the occurrence of cells that differ in their genetic component from other cells of the body.

Polygeny refers to a single characteristic that is controlled by more than two genes. (it is also known as multifactorial inheritance).

Q.13 In a certain taxon of insects some have 17 chromosomes and the others have 18 chromosomes. The 17 and 18 chromosome-bearing organisms are

(a) males and females, respectively

(b) females and males, respectively

(c) all males

(d) all females

Ans. ***(a)*** Males and females respectively, Certain insects, such as cockroach, and some roundworms, comes under XO type of sex determination. The Y-chromosome is missing so that the male has only one sex chromosome, *i.e.*, 'X'.

The condition in the male is XO (O means absence of one sex chromosome) and in the female it is XX, thus males showing 17 chromosomes while females show 18 chromosome.

Q.14 The inheritance pattern of a gene over generations among humans is studied by the pedigree analysis. Character studied in the pedigree analysis is equivalent to

(a) quantitative trait (b) mendelian trait

(c) polygenic trait (d) maternal trait

Thinking Process A pedigree is a family tree that shows the relationships among parents and children across several generations as well as the inheritance pattern of a particular phenotyphic character.

Ans. ***(b)*** Character understanding of mendelian inheritance in humans is gained by analysis of family pedigrees or the results of matings that have already occured. By analysing a pedigree, it becomes easy to predict how the trait is inherited.

It is a visual tool for documenting the biological relationship in families and to determine the mode of inheritance (dominant, recessive etc.,) of genetic diseases.

Whereas quantitative trait, polygenic trait and maternal traits are not studied by pedigree analysis. Quantitative traits are influenced by multiple genes and show continuous variation (*i.e.*, height, weight). Polygenic traits are another exception to Mendels rule, which occurs when a trait is controlled by more than one gene. This means that each dominant allele adds to the expression of the next dominant allele. Maternal traits are the traits inherited and expressed from the maternal parent to the subsequent offsprings.

Q.15 It is said that Mendel proposed that the factor controlling any character is discrete and independent. This proposition was based on the

(a) results of F_3-generation of a cross
(b) observations that the offspring of a cross made between the plants having two contrasting characters shows only one character without any blending
(c) self-pollination of F_1 offsprings
(d) cross-pollination of F_1-generation with recessive parent

Ans. ***(b)*** Law of segregation states that the factors or alleles of a pair segregate from each other during gamete formation, such that a gamete receives only one of the two factors. They do not show any blending.

Q. 16 Two genes 'A' and 'B' are linked. In a dihybrid cross involving these two genes, the F_1 heterozygote is crossed with homozygous recessive parental type (aa bb). What would be the ratio of offspring in the next generation?

(a) 1 : 1 : 1 : 1 (b) 9 : 3 : 3 : 1 (c) 3 : 1 (d) 1 : 1

Thinking Process When a progeny of F_1 is crossed with the homozygous recessive parent, it is called test cross.

Ans. ***(d)*** 1 : 1 It can be explained by the following test cross.

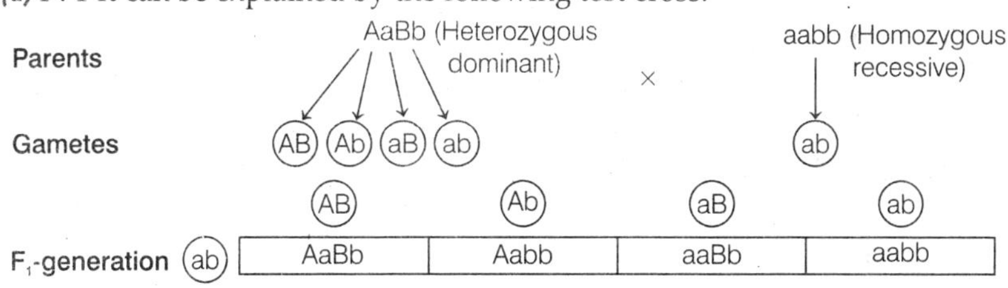

The offspring genotypes are : AaBb and aabb (parental types)
Aabb and aaBb (recombinant types)

Due to the linkage, the parental types are more common, leading to a 1 : 1 ratio of parental to recombinant types.

Q.17 In the F_2-generation of a Mendelian dihybrid cross the number of phenotypes and genotypes are

(a) phenotypes-4, genotypes-16
(b) phenotypes-9, genotypes-4
(c) phenotypes-4, genotypes-8
(d) phenotypes-4, genotypes-9

Ans. ***(d)*** Mendel's dihybrid cross

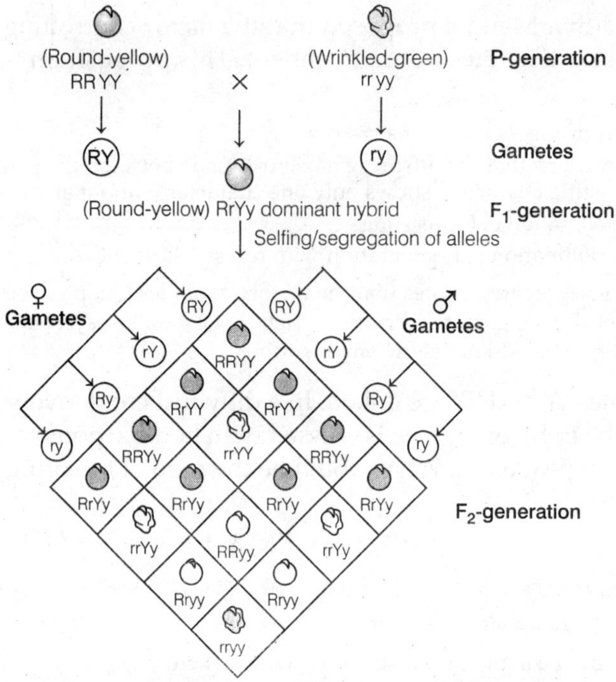

Phenotypic ratio Round-yellow : Round-green : Wrinkled-yellow : Wrinkled-green

9 : 3 : 3 : 1

↓ 4 (phenotypes)

Genotypic ratio 1 : 2 : 2 : 4 : 1 : 2 : 1 : 2 : 1

↓ 9 (genotypes)

Results of a dihybrid cross where the two parents differed in two pairs of contrasting traits : seed colour and seed shape.

Q.18 Mother and father of a person with 'O' blood group have 'A' and 'B' blood group respectively. What would be the genotype of both mother and father?

(a) Mother is homozygous for 'A' blood group and father is heterozygous for 'B'
(b) Mother is heterozygous for 'A' blood group and father is homozygous for 'B'
(c) Both mother and father are heterozygous for 'A' and 'B' blood group respectively
(d) Both mother and father are homozygous for 'A' and 'B' blood group respectively

Thinking Process The child with blood group O will have homozygous recessive alleles. Therefore, both the parents should be heterozygous, *i.e.*, the genotype of father will be $I^A i$ and of mother will be $I^B i$.

Ans. *(c)* When a cross is carried out between heterozygous father (for blood group B) with genotype $I^B i$ and heterozygous mother (of blood group A) with genotype $I^A i$ to get four children with different blood groups.

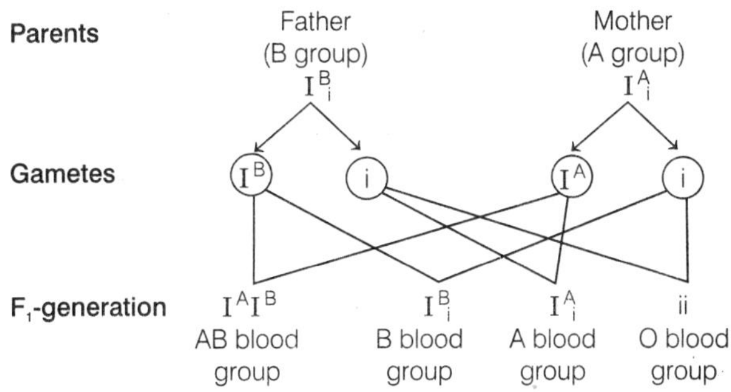

All the four blood groups are controlled by three allelic genes I^A, I^B, i and thus it shows phenomenon of multiple allelism. Both I^A and I^B is dominant over i.

Very Short Answer Type Questions

Q.1 What is the cross between the progeny of F_1 and the homozygous recessive parent called? How is it useful?

Ans. When a progeny of F_1 is crossed with the homozygous recessive parent, it is called test cross. Test cross between hybrid dominant individuals with recessive parent is shown below

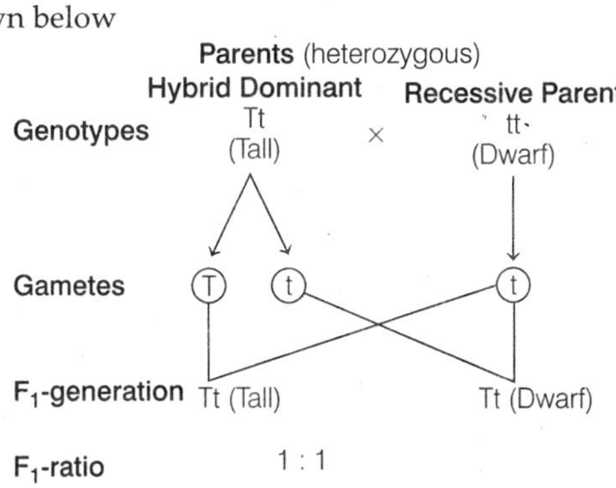

Such a cross is useful to determine the genotype of an unknown trait, *i.e.*, whether it is heterozygous or homozygous dominant for the trait.

Q.2 Do you think Mendel's Laws of inheritance would have been different in the characters that he chose were located on the same chromosome.

Ans. If the characters are present on the same chromosome, they would not assort independently. Percentage of linkage depends on the distance between the genes. So, if mendel choose the characters present on the same chromosome, then his observations would have been altered.

Q 3 Enlist the steps of controlled cross-pollination. Would emasculation be needed in a cucurbit plant? Give reasons for your answer.

Thinking Process Controlled cross-pollination is one of the major approaches of crop improvement programme. In such experiments it is important to make sure that only the desired pollen grains are used for pollination and the stigma is protected from contamination (from unwanted pollen).

Ans. Steps of controlled cross-pollination are

(i) Selection of parents with desired characters.

(ii) Emasculation, *i.e.*, if the female parent bears bisexual flowers, anther should be removed by forceps before dehiscence.

(iii) Bagging, *i.e.*, emasculated flowers have to be covered with a bag of suitable size, generally made up of butter paper, to prevent contamination of its stigma with unwanted pollen.

(iv) When the stigma of bagged, the flower attains receptivity, mature pollen grains collected from anthers of the male parent are dusted on the stigma

(v) The flowers are rebagged and the fruits are allowed to develop.

Emasculation is not always needed in a cucurbit plant. Emasculation is essential only in case of bisexual flowers to prevent self-pollination. In case of cucurbit plant, female parent produces usually unisexual flowers but may sometimes have bisexual flowers as well.

Note If the female parent produces unisexual flowers, there is no need for emasculation. The female flower buds are bagged before the flowers open. When the stigma becomes receptive, pollination is carried out using the desired pollen and the flower rebagged.

Q.4 A person has to perform crosses for the purpose of studying inheritance of a few traits/characters. What should be the criteria for selecting the organisms?

Ans. The criteria for selecting the organism to study inheritance are

(i) Easily visible and different traits

(ii) Short life span

(iii) Simple pollination procedure

(iv) Organisms must be true breeds

(v) Mating of gametes has to be random

(vi) Can be easily manipulated

(vii) Clear differentiation of sex and characteristics

(viii) Produce large number of progeny.

Q.5 The pedigree chart given below shows a particular trait which is absent in parents but present in the next generation irrespective of sexes. Draw your conclusion on the basis of the pedigree.

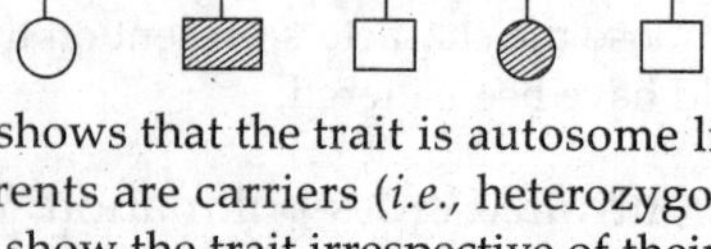

Ans. The pedigree chart shows that the trait is autosome linked and recessive in nature. But, the parents are carriers (*i.e.*, heterozygous) hence, among the offsprings only few show the trait irrespective of their sexes. The other offsprings are either normal or carrier.

Q.6 In order to obtain the F_1-generation Mendel pollinated a pure-breeding tall plant with a pure-breeding dwarf plant. But for getting the F_2-generation, he simply self-pollinated the tall F_1 plants. Why?

Ans. Characters segregate during gamete formation. Pure-breeding parents give rise to F_1 with heterozygous conditions.

Only self-pollination of heterozygotes can result in all possible recombinations of characters in progeny as mating is random. It also helps to study the effects of dominant and recessive allele of gene.

Q.7 'Genes contain the information that is required to express a particular trait.' Explain.

Ans. Genes contain the information required to express a particular trait becaue genes code for proteins which in turn performs various functions. It can be explained by the following experiment.

G Beadle and **E Tatum** set an experiment to prove that one gene possess a particular trait and is responsible for the production of one enzyme or protein. They performed their experiment on *Neurospora crassa* which were nutritionally mutant.

It was proved that a single protein contains several polypeptide and each polypeptide is controlled by a separate gene. Thus, each gene expresses a particular trait.

This theory was called one gene-one enzyme or one gene-one polypeptide hypothesis. But after the discovery of cistron (the functional unit of gene), the theory was named as one cistron-one polypeptide hypothesis.

Q.8 How are alleles of particular gene differ from each other? Explain its significance.

Ans. Alleles are polymorphs that differ in their nucleotide sequence resulting in contrasting phenotype expression. These differences are caused by mutations in the genetic DNA.

Alleles are the alternative forms of a same gene for, *e.g.*, genes for height have two allele, one for dwarfness (t) and one for tallness (T).

Significance

(i) A character may have two or more contrasting phenotypic expression, thus resulting variation in the population.

(ii) These are used in the studies of inheritance and in understanding their behaviour.

(iii) This contribute to genetic diversity and evolution.

Q.9 In a monohybrid cross of plants with red and white flowered plants. Mendel got only red flowered plants. On self-pollinating these F_1 plants got both red and white flowered plants in 3:1 ratio. Explain the basis of using RR and rr symbols to represent the genotype of plants of parental generation.

Ans.

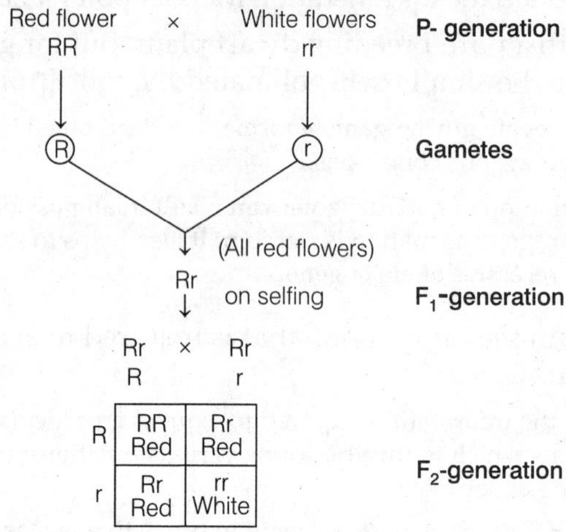

Phenotypic ratio Red flower : White flower 3 : 1

Genotype ratio RR : Rr : rr 1 : 2 : 1

Generally, upper case letters are used as symbols for dominant and lower case letters for recessive traits of the same gene (alleles). The experiment shows that it is a monohybrid cross with 3 : 1 ratio in F_2-generation. The red and white traits are identical to their parents and did not show any blending.

This shows parents must be true-breeds. As parents are diploid and homologous chromosomes carry alleles with similar type they are represented with RR and rr.

Q.10 For the expression of traits genes provide only the potentiality and the environment provides the opportunity. Comment on the veracity of the statement.

Thinking Process Phenotype = Genotype + Environment
(Trait) (potentiality) (opportunity)

Ans. Genes are not the only factors that determine phenotype. Environment also plays an important role in the expression of traits. Genes are actually quite active throughout human lives, switching their expression on and off in response to the environment.

Besides the effect of internal factors like hormones and metabolism on gene expression, external factors like temperature, light, nutrition, etc., also affect the gene expression and ultimately exhibiting phenotypic changes.

Therefore, it can be said that genes provide only the potentiality and the environment provides the opportunity for the expression of traits.

Q.11 A, B, D are three independently assorting genes with their recessive alleles a, b, d, respectively. A cross was made between individuals of Aa bb DD genotype with aa bb dd. Find out the type of genotypes of the offspring produced.

Ans. The given cross Aa bb DD X aa bb dd, is a trihybrid cross. Accordingly the type of offspring produced would be,

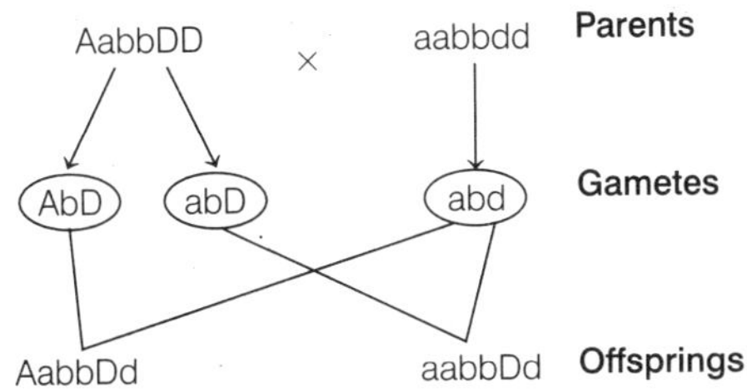

Therefore, the offsprings produced would be AabbDd and aabbDd.

Q.12 In our society a woman is often blamed for not bearing male child. Do you think it is right? Justify.

Thinking Process The sex determining chromosome in case of humans is of XY type.

Ans. It is unfortunate that in today's society women are blamed for giving birth to female children and have been ostracised and ill-treated because of this false notion. Out of 23 pairs of chromosomes present, 22 pairs are exactly same in both males and females, these are the autosomes and only one pair is responsible for determining sex, the sex chromosomes.

The sex of a child is determined by the type of sperm that fertilised with the egg. 50 per cent of the total sperm produced carry the X-chromosome and the rest 50% has Y-chromosome besides the autosomes. Females, however, produce only one type of ovum with an X-chromosome. There is an equal probability of fertilisation of the ovum with the sperm carrying either X or Y-chromosome.

In case when the ovum fertilises with a sperm carrying X-chromosome the zygote develops into a female (XX) and the fertilisation of ovum with Y-chromosome carrying sperm results into a male offspring. Thus, it is evident that it is the genetic makeup of the sperm (male) that determines the sex of the child.

It is also evident that in each pregnancy there is always 50% probability of having either a male or a female child. Therefore, it is not correct to blame women for bearing female children.

Q.13 Discuss the genetic basis of wrinkled phenotype of pea seed.

Ans. Seed shape is determined by a single gene, with the allele (R) for round peas dominant over the allele (r) for wrinkled peas (recessive trait). If the alleles for the gene controlling the seed shape are homozygous in a plant, it will show the character or phenotype of same alleles, *i.e.*,-RR- round seed, rr-wrinkled seed. On the other hand, if the alleles of gene are heterozygous. They will express the phenotype of dominant allele.

Rr-Round seed (R-round is dominant and r- wrinkled is recessive). Thus the genetic basis of wrinkled phenotype of pea seed is the homozygous recessive genotype rr.

Q.14 Even if a character shows multiple allelism, an individual will only have two alleles for that character. Why?

Ans. Multiple alleles are the multiple forms of a gene which occur on the same gene locus, but distributed in different organisms in the gene pool. However, an organism carry only two alleles and the gamete have only one allele.

Despite multiple allelism, an individual will have only two alleles because an individual develops from a zygote which is the result of fusion of sperm (carrying father set of (n)haploid chromosomes) and an egg (carrying mother set of haploid chromosomes).

Sperm and an egg have only one gene (allele) for each trait. A zygote when becomes diploid, have two alleles for each trait. It is the maximum number of alleles an individual can have. *e.g.*, genes of blood groups. Multiple alleles are created when there are many gene variation of a single gene. These alleles combine to create different phenotype.

Q.15 How does a mutagen induce mutation? Explain with example.

Ans. Mutagens may be physical, *i.e.*, ionising radiations (X-ray, UV rays, gamma rays,) chemicals, (*i.e.*, hydroxyl radicals, H_2O_2, etc.,) or biological (such as virus). A mutagen can induce mutation by inducing, a change in the base sequence of DNA by insertion, deletion or substitution during replication. *e.g.*, a single base sequence substitution at the sixth codon of the β-globin gene changes the codon from GAG to GUG. This results in the substitution of glutamic acid (Glu) by valine (Val) at the sixth position of the β-globin chain of the haemoglobin molecule.

The mutant haemoglobin molecule undergoes polymerisation under low oxygen tension causing the change in the shape of the RBC from biconcave disc to the elongated sickle, *i.e.*, like structure which is not functional. This condition is known as sickle cell anemia.

Short Answer Type Questions

Q.1 In a Mendelian monohybrid cross, the F_2-generation shows identical genotypic and phenotypic ratios. What does it tell us about the nature of alleles involved? Justify your answer.

Thinking Process In a monohybrid cross starting with parents which are homozygous dominant and homozygous recessive, F_1 would be heterozygous for the trait and would express the dominant allele. But in case of incomplete dominance the result will be different.

Ans. In case of incomplete dominance, a monohybrid cross shows identical phenotypic and genetypic ratio, for example in Snapdragon. If a cross is made between red flowered and white flowered plants, the F_1 progeny will be pink flowered. Self pollination of F_1 pink flowered plants gives F_2 progeny of Red, pink and white flowered plants in the ratio of 1 : 2 : 1.

RR (red) × rr (white)
↓
Rr
All pink — **F_1-generation**

Rr X Rr — **Selfing**
↓

	RR	rR	rR	rr	
					F_2-generation
Phenotypic ratio	Red	Pink	Pink	White	
Genotypic ratio	1	2		1	

Here, the phenotypic and genotypic both ratios are the same. So, we can conclude that when genotypic and phenotypic ratios are the same, alleles show incomplete dominance. *i.e.*, none of the two alleles shows dominance thus producing hybrid intermediate from the expression of two homozygous alleles.

Q.2 Can a child have blood group 'O' if his parents have blood group 'A' and 'B' Explain.

Thinking Process The child with blood group O will have homozygous recessive alleles. Therefore, both the parents should be heterozygous, *i.e.*, genotype of father will be I^A i, or I^B i and of mother will be I^A i or I^B i .

Ans. A child can have blood group O in the following two cases

Case I When father is I^A i and mother is I^B i.

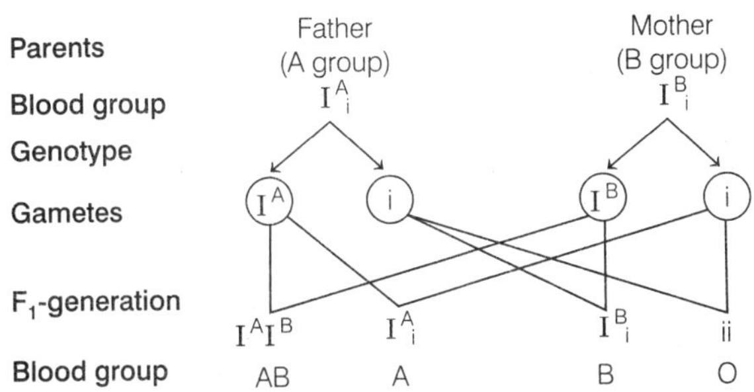

The offsprings will have the above possible blood groups. *i.e.*, AB, A, B and O

Case II When father is I^B i and mother is I^A i.

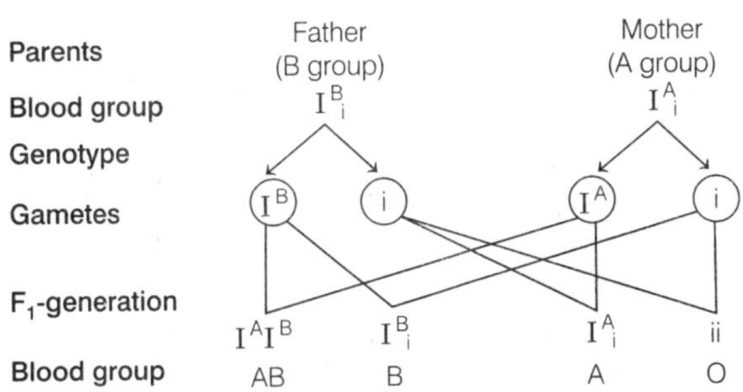

The offsprings will have the above possible blood groups, *i.e.*, AB, A, B and O. Thus, a child can have blood group 'O' if parents have heterozygous alleles for group 'A' and 'B'.

Q.3 What is Down's syndrome? Give its symptoms and cause. Why is it that the chances of having a child with Down's syndrome increases if the age of the mother exceeds forty years?

Ans. Down's syndrome is a human genetic disorder caused due to trisomy of chromosome number 21. Such individuals are aneuploid and have 47 chromosomes, *i.e.*, $(2n+1)$

Symptoms of down's syndrome are

(i) Mental retardation, retarded psychomotor development.
(ii) Growth abnormalities
(iii) Constantly open mouth, small round head, broad forehead.
(iv) Dwarfness, etc., gonads and genitalia are under developed
(v) Protruded, furrowed tongue
(vi) Short life expectancy

The reason for the disorder is the non-disjunction (failure to separate) of homologous chromosome (a pair 21 during meiotic division). The chances of having a child with Down's syndrome increases with the age of the mother (over 40 years) because age adversely affects meiotic behaviour of chromosomes.

Q.4 How was it concluded that genes are located on chromosomes?

Ans. Chromosome theory of inheritance was proposed by **Sutton** and **Boveri** independently in 1902. The theory believes that chromosomes are vehicles of heriditary information, possess Mendelian factors or genes and it is the chromosomes which segregate and assort independently during transmission from one generation to the next. They observed that the movement of genes and chromosomes were similar during meiosis. Their work was confirmed by **Morgan** when he studied sex linked inheritance of eye colour in ***Drosophila***. Thus concluding that genes are located on chromosomes.

Q.5 A plant with red flowers was crossed with another plant with yellow flowers. If F_1 showed all flowers orange in colour, explain the inheritance.

Thinking Process If any of the alleles does not fully dominate in a heterozygous condition, it is called incomplete dominance.

Ans. Incomplete dominance is the inheritance pattern where neither of the two alleles shows complete dominance. Thus, producing intermediate hybrid between the expression of two alleles in heterozygous state. In this case, a new phenotype in between the two original phenotype appears. Which is the characteristic of incomplete dominance

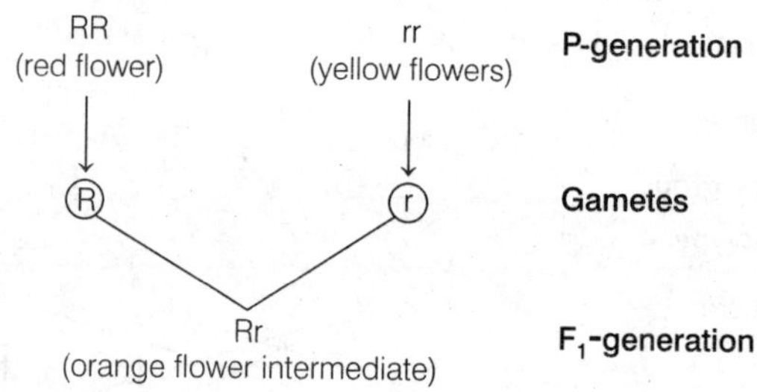

Q.6 What are the characteristic features of a true-breeding line?

Ans. True breeding is a stable inheritance and expression of a trait for several generations as a result of continuous self-pollination. This is because the organisms are homozygous for the traits.

Characteristic features of a true-breeding line

(i) They are used as parents in artificial hybridisation as they provide gametes with all similar traits.

(ii) Homozygous recessive plants are used in test cross to determine the genotype.

(iii) It promotes accumulation of superior genes.

Q.7 In peas,tallness is dominant over dwarfness, and red colour of flowers is dominant over the white colour. When a tall plant bearing red flowers was pollinated with a dwarf plant bearing white flowers, the different phenotypic groups were obtained in the progeny in numbers mentioned against them

Tall, Red = 138
Tall, White = 132
Dwarf, Red = 136
Dwarf, White = 128

Mention the genotypes of the two parents and of the four offspring types.

Ans. The result shows that the four types of offspring are in a ratio of 1:1:1:1. Such a result is observed in a test cross progeny of a dihybrid cross. Such cross has one parent with genotype double recessive (ttrr) and another parent with double hybrid (TtRr).

The cross can be represented as

Parents Tall and red (TtRr) × Dwarf and white (ttrr)

Offsprings

♂ / ♀	TR	Tr	tR	tr
tr	TtRr (tall and red)	Ttrr (tall and white)	ttRr (dwarf and red)	ttrr (dwarf and white)

Q.8 Why is the frequency of red-green colourblindness is many times higher in males than that in the females?

Ans. Colour blindness show X-linked sex inheritance. For becoming colourblind, the female must have the allele on both the X-chromosomes. If only one X-chromosome of female possess allele for colour blind character then she will becomes the carrier for this characteristic.

But males develop colour blindness when their sole X-chromosome has the allele for it. Thus males are more prone to colour blindness because they only have one X-chromosome while females with two x-chromosomes. This is a rare disorder due to large scale heterozygosity in human population.

Q.9 If a father and son are both defective in red-green colour vision, is it likely that the son inherited the trait from his father? Comment.

Ans. Gene for colour blindness is X-chromosome linked, and sons receive their sole X-chromosome from their mother, not from their father. Therefore male to male inheritances is not possible for X-linked traits in humans.

In the given case the mother of the son must be a carrier (heterozygous) for colour blindness gene, thus transmitting the gene to her son.

Q.10 Discuss why *Drosophila* has been used extensively for genetical studies?

Ans. **Morgan** worked with the tiny fruit flies, *Drosophila melanogaster*, which were found to be suitable for genetical studies due to the following characteristics

(i) They could be grown on simple synthetic medium in the laboratory like cream of wheat, molasses and agar.

(ii) They complete their life-cycle in about two weeks and can be bred throughout the year.

(iii) A single mating could produce a large number of progeny flies.

(iv) A clear differentiation of the sexes–the male and female flies are easily distinguishable due to their larger size.

(v) It has many types of variations (hereditary) that can be seen with low power microscopes.

(vi) Does not require any big space and can be reared in bottles.

(vii) They have large number of easily recognisable traits.

Q.11 How do genes and chromosomes share similarity from the point of view of genetical studies?

Ans. From the point of view of genetical studies, both genes and chromosomes are essential to the process of inheritance.

They share following similarities

(i) Both carry genetic information.
(ii) Involved in inheritance of traits.
(iii) Follow principle of segregation and independent assortment.
(iv) Contribute to genetic variation.

Q.12 What is recombination? Discuss the applications of recombination from the point of view of genetic engineering.

Ans. Recombination refers to the generation of new combination of genes which is different from the parental types. It is produced due to crossing over that occurs during meiosis, prior to gamete formation.

Applications of Recombination

(i) It is a means of introducing new combinations of genes and hence new traits.
(ii) It increases variability which is useful for natural selection and under changed environment.
(iii) Since, the frequency of crossing over depends upon the distance between the two genes, the phenomenon is used for preparing linkage chromosome maps.
(iv) It has proved that genes lie in a linear fashion in the chromosome.
(v) Breeders have to select small or large population for obtaining the required cross-overs. For obtaining cross-overs between closely linked genes, a very large population is required.
(vi) Useful recombinations produced by crossing over are picked up by breeders to produce useful new varieties of crop plants and animals. For example, the green revolution has been achieved in India due to this selective picking up of useful recombinations. Operation flood or white revolution is also being carried out on the similar lines.

Q.13 What is artificial selection? Do you think it affects the process of natural selection? How?

Ans. Artificial selection (or selective breeding) describes intentional breeding for certain traits or combination of traits by humans, for exploiting the variations existing among species. It is of three types-mass selection, pure-line selection and clonal selection. Yes, it affects the process of natural selection. Natural selection selects for/or against traits based on their effect on the fitness of the organism. In artificial selection, traits are selected based on human preference for improving traits.

The process of natural selection leads to evolutionary change in the expression of the trait in the population, whereas the artificial selection, though being the same process, involves the traits preferred by humans for its own benefit. It is a much faster process than the natural selection but it may impose threat on diversity in long run making it unfit to the environment.

Q.14 With the help of an example differentiate between incomplete dominance and co-dominance.

Ans. Incomplete dominance is a phenomenon where two contrasting alleles are present together but neither of the alleles is dominant over other and the phenotype formed is intermediate of the two alleles.

e.g., the kind of inheritance in the dog flower (Snapdragon or *Antirrhinum* species) in which the intermediate trait is expressed in F_1-generation.

Cross showing incomplete dominance

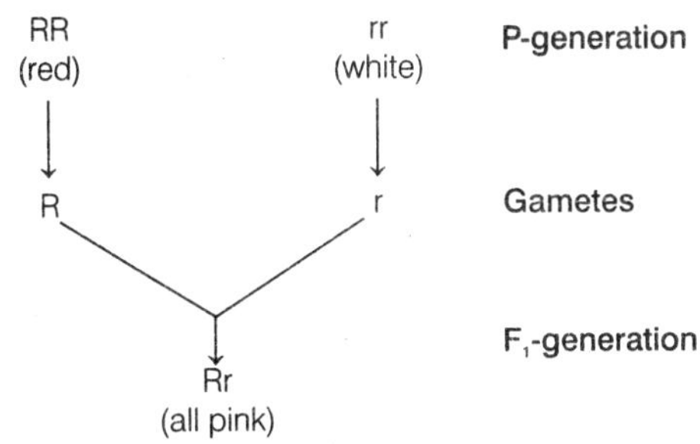

Codominance is a phenomenon in which when two contrasting alleles are present together and both of the alleles express themselves.

e.g., ABO blood group in humans where both A and B alleles are expressed to produce RBC surface antigens A and B.

Blood group showing co-dominance

Genotype	Surface Antigen	Blood Group
I^Ai (dominance)	A	A
I^AI^A	A	A
I^Bi (dominance)	B	B
I^BI^B	B	B
I^AI^B (co-dominance)	AB	AB
ii	—	O

Q.15 It is said, that the harmful alleles get eliminated from population over a period of time, yet sickle-cell anaemia is persisting in human population. Why?

Ans. Sickle-cell anaemia is an autosomal recessive disease caused by substitution in β-globin chain of haemoglobin (oxygen carrying protein in blood cells).

Despite the disease's lethal symptoms, it protects the carrier from malaria because malaria parasite is unable to efficiently infect RBC having Hb^AHb^S haemoglobin. Its allele are most common in the people of African descent (about 7% people of African descent carry an allele) and some other are as where malaria in prevalent.

Long Answer Type Questions

Q.1 In a plant tallness is dominant over dwarfness and red flower is dominant over white. Starting with the parents work out a dihybrid cross. What is standard dihybrid ratio? Do you think the values would deviate if the two genes in question are interacting with each other?

Ans.

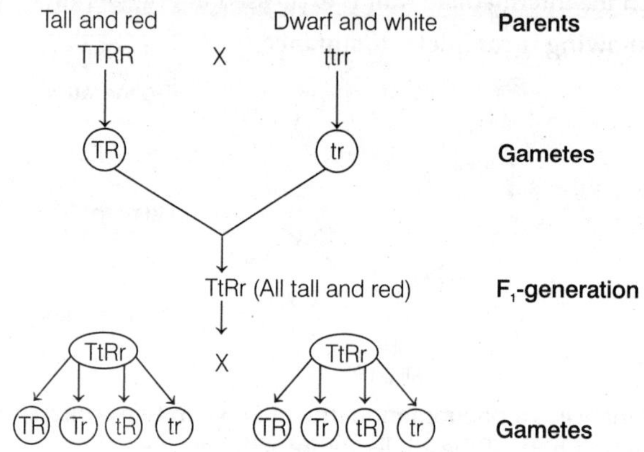

F_2-generation

	TR	Tr	tR	tr
TR	TTRR Tall, Red	TTRr Tall, Red	TtRR Tall, Red	TtRr Tall, Red
Tr	TTRr Tall, Red	TTrr Tall, White	TtRr Tall, Red	Ttrr Tall, White
tR	TtRR Tall, Red	TtRr Tall, Red	ttRR Dwarf, Red	ttRr Dwarf, Red
tr	TtRr Tall, Red	Ttrr Tall, White	ttRr Dwarf, Red	ttrr Dwarf, White

The standard dihybrid ratio is 9:3:3:1.

Yes, the values will show deviation if the two genes in the above case are interacting with each other. When the genes are linked, they do not assort independently but remain together in the gametes and the offsprings, give a dihybrid ratio of 3:1 and show a test cross ratio of 1:1 instead of 1:1:1:1.

Q.2 (a) In humans, males are heterogametic and females are homogametic, Explain. Are there any examples where males are homogametic and females heterogametic?

(b) Also describe as to, who determines the sex of an unborn child? Mention whether temperature has a role in sex determination.

Ans. (a) The term homogametic and heterogametic refers to the organism containing one type of sex chromosome (*homo*-same) or two different types of sex chromosomes (*hetero*-different). Humans show XX/XY type of sex determination, *i.e.*, females contain 2 copies of X-chromosome and males contain 1 X and 1 Y-chromosome. Therefore, ova produced by females contain the same sex chromosome, *i.e.*, X.

On the other hand the sperms contain 2 different types of chromosomes, *i.e.*, 50% sperms have X and 50% have Y-chromosomes (meiosis). Therefore, the sperms are different with respect to the composition of sex chromosome.

In case of humans, females are considered to be homogametic while males are heterogametic. Yes, there are examples where males are homogametic and females are heterogametic. In some birds the mode of sex determination is denoted by ZZ (males) and ZW (females) type. Certain moths and butterflies also show homogametic males and heterogametic females.

(b) As a rule the heterogametic organism determines the sex of the unborn child. In case of humans, since males are heterogametic it is the father and not the mother who decides the sex of the child. Temperature plays a role in sex determination in some animals like crocodiles, lower temperature favour development of female offsprings and higher temperatures lead to development of male offsprings.

Q.3 A normal visioned woman, whose father is colour blind, marries a normal visioned man. What would be probability of her sons and daughters to be colour blind? Explain with the help of a pedigree chart.

Ans. Colour blindness is X linked recessive disorder. The defected gene is present on 'X' chromosome. As males have only one X chromosome, males are commonly diseased but females are carrier. The genotype of parents are

Mother ⟶ XX

Father ⟶ XY

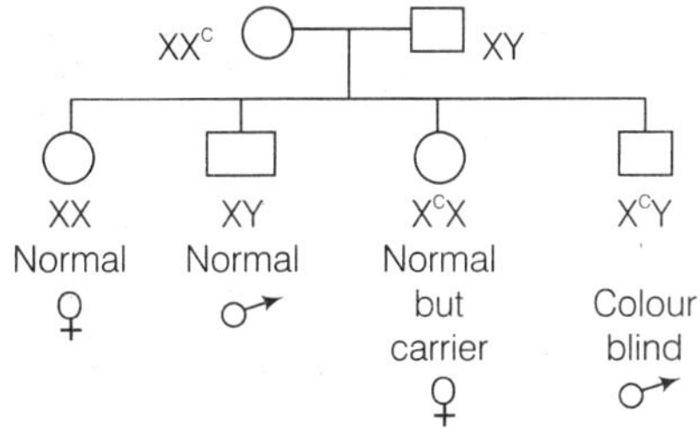

50% daughters are normal visioned but 50% will be carriers.

50% of sons are likely to be colour blind and 50% are normal visioned.

Q.4 Discuss in detail the contributions of Morgan and Sturvant in the area of genetics.

Ans. **T H Morgan** (1866-1945) was given the Nobel Prize in 1933.

His contributions are

(i) Morgan worked on fruit fly, *Drosophila melanogaster* and provide experimental verification of the chromosomal theory of inheritance.

(ii) He stated and established that genes are located on the chromosomes.

(iii) He established the principle of linkage, crossing over, sex-linked inheritance and discovered the relation between gene and chromosome.

(iv) He established the technique of chromosome mapping.

(v) He observed and worked on mutation.

Alfred Henry Sturtevant (1891-1970) student of Morgan was given the National Medal of Science in 1967. His contributions are

(i) He constructed the first genetic map of a chromosome while working on the *Drosophila* genome.

(ii) His main contributions to science include his analysis of genetic 'linkage groups,' which became classical method of chromosome mapping that is still used today. He also determined that genes were arranged on chromosomes in a linear fashion, like beads on a necklace. He also showed that the gene for any specific trait was in a fixed location (locus).

(iii) His work on *Drosophila* proved that two closely related species showed newly recurring mutations that were allelic and thus probably identical. His work also helped to determine genetic role in sexual selection and development and displayed the importance of chromosomal crossing over in mutations.

(iv) One of Sturtevant's principal contributions was his introduction to the concept that the frequency of crossing over between two genes could help to determine their proximity on a linear genetic map. His experiments determined that the frequency of double crossing over can be used to deduce gene order.

Q.5 Define aneuploidy. How is it different from polyploidy? Describe the individuals having following chromosomal abnormalities.

(a) Trisomy of 21st Chromosome (b) XXY (c) XO

Ans. Aneuploidy is the numerical change in the chromosome number in the genome of an individual which occurs due to non-disjunction, resulting in gain or loss of one or more chromosomes during meiosis.

Aneuploidy is different from polyploidy. Polyploidy is a phenomenon in which the organisms contain more than two sets of chromosomes. *i.e.*, $3n$, $4n$etc. Example of such organisms are certain fishes and salamanders and is commonly found in plants like grapes, banana.

Chromosomal Abnormalities

(a) Down's syndrome is an autosomal disorder that is caused by the trisomy of chromosome 21. The individual is short statured with round head, open mouth, protruding tongue, short neck, slanting eyes, and broad short hands. The individual also shows retarded mental and physical growth,under developed gonads and genitals, etc.

(b) Klinefelter's syndrome is the chromosomal disorder that is caused by the presence of an additional copy of X-chromosome resulting in the karyotype 44+XXY. In this disorder sex of the individual is masculine but possess feminine characters also. The individual shows gynaecomastia, *i.e.*, development of breasts. The individual will be often sterile having poor beard growth and feminine pitched voice.

(c) Turner's syndrome (XO) is the chromosomal disorder that is caused by the absence of one of the X-chromosomes, resulting in the karyotype 44+XO.

In this disorder the individual (female) will be sterile with rudimentary ovaries. Other symptoms include shield-shaped thorax, webbed neck, poor development of breasts, short stature, small uterus and puffy fingers.

Chapter 06

Molecular Basis of Inheritance

Multiple Choice Questions (MCQs)

Q.1 In a DNA strand the nucleotides are linked together by

(a) glycosidic bonds (b) phosphodiester bonds
(c) peptide bonds (d) hydrogen bonds

Ans. *(b)* In a DNA strand, the nucleotides are linked together by 3′–5′ phosphodiester linkage (bonds) to form a dinucleotide. More nucleotides can be joined in such a manner to form a polynucleotide chain.

Q.2 A nucleoside differs from a nucleotide. It lacks the

(a) base (b) sugar
(c) phosphate group (d) hydroxyl group

Ans. *(c)* A nucleoside differs from a nucleotide as it lacks the phosphate group. A nitrogenous base is attached to the pentose sugar by an N-glycosidic linkage to form a nucleoside, *i.e.*, Nucleoside = Nitrogen base + Pentose sugar.

When a phosphate group is attached to the 5′-OH of a nucleoside through phosphoester linkage, a nucleotide is formed, *i.e.*, Nucleotide = Nitrogen base + Pentose sugar + Phosphate (PO_4^{3-}).

Q.3 Both deoxyribose and ribose belong to a class of sugars called

(a) trioses (b) hexoses
(c) pentoses (d) polysaccharides

Ans. (c) Both deoxyribose and ribose belong to the class-pentoses. Pentose sugar contains five carbon sugar molecule .

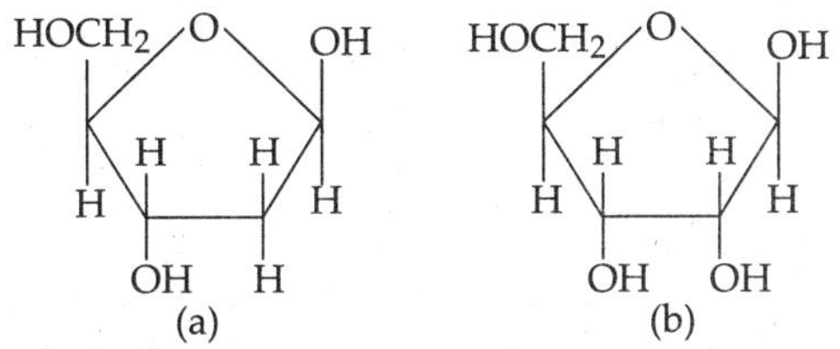

Structure of (a) deoxyribose (b) ribose sugar

Q.4 The fact that a purine base always pairs through hydrogen bonds with a pyrimidine base in the DNA double helix leads to

(a) the antiparallel nature
(b) the semiconservative nature
(c) uniform width throughout DNA
(d) uniform length in all DNA

Ans. *(c)* The diameter of the strand is always constant due to a pairing of purine (adenine and guanine) and pyrimidine (cytosine and thymine). This specific bonding gives uniform width to the DNA.

Q.5 The net electric charge on DNA and histones is

(a) both positive
(b) both negative
(c) Both (a) and (b)
(d) zero

Ans. *(c)* DNA consists of a nitrogenous base, pentose sugar and a phosphate group. DNA has negative charge due to the presence of phosphate group (PO_4^{3-}).

Histones are rich in the basic amino acid residues, lysines and arginines, which carry positive charges in their side chains. Therefore, histones are positively charged.

Q.6 The promoter site and the terminator site for transcription are located at

(a) 3′ (downstream) end and 5′ (upstream) end, respectively of the transcription unit
(b) 5′ (upstream) end and 3′ (downstream) end, respectively of the transcription unit
(c) the 5′ (upstream) end
(d) the 3′ (downstream) end

Ans. *(b)* The promoter is the binding site for RNA polymerase for initiation of transcription.

The promoter is located towards 5′-end (upstream) of the structural gene of coding strands and provides the binding site for RNA polymerase whereas, terminator is present at 3′-end (downstream) of the structural gene.

Q.7 Which of the following statements is the most appropriate for sickle-cell anaemia?

(a) It cannot be treated with iron supplements
(b) It is a molecular disease
(c) It confers resistance to acquiring malaria
(d) All of the above

Ans. *(d)* All of the above statements about sickle cell anaemia are true as,

Sike cell anaemia is not caused by iron deficiency, so iron supplements would not be an effective treatment.

It is a molecular disease caused by a mutation in the haemoglobin gene.

Sickle-cell anemia confers resistance to malaria because heterozygotes individuals, having both types of haemoglobin, show resistance to malaria infection because *P. falciparum* cannot effectively infect elongated sickle structured RBC.

Q.8 Which of the following is true with respect to AUG

(a) it codes for methionine only
(b) it is also an initiation codon
(c) it codes for methionine in both prokaryotes and eukaryotes
(d) All of the above

Thinking Process Three adjacent nitrogenous bases constitute a codon which specifies the placement of one amino acid, in a polypeptide chain.

Ans. *(d)* All the above statements are true about AUG as polypeptide synthesis is signalled by initiation codon AUG. It codes for methionine in prokaryotes and eukaryotes. Since, there are 64 triplet codons and only 20 amino acids, the incorporation of some amino acids must be influenced by more than one codon.

Only tryptophan (UGG) and methionine (AUG) are specified by single codons.

Q.9 The first genetic material could be

(a) protein (b) carbohydrates (c) DNA (d) RNA

Ans. *(d)* RNA was the first genetic material. It is essential for life processes such as metabolism, translation, splicing, etc.

RNA used to act as a genetic material as well as a catalyst (there are some important biochemical reactions in living systems that are catalysed by RNA catalysts and not by protein enzymes). But, RNA being a catalyst was reactive and hence unstable.

Therefore, DNA has evolved from RNA with chemical modifications that make it more stable. DNA being double-stranded and having complementary strand further resists changes by evolving a process of repair mechanism.

Q.10 With regard to mature *m*RNA in eukaryotes

(a) exons and introns do not appear in the mature RNA
(b) exons appear but introns do not appear in the mature RNA
(c) introns appear but exons do not appear in the mature RNA
(d) both exons and introns appear in the mature RNA

Ans. *(b)* In eukaryotes, the monocistronic structural genes have interrupted sequences *i.e.*, the genes in eukaryotes are split. The coding sequences or expressed sequences are defined as exons.

These sequences (exons) appear in mature or processed RNA. The exons are interrupted by introns or intervening sequences which do not appear in mature or processed RNA.

Q.11 The human chromosome with the highest and least number of genes in them are respectively

(a) chromosome 21 and Y (b) chromosome 1 and X
(c) chromosome 1 and Y (d) chromosome X and Y

Ans. *(c)* In humans, chromosome 1 has highest number of genes (2968 approx.) and the Y has the least number of (231 approx.) genes.

Q.12 Who amongst the following scientists had no contribution in the development of the double helix model for the structure of DNA?

(a) Rosalind Franklin (b) Maurice Wilkins
(c) Erwin Chargaff (d) Meselson and Stahl

Ans. *(d)* **Matthew Meselson** and **Franklin Stahl** performed experiments on *E.coli* to prove that DNA replication is semi-conservative. But, had no contribution the development of double helix model of DNA.

James Watson and **Francis Crick**, based on the *X*-ray diffraction data produced by **Maurice Wilkins** and **Rasalind Franklin**, proposed the simple, but famous double helix model for the structure of DNA.

Erwin Chargaff observed that for a double-stranded DNA, the ratios between adenine and thymine and guanine and cytosine are constant and equals to one.

Q.13 DNA is a polymer of nucleotides which are linked to each other by 3′–5′ phosphodiester bond. To prevent polymerisation of nucleotides, which of the following modifications would you choose?

(a) Replace purine with pyrimindines
(b) Remove/Replace 3′ OH group in deoxy ribose
(c) Remove/Replace 2′ OH group with some other group in deoxy ribose
(d) Both (b) and (c)

Ans. *(b)* The enzyme DNA polymerase (for DNA polymerisation) progressively adds deoxyribonucleotides to the free 3′-end of the growing polynucleotide chain. This ensures that the replication of the 3′–5′ strand of the DNA molecule is continuous (growth of the new strand in 5′ → 3′ direction).

So, to prevent polymerisation of nucleotides 3′ OH group in deoxyribose should be replaced/removed.

Q.14 Discontinuous synthesis of DNA occurs in one strand, because

(a) DNA molecule being synthesised is very long
(b) DNA dependent DNA polymerase catalyses polymerisation only in one direction (5′→ 3′)
(c) it is a more efficient process
(d) DNA ligase has to have a role

Thinking Process The replication of 3′ → 5′ strand is continuous and it is called leading strand, while the replication of second strand (5′→ 3′ strand) of the DNA molecules is discontinuous and it is known as the lagging strand.

Ans. *(b)* DNA polymerase adds deoxyribonucleotides to the free 3′-end of the growing polynucleotide chain. This ensures that the replication of the 3′→ 5′ strand of the DNA molecule is continuous (growth of the new strand in 5′ → 3′ direction).

Since, DNA dependent DNA polymerase catalyses polymerisation only in one direction (5′ → 3′ leading strand), discontinuous synthesis of DNA occurs in the other direction on the other strand, *i.e.*, lagging strand.

Q.15 Which of the following steps in transcription is catalysed by RNA polymerse?

(a) Initiation
(b) Elongation
(c) Termination
(d) All of these

Ans. *(b)* The DNA dependent RNA polymerase helps in DNA transcription by catalysing the polymerisation in only one direction, *i.e.*, $5' \rightarrow 3'$.

Q.16 Control of gene expression in prokaryotes takes place at the level of

(a) DNA-replication
(b) transcription
(c) translation
(d) None of these

Thinking Process Regulation of gene expression refers to a very broad term that may occur at various levels. It is a process by which information encoded in a gene is used for directing the polypeptide formation.

Ans. *(b)* Transcription is the main level at which control of gene expression takes place in prokaryotes.

This is because the regulation of transcription allows the cells to control which genes are transcribed into RNA and than proteins.

Key mechanisms of transcriptional control in prokaryotes include operons and regulatory proteins (like repressors or activators). This influences RNA prymerase's ability to intiate transcription.

Q.17 Which of the following statements is correct about role of regulatory proteins in the transcription of prokaryotes?

(a) They only increase expression
(b) They only decrease expression
(c) They interact with RNA polymerase but do not affect the expression
(d) They can act both as activators and as repressors

Thinking Process Regulatory protein is a term used in genetics to describe a protein involved in regulating gene expressions. There are often needed to switch a gene on (activator) or to switch off a gene (represssor).

Ans. *(d)* Statement (d) is correct as regulatory proteins can act as both activators and repressors.

Statements (a), (b) and (c) are incorrect and be corrected as

Regulatory proteins increases as well as decreases gene expression.

They interact with RNA polymerase and affect the expressions as well. This can be achieved by either activating or repressing transcription.

Q.18 Which was the last human chromosome to be completely sequenced?

(a) Chromosome 1
(b) Chromosome 11
(c) Chromosome 21
(d) Chromosome-X

Ans. *(a)* Chromosome 1 was the last completed chromosome. It was sequenced two decades after the beginning of the human Genome Project (HGP). As chromosome 1 was the largest human chromosome and had complex regions, which made is difficult to sequence.

Q.19 Which of the following are the functions of RNA?

(a) It is carrier of genetic information from DNA to ribosomes synthesising polypeptides
(b) It carries amino acids to ribosomes
(c) It is a constituent component of ribosomes
(d) All of the above

Thinking Process RNA is a single chain of polyribonucleotide, which functions as carrier of coded genetic or hereditary information from DNA to cytoplasm for taking part in protein and enzyme synthesis.

Ans. ***(d)*** All the above statements are true about functions of RNA as *r*RNA, *m*RNA and *t*RNA are major classes of RNA*s* that are involved in gene expression.
It is a constituent component of ribosomes. This refers to *r*RNAs as they bind protein molecules and give rise to ribosomes.
It is a carrier of genetic information from DNA to ribosomes synthesing polypeptides. This refers to *m*RNA, which codes.

It carries amino acids to ribosomes. This refers to *t*RNA, which is called soluble or adaptor RNA and carries amino acids to *m*RNA during protein synthesis.

Q.20 While analysing the DNA of an organism a total number of 5386 nucleotides were found out of which the proportion of different bases were Adenine = 29%, Guanine = 17%, Cytosine = 32%, Thymine = 17%. Considering the Chargaffs rule it can be concluded that

(a) it is a double-stranded circular DNA
(b) it is single-stranded DNA
(c) it is a double-stranded linear DNA
(d) No conclusion can be drawn

Ans. ***(b)*** According to Chargaff's rules of base pairing,

(i) The amount of adenine is always equal to the amount of thymine and the amount of guanine is always equal to the amount of cytosine.
(ii) Adenine is joined to thymine with two hydrogen bonds and guanine is joined to cytosine by three hydrogen bonds.
(iii) The ratio of adenine to thymine and that of guanine to cytosine is always equal to one,

i.e.,
$$\frac{A}{T} = \frac{G}{C} = 1$$

In the given organism, the DNA is not following the Chargaff's rule, hence it can be concluded that it is a single-stranded DNA, not double-stranded.

Q.21 In some viruses, DNA is synthesised by using RNA as template. Such a DNA is called

(a) A-DNA
(b) B-DNA
(c) cDNA
(d) *r*DNA

Ans. ***(c)*** In some viruses, like retroviruses (*e.g.*, HIV), an enzyme called reverse transcriptase is used to generate complementary DNA (*c*DNA) from an RNA template. This process is termed as reverse transcription.

Q.22 If Meselson and Stahl's experiment is continued for four generations in bacteria, the ratio of $N^{15}/N^{15}:N^{15}/N^{14}:N^{14}/N^{14}$ containing DNA in the fourth generation would be

(a) 1:1:0 (b) 1:4:0 (c) 0:1:3 (d) 0:1:7

Ans. ***(d)*** Meselson and Stahl found that DNA of the first generation was hybrid or intermediate (^{15}N and ^{14}N). It settled in caesium chloride at a level higher than the fully labelled DNA of parent bacteria (^{15}N ^{15}N).

The second generation of bacteria after 40 minutes, contained two types of DNA, 50% light (N^{14} N^{14}) and 50% intermediate (N^{15} N^{14}).

The third generation of bacteria after 60 minutes contained two types of DNA, 25% intermediate (N^{15} N^{14}) and 75% light (N^{14} N^{14}) in 1:3 ratio.

The fourth generation after 80 minutes contained 12.5% N^{15} N^{14} and 87.5% N^{14} N^{14} DNA in 1:7 ratio.

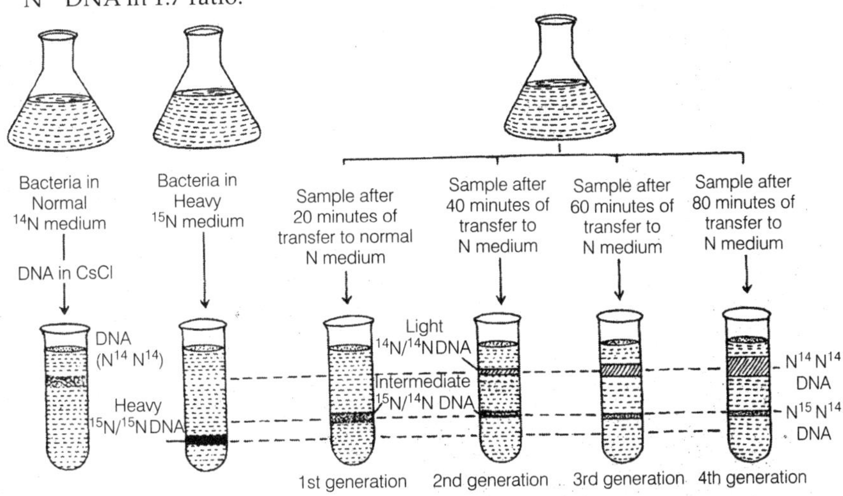

Meselson and Stahl's experiment

Q.23 If the sequence of nitrogen bases of the coding strand of DNA in a transcription unit is

5' - A T G A A T G - 3',

the sequence of bases in its RNA transcript would be

(a) 5′ - A U G A A U G - 3′ (b) 5′ - U A C U U A C - 3′

(c) 5′ - C A U U C A U - 3′ (d) 5′ - G U A A G U A - 3′

Ans. ***(a)*** The transcription will take place as follows

5′ - A T G A A T G - 3′ (coding strand)

↓

5′- T A C T T A C - 3′ (complementary strand)

↓

5′ -A U G A A U G - 3′ (RNA)

Q.24 The RNA polymerase holoenzyme transcribes
(a) the promoter, structural gene and the terminator region
(b) the promoter and the terminator region
(c) the structural gene and the terminator regions
(d) the structural gene only

Thinking Process In prokaryotes, the structural gene is polycistronic and continuous. In bacteria (prokaryotes), the transcription of all the three types of RNA (*m*RNA, *t*RNA and *r*RNA) is catalysed by single DNA dependent enzyme, called the RNA polymerase.

Ans. ***(c)*** In *E. coli* bacterium, the RNA polymerase transcribes the structural and the terminator regions. The transcription is completed in three steps.

Initiation σ (sigma) factor recognises the start signal and promotor region on DNA, which then along with RNA polymerase binds to the promoter to initiate transcription.

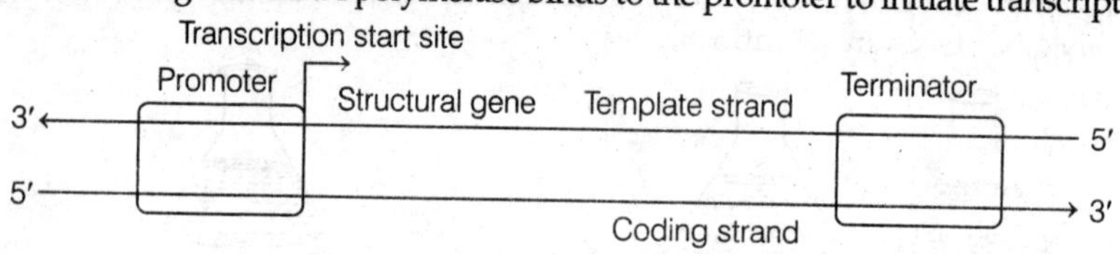

Schematic structure of a transcription unit

Elongation The RNA polymerase after initiation of RNA transcription loses the σ factor but continues the polymerisation of ribonucleotides to form RNA.

Termination Once the RNA polymerase reaches the termination region of DNA, the RNA polymerase is separated from DNA-RNA hybrid, as a result nascent RNA separates. This process is called termination which is facilitated by a termination factor ρ (rho).

Q.25 If the base sequence of a codon in *m*RNA is 5'-AUG-3', the sequence of *t*RNA pairing with it must be
(a) 5′ - UAC - 3′ (b) 5′ - CAU - 3′ (c) 5′ - AUG - 3′ (d) 5′ - GUA - 3′

Ans. ***(b)*** 5′ - CAU - 3′

5′ - A U G - 3′ (codon in *m*RNA)
| | |
5′ - U A C - 3′ (*t*RNA)

If the mRNA codon is 5′ AUG 3′ then the tRNA anticodon will be 3′ - UAC - 5′. The base sequences are usually read in 5′→ 3′ direction. Therefore *t*RNA anticodon in the 5′→ 3′ direction is 5′ - CAU - 3′.

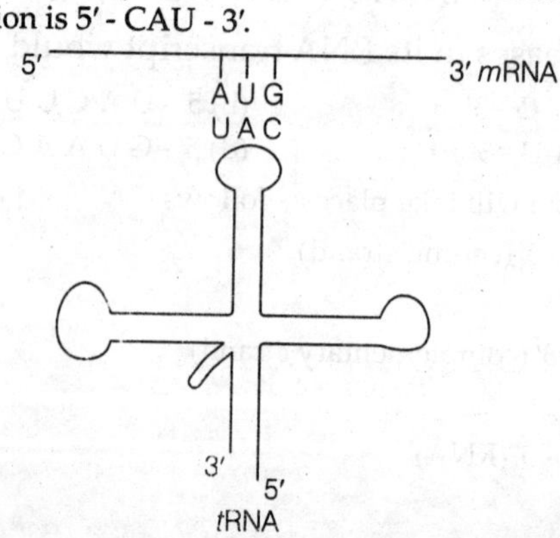

Q.26 The amino acid attaches to the *t*RNA at its

(a) 5′-end (b) 3′-end (c) Anti codon site (d) DHU loop

Ans. ***(b)*** AA-binding site (amino acid binding site) lies at the 3′ end, opposite to the anticodon that has complimentary bases to the code. It is the site where amino acid attaches to the *t*RNA.

Q.27 To initiate translation, the *m*RNA first binds to

(a) the smaller ribosomal sub-unit (b) the larger ribosomal sub-unit
(c) the whole ribosome (d) No such specificity exists

Thinking Process The cellular factory responsible for synthesising proteins is the ribosome.

Ans. ***(a)*** To initiate translation *m*RNA first binds to the smaller ribosomes subunit. The ribosome consists of structural RNAs and about 80 different proteins. In its inactive state, it exists as two subunits, a large subunit and a small subunit. When the smaller subunit encounters the *m*RNA, the process of translation of the *m*RNA to protein begins.

Q.28 In *E. coli*, the *lac* operon gets switched on when

(a) lactose is present and it binds to the repressor
(b) repressor binds to operator
(c) RNA polymerase binds to the operator
(d) lactose is present and it binds to RNA polymerase

Ans. ***(a)*** In *E. coil* the *lac* operon gets switched on when lactose is present and it binds to the repressou. The presence of lactose triggers the expression of lac operon.

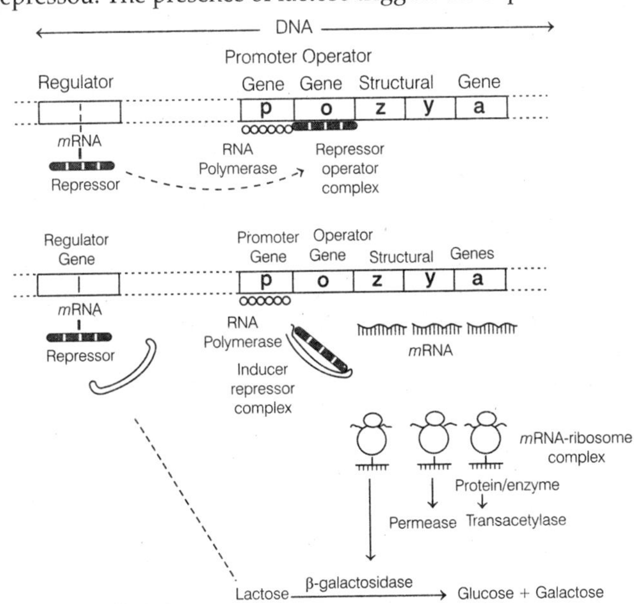

Jacob and Monod model of an inducible operon

In case presence of lactose

(i) Lactose acts as an inducer which binds to the repressor and forms an inactive repressor.

(ii) The repressor fails to bind to the operator region.

(iii) The RNA polymerase binds to the operator and transcript *lac* *m*RNA.

(iv) *lac* *m*RNA is polycistronic, *i.e.*, produces all three enzymes, β-galactosidase, permease and transacetylase.

(v) The *lac* operon is switched on.

Very Short Answers Type Questions

Q.1 What is the function of histones in DNA packaging?

Ans. Functions of histones in DNA packaging are as follows

(i) Histones form an octamer unit that participate in primary packaging of DNA.

(ii) Basic histone proteins neutralise the acidic DNA molecule.

(iii) Fifth histone (H_1) helps in coiling of DNA strand. It binds the DNA between nucleosomes.

Q.2 Distinguish between heterochromatin and euchromatin. Which of the two is transcriptionally active?

Ans. Densely packed, thicker and dark stained chromatin regions are called hetrochromatin, while, loosely packed, thin and light stained regions are called euchromatin.

Euchromation is transcriptionally active and is transcribed into *m*RNA. Due to very tight coiling heterochromatin can not be transcribed and is in inert or inactive form.

Q.3 The enzyme DNA polymerase in *E.coli* is a DNA dependent polymerase and also has the ability to proofread the DNA strand being synthesised Explain. Discuss the dual polymerase.

Ans. In *E. coil*, the enzyme DNA polymerase plays a critical role in DNA replication. It is both a DNA dependent polymerase and as the ability to proof read the newly synthesised strand. This contributes to high accuracy during DNA replication.

This dual function of DNA polymerase is essential for both the synthessis of the new DNA and correction of errors during replication.

Q.4 What is the cause of discontinuous synthesis of DNA on one of the parental strands of DNA? What happens to these short stretches of synthesised DNA?

Ans. DNA synthesis is discontinuous on one of the parental strands of DNA. Synthesis of DNA always takes place in $5' \rightarrow 3'$ direction. In a double stranded DNA, both strands are anti parallel and complementary. During DNA synthesis both strands cannot act as templates, only one strand (the leading strand) with the polarity, $3' \rightarrow 5'$ can synthesis continous complementary strand. The other strand, (the lagging strand) *i.e.*, $5' \rightarrow 3'$ has to be synthesised in small stretches in opposite direction. These small stretches called Okazaki fragments (the short fragments) are joined together by DNA ligase enzyme that closes the nicks.

Q.5 Given below is the sequence of coding strand of DNA in a transcription unit 3′-AATGCAGCTATTAGG-5′ write the sequence of

(a) its complementary strand

(b) the *m*RNA

Ans. According to base complementary rules,

(a) 5'TTACGTCGATAATCC-3'

(b) The *m*RNA uses the base uracil (U) rather than thymine (T). So, in RNA the base pairs are

Adenine (A) pairs with uracil (U)

Guanine (G) pairs with cytosine (C).

*m*RNA sequence 5′-3″AAUGCAGCUAUUAGG5″-3′

Q.6 What is DNA polymorphism? What is it important to study it?

Ans. DNA polymorphism refers to the variation in DNA sequences arising through mutation, often occurring non-coding sequences.

A special type of polymorphism, called VNTR (Variable Number of Tandem Repeats), is composed of repeated copies of a DNA sequence that lie adjacent to one another on the chromosome. Since, polymorphism is the basis of genetic mapping of human genome, therefore, it forms the basis of DNA fingerprinting as well. The single nucleotide polymorphisms are used in locating diseases and tracing of human history as well as in case of paternity testing.

Q.7 Based on your understanding of genetic code, explain the formation of any abnormal haemoglobin molecule. What are the known consequences of such a change?

Thinking Process It is the case of sickle-cell anaemia.

Ans. Formation of abnormal haemoglobin molecule is known as sickle cell anaemia. This happens due to point a mutation in β-globin chain of haemoglobin molecule. This happens when the glutamic acid (Glu) is replaced by valine (Val) at the sixth position in the chain. Under stressful conditions such as low oxygen, erythrocytes lose their circular shape and become sickle-shaped. As a result, the cells cannot pass through narrow capillaries. Blood capillaries are clogged and thus affect blood supply to different organs.

Q.8 Sometimes cattle or even human beings give birth to their young ones that are having extremely different sets of organs like limbs/position of eye(s) etc. Comment.

Ans. Sometimes cattle or even human beings give birth to their young ones that are having extremely different of organs like limbs/position of eye etc. It happens due to the disturbance in coordinated regulation and sequential expression in sets of genes, which are associated with organ development.

Q.9 In a nucleus, the number of ribonucleoside triphosphates is 10 times the number of deoxy ribonucleoside triphosphates, but only deoxy ribonucleotides are added during the DNA replication. Suggest a mechanism.

Ans. In a nucleus, the number of ribonucleoside triphosphate is 10 times the number of deoxy ribonucleoside triphosphates. However, only deoxyribonucleotides are added during DNA replication because the DNA polymerase enzyme is highly specific to recognise only deoxy ribonucleoside triphosphates. Therefore, it cannot hold RNA nucleotides.

Q.10 Name a few enzymes involved in DNA replication other than DNA polymerase and ligase. Name the key functions for each of them.

Ans. The enzymes involved in DNA replication other than DNA polymerase and ligase are listed below with their functions.

(i) Helicase—Opens the helix by breaking hydrogen bonds between the strands.

(ii) Topoisomerases—Removes the super coiling of DNA, unwinding, cutting and resealing of DNA strands

(iii) Primase—Synthesises RNA primer

(iv) Telomerase—To synthesise the DNA of telomeric end of chromosomes.

Q.11 Name any three viruses which have RNA as the genetic material.

Ans. In some viruses, RNA is the genetic material, *e.g.*, Tobacco mosaic viruscs, QB bacteriophage, HIV, influenza virus, etc.

Short Answer Type Questions

Q.1 Define transformation in Griffith's experiment. Discuss how it helps in the identification of DNA as the genetic material.

Ans. In **Griffith's experiment**, transformation can be defined as a change in the genetic constitution of an organism by picking up DNA from the environment (from dead organisms).

Transformation helps in identification of DNA as a genetic material. When heat was used to kill the virulent bacteria, they died but not their genetic material (DNA). This DNA when picked up by non-virulent bacteria made them capable of causing infection. Since, ability to cause infection could be passed on by these organisms to their progeny, it was concluded that DNA was the material that was inherited.

Q.2 Who revealed biochemical nature of the transforming principle?

Ans. Oswald Avery, Colin MacLeod and Maclyn McCarty revealed biochemical nature of the transforming principle. They also reported **Griffith's experiment** in an *in vitro* system in order to determine biochemical nature of transforming principle. It was also reported that DNA from the heat-killed S-type bacteria caused the transformation of non-virulent R-type bacteria into virulent S-type bacteria. They also discovered that proteases and RNase did not affect transformation while DNase inhibited the process. They concluded that DNA is the hereditary material.

Q.3 Discuss the significance of heavy isotope of nitrogen in the Meselson and Stahl's experiment.

Thinking Process **Meselson** and **Stahl** used heavy isotope of ^{15}N in the nutrient medium to grow *Escherichia coli (E. coli)*, for several generations.

Ans. The significance of heavy nitrogen isotope in Meselson and Stahl's expriment is as follows

(i) The heavy DNA molecule containing ^{15}N was easily distinguisable.

(ii) It could be easily seperated from the lighter nitrogen ^{14}N based on density gradient.

(iii) Use of light and heavy nitrogen made it easy to identify transfer of DNA through subsequent generations.

Q.4 Define a cistron. Giving examples differentiate between monocistronic and polycistronic unit.

Ans. A cistron is stretch of base sequences that codes for one polypeptide. It is equivalent to a structural gene. It may also code for a tRNA, rRNA molecule or may perform other specific functions including regulating functions of other cistrons.

A cistron is equivalent to a gene.

Monocistronic transcription unit will have all the regulatory and coding sequences for a single polypeptide, whereas polycistronic may have coding sequences for more than one polypeptide.

In eukaryotic cells almost all the messenger RNAs are monocistronic. In prokaryotes, *lac* operon coding sequence would be an example of polycistronic DNA region.

Q.5 Give any six features of the human genome.

Ans. Salient features of human genome as a follows (any six)

(i) The human genome contains 3164.7 million nucleotide bases.

(ii) The average gene consists of 30,000 the largest know human gene being dystrophin at 2.4 million bases.

(iii) The total number of genes is estimated to be 30,000 and 99.9% nucleotide bases are exactly the same in all people.

(iv) The functions are unknown for over 50% of the discovered genes.

(v) Less than 2% of the genome codes for proteins.

(vi) The human genome contains large repeated sequences.

(vii) The repeated sequence is thought to have no direct coding functions but they throw light on chromosome structures, dynamics and evolution.

(viii) Chromosome I has most genes (2968) and the Y has the fewest genes (231).

(ix) Scientists have identified about 1.4 million locations where single base DNA sequence differences called **SNPs** or Single Nucleotide Polymorphisms occur in humans.

Q.6 **During DNA replication, why is it that the entire molecule does not open in one go? Explain replication fork. What are the two functions that the monomers (dNTPs) play?**

Ans. While replicating, the entire DNA molecule does not open up. This is done to keep the whole molecule stabilised. Unwiding creates tension in the molecule as uncoiled parts.

It has to be fast and accurate. The DNA is opened at specific site called origin of replication (ori). The replication proceedes in a bidirectional manner from these origins and only small DNA fragments unwound at a time. The replication occurs at a small opening of the DNA helix. This is known as replication fork. It gives an appearance of Y-shaped structure.

The two functions that the monomer units of NTPs play are :

(i) They pair up with exposed nucleotides of the template strand and make phosphodiester linkages and release a pyrophosphate.

(ii) NTPs supply high-energy phosphate bonds needed to form phosphodiester linkages in growing chain.

Q.7 **Retroviruses do no follow central dogma. Comment.**

Ans. Retroviruses do not follow central dogma., (*i.e.*, DNA $\xrightarrow{\text{transcription}}$ RNA $\xrightarrow{\text{translation}}$ Protein) because their genetic material is not DNA. Instead they have RNA. The RNA is converted to DNA by the enzyme reverse transcriptase which is a deviation from the typical central dogma.

Q.8 **In an experiment, DNA is treated with the compound which tends to place itself amongst the stacks of nitrogenous base pairs. As a result of this, the distance between two consecutive base increases. From 0.34–0.44 nm calculate the length of DNA double helix (which has 2×10^9 bp) in the presence of saturating of this compound.**

Ans. The length of DNA double helix = $2 \times 10^9 \times 0.44/$ nm. = $2 \times 10^9 \times 0.44 \times 10^{-9}$ /bp (1 m = 10^{-9} nm)

$$= 0.88 \text{ m}$$

Q.9 **What would happen if histones were to be mutated and made rich in acidic amino acids such as aspartic acid and glutamic acid in place of basic amino acids such as lysine and arginine?**

Ans. If histones were mutated and made rich in acidic amino acids, they will not be able to serve the purpose of keeping the DNA coiled around them. This is because DNA is negatively charged molecule and histones are positively charged because of basic amino acids.

So, they are attracted to each other. If histones become negatively charged, instead of binding, they will rather repel DNA. The packaging of DNA in eukaryotes would not happen. Consequently, the chromatin fibre would not be formed.

Q.10 Recall the experiments done by Frederick Griffith, Avery, MacLeod and McCarty, where DNA was speculated to be the genetic material. If RNA, instead of DNA was the genetic material, would the heat killed strain of *Pneumococcus* have transformed the R-strain into virulent strain? Explain.

Ans. RNA is more liable as it is not thermostable and prone to degradation (owing to the presence of 2'OH group in its ribose). Hence, heat-killed S-stain may not have retained its ability to transform the R-strain into virulent form if RNA was its genetic material.

Q.11 You are repeating the Hershey-Chase experiment and are provided with two isotopes ^{32}P and ^{15}N (in place of ^{35}S in the original experiment). How does you expect your results to be different?

Ans. Use of ^{15}N will be inappropriate because method of detection of ^{32}P and ^{15}N is different (^{32}P being a radioactive isotope while ^{15}N is non-radioactive but is the heavier isotope of nitrogen). Even if ^{15}N was radioactive then its presence would not provide exclusive result as it is detected, both inside the cell (^{15}N incorporated as nitrogenous base in DNA) as well as in the supernatant, because ^{15}N would also get incorporated in amino group of amino acids in proteins. Hence, the use of ^{15}N would not give any conclusive results.

Q.12 There is only one possible sequence of amino acids when deduced from a given nucleotides. But multiple nucleotides sequence can be deduced from a single amino acid sequence. Explain this phenomena.

Ans. Some amino acids are coded by more then one codon (known as degeneracy of codons), hence, on deducing a nucleotide sequence from an amino acid sequence, multiple nucleotide sequence will be obtained, e.g., Ile (Isoleucine) has three codons AUU, AUC, AUA. Hence, a dipeptide Met-Ile can have the following nucleotide sequence.

(i) AUG-AUU (ii) AUG-AUC (iii) AUG-AUA

And if, we deduce amino acid sequence from the above nucleotide sequences, all the three will code for Met-Ile.

Q.13 A single base mutation in a gene may not 'always' result in loss or gain of function. Do you think the statement is correct? Defend your answer.

Ans. The statement is correct. Because of degeneracy of codons, mutations at third base of codon, usually does not result into any change in phenotype. This is called silent mutations. eg. AGA, AGG and AGC all code for the same amino acid (Arginine). On other hand, if codon is changed in away that now it specifies another amino acid, it may affect other the protein function as it happens in case of β-globin chain of haemoglobin protein. In this chain, a substitution of valine instead of glutamic acid causes change in its structure and function, and resulting into sickle-cell trait.

Q.14 A low level of expression of *lac* operon occurs at all the time. Can you explain the logic behind this phenomena.

Ans. In the complete absence of expression of lac operon, permease will not be synthesised which is essential for transport of lactose from the medium into the cells. And if lactose cannot be transported into the cell, then it cannot act an inducer. Hence, it cannot relieve the lac operon from its repressed state. Therefore, a low level of expression of the lac operon occurs as constantly to maintain a baseline level of permease production, ensuring that lactose can be transported into the cell when available.

Q.15 How has the sequencing of human genome opened new windows for treatment of various genetic disorders. Discuss amongst your classmates.

Thinking Process In 1990, US department of energy and National Institute of Health Embarked and Coordinated on the project of sequencing human genome called HGP or Human Genome Project.

Ans. The sequencing of human genome helped in enhancing the basic understanding of genetics and immunity to various disorders. Various genes that cause genetic disorders were identified with the help of this project. It was found that more than 1200 genes are responsible for common human cardiovascular diseases, endocrine diseases (like diabetes), neurological disorders (like Alzeimer's disease), cancers and many more.

These diseases can be treated easily by knowing the particular gene responsible for the particular disease.

Q.16 The total number of genes in humans is far less (< 25,000) than the previous estimate (up to 140,000 gene). Comment.

Ans. The total number of genes is estimated at 25,000 much lower than previous estimates of 140000 that had been based on extrapolations from gene-rich areas as opposed to a composite of gene-rich and gene-poor areas. Almost all (99.9%) nucleotide bases are exactly the same in all people. Functions for over 50% discovered genes are not known yet. Scientists have identified about 1.4 million locations where single-base DNA difference (SNPs or Single Nucleotide Polymorphisms) occur in humans. This information promises to revolutionise the processes of finding chromosomal locations for disease-associated sequence and tracing human history.

Q.17 Now, sequencing of total genomes is getting less expensive day by day. Soon it may be affordable for a common man to get his genome sequenced. What in your opinion could be the advantage and disadvantage of this development?

Ans. Human genome helps to find out the complete genome sequence of the human. It has many advantages and disadvantages.

Advantages It provides the knowledge of the effects of variations of DNA among individuals and can revolutionise the ways to diagnose, treat and prevent many diseases that affect humans. It also provides clues to the understanding of human biology.

It helps to find out the human evolution. Identification through DNA forensics is also possible. Finding metabolic defects and their cumulative effects. It has tendency to catch degenrative diseases at a particular age.

Disadvantages People might discover that they carry untreatable genetic disease. People may abuse the knowledge obtained from the HGP. Problem can occur for the ownership of the genetic test result and the patenting of human genes and DNA. People believe that they are special and unique in their own ways and may wish to remain like that. All efforts of the person will be directed towards improving onis genetic set up.

Q.18 Would it be appropriate to use DNA probes such as VNTR in DNA fingerprinting of a bacteriophage?

Ans. Bacteriophage does not have repetitive sequences such as VNTRs in its genome, as its genome is very small and have all the coding sequence. DNA finger printing is not done for phages.

Q.19 During *in vitro* synthesis of DNA, a researcher used 2′, 3′-dideoxy cytidine triphosphate as raw nucleotide in place of 2′-deoxy cytidine. What would be the consequence?

Ans. The consequence would be that the further polymerisation would not occur, as the 3′ OH on sugar is not there to add a new nucleotide for forming ester bond.

Q.20 What background information did Watson and Crick have made available for developing a model of DNA? What was their contribution?

Ans. **Watson** and **Crick** had the following informations which helped them to develop a model of DNA.

(i) **Chargaff's** Law suggesting A = T and C = G

(ii) **Wilkins** and **Rosalind Franklin's work on DNA crystal's X-ray diffraction** studies about DNAs physical structure. (X-ray crystallography)

(iii) Concluding are the information **Watson** and **Crick** proposed

(a) Pattern of complementary bases pair

(b) Semi-conservative replication

(c) Mutation through tautomerism

Q.21 What are the functions of

(i) methylated guanosine cap? (ii) poly-A 'tail' in a mature on RNA?

Ans. (i) Methylated guanine cap helps in binding of mRNA to smaller ribosomal sub-unit during initiation of translation.

(ii) Poly-A tail provides longevity to mRNA's life. Tail length and longevity of *m*RNA are positively correlated.

Q.22 Do you think that the alternate splicing of exons may enable a structural gene to code for several isoproteins from one and the same gene? If yes, how? If not, why so?

Ans. Yes, alternative splicing of exons enable a structural gene code for several isoforms. This alternate splicing of exons is sex-specific, tissue-specific and even developmental stage-specific. By such alternate splicing of exons, a single gene may encode for several isoproteins and/ or proteins of similar class.

In absence of such a kind of splicing, there should have been new genes for every protein or isoprotein. Such an extravagancy has been avoided in natural phenomeon by way of alternate splicing.

Q.23 Comment on the utility of variability in number of tandem repeats during DNA fingerprinting.

Ans. Variability in the number of tandem repeats provides many copies of the sequence for finger-printing and variability in nitrogen base sequences present in them. Being individual-specific, this proves to be useful in the process of DNA fingerprinting.

Long Answer Type Questions

Q.1 Give an account of Hershey and Chase experiment. What did it conclusively prove? If both DNA and proteins contained phosphorus and sulphur do you think the result would have been the same?

Ans. **Hershey** and **Chase** conducted experiments on bacteriophage to prove that DNA is the genetic material.

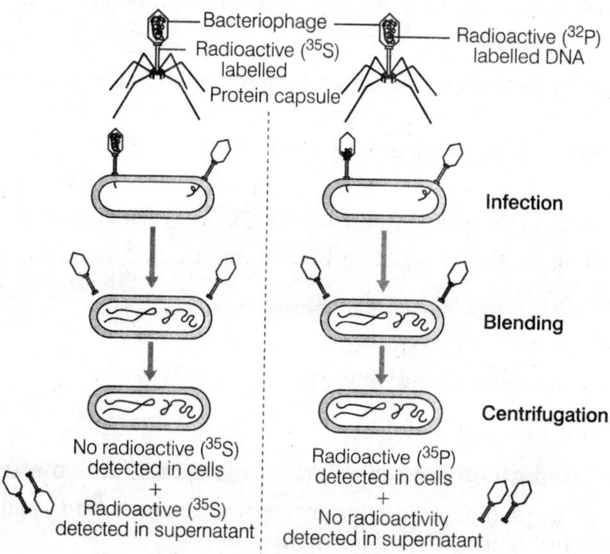

Hershey and Chase experiment

(i) Some bacteriophage virus were grown on a medium that contained radioactive phosphorus (^{32}P) and some in another medium with radioactive sulphur (^{35}S).

(ii) Viruses grown in the presence of radioactive phosphorus (^{32}P) contained radioactive DNA.

(iii) Similar viruses grown in presence of radioactive sulphur (^{35}S) contained radioactive protein.

(iv) Both the radioactive virus types were allowed to infect *E. coli* separately.

(v) Soon after the infection, the bacterial cells were gently agitated in blender to remove viral coats from the bacteria.

(vi) The culture was also centrifuged to separate the viral particle from the bacterial cell.

Observations and Conclusions

(i) Only radioactive ^{32}P was found to be associated with the bacterial cell, whereas radioactive ^{35}S was only found in surrounding medium and not in the bacterial cell.

(ii) This indicates that only DNA and not protein coat entered the bacterial cell.

(iii) This proves that DNA is the genetic material which is passed from virus to bacteria and not protein.

If both DNA and proteins contained phosphorus and sulphur, the result might change.

Q.2 During the course of evolution why DNA was choosen over RNA as genetic material. Give reasons by first discussing the desired criteria in a molecule that can act as genetic material and in the light of biochemical differences between DNA and RNA.

Ans. A molecule that can act as a genetic material must fulfil the following

(i) It should be able to generate its replica (replication).

(ii) It should chemically and structurally be stable.

(iii) It should provide the scope for slow changes (mutation) that are required for evolution.

(iv) It should be able to express itself in the form of Mendelian inheritance.

Biochemical differences between DNA and RNA

(i) Both nucleic acid (DNA and RNA) are able to direct their duplication proteins but RNA is reactive, it also acts are catalyst, hence DNA is less reactive and structurally more stable than RNA.

(ii) Presence of thymine at the place of uracil also confers additional stability to DNA.

Hence, DNA was preferred as a genetic material during course of evolution due to its stability and reliability.

Q.3 Give an account of post transcriptional modifications of a eukaryotic *m*RNA.

Thinking Process Post-transcriptional modifications include the modification of the *m*RNA transcript synthesised by RNA polymerase II (in eukaryotes).

Ans. The primary transcripts are non-functional, containing both the coding region, (exon) and non-coding region, (intron) in RNA and are called heterogenous RNA or *hn*RNA.

The *hn*RNA undergoes two additional processes called **capping** and **tailing**.

In capping, an unusual nucleotide, methyl guanosine triphosphate is added to the 5′-end of *hn*RNA.

In tailing, adenylate residues (about 200-300) are added at 3′-end in a template independent manner.

Now the *hn*RNA undergoes a process where the introns are removed and exons are joined to form *m*RNA by the process called **splicing**.

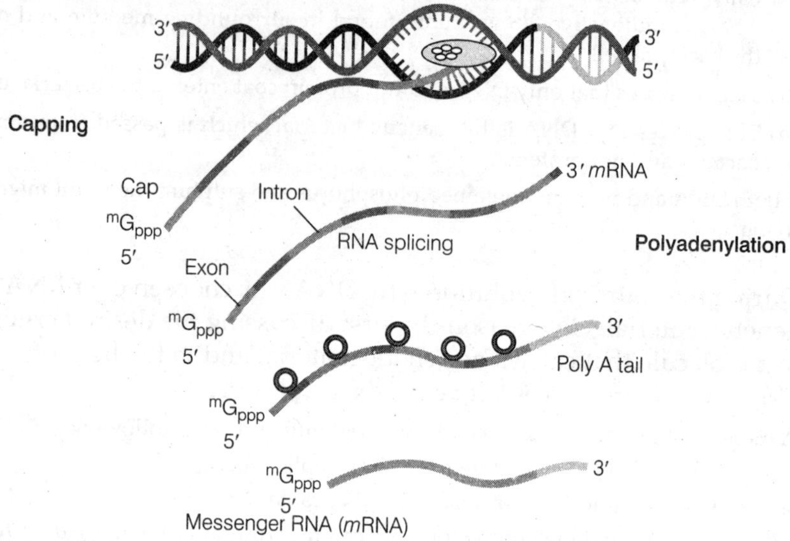

Diagram representation of a post transcriptional modification in eukaryotes

Note In prokaryotes, *m*RNA does not require any processing.

Q.4 Discuss the process of translation in detail.

Thinking Process Translation is the process of synthesis of protein from *m*RNA with the help of ribosome. A translational unit in *m*RNA comprises of a start codon, region coding for a polypeptide, a stop codon and Untranslated Regions (UTRs) at both 5′-end and 3′-end for efficient process.

Ans. *There are three-stages of protein synthesis*

(i) **Initiation**

Assembly of Ribosomes on *m*RNA

In prokaryotes, initiation requires the large and small ribosome subunits, the *m*RNA, initiation *t*RNA and three Initiation Factors (IFs).

Activation of Amino Acid

Amino acids become activated by binding with aminoacyl *t*RNA synthetase enzyme in the presence of ATP.

$$\text{Amino acid (AA)} + \text{ATP} \xrightarrow[\text{synthetases}]{\text{Aminoacy } t\text{RNA}} \text{Aminoacyl-AMP-Enzyme complex} + P_i$$

Transfer of Amino Acid to *t*RNA

The AA-AMP-enzyme complex formed reacts with specific *t*RNA to form aminoacyl *t*RNA complex.

$$\text{AA-AMP-Enzyme complex} + t\text{RNA} \longrightarrow \text{Aminoacyl } t\text{RNA} + \text{AMP} + \text{Enzyme.}$$

The cap region of *m*RNA binds to the smaller subunit of ribosome.

The ribosome has two sites, A-site and P-site. The smaller subunit first binds the initiator *t*RNA then and then binds to the larger subunit so, that initiation codon (AUG) lies on the P-site.

The initiation *t*RNA, *i.e.*, methionyl *t*RNA then binds to the P-site.

(ii) **Elongation** : Another charged aminoacyl *t*RNA complex binds to the A-site of the ribosome. Peptide bond formation and movement along the *m*RNA called translocation. A peptide bond is formed between carboxyl group (—COOH) of amino acid at P-site and amino group (—NH) of amino acid at A-site by the enzyme peptidyl transferase. The ribosome slides over *m*RNA from codon to codon in the 5′→3′ direction. According to the sequence of codon, amino acids are attached to one another by peptide bonds and a polypeptide chain is formed.

(iii) **Termination :** When the A-site of ribosome reaches a termination codon which does not code for any amino acid, no charged *t*RNA binds to the A-site.

Dissociation of polypeptide from ribosome takes place which is catalysed by a '**release factor**'. There are three **termination codons,** *i.e.*, UGA, UAG and UAA.

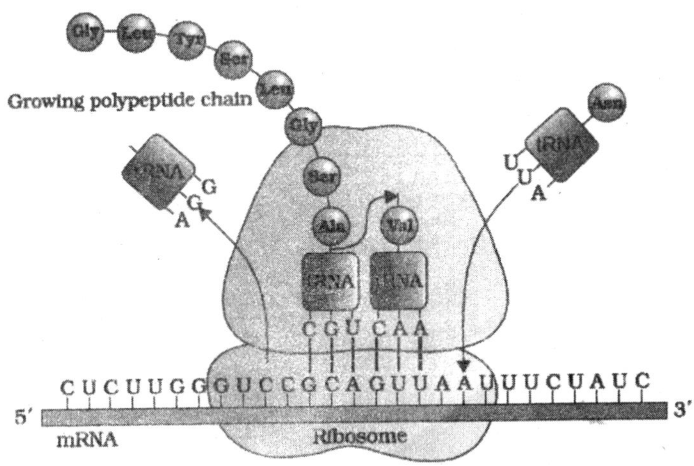

Process of translation

Q.5 Define an operon, giving an example, explain an inducible operon.

Ans. An operon is a unit of prokaryotic gene expression which includes coordinately regulated (structural) genes and control elements which are recognised by regulatory proteins.

Components of an Operon

(i) **Structural gene** The fragment of DNA which transcribe *m*RNA for polypeptide synthesis.

(ii) **Promoter** The sequence of DNA where RNA polymerase binds and initiates transcription of structural genes is called promoter.

(iii) **Operator** The sequence of DNA adjacent to promoter where specific repressor protein binds is called operator.

(iv) **Regulator gene** The gene that codes for the repressor protein that binds to the operator and suppresses its activity as a result of which transcription will be switched off.

(v) **Inducer** The substrate that prevents the repressor from binding to the operator, is called an inducer. As a result transcription is switched on. It is a chemical of diverse nature like metabolite, hormone substrate, etc.

Inducible Operon System An inducible operon system is a regulated unit of genetic material which is switched on in response to the presence of a chemical. *e.g.*, the lactose or *lac*-operon of *E.coli*.

The lactose operon The *lac z, y, a* genes are transcribed from a *lac* transcription unit under the control of a single promoter. They encode enzyme required for the use of lactose as a carbon source. The *lac i* gene product, the lac repressor, is expressed from a separate transcription unit upstream from the operator.

lac operon consists of **three structural genes** (z, y and a), operator, promoter and a separate regulatory gene.

The three structural genes (*a, y* and *z*) transcribe a polycistronic *m*RNA.

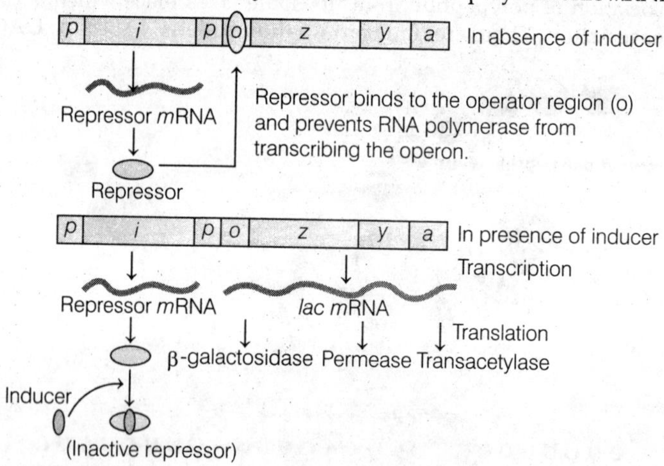

The *Lac* operon

Gene *z* codes for β-galactosidase (β-gal) enzyme which breaks lactose into galactose and glucose.

Gene *y* codes for permease, which increases the permeability of the cell to lactose.

Gene *a* codes for enzyme transacetylase, which catalyses the transacetylation of β-galactosides.

When Lactose is Absent

(i) When lactose is absent, *i* gene regulates and produces repressor *m*RNA which translate repression.

(ii) The repressor protein binds to the operator region of the operon and as a result prevents RNA polymerase to bind to the operon.

(iii) The operon is **switched off.**

When Lactose is Present

(i) Lactose acts as an inducer which binds to the repressor and forms an inactive repressor.

(ii) The repressor fails to bind to the operator region.

(iii) The RNA polymerase binds to the operator and transcript *lac m*RNA.

(iv) *lac m*RNA is polycistronic, *i.e.*, produces all three enzymes, β-galactosidase, permease and transacetylase.

(v) The *lac* operon is **switched on.**

Q.6 'There is a paternity dispute for a child'. Which technique can solve the problem? Discuss the principle involved.

Ans. DNA fingerprinting is the technique used in solving the paternity dispute for a child. DNA profiling was developed by Jeffreys et al (1985). DNA fingerprinting is a technique of determining nucleotide sequences of certain areas of DNA which are unique to each individual.

The basis of DNA fingerprinting is DNA polymorphism. Although the DNA from different individuals is more alike than different, there are many regions of the human chromosomes that exhibit a great deal of diversity. Such variable sequences are termed 'polymorphic' (meaning many forms).

A special type of polymorphism, called VNTR (Variable Number of Tandem Repeats), is composed of repeated copies of a DNA sequence that lie adjacent to one another on the chromosome. Since, polymorphism is the basis of genetic mapping of human. Mutations keep on accumulating in generation after generation. Most of the mutations are located in region of satellite DNA and is the source of VNTR. Each child receives 50% of DNA from each parent. Hence, each the individual has a distinct combination of VNTR.

Q.7 Give an account of the methods used in sequencing the human genome.

Ans. Sequencing of human genome has made it possible to understand the link between various genes and their functions. If there are any gene defects that express as disorders or that increase the susceptibility of an individual to a disease then specific gene therapies can be worked out.

Methodologies of human genome sequencing

The methods involve two major approaches

(i) **Expressed Sequence Tags** (ESTs) This method focusses on identifying all the genes that are expressed as RNA.

(ii) **Sequence annotation** It is an approach of simply sequencing the whole set of genome that contains all the coding and non-coding sequences, and later assigning different regions in the sequence with functions.

For sequencing, first the total DNA from cell is *i.e.,* solated and broken down in relatively small sizes as fragments.

These DNA fragments are cloned in suitable host using suitable vectors. When bacteria is used as vector, they are called Bacterial Artificial Chromosomes (BAC) and when yeast is used as vector, they are called Yeast Artificial Chromosomes (YACs).

Frederick Sanger developed a principle according to which the fragments of DNA are sequenced by automated DNA sequences.

On the basis of overlapping regions on DNA fragments, these sequences are arranged accordingly. For alignment of these sequences, specialised computer-based programmes were developed.

Finally, the genetic and physical maps of the genome were constructed by collecting information about certain repetitive DNA sequences and DNA polymorphism, based on endonuclease recognition sites.

Q. 8 List the various markers that are used in DNA fingerprinting.

Ans. Dr. Alec Jeffreys developed the technique of DNA fingerprinting in an attempt to identify DNA marker for inherited diseases.

Markers for DNA finger printing are

(1) Satellite DNA
(2) Restriction endonuclease
(3) Fluorescent dye for separation of VNTR
(4) Southern blotting
(5) Radioactive DNA probes
(6) X-ray films

Q. 9 Replication was allowed to take place in the presence of radioactive deoxynucleotides precursors in *E.coli* that was a mutant for DNA ligase. Newly synthesised radioactive DNA was purified and strands were separated by denaturation. These were centrifuged using density gradient centrifugation. Which of the following would be a correct result?

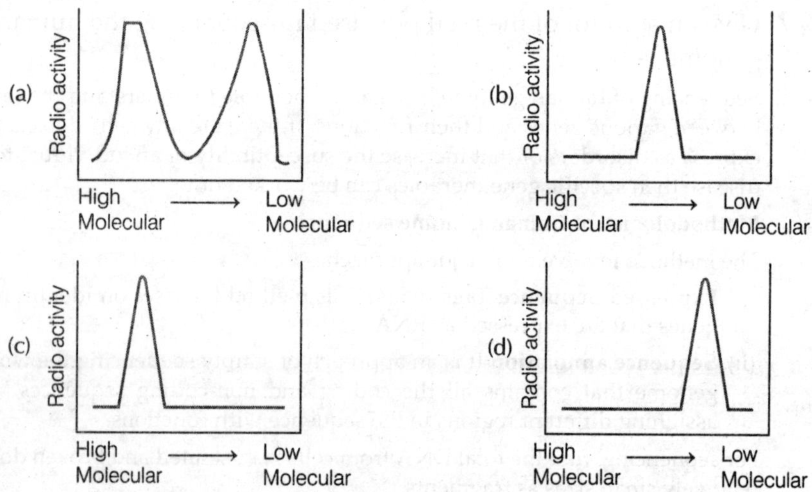

Ans. In above case, as *E.coli* is a mutant for DNA ligase, it will result in no further joining of Okazaki fragments on lagging strand.

This will ultimately result into the formation of both high molecular weight fragments (on leading strands) and low molecular weight fragments (on lagging strand). Hence, only the graph (a) could be the appropriate result after centrifugation.

Chapter

07 Evolution

Multiple Choice Questions (MCQs)

Q.1 Which of the following is used as an atmospheric pollution indicator?

(a) Lepidoptera
(b) Lichens
(c) *Lycopersicon*
(d) *Lycopodium*

Ans. ***(b)*** Lichens are used as an atmospheric pollution indicator. They do not grow in areas that are polluted, as they are sensitive (especially phycobiont) to oxides of nitrogen and sulphur, hence unable to synthesise organic food and do not grow well.

Whereas lepidoptera belongs to an order of Insects.

Lycopersicon It is scientific name of tomato.

Lycopodium It is a pteridophyte.

Q.2 The theory of spontaneous generation stated that

(a) life arose from living forms only
(b) life can arise from both living and non-living
(c) life can arise from non-living things only
(d) life arises spontaneously, neither from living nor from the non-living.

Ans. ***(c)*** The theory of spontaneous generation stated that life can arise from non-living things only. It is also known as abiogenesis.

Q.3 Animal husbandry and plant breeding programmes are the examples of

(a) reverse evolution
(b) artificial selection
(c) mutation
(d) natural selection

Ans. ***(b)*** 'Artificial selection' is a process in which the breeder chooses to perpetuate only those forms that have certain desirable inheritable characteristics. It is also known as selective breeding.

Whereas **mutation** is a sudden change in DNA sequence due to mutagenic agents such as chemicals and radiations.

Natural selection is a gradual process by which biological traits become either more or less common in a population as a function of the effect of the changing environment.

Reverse evolution or devolution is a notion that species can change into more primitive forms over time. Which is not widely accepted in modern biology.

Q.4 Palaeontological evidences for evolution refer to the

(a) development of embryo
(b) homologous organs
(c) fossils
(d) analogous organs

Thinking Process The study of fossils is called Palaeontology.

Ans. *(c)* Palaeontological evidences for evolution refer to the evidences from fossils. Fossils are the preserved remains or traces of organisms from the distant past. The development patterns of embryo refer to embryological evidences of evolution.

Homologous and analogous organs provide evidences for comparative anatomy and morphology.

Q.5 The bones of forelimbs of whale, bat, cheetah and man are similar in structure, because

(a) one organism has given rise to another
(b) they share a common ancestor
(c) they perform the same function
(d) the have biochemical similarities

Ans. *(b)* The bones of forelimbs of whale, bat, cheetah and man are similar in structure, because they have a common ancestor.

These are homologous organs which have different functions across diverse forms, but are developed along same basic pattern. These organs arise due to divergent evolution.

Q.6 Analogous organs arise due to

(a) divergent evolution
(b) artificial selection
(c) genetic drift
(d) convergent evolution

Ans. *(d)* Analogous organs arise due to convergent evolution. These are the organs which have similar functions, but are different in their structural details and origin, *e.g.*, wings of insect and bird.

The other three options are incorrect, because divergent evolution give rise to homologous organs, genetic drift can contribute to speciation and artificial selection is used to produce improved varieties of animals and plants.

Q.7 $(p + q)^2 = p^2 + 2pq + q^2 = 1$, represents an equation used in

(a) population genetics
(b) Mendelian genetics
(c) biometrics
(d) molecular genetics

Ans. *(a)* $(p + q)^2 = p^2 + 2pq + q^2 = 1$ represents an equation used in population genetics. It is a mathematical representation of 'Hardy-Weinberg principle'. This principle states that in absence of evolutionary forces the allele frequencies in a population are stable and are constant from generation to generation, *i.e.*, the gene pool remains a constant.

Q.8 Appearance of antibiotic-resistant bacteria is an example of

(a) adaptive radiation
(b) transduction
(c) pre-existing variation in the population
(d) divergent evolution

Ans. *(c)* Appearance of antibiotic-resistant bacteria is an example of pre-existing variation in the population. When a bacterial population encounters a particular antibiotic, those sensitive to it die. But some bacteria having mutations become resistant to the antibiotic. Soon, the resistance providing genes become widespread and the entire population becomes resistant. It is not due to adaptive radiation because adaptive radiation is development of different functional structures from a common ancestral form which is also known as divergent evolution. While transduction is a process whereby, foreign DNA is introduced into another cell *via* a viral vector.

Q.9 Evolution of life shows that life forms had a trend of moving from

(a) land to water
(b) dryland to wet land
(c) freshwater to sea water
(d) water to land

Ans. *(d)* Evolution of life shows that life forms had a trend of moving from water to land. Life first emerged in the oceans, so mostly early organisms lived in water. The early vertebrates were fishes (which lived in only water). Some fishes gradually evolved into amphibians (can live both on land and in water). Certain amphibians then evolved into the reptiles (live on land) some of the latter finally evolved into birds (can fly) and then mammals. Thus, showing life forms moved from water to land.

Q.10 Viviparity is considered to be more evolved because

(a) the young ones are left on their own
(b) the young ones are protected by a thicks shell
(c) the young ones are protected inside the mother's body and are looked after they are born leading to more chances of survival
(d) the embryo takes a long time to develop

Ans. *(c)* Viviparity is considered to be more evolved because the young ones are protected inside the mother's body and are looked after once they are born, leading to more chances of survival. The young one are protected from environmental pressures and predation, *e.g.*, mammals.

However, in oviparity, the female lays fertilised or unfertilised eggs covered by a hard calcareous shell in a safe place in the environment. The chances of survival are less as the young ones are left on their own.

Q.11 Fossils are generally found in

(a) sedimentary rocks (b) igneous rocks (c) metamorphic rocks (d) any type of rock

Ans. *(a)* Fossils are generally found in sedimentary rocks, which are formed by the gradual deposition of silt, sand or calcium carbonate over millions of years in regions such as lakes or sea. During their formation, the dead animals are carried to the sea or large lake, sink down and get burried in the rocks. Sedimentary rocks form at low temperatures and pressure compared to igneous metamorphic rocks that don't destroy fossil remains. The animals, thus preserved in the rocks, are converted into fossils.

Q.12 For the MN-blood group system, the frequencies of M and N alleles are 0.7 and 0.3, respectively. The expected frequency of MN-blood group bearing organisms is likely to be

(a) 42% (b) 49% (c) 9% (d) 58%

Ans. ***(a)*** The expected frequency of MN blood group bearings organisms is likely to be 42%.

According to Hardy-Weinberg equation, $p^2 + 2pq + q^2 = 1$

where, p = Frequency of M alleles,

p^2 = Frequency of homozygous dominant individuals.

q = frequency of N alleles

q^2 = Frequency of homozygous recessive individuals.

$2Pq$ = Frequency of heterozygous individuals (MN).

So, $(0.7)^2 + (0.3)^2 + 2\ pq = 1$

$0.49 + 0.09 + 2\ (0.7 \times 0.3) = 1$

$\therefore\ 2pq = 0.42$ = Frequency of heterozygous individuals. *i.e.,* 42%

Q.13 Which type of selection is industrial melanism observed in moth, *Biston betularia* ?

(a) Stabilising (b) Directional (c) Disruptive (d) Artificial

Ans. ***(b)*** Directional selection is observed in moth, *Biston betularia* is industrial melanism. It occurs when a populations genetic variance shift towards a new phenotype in response to environmental changes.

The other options are incorrect because : in stabilising selection, average sized individuals are favoured. (*e.g.,* weight of new-born babies) and in disruptive selection both extremes are favoured, while intermediate varieties are eliminated, *e.g.,* black bellied seed cracker, *Pyrenestes ostrinus.*

In artificial selection, the individuals with desirable characteristics are deliberately selected to produce a progeny with all those characteristics.

Q.14 The most accepted line of descent in human evolution is

(a) *Australopithecus* → *Ramapithecus* → *Homo sapiens* → *Homo habilis*
(b) *Homo erectus* → *Homo habilis* → *Homo sapiens*
(c) *Ramapithecus* → *Homo habilis* → *Homo erectus* → *Homo sapiens*
(d) *Australopithecus* → *Ramapithecus* → *Homo erectus* → *Homo habilis* → *Homo sapiens*

Ans. ***(c)*** The most accepted line of descent in human evolution is *Ramapithecus*→ *Homo habilis*→ *Homo erectus*→ *Homo sapiens.*

Human Evolution	Characteristics
Ramapithecus	Arise about 14-15 mya, walked erect on its hind legs, arise from *Dryopithecus.*
Australopithecus	Arise from 4-5 mya in caves, had omnivorous diet. Fully bipedal hominid
Homo habilis	First human like being Did not eat meat
Homo erectus	Lived about 1.5 mya and ate meat
Homo sapiens	Evolved around 10000 years ago. Erect posture and limbs straight.

Q.15 Which of the following is an example for link, species?

(a) Lobe fish (b) Dodo bird (c) Sea weed (d) Chimpanzee

Ans. ***(a)*** Lobe fish is an example for link species. It connects fish and amphibians. About 350 mya, fish with stout and strong fins could move on land and go back to water. These were called lobe finned fish and they evolved into the first amphibians that lived on both land and water, *e.g.*, coelocanth.

Whereas dodo is an extinct flightless bird. Sea weed is multicellular benthic marine algae, while chimpanzees are the closest living relatives of humans.

Q.16 Match the scientists listed under column I with ideas listed column II.

	Column I		Column II
A.	Darwin	1.	Abiogenesis
B.	Oparin	2.	Use and disuse of organs
C.	Lamarck	3.	Continental drift theory
D.	Wagner	4.	Evolution by natural selection

Codes

	A	B	C	D		A	B	C	D
(a)	1	4	2	3	(b)	4	1	2	3
(c)	2	4	3	1	(d)	4	3	2	1

Ans. ***(b)*** The correct sequence is A-4, B-1, C-2 and D-3

Darwin is associated with evolution by natural selection. According to this theory in the struggle for existence, the individuals which have more favourable variations will survive and reproduce, while others, which have less favourable or unfavourable variations will not peripetuate.

Oparin put forth abiogenesis theory. According to abiogenesis, life is originated from the non-living things spontaneously.

Lamarck proposed the idea of the use and disuse of organs which is one of the important principle of Lamarckism. Wagner proposed continental drift theory. It states that part of the Earth's crust slowly drift atop a liquid core forming different continents. As these continents had different environmental conditions, so plants and animals evolved accordingly.

Q.17 In 1953 SL Miller created primitive earth conditions in the laboratory and gave experimental evidence for origin of first form of life from pre-existing non-living organic molecules. The primitive earth conditions created include

(a) low temperature, volcanic storms, atmosphere rich in oxygen
(b) low temperature, volcanic storms, reducing atmosphere
(c) high temperature, volcanic storms, non-reducing atmosphere
(d) high temperature, volcanic storms, reducing atmosphere containing CH_4, NH_3 etc.

Ans. ***(d)*** The Miller – Urey experiment tested for the occurrence of chemical evolution by stimulating hypothetical conditions present on early earth.

These primitive earth conditions include high temperature, volcanic storms and reducing environment containing methane (CH_4), ammonia (NH_3), hydrogen (H_2) and water (H_2O).

They ultimately found that a large number of simple organic compounds including some amino acids such as alanine, glycine and aspartic acid can be synthesised as during chemical origin of life.

Q.18 Variations during mutations of meiotic recombinations are

(a) random and directionless (b) random and directional
(c) random and small (d) random, small and directional

Ans. *(a)* Variations during mutations of meiotic recombinations are random and directionless. Hugo de Vries based on his work on evening primrose stated that it is mutation which causes sudden appearance of variations that results in speciation. He stated that mutations are sudden, heritable and persistent in successive generation. He contradicted Darwinian variations that are small and directional.

Very Short Answer Type Questions

Q.1 What were the characteristics of life forms that had been fossilised?

Thinking Process Fossils are formed and preserved over times so, all organisms are not equally likely to be fossilised. It is based towards organisms with hard parts such as bones of vertebrates or calcareous exoskeleton of invertebrates.

Ans. The organisms with hard parts are likely to be fossilised, (teeth, bones, shells) than those who do not have such parts. The harder the material, better it would be preserved but soft parts fossils occur rarely, *e.g.*, birds and pterosaurs have very light bones, hollowed out and specialised for flight.

So, they have sparser fossil record as compared to mammals, whose bones are partially mineralised during life.

Q.2 Did aquatic life forms get fossilised? If, yes where do we come across such fossils?

Thinking Process The geological changes that took place over time transformed many water-bodies into solid rocks and mountains, so fossils of aquatic organism are more likely to be found in mountains.

And. Yes, aquatic forms of life do get fossilised. Infact, there are more fossils of aquatic organism than terrestial forms. Such fossils of sea creatures are found in mountains as opposed to deep sea beds. This is because the sedimentary rocks in which the fossils are found used to be at the bottom of oceans. Due to the changes in the crustal plates over time, the ocean sediments were pushed up to form mountains.

Q.3 What are we referring to? When we say 'simple organisms' or 'complex organisms'?

Ans. These terms are used to classify organisms according to their evolutionary history. Simple organisms refer to those organisms that have simple structural and functional organisation and are considered to be primitive, whereas complex organisms refer to those organisms that have higher and complex levels of structural and functional organisation. Complex organisms are more advanced and believed to have arisen from simple organism.

Q.4 How do we compute the age of a living tree?

Ans. To estimate the age of a living tree, following steps are required

(i) Measure the circumference of the tree trunk (at about 4.5 feet above the ground).

(ii) Calculate the diameter of the trunk. This is done by dividing the circumference by 3.14(π). Divide this (*i.e.*, diameter) by 2 to get the radius.

(iii) Determine the growth factor. A tree's growth factor is the measurement of the width it gains annually. The trees's growth factor can be seen from the data available or by measuring the rings of a dead tree from the same species.

(iv) Carbon dating

(v) Counting the number of growth rings at the base of trunk with the help of increment borer.

Q.5 Give an example for convergent evolution and identify the features towards which they are converging.

Ans. When unrelated animals converging to the same form or structure, that is very adaptive in their common environment. It is called **convergent evolution,** *e.g.*, Australian marsupials and placental mammals.

Such as placental wolf and Tasmanian wolf these two sub-classes of mammals have adapted in similar ways to a particular food supply, locomotor skill or climate.

Q.6 How do we compute the age of a fossil?

Ans. The age of a fossil can be computed by **radioactive dating** (also called radiometric dating). It is a technique based on a comparison between the observed abundance of a naturally occurring radioactive isotope and its decay products, using known decay rates.

Among the best known techniques are radiocarbon dating, potassium-argon dating and uranium lead dating.

Q.7 What is the most important pre-condition for adaptive radiation?

Ans. Pre-condition for adaptive radiation is the presence of a geographical and physical barrier between population of same species allows for isolation and ecological oppurtunity leading to the accupation of unfilled niches.

Q.8 How do we compute the age of a rock?

Ans. The age of a rock in years is called its absolute age. It is determined by the natural radioactive decay of certain elements, *e.g.*, uranium, when decays turns into lead. The parent atoms of uranium are converted into daughter atoms of lead over a fixed interval of time. This interval is the **decay constant**.

The ratio of parent-daughter atoms changes in a quantity that can be measured.

The **radioactive half-life** (the amount of time required for one half of the parent atoms to be converted to daughter atoms) is used to calculate the age of the rock.

The Potassium-Argon transformations can also be used.

Q.9 When we talk of functional macromolecules (*e.g.*, proteins as enzymes, hormones, receptors, antibodies etc), towards what are they evolving?

Ans. Functional macromolecules are evolving towards creation of a complex organism. There are various evidences that are common to simple and complex forms of which indicate common ancestry, *e.g.*, histones protein tend to be well preserved among all eukaryotes, from amoebas to blue whale or to humans, with only one or two amino acids different.

The genetic code is nearly identical for all known life forms, from bacteria to archaea, animals and plants.

Q.10 In a certain population, the frequency of three genotypes is as follows

Genotypes	BB	Bb	bb
Frequency	22%	62%	16%

What is the likely frequency of B and b alleles?

Thinking Process According to Hardy-Weinberg equilibrium, $p^2 + 2pq + q^2 = 1$.

Ans. The likely frequency of B = BB + 1/2 Bb = $\left[22 + \frac{62}{2}\right]\% = 53\%$

The likely frequency of b = bb + 1/2Bb = $\left[16 + \frac{62}{2}\right]\% = 47\%$

Q.11 Among the five factors that are known to affect Hardy-Weinberg equilibrium, three factors are gene flow, genetic drift and genetic recombination. What are the other two factors?

Ans. The other two factors that affect Hardy-Weinberg equilibrium are mutation and natural selection.

Mutation is a sudden heritable change in an organism which is generally due to change in the base sequence of the nucleic acid in the organism's genome.

Natural selection is a phenomenon by which organisms possessing heritable variations enabling their better survival reproduce and leave greater number of progeny than their counterpart.

It can lead to stabilisation (in which more individuals acquire mean character value), directional change (more individuals acquire value other than the mean character value) or disruption (more individuals acquire peripheral character value at both ends of the distribution curve).

Q.12 What is founder effect?

Ans. The founder effect occurs when a small number of individuals become isolated from a larger population to form a new population at some distance away from their place of origin. The original drifted population becomes **founders** and this effect is called **founder effect.**

Q.13 Who among the *Dryopithecus* and *Ramapithecus* was more man like?

Ans. *Ramapithecus* was more man-like. It walked erect on its hind legs, ate hard nuts and seeds like modern human and had jaws and teeth similar to humans. It arose from *Dryopithecus*, which was considered to be a common ancestor of human and apes.

Whereas *Dryopithecus* was more ape-like with same length of arms and legs.

Q.14 By what Latin name, the first Hominid was known?

Ans. The first hominid was known as *Homo habilis*. Their brain capacities were between 650-800cc. They probably did not eat meat.

Q.15 Among *Ramapithecus, Australopithecines* and *Homo habilis* who probably did not eat meat?

Ans. *Homo habilis* probably did not eat meat. This creature was the first human like being, with brain capacities between 650-800cc.

Short Answer Type Questions

Q.1 Louis Pasteur's experiments, if you recall, proved that life can arise from only pre-existing life. Can we correct this as life evolves from pre-existent life or otherwise we will never answer the question as to how the first forms of life arose? Comment.

Ans. Yes, we can correct this as life evolves from pre-existent life. The first life that appeared on earth was apparently the result of chemical evolution, *i.e.*, the life originated from inorganic molecules which formed organic molecules, further forming complex compounds.

This finally resulted into simple cells and then simple organisms, wherein complexity developed with time. However, once life originated, abiogenesis could not follow, and hence, life evolved further only through biogenesis, *i.e.*, pre-existent life gave rise to new life.

Q.2 The scientists believe that evolution is gradual. But extinction, part of evolutionary story, are 'sudden' and 'abrupt' and also group-specific. Comment whether a natural disaster can be the cause for extinction of species.

Ans. *Yes*, a natural disaster can be the cause for extinction of species. As new species evolve to fit ever changing ecological niches, and older species who do not adopt fade away. But, the rate of extincition is far from constant. In last 500 million years, 50 - 90% or more of all species on earth have disappeared in a geological blink of the eye.

Many times, these mass extinctions had been the consequence of a natural disaster such as volcanic eruptions or the impact of large asteroids or comets. The most studied mass extinction between the Cretaceous and Palaeocene periods about 65 million years ago, killed off the dinosaurs and made room for mammals to rapidly diversify and evolve. The cause is suspected to be volcanic eruptions and impact of large asteroids or comets striking the earth.

Q.3 Why is nascent oxygen supposed to be toxic to aerobic life forms?

Ans. Nascent oxygen is a permanent oxidising agent. It is highly reactive and can react readily with different kind of molecules including DNA, proteins present in the cells of aerobic life forms.

It is thus, considered toxic if it reacts with DNA, it can lead to mutations and defective proteins, both structural and functionally. Similarly if it reacts with proteins and enzymes, they are degraded and many metabolic pathways may be impaired.

Q.4 While creation and presence of variation is directionless, natural selection is directional as it is in the context of adaptation. Comment.

Ans. The creation and presence of variations is directionless in regard that they occur randomly and spontaneously Variations develop in organisms due to recombination fusion of gametes and mutations. But the variations which are helpful in the adaptations of an organism towards its surroundings would be passed on to next generations.

Natural selection is the most critical evolutionary process, which can be considered directional as it leads to only one path that is selection and perpetuation of better adapted individuals. Natural selection leads to survival of the fittest and disappearance of all those organisms which do not fit in the prevailing environmental conditions.

Q.5 The evolutionary story of moths in England during industrialisation reveals, that 'evolution is apparently reversible'. Clarify this statement.

Thinking Process The peppered moths were initially white coloured, then black coloured due to industrialisation. In recent years, the light coloured moths are increasing in population again.

Ans. During the last century in the industrial regions of England, a light coloured peppered moth *Biston betularia* was found on the bark of trees. The tree bark was covered by whitish lichens, so light coloured moths escaped unnoticed from predatory birds. After industrialisation, barks got covered by soot, so the white moths were selectively picked up by birds. However, the black coloured moths escaped unnoticed against a dark background and became abundant. Thus evolution of white winged moth reversed due to industrialisation reveals, that 'evolution is apparently reversible'

Q.6 Comment on the statement that 'evolution and natural selection are end result or consequence of some other processes, but themselves are not processes'.

Ans. Evolution helps to understand the history of life. It can be viewed as both a pattern of evolutionary change and as a process as well.

The world with, all the inanimate and animate, is only the success stories of evolution. On the other hand, when the story of life is described on earth, evolution is seen as a consequence of a process called natural selection. Natural selection is the outcome of favourable variations among organisms and environmental conditions.

Thus, both evolution and natural selection are involved in development of variation suited to the individuals in a particular environmental and formation of new form of life can be described through these processes.

Q.7 State and explain any three factors affecting allele frequency in populations.

Ans. Factors affecting allele frequency in populations are as described below

(i) **Mutations** These are sudden heritable changes which are supposed to be the primary source of genetic variation. They are of following two types

(a) Chromosomal mutations arise due to changes in chromosome number or changes in structure.

(b) Gene mutations involve changes in gene structure and expression due to addition, deletion, substitution or inversion of nucleotides.

(ii) **Non-random Mating** Repeated mating between individuals of certain selected traits changes the gene frequency, *e.g.*, selection of more brightly coloured male bird by a female bird may increase the gene frequency of bright colour in the next generation.

(iii) **Gene Flow (Gene Migration)** It is the movement of alleles into and out of a gene pool. Breeding of immigrants with the host population adds new alleles to the gene pool of the host population.

Q.8 Gene flow occurs through generations. Gene flow can occur across language barriers in humans. If we have a technique of measuring specific allele frequencies in different population of the world, can we not predict human migratory patterns in pre-history and history? Do you agree or disagree? Provide explanation to your answer.

Ans. *Yes*, we agree. Gene flow occurs when a section of population emigrates or immigrates. As the gene flow occurs through geographical barriers over generations, by studying specific allelic frequencies in various populations of the world, we can predict the human migratory patterns in pre-historic and historic era.

There have been projects undertaken such as Human Genographics Project, which uses data from studies on specific genes, chromosomes and mitochondrial DNA to trace the evolutionary history and migratory patterns of humans.

Q.9 How do you express the meaning of words like race, breed, cultivars or variety?

Ans. The meaning of the given words are as given below

Race It is a classification system used to categorise humans into large and distinct populations or groups by anatomical, cultural, linguistic, geographical, historical and for religious relationship. *e.g.*, Mongoloid, Caucasoid, negroid races of modern human. These are members of different races of the same species that can interbreed.

Breed It is a specific group of domestic animals or plants having homogenous appearance, homogenous behaviour and other characteristics that distinguish it from other animals or plants of the same species and that were arrived at through selective breeding. *e.g.*, Leghorn breed of poultry.

Cultivar It is a plant or grouping of plants selected for desirable characteristics that can be maintained by propogation. 'Cultivar' stands for 'cultivated variety'. *e.g.*, Pusa Gaurav is a cultivar of mustard.

Variety A taxonomic category below species similar to race but used for plants. *e.g.*, Cauliflower, Cabbage.

Q.10 When we say 'survival of the fittest', does it mean that

(a) those which are fit only survive

(b) those that survive are called fit? Comment.

Thinking Process Those individuals which survive and reproduce in their respective environment are called fit.

Ans. In the struggle for existence, the individuals which have more favourable variations will enjoy a competitive advantage over others which have less favourable or unfavourable variations. They are considered fit and thus, will survive and reproduce. Such individuals produce more progeny (with more fit individuals) than others who are less adapted in that environment.

Q.11 Enumerate three most characteristic criteria for designating a Mendelian population.

Ans. Characteristic criteria for designating a Mendelian population are as follows

(i) Population must be sufficiently large.

(ii) Population must have potentialities for free flow of genetic material among individuals, through sexual reproduction.

(iii) Migration should either be nil or negligible.

Q.12 'Migration may enhance or blur the effects of selection' comment.

Ans. The movement of individuals from one place to another is called migration. It can be the movement of individuals to a different populations (*i.e.*, emigration) or movement of individual into a particular population (*i.e.*, immigration) Migration may bring in more such alleles, that bestow upon the individuals, such adaptations or traits which are selected by nature. Thus, enhancing the effect of selection. Similarly, emigration may lead to removal of such alleles that confer better adaptations. Immigration may also bring in those alleles which confer the traits that are not selected by nature, *i.e.*, blur the effects of selection.

Hence, it is justifiable to say that 'migration may enhance or blur the effects of selection.'

Long Answer Type Questions

Q.1 Name the law that states that the sum of allelic frequencies in a population remains constant. What are the five factors that influence these values?

Ans. **Hardy-Weinberg Principle** states that the sum of allelic frequencies in a population is stable and is constant from generation to generation, *i.e.*, the gene pool (total genes and their alleles in a population remains constant in the absence of disturbing factors. This is called genetic equilibrium. The sum total of all the allelic frequencies is one. Hardy Weinberg equation : $(p+q)^2 = p^2 + 2pq + q^2 = 1$

Five factors that influence these values are

(i) **Gene Migration or Gene Flow** When migration of a section of population to another place occurs, gene frequencies change in the original as well as in the new population. New genes or alleles are added to the new population while alleles are lost from the old population. There would be gene flow if this gene migration, happens multiple times.

(ii) **Genetic Drift** It refers to the elimination of the genes of certain traits when a section of population migrates or dies out due to a natural calamity. It is an evolutionary force operating in small populations whereby gene frequency changes by chance leadings to loss of some genes or gain of others irrespective of their selective advantages or disadvantages.

(iii) **Mutation** The sudden heritable change which is directionless in gene is called mutation. It alters the genetic frequency or genetic make up of an individual.

(iv) **Genetic Recombination** This phenomenon occurs during gamete formation when chromosomes pass from parents to offsprings which show new combination of characteristics.

(v) **Natural Selection** It is a phenomenon by which some members of population having traits that enable them to grow and reproduce at higher rates are favoured. Hence, they leave more surviving offspring in the next generation than others.

Q.2 Explain divergent evolution in detail. What is the driving force behind it?

Ans. Divergent evolution occurs when there are two organisms or species having common ancestors but different characteristics due to adaptation. The driving force behind it is adaptations to new habitat and the prevailing environmental conditions. As the original population increases in size, it spreads out from its centre of origin to explore new habitats and food resources.

In time this results in a number of populations each adapted to its particular habitat, eventually these populations will differ from each other sufficiently to become new species.

A good example of this process is the evolution of the australian marsupials into species adapted as carnivores, herbivores, burrowers, fliers, etc. Another example is that of pentadactyl limb found in mammals.

The flipper of a seal, wing of a bat, forelimb of a male, front legs of horse and the arm of a man perform different functions, but exhibit the same structural plan including same pentadactyl pattern of bones.

Q.3 You have studied the story of peppered moths in England. Had the industries been removed, what impact could it have on the moth population? Discuss.

Thinking Process Prior to industrialisation, the light coloured moths were prevalent and well adapted to lichen covered trunks of trees.

Ans. In the population of peppered moth two variants exist : the dark and the light coloured. Before industrialisation, the light coloured moths were prevalent because they blended well with the lichen covered bark of the trees.

The predators were unable to spot them and hence, their population were more in number. With industrialisation, the barks got covered with soot. The growth of lichens reduced, the light coloured moths were thus, spotted by the predators and their number decreased. However, the black variants were camouflaged better on soot covered barks and their number increased drastically.

If the industries were removed, the population of black moths would have declined because air pollution will disappear and lichen will reappear on tree trunk and they would not be able to camouflage against a light background (no black soot). Therefore, the dark variants would be spotted better by predators and be eaten more frequently.

Q.4 What are the key concepts in the evolution theory of Darwin?

Ans. Key concepts of Darwin's theory of evolution are as follows

(i) **Over Production** Living beings have an innate ability of producing own kind for the continuity of race. It has been observed that more individuals of each kind are produced than could possibly survive.

(ii) **Struggle for Existence** Individuals multiply in geometric ratio, whereas space and food remain almost limited.

(iii) **Variations** Members of a population vary in size, form and other characteristics even though they look superficially similar, no two individuals are alike. These variations are gradual and those with adaptive value are passed on to next generation.

(iv) **Survival of the Fittest and Natural Selection** During struggle for existence only those individuals could survive who exhibited beneficial variations and adapt better to changing environment. This is known as natural selection.

(v) **Origin of Species** Natural Selection results in modification of traits within a lineage, which over a period of long time can bring about evolution of original species into new one.

Q.5 Two organisms occupying a particular geographical area (say desert) show similar adaptive strategies. Taking examples, describe the phenomenon.

Ans. This phenomenon indicated in the question is convergent evolution whereby organisms, not closely related, evolve similar traits independently as a result of adaptation to similar environment. *e.g.,*

(i) **Streamlined shape of sharks and dolphins** : The former is a fish, while dolphin is a mammal, but both of them depend on swift movement through the water, so a streamlined shape is essential. Thus, it is the similar habitat that resulted in selection of similar adaptive features in different groups of organisms, but toward the same function.

(ii) **Spines (modified leaves) and thorns (modified stems)** : Both structures look similar and provide protection to the plant, but the plants to which they belong are distantly related.

(iii) Desert has several types of drought resistant perennial plants also called **succulents**, eg. orchids, agaves, etc. All of them store mucilage and water.

Q.6 We are told that evolution is a continuing phenomenon for all living things. Are humans also evolving? Justify your answer.

Ans. Evolution is a continous process. Microevolution goes on continuously and there are inheritable gradual changes in population of organisms. New research suggests that despite modern technology and industrialisation, 'humans continue to evolve'. In the last 10,000 years or so, the pace of our evolution has speeded up 100 times creating more mutations in our genes and hence, greater natural selection.

Some clues that show humans are evolving are

(i) **Lactose Tolerance** Historically the gene that regulated human's ability to digest lactose used to shut down as infants are weaned off of their mother's breast milk. However, adult human in regions of Africa and Northern Europe developed the ability to tolerate lactose in their diets as recent as 5,000 or 6,000 years ago due to mutations.

(ii) **Wisdom Teeth** Our ancestors had much bigger jaws than we do because of eating habits. Today our jaws are much smaller and wisdom teeth are often impacted. Estimates say that they will disappear in the coming population.

(iii) **Enhanced reproductive period** The reproductive period was much less in earlier humans.

(iv) **Increased life expectancy** The average life expectancy is doubled than what it was 1000 years ago.

Q.7 Had Darwin been aware of Mendel's work? Would he been able to explain the origin of variations. Discuss.

Ans. *Yes,* had Darwin been aware of Mendel's work, he would have been able to explain the origin of variations. Darwins observation of different forms of an individual in a population could be related to the presence of different forms of alleles of a gene, as explained by Mendel's principles of inheritance. The gene are expressed because the most adaptive traits are selected naturally and become more abundant than those that are expressed as less adaptive traits. Over the time, the accumulation of these traits might change the species to such an extent that it develops into a new one and adapted to the specific environment.

Chapter 08

Human Health and Disease

Multiple Choice Questions (MCQs)

Q.1 The term 'Health' is defined in many ways. The most accurate definition of the health would be

(a) health is the state of body and mind in a balanced condition
(b) health is the reflection of a smiling face
(c) health is a state of complete physical, mental and social well-being
(d) health is the symbol of economic prosperity.

Ans. *(c)* Health does not, simply mean 'absence of disease' or 'physical fitness'. It can be defined as a state of complete physical, mental and social well being. When people are healthy, they are happy and more efficient at work.

This increases productivity and brings economic prosperity. It also increases longevity of people and reduces infant and maternal mortality.

Q.2 The organisms which cause diseases in plants and animals are called

(a) pathogens
(b) vectors
(c) insects
(d) worms

Ans. *(a)* A wide range of organisms including bacteria, viruses, fungi, protozoans, helminths, etc., cause diseases in plants and animals including humans. Such disease causing organisms are called pathogens. These pathogens can enter into the body through various routes, multiply and interfere with the normal vital activities thus, resulting in morphological and functional damage.

Q.3 The clinical test that is used for diagnosis of typhoid is

(a) ELISA test
(b) ESR test
(c) PCR test
(d) Widal test

Thinking Process Typhoid fever is caused by pathogenic bacterium *salmonella typhi.*

Ans. *(d)* Typhoid fever could be confirmed by **Widal test**, while **ELISA** (Enzyme Linked Immunosorbent Aassy) is widely used as diagnostic test for AIDS, **PCR test** is used to amplify the genome sequences of organisms.

Whereas **ESR** (Erythrocyte Sedimentation Rate) test is a type of blood test.

Q.4 Diseases are broadly grouped into infectious and non-infectious diseases. In the list given below, identify the infectious diseases.

I. Cancer　　II. Influenza

III. Allergy　　IV. Smallpox

(a) I and II　　(b) II and III

(c) III and IV　　(d) II and IV

Ans. ***(d)*** The diseases that are transmitted from one person to another are called infectious diseases, these includes influenza and small pox. While, cancer and allergy are the non-communicable diseases that remain confined to the person who suffers from this disease. Hence, these cannot transmitted from infected person to a healthy person.

Q.5 The sporozoites that cause infection when a female *Anopheles* mosquito bites a human being are formed in

(a) liver of human

(b) RBCs of mosquito

(c) salivary glands of mosquito

(d) intestine of human

Thinking Process Malaria is caused by a **protozoan**, *Plasmodium*. The vector of Plasmodium is female *Anopheles* mosquito which transfers the sporozoites (infectious form) to the human body through bite.

Ans. ***(c)*** Parasite enter the female *Anopheles* mosquito when the mosquito bites an infected person. These parasite then multiply in the stomach wall of the female *Anopheles* to form sporozoites. These sporozoites are then stored in the salivary glands of mosquito.

Q.6 The disease chikungunya is transmitted by

(a) house flies　　(b) *Aedes* mosquitoes

(c) cockroach　　(d) female *Anopheles*

Thinking Process Diseases like dengue and chikungunya are transmitted through vectors like insects.

Ans. ***(b)*** *Chikungunya* is transmitted by these vector *Aedes* mosquitoes. Whereas housefly is the vector for cholera. Cockroach is a carrier of food and waterborne diseases. Female *Anopheles* is responsible for spreading malaria.

Q.7 Many diseases can be diagnosed by observing the symptoms in the patient. Which group of symptoms are indicative of pneumonia?

(a) Difficulty in respiration, fever, chills, cough and headache

(b) Constipation, abdominal pain, cramps and blood clots

(c) Nasal congestion and discharge, cough, sore throat and headache

(d) High fever, weakness, stomach pain, loss of appetite and constipation.

Ans. ***(a)*** Symptoms indicative of pneumonia and other diseases are given below.

Symptoms	Diseases
Difficulty in respiration, fever, chills, cough and headache.	Pneumonia
Constipation, abdominal, pain, cramp and blood dots	Amoebiasis
Nasal congestion and discharge, cough, sore throat and headache.	Common cold /influenzae
High fever, weakness, stomach pain, loss of appetite and constipation	Typhoid

Mistake Alert! *Students should carefully learn the diseases and their related symptoms and must not get confused while, answering.*

Q.8 Cancer causing genes are

(a) structural genes
(b) expressor genes
(c) oncogenes
(d) regulatory genes

Ans. ***(c)*** Normal cells have genes called cellular oncogenes or proto-oncogenes which are present in an inactivated state, but under certain conditions, like mutation, these get transformed in to cancer causing oncogens. Whereas structural genes, expressor genes and regulatory genes are responsible for regulation of gene expression (operon model).

Q.9 In malignant tumours, the cells proliferate, grow rapidly and move to other parts of the body to form new tumours. This stage of disease is called

(a) metagenesis
(b) metastasis
(c) teratogenesis
(d) mitosis

Ans. ***(b)*** Metastasis refers to the spread of cancer cells from original tumor site to other parts of the body (forming secondary tumors) where as teratogenesis is related to congenital diseases. Mitosis is a type of cells division while metagenesis refers to alternation of generation in plants and animals.

Q.10 When an apparently healthy person is diagnosed as unhealthy by a psychiatrist, the reason could be that

(a) the patient was not efficient at his work
(b) the patient was not economically prosperous
(c) the patient shows behavioural and social maladjustment
(d) he does not take interest in sports

Ans. ***(c)*** Health can be defined as a state of complete physical, mental and social well being. So, when an apparently healthy person is diagnosed as unhealthy by a psychiatrist, the reason could be that the patient shows behavioural and social maladjustment due to mental discomfort.

If a patient is not efficient at his or her work and do not show interest in routine social and sports activities it means that he or she is not physically well and require treatment by a psychiatrist.

Q.11 Which of the following are the reason(s) for rheumatoid arthritics? Choose the correct option.

I. The ability to differentiate pathogens or foreign molecules from self-cells increases.

II. Body attacks self cells

III. More antibodies are produced in the body

IV. The ability to differentiate pathogens or foreign molecules from self cells is lost

(a) I and II (b) II and IV (c) III and IV (d) I and III

Thinking Process Rheumatoid arthritis, which affects many people in our society is an auto-immune disease.

Ans. *(b)* Rheumatoid artheritis is an autoimmune disease in which the immune system of a person attacks self cells. In this candition. The body's ability to differentiate pathogens or foregin molecules from self cells is lost. This results in damage to the body.

Q.12 AIDS is caused by HIV. Among the following, which one is not a mode of transmission of HIV?

(a) Transfusion of contaminated blood (b) Sharing the infected needles
(c) Shaking hands with infected persons (d) Sexual contact with infected persons

Ans. *(c)* Transmission of HIV-infection generally occurs by the following

(i) Sexual contact with an infected person
(ii) Transfusion of contaminated blood
(iii) Sharing infected needles as in the case of intravenous drug abusers
(iv) Infected mother to her child through placenta.

Q.13 'Smack' is a drug obtained from the

(a) latex of *Papaver somniferum* (b) leaves of *Cannabis sativa*
(c) flowers of *Dhatura pinata* (d) fruits of *Erythroxyl coca*

Ans. *(a)* Heroin, commonly called smack, is chemically diacetyl morphine which is a white, odourless, bitter, crystalline compound. This is obtained by acetylation of morphine, extracted from the latex of poppy plant (*Papaver somniferum*), and leaves of *cannabis sativa* commonly called bhang produces cannabinoids.

Active chemical of Dhatura flower is tropane alkaloids mainly scopolamines, hyoscyamine and atropine.

Cocaine is extracted from the dried leaves and young twigs of *Erythroxyl coca.*

Mistake Alert! *Students should be very particular while, learning about the name of the drugs and where they are extracted from.*

Q.14 The substance produced by a cell in viral infection that can protect other cells from further infection is

(a) serotonin (b) colostrum (c) interferon (d) histamine

Thinking Process Innate immunity is non-specific type of defense mechanism of the body which is present at the time of birth. This is accomplished by providing different types of barriers to prevent the entry of the foreign agents into the body.

Ans. *(c)* Interferons are the proteins secreted by virus infected cells, which protect non-infected cells from further viral infection.

Whereas serotonin is a neurotransmitter carries messages between nerve cells in the brain and body. Colostrum is the milk produced during initial days by a lactating mother's and contains antibodies which protect the newborn against diseases. Histamine is also a neurotransmitter involved in inflammatory response.

Q.15 Transplantation of tissues/organs to save certain patients often fails due to rejection of such tissues/organs by the patient. Which type of immune response is responsible for such rejections?

(a) Auto-immune response
(b) Humoral immune response
(c) Physiological immune response
(d) Cell-mediated immune response

Ans. *(d)* Transplantation is the replacement of a diseased organ or tissue of an individual with healthy organ or tissue of same or another individual. These transplants or graft get rejected if it is recognised as foreign antigen by the body's immune systems.

Cell mediated immune response, mediated by T-lymphocyte is able to differentiate between self and non-self cells/organ. This type of immune response recognise the body's non-cells or other tissue or organs from other individual as foreign antigen and cause rejection of the graft.

Q.16 Antibodies present in colostrum which protect the new born from certain diseases is of

(a) IgG type
(b) IgA type
(c) IgD type
(d) IgE type

Ans. *(b)* Colostrum, the yellowish fluid secreted by mother's during the initial days of lactation has abundant antibodies (IgA) to protect the infant from several diseases.

While IG immunoglobulin (antibody) is most abundant (approximately 80%) antibody in human and found is in blood and extracellular fluid. Whereas IgD and IgE constitute 2-3% of total antibodies. IgD is found in bodily secretions and IgE is associated with allergies.

Q.17 Tobacco consumption is known to stimulate secretion of adrenaline and noradrenaline. The component causing this could be.

(a) nicotine
(b) tannic acid
(c) curaimin
(d) catechine

Ans. *(a)* Tobacco contains large number of chemical substances including nicotine. It is an alkaloid that stimulates the adrenal gland to release adrenaline and noradrenaline which in turn increases blood pressure and heart rate.

Tannic-acid is a type of polyphenol used as a astringent.
Curaimin, is a pain reliever
Catechine derived from catechu is an antioxidant.

Q.18 Anti-venom against snake poison contains

(a) antigens
(b) antigen-antibody complexes
(c) antibodies
(d) enzymes

Ans. *(c)* Snake anti-venom is a biological product that typically consists of venom neutralising antibodies derived from a host animal, such as a horse or sheep. It dose not contain antigen or antigen-antibody complex or enzyme.

Q.19 Which of the following is not a lymphoid tissue?

(a) Spleen (b) Tonsils (c) Pancreas (d) Thymus

Ans. ***(c)*** The Pancreas is a gland which has both endocrine and exocrine functions. Lymphoid organs are the organs where origin and/or maturation and proliferation of lymphocytes occurs. Spleen, thumus and tonsilles are lymphoid organs.

Q.20 Which of the following glands is large sized at birth but reduces in size with ageing?

(a) Pineal (b) Pituitary (c) Thymus (d) Thyroid

Ans. ***(c)*** The thymus is quite large at the time of birth (for maturation of T-cells) but keeps reducing in size with age and by the time puberty is attained it reduces to a very small size. While the size of pineal gland (located at brain), pituitary gland (in brain), thyroid (located infront of neck) remains constant with ageing.

Q.21 Haemozoin is a

(a) precursor of haemoglobin

(b) toxin released from *Streptococcus* infected cells

(c) toxin released from *Plasmodium* infected cells

(d) toxin released from *Haemophilus* infected cells

Ans. ***(c)*** Haemozoin is a toxin released by *Plasmodium* species, which is responsible for the chills and high fever recurring every three to four days during malaria. The *Plasmodium* enters the human body as sporozoites and multiply within the liver cells, resulting in the rupture of the RBCs. This results in the release of haemozin. While *Streptococcus* produces hemolysines and *Haemophilus* produces cytolethal distending toxin (HdCDT) which inhibts mammalian cell proliferation.

Q.22 One of the following is not the causal organism for ringworm

(a) *Microsporum* (b) *Trichophyton* (c) *Epidermophyton* (d) *Macrosporum*

Ans. ***(d)*** Ringworm infection is caused by fungi belonging to the genera *Microsporum, trichophyton* and *Epidermophyton*.

Q.23 A person with sickle–cell anaemia is

(a) more prone to malaria (b) more prone to typhoid

(c) less prone to malaria (d) less prone to typhoid

- **Concept Insight** Sickle–cell anaemia is an autosome-linked recessive trait that can be transmitted from heterozygous carrier parents to the offspring.

Ans. ***(c)*** A person suffering from sickle–cell anaemia is resistant to malarial parasite. RBCs of sickle–cell anaemic patients is distored in shape and hence Plasmodium is not able to survive in sickle shaped.

Very Short Answer Type Questions

Q.1 Certain pathogens are tissue/organ specific. Justify the statement with suitable example.

Ans. Certain pathogens are tissue or organ specific as they are adapted to overcome the resistance mechanisms of those tissues and organs, *e.g., Plasmodium* infects liver cells and red blood cells in humans where as Mycobacterium tuberculosis targets lungs.

Q.2 The immune system of a person is suppressed. In the ELISA test, was found positive to a pathogen.

(a) Name the diseases the patient is suffering from.
(b) What is the causative organisms?
(c) Which cells of body are affected by the pathogen?

Ans. (a)The patient is suffering from AIDS.

(b) AIDS is caused by Human Immuno deficiency Virus (HIV). It is a retro virus containing RNA as genetic material.

(c) Macrophages and helper T-cells are affected by the pathogen.

Q.3 Where are B-cells and T-cells formed? How do they differ from each other?

Ans. Lymphocytes are of two types i.e., T-lymphocytes or T-cells and B-lymphocytes or B-cells. Both type of lymphocytes and other cells of the immune system are produced in the bone marrow.

B and *T*-cells are different from each other in the following aspects

B-lymphocytes (B-cell)	**T-lymphocytes** (T-cell)
They mature in bone marrow.	They mature in thymus gland.
They produce antibody against antigen.	They directly attack the antigen and help B-cells to produce antibody.
They do not respond to organ transplantation.	They respond to organ transplantation.

Q.4 Given below are the pairs of pathogens and the diseases caused by them. Which out of these is not a matching pair and why?

(a)	Virus	Common cold
(b)	*Salmonella*	Typhoid
(c)	*Microsporium*	Filariasis
(d)	*Plasmodium*	Malaria

Ans. ***(c)*** *Wuchereria bancrofti* and *W. malayi*, the filarial worms cause a slowly developing chronic inflammation of the organs in which they live for many years, usually the lymphatic vessels of the lower limbs and the disease is called elephantiasis or filariasis. Fungi belonging to the genera *Microsporium, Trichophyton* and *Epidermophyton* are responsible for ringworms which is one of the most common infectious diseases in man.

Q.5 What would happen to immune system, if thymus gland is removed from the body of a person?

Thinking Process Thymus is the primary lymphoid organ. In thymus gland, immature lymphocytes differentiate into antigen-sensitive lymphocytes.

Ans. T-lymphocytes gets differentiated in the thymus gland and are responsible for the Cell Mediated Immunity (CMI). If thymus gland is removed from the body of a person, the immune system will become weak. As a result the person's body become prone to infectious diseases.

Q.6 Many microbial pathogens enter the gut of humans along with food. What are the preventive barriers to protect the body from such pathogens? What type of immunity do you observe in this case?

Ans. Many microbial pathogens enter the gut of humans along with food.

The preventive barriers to protect the body from such pathogens are as follows

(i) The mucus coating of the epithelium lining of the gut helps in trapping microbes, entering the body.

(ii) Saliva in the mouth and hydrochloric acid in gastric juice secreted by stomach prevent microbial growth.

This type of immunity is innate immunity. It is present from birth and is inherited from parents. The innate immunity remains throughout life.

Q.7 Why is mother's milk considered the most appropriate food for a new born infant?

- **Concept Insight** Colostrum is the first yellowish milk secreted during initial days of lactation.

Ans. Colostrum contains all necessary nutrients and several antibodies (especially IgA) which are absolutely essential for developing resistance, against pathogen, in the new-born babies. This provides passive immunity and protect the infant for few months after birth.

Q.8 What are interferons? How do interferons check infection of new cells?

Ans. Interferons are natural proteins produced by the immune cells in responce to foreign agents such as virus, tumour cells and parasites. These type of barriers of innate immunity is called cytokine barrier. Interferons protect the non-infected cells from further viral infection.

Q.9 In the figure, structure of an antibody molecule is shown. Name the parts *A*, *B* and *C*.

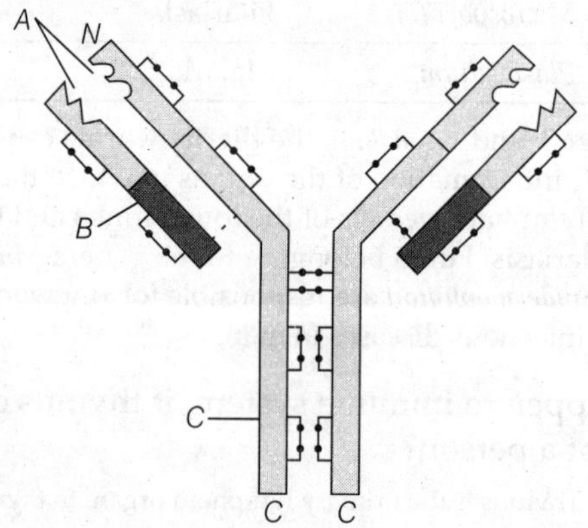

Ans. The names of the parts are given below

A - Antigen binding site

B - Light chain

C - Heavy chain

Q.10 If a regular dose of drug or alcohol is not provided to an addicted person, he shows some withdrawal symptoms. List any four such withdrawal symptoms.

Ans. The withdrawal symptoms shown by an addicted person when not provided with drug or alcohol includes the following :

(i) anxiety (ii) shakiness

(iii) nausea (iv) sweating

Q.11 Why is it that during changing weather, one is advised to avoid closed, crowded and air conditioned places like cinema halls etc?

Ans. During changing weather one is advised to avoid crowded places, because changing seasons are the time when infectious agents are more prevalent as moist condition favoures pathogen to grow faster. People are more vulnerable as their body system is busy in adapting the changing environmental conditions like temperature humidity, etc and they get infected by the pathogen easily.

Q.12 The harmful allele of sickle-cell anaemia has not been eliminated from human population. Such afflicted people derive some other benefit. Discuss.

Ans. Sickle-cell anaemia still persists in the population despite being harmful because this mutation can also be beneficial in certain conditions. The mutant Hb^S type haemoglobin is found at high frequencies (upto 20% and above) in the tropical Africa. It is known that heterozygotes (Hb^A/Hb^S), having both types of alleles show resistance to malarial infection because malarial parasite can not survive in sickle shaped RBCs. In contrast, individuals homozygous for normal haemoglobin (Hb^A/Hb^A) suffer high mortality rates in early childhood due to malarial infection. Thus, the allele for sickle cells has been maintained because heterozygotes have a higher survival success than either of the two possible homozygotes.

Q.13 Lymph nodes are secondary lymphoid organs. Explain the role of lymph nodes in our immune response.

Ans. Lymph nodes are small solid structures present at different points along the lymphatic system. Lymph nodes serves to trap the microorganisms or other antigens that enter the lymph and tissue fluid. Antigens trapped in the lymph nodes activate the lymphocytes and produce an immune response.

Q.14 Why is an antibody molecule represented as H_2L_2?

Ans. Each antibody molecule has four peptide chains, two small chains called light chains (represented by L) and two longer chains called heavy chains (represented by H). Hence, an antibody is represented as H_2L_2.

Q.15 What does the term 'memory' of the immune system mean?

Ans. When the body encounters a pathogen for the first time, it mounts an immune response by generating antibodies. This response is of low intensity. Subsequent encounter with the same pathogen elicits a highly intensified secondary response. This is due to the fact that the body appears to have memory of the first encounter. This type of secondary immune response is elicited by memory T-cells and B-cell which are ready to mount a rapid and vigorous attack as soon as the same pathogen infects the body again.

Q.16 If a patient is advised anti retroviral therapy, which infection is he suffering from? Name the causative organism.

Ans. The patient is most likely suffering from AIDS. The causative agent is HIV virus, a member of 'retrovirus group'.

Short Answer Type Questions

Q.1 Differentiate between active immunity and passive immunity.

Ans. Differences between active immunity and passive immunity are as follows

Active Immunity	Passive Immunity
It is developed due to contact with pathogen or its antigen.	It is developed when ready-made antibodies are injected into the body.
It has no side effects .	It may cause a reaction.
It is slow but long lasting.	It is fast but lasts only for few days.
It takes time to develop its response.	It is used when the immune response has to be faster.
E.g., vaccination for polio, etc	*E.g.*, administration of tetanus antitoxins, etc.

Q.2 Differentiate between bening tumour and malignant tumour.

Ans. Differences between bening tumour and malignant tumour are as follows

Benign Tumour	Malignant Tumour
It is a non-cancerous tumour.	It is a cancerous tumour.
Benign tumour does not show metastasis and is non-invasive.	It shows metastasis and thus invades other body parts.
It stops growing after reaching a certain size.	Malignant tumour shows indefinite growth.
It is less fatal to the body.	It is more fatal to the body.

Q.3 Do you consider passive smoking is more dangerous than active smoking? Why?

Ans. Passive smoking is more dangerous than active smoking because it exposes the person to untiftered side stream smoks, which contain higher concentration of toxin and carcinogens.

Passive or second hand smoking means being in the same room or place, where someone is smoking and getting exposed to smoke in the surrounding air.

Once inhaled, the smoke can trigger release of mucus in the bronchioles that blocks the airways. This induces coughing and prolonged exposures can also lead to bronchitis, emphysema, respiratory tract infections and eventually lung cancer.

Q.4 'Prevention is better than cure'. Comment.

Ans. Prevention is always better than cures because some diseases cause extensive damage to the body tissues or organs and have a

(i) negative effect on their capacity to function.
(ii) permanent or long term debilitating effect.
(iii) negative mental and psychological effect.
(iv) financial burden.

Prevention, therefore is easier and effective, than cure of a disease.

Q.5 Explain any three preventive measures to control microbial infections.

Ans. Preventive measures to control microbial infection include the following

(i) Maintenance of personal and public hygiene by
  (a) proper cleanliness standards and practices .
  (b) proper disposal of waste.
  (c) periodic cleaning of water reservoirs, etc.

(ii) Control or elimination of vectors that transmit diseases by
  (a) checking water stagnation and garbage accumulation.
  (b) using disinfectants or biological methods to check their breeding and spread.

(iii) Proper immunisation by vaccination, wherever available to control or completely eradicate infectious diseases.

Q.6 In the given flow diagram, the replication of retro virus in a host is shown. Observe and answer the following questions.

(a) Fill in (A) and (B)
(b) Why is the virus called retrovirus?
(c) Can the infected cell survive, while viruses are being replicated and released?

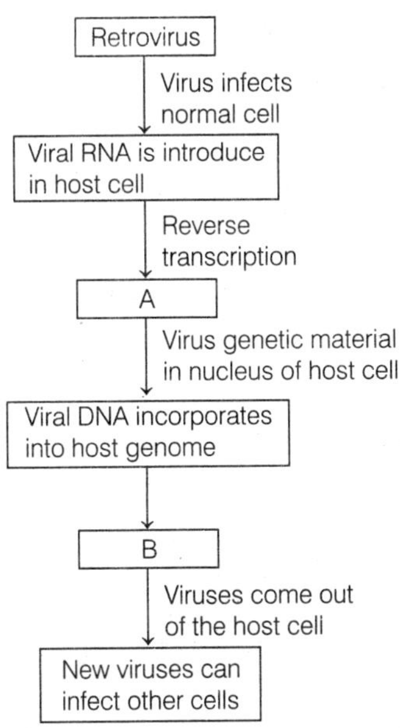

Ans. *(a)* A. Viral DNA produced by reverse transcriptase.

B. New viral RNA produced by infected cell.

(b) The virus is called retrovirus because it does not follow the central dogma of biology (DNA → RNA → Proteins).

Its genetic material is RNA that is transcribed to DNA using enzyme reverse transcriptase.

(c) Yes, the infected cell can temporarily survive, while viruses are being replicated and released.

Q.7 'Maintenance of personal and public hygiene is necessary for prevention and control of many infectious diseaes'. Justify the statement giving suitable examples.

Ans. Diseases which are easily transmitted from one person to another, are called infectious diseases.

For prevention and control of such diseases, maintenance of personal and public hygiene is necessary, for this purpose, some common preventive measures should be taken which are as follows

(i) **Education** People should be educated about communicable disease to protect themselves from such diseases.

(ii) **Isolation** The infected person should be kept isolated to minimises the spread of infection.

(iii) **Vaccination** People should get vaccination on time to avoid infection.

(iv) **Sanitation** The sanitation should be improved to avoid spread of infection from polluted water, contaminated food, etc.

(v) **Eradication of Vectors** The breeding places of vectors must be destroyed and adult vectors should be killed by suitable methods.

(vi) **Sterilisation** The patient's surroundings and articles of use should be completely sterilised to reduce the chances of infection.

Q.8 The following table shows certain diseases, their causative organisms and symptoms. Fill the gaps.

Diseases	Causative organisms	Symptoms
1. Ascariasis	*Ascaris*	—
2. —	*Trichophyton*	Appearance of dry, scaly lesions on various parts of the body
3. Typhoid	—	High fever, weakness, headache, stomach pain and constipation.
4. Pneumonia	*Streptococcus pneumoniae*	—
5. —	*Rhino viruses*	Nasal congestion and discharge, sorethroat, cough headache
6. Filariasis	—	Inflammation in lower limbs

Ans.

Diseases	Causative organisms	Symptoms
1. **Ascariasis**	*Ascaris*	Internal bleeding, muscular pain, fever, anaemia and blokage of the instestinal passage.
2. Ring worms	*Microsporum, Trichophyton and Epidermophyton*	Appearance of dry, scaly lesions on various parts of the body such as skin, nails and scalp.
3. Typhoid	*Salmonella typhi*	High fever, weakness, stomach pain constipation, headache and los of appetite. Intestinal perforation and death may occur in severe cases.
4. Pneumonia	*Streptococcus pneumoniae and Haemophilus influenzae*	Fever, chills, cough and headache. In severe cases, the lips and finger nails may turn gray to bluish in colour
5. Common cold	*Rhinoviruses*	Nasal congestion and discharge, sore throat, hoarseness, cough, headache tiredness.
6. Filariasis	*Wuchereria (W. bancrofti and W. malayi)*	Chronic inflammation and deformation of the organs and genital organs.

Q.9 The outline structure of a drug is given below.

(a) Which group of drugs does this represent?

(b) What are the modes of consumption of these drugs?

(c) Name the organ of the body which is affected by consumption of these drugs.

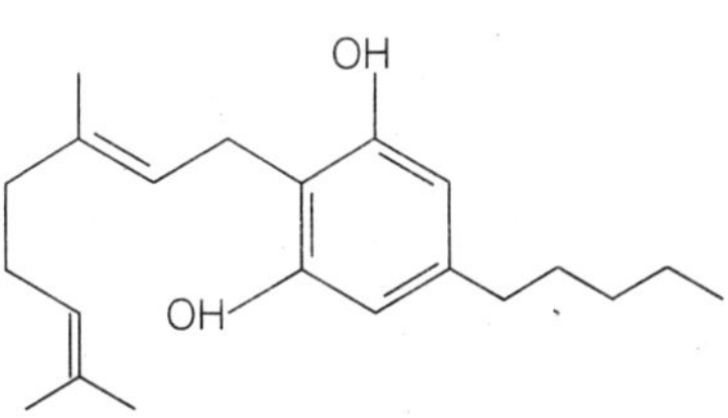

Ans. (a) It represents cannabinoids group of drugs.

(b) Mode of consumption–nasal inhalation or oral intake.

(c) Organs affected–heart and cardiovascular system.

Q.10 Give the full form of CT and MRI. How are they different from each other? Where are they used?

Ans. CT-Computed Tomography. It uses X-rays to generate 3-D images of internal organs. MRI–Magnetic Resonance Imaging. It uses strong magnetic fields and non-ionising radiations to detect pathological and physiological changes in the living tissue accurately. Both of these imaging techniques are used in detection of cancer and other abnormalaties.

Q.11 Many secondary metabolites of plants have medicinal properties. It is their misuse that creates problems. Justify the statement with an example.

Ans. Drugs like barbiturates, amphetamines, benzodiazepines, lysergic acid diethylamides (LSD) and other similar drugs, are normally used as medicines to help patients coping with mental illnesses like depression and insomnia. Morphine is a very effective sedative and painkiller and is very useful in patients who have undergone surgery.

Misuse of plant metabolites, fruits and seeds in amounts/frequency more than prescribed for medicinal purposes can impair one's physical, physiological or functional behaviour creating problem for the society and slowly moves towards the death.

Q.12 Why cannabinoids are banned in sports and games?

Ans. Cannabionoids may enhance the performance of athletes and smoking cannabis may also decrease anxiety, fear, depression, tension etc. and also improves self confidence, relaxation, well-being and sleep.

These effects may allow the athletes to perform better especially under pressure and may reduce stress, experienced before and during competition.

Morever, cannabinoids increases bronchodialation and may have analgesic or pain relieving properties which could permit athletes to work during injury. Moreover, long term use of cannabinoids causes various hazards to the health of abuser. Therefore, use of cannabinoids by a sportsperson is not justified, as it leads to unfair competition. Hence, their use is strictly banned in sports and games.

Q.13 What is secondary metabolism?

Ans. Secondary metabolism (also called specialised metabolism) refers to the production of producing small molecules and pathways that are not absolutely required for the survival of the organism but provide fitness advantage in a given ecological contact.

In case of plant, metabolites aid in the growth and development of plants. It also facilitates the primary metabolism.

Q.14 Drugs and alcohol give short-term 'high' and long-term 'damages' Discuss.

Ans. Curiosity, need for adventure, excitement and experimentation, constitute common causes, which motivate youngsters towards drug and alcohol use.

The frequent use of drugs/alcohols drive people to take them even when these are not needed, or even their use becomes self-destructive.

Short-term effects of drugs/alcohols

- A relaxing effect
- Reduced tension
- Lowered inhibitions
- Poor concentration
- Slow reflexes
- Slow reaction time

- Reduced coordination
- Slower brain activity
- Sensations and perceptions that are less clear

Long-term effects of drugs/alcohols

- Disrupts normal brain development
- Liver damage and cirrhosis of the liver
- Brain cells die, decreasing brain mass
- Stomach and intestinal ulcers and destroyed organs
- Blood pressure increases, causing heart disease, heart attack or stroke
- Male sperm production decreases
- Lower levels of iron and vitamin-B, causing anaemia
- Alcoholism
- Death
- Fatal alcohol syndrome in unborn children

Q.15 Diseases like dysentery, cholera, typhoid, etc., are more common in over crowded human settlements. Why?

Ans. Dysentery, cholera and typhoid are more common in crowded settlements because these are infectious in nature and can spread easily from person to person. For instance water bodies of these areas are generally unhygenic and contaminated with the excreta of infected people which causes the spread of infection to other people.

Q.16 From which plant cannabiniods are obtained? Name any two cannabinoids. Which part of the body is effected by consuming these substances?

Ans. Cannabinoids are obtained from the inflorescence, leaves, resins and flowers of hemp plants. *Cannabis sativa.*

Marijuana, hashish, charas, ganja are the common examples of some cannabinoids. These chemicals interact with cannabinoid receptors of the body, mainly present in the brain. Cardiovascular system of the body is effected adversly by consuming these substances.

Q.17 In the metropolitan cities of India, many children are suffering from allergy/asthma. What are the main causes of this problem. Give some symptoms of allergic reactions.

Thinking Process Allergy is the exaggerated response of the immune system in response to certain antigens present in the environment.

Ans. In metropolitan cities lifestyle is responsible in lowering the immunity and sensitivity to allergens. More polluted environment with and other air borne pollutants dust increases the chances of allergy in children. Some symptoms of allergic reactions are sneezing, watery eyes, running nose and difficulty in breathing.

Q.18 **What is the basic principle of vaccination? How do vaccines prevent microbial infections? Name the organism from which hepatitis-B vaccine is produced.**

Ans. The principle of vaccination is based on the property of 'memory' of immune system.

In vaccination, a preparation of antigenic proteins, or inactivated or live attenuated but (weakened) pathogens are introduced into the body. The antigens generate primary immune response by producing antibodies along with memory B-cells and T-cells.

When the vaccinated person is attacked by the same pathogens, the existing memory B-cells and T-cells recognise the antigen and overwhelm the invaders with massive production of lymphocytes and antibodies.

Hepatitis-B vaccine is the vaccine produced from yeast.

Q.19 **What is cancer? How is a cancer cell different from the normal cell? How do normal cells attain cancerous nature?**

Ans. An abnormal and uncontrolled division of cells is termed as cancer. Genes called cellular oncogenes (c-onc) or proto-oncogens present in normal cells when activated under certain conditions lead oncogenic transformation of the normal cells, leading to cancer.

A cancer cell is different from the normal cell in following ways

Cancer cell	Normal cell
Cancer cells divide in an uncontrolled manner.	Normal cells divide in a controlled manner.
The cells do not show contact inhibition.	The cells show contact inhibition.
Life span is indefinite.	Life span is definite.

Q.20 **A person shows strong unusual hypersensitive reactions when exposed to certain substances present in the air. Identify the condition. Name the cells responsible for such reactions. What precaution should be taken to avoid such reactions.**

Ans. If a person is hypersensitive to certain substance present in the air, he or she may be allergic to it.

Mast cells release certain chemicals, *e.g.*, histamine and serotonin, in response to this substance, that result in allergic reaction.

Precaution taken to prevent such reaction is to avoid the allergens responsible for a particular allergy.

Q.21 **For an organ transplant, it is an advantage to have an identical twin. Why?**

Ans. For an organ transplant, it is an advantage to have an identical twin because the organ will have same surface markers. Therefore, the recipient's immune system will not identify it as foreign and will not react against it. This will lead to lesser chances of organ rejection. In case of different surface markers, the immune system starts a reaction, killing the foreign tissue or rejecting the graft..

Q.22 What are lifestyle diseases? How are they caused? Name any two such diseases.

Ans. Lifestyle disease are noncommunicable disease. These are caused by some specific food habits, work related posture or exposure to harmful radiations or substances, lack of physical exercise, mental stress, etc.

The life style disease include cancer, alcoholism, heart disease, etc.

Q.23 If there are two pathogenic viruses, one with DNA and other with RNA, which would mutate faster? And why?

Ans. Pathogenic virus with RNA as a genetic material will mutate faster than the one with DNA as genetic material because of the following reasons

(i) RNA is chemically and structurally unstable. Uracil present in RNA is less stable than thymine in DNA.

(ii) RNA is highly reactive, labile and is easily degradable.

Long Answer Type Questions

Q.1 Represent schematically the life-cycle of a malarial parasite.

Ans. The life-cycle of a malarial parasite is as follows

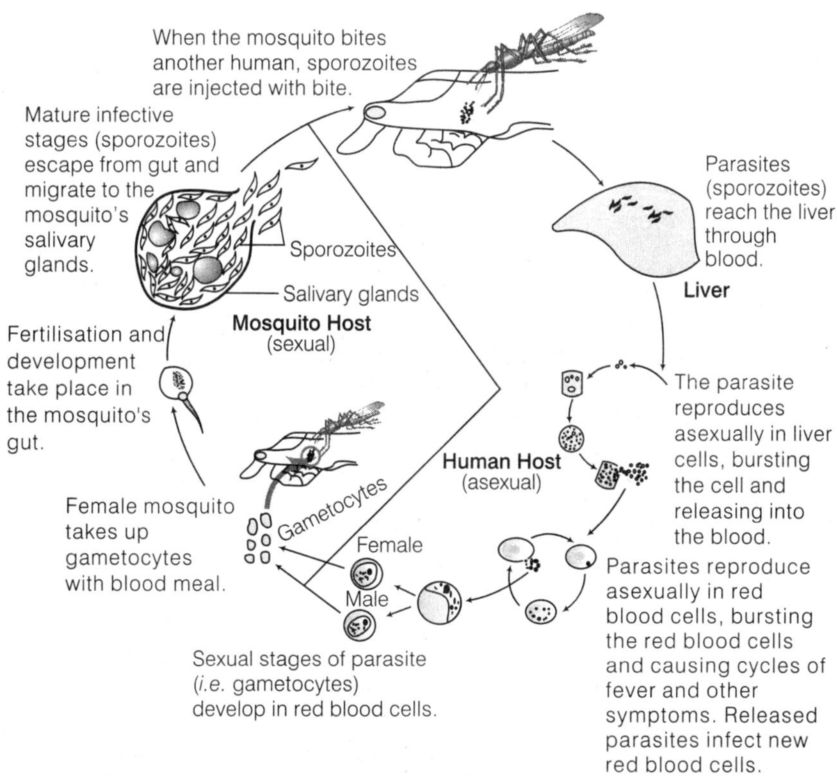

Life cycle of *Plasmodium*

Q.2 Compare the life style of people living in the urban areas with those of rural areas and briefly describe how the life style affects their health.

Ans. In terms of health, the lifestyles in urban and rural areas differ significantly:

Urban Areas Higher risk of chronic diseases: Due to sedentary habits, poor diets, and high levels of pollution, urban residents are at a greater risk for heart disease, obesity, diabetes, and respiratory conditions.

Stress-related issues The fast-paced lifestyle and work pressures can lead to mental health problems like anxiety, depression, and stress-related disorders. **Better healthcare access** Urban areas typically have more hospitals and healthcare facilities, leading to faster diagnosis and treatment of health issues.

Rural Areas Better physical health: Rural residents tend to engage in more physical activity, which can lower the risk of obesity and cardiovascular diseases. **Lower risk of pollution-related diseases:** Cleaner air and environment in rural areas contribute to fewer respiratory issues.

Limited healthcare access Health issues may go undiagnosed or untreated due to fewer healthcare facilities, leading to higher risks of complications from preventable diseases. Overall, urban lifestyles are often linked to higher risks of chronic diseases and mental health issues due to stress and environmental factors, while rural lifestyles may have advantages in terms of physical activity and cleaner surroundings but suffer from limited healthcare access.

Q.3 Why do some adolescents start taking drugs. How can this be avoided?

Ans. Some of the reasons why adolescents and youngsters starts taking drugs are as follows

(i) Curiosity of child motivates him/her to do experiment.
(ii) For adventure and excitement.
(iii) Peer group pressure.
(iv) To overcome frustration and depression, due to failure in examinations or in other activities.
(v) Unstable or unsupportive family structures.

The following measures can be taken to avoid drug *abuses*

(i) Avoid undue pressure on child to perform beyond his or her capability in studies, sports or any other activities.
(ii) Education and counselling are very important to face problem of stress and failure in life.
(iii) Seeking help from parents, elders and peers. This would help the young to share their feelings and concern.
(iv) Looking for danger signs and taking appropriate measures to treat them.
(v) Seeking professional and medical help for de-addiction and rehabilation.

Q.4 In your locality, if a person is addicted to alcohol, what kind of behavioural changes do you observe in that person? Suggest measures to over come the problem.

Ans. If a person is addicted to alcohol, it will give rise to some behavioural changes in that person. Alcoholic drinks are costly and most drinkers, because of their selfish habits, deprive their children and other members of the family for basic needs. The drinking of alcohol is invariably associated with social crimes and dissolution of moral and cultural inhibitions. Violence and other corrupt practices occur in the community are often directly or indirectly due to the consumption of alcohol.

Measures that should be taken to overcome the above mentioned problem are

(i) **Avoid Undue Peer Pressure** Every person has his or her own choices and personality, which should be kept in mind. So he/she should not be pressed unduly to do beyond his/her capacities, in work condition and other in social get together or activities.

(ii) **Education and Counselling** Helps to overcome the problems like stresses, disappointments and failure in life. One should utilise some energy in some beneficial activities like sports, music, reading, yoga and other extra curricular activities.

(iii) **Seeking Help from Parents and Peers** In case of minors, whenever, there is any problem, one should seek help and guidance from parents and peers. Help should be taken from close and trusted friends. This would help young to share their feelings of anxiety and wrong doings.

(iv) **Looking for Danger Signs** If friends find someone using drugs or alcohol, they should bring this to the notice of parents or teacher so that appropriate measures can be taken to diagnose the illness and the causes. This would help in taking proper remedial steps or treatment.

(v) **Seeking Professional and Medical Help** Highly qualified psychologists, psychiatrists as well as de-addiction and rehabilitation programmes can help individuals who are suffering from drug/alcohol abuse.

If such help is provided to the affected persons, with sufficient efforts and will power, the patient could be completely cured and lead normal and healthy life.

Q.5 What are the methods of cancer detection? Describe the common approaches for treatment of cancer.

Ans. Early detection of cancer is essential. The methods of cancer detection and diagnosis are as follows.

(i) Biopsy and histo-pathological studies of the tissue/ blood/ bone marrow.
(ii) Tests for increased cell counts (in the case of leukaemia blood cancer).
(iii) Techniques like radiography (use of X-rays), CT (computed tomography) and MRI (Magnetic Resonance Imaging) to detect cancers of the internal organs.
(iv) Detection of cancer specific antigens.
(v) Molecular biology techniques to detect genes in individuals with inherited susceptibility to certain cancers.

The common approaches for treatment of cancer as follows

(i) Surgical removal of tumour.
(ii) Irradiation of tissue to kill cancerous cells.
(iii) Immunotherapy using interferon to boost the killing of cancer cells.

Q.6 Drugs like LSD, barbiturates, amphetamines, etc., are used as medicines to help patients with mental illness. However, excessive doses and abusive usage are harmful. Enumerate the major adverse effects of such drugs in humans.

Ans. Harmful effects of drugs like LSD, barbiturates, are as follows

(i) Anxiety, shakiness, nausea sweating and loss of mind control.

(ii) Reckless behaviour, vandalism and violence.

(iii) Lack of interest in personal hygiene, fluctuations in weight and appetite.

(iv) Withdrawal, isolation, depression, fatigue and aggressive behaviour.

(v) Problems in social adjustment.

(vi) Withdrawal symptoms can be severe and life threatening.

(vii) Excessive doses of drugs may lead to coma and death may also occur due to respiratory failure, heart failure or cerebral haemorrhage.

Q.7 What is Pulse Polio Programme of Government of India? What is OPV? Why is it that India is yet to eradicate polio?

Ans. Pulse Polio is an immunisation campaign established by the Government of India in 1995-96 to eradicate poliomyelitis (polio) in India by vaccinating all children under the age of five years orally against polio virus.

This project deals with the ways to fight poliomyelitis through a large scale immunisation programme, co-operating with various international institutions, state governments and Non-Governmental Organisations. In 1995, following the polio eradication initiative of World Health Organisation (1988), India launched Pulse Polio Immunisation Program along with Universal Immunisation Program which aimed at 100% coverage.

Oral Polio Vaccine

Oral Polio Vaccine (OPV) is a live-attenuated vaccine, produced by the passage of the virus through non-human cells at a sub-physiological temperature, which produces spontaneous mutations in the viral genome.

OPV also proved to be superior in administration, eliminating the need for sterile syringes and making the vaccine more suitable for mass vaccination campaigns. OPV also provides long lasting immunity than the salk vaccine.

One dose of OPV produces immunity to all three poliovirus serotypes

In India the main obstacle in the eradication of polio had been the refusal of polio vaccine by certain communities on account of illiteracy and misinformation.

Q.8 What are recombinant DNA vaccines? Give two examples of such vaccines. Discuss their advantages.

Ans. Recombinant DNA vaccines are made up of a small circular DNA (plasmid) that has very tiny piece of pathogen DNA incorporated in it to produce one or two specific proteins of the pathogen. This recombinant DNA is introduced into the bacteria or yeast cells, where it uses the cell's machinery to produce polypeptides of pathogen. These are used as vaccine to trigger a range of immune responses.

Two examples of recombinant DNA vaccines are as follows.

(i) Hepatitis-B vaccine produced from yeast.

(ii) Bird flu DNA vaccine.

Advantages

(i) Recombinant DNA vaccines are advantageous over killed or attenuated vaccines since, they does not get virulent or mutated again as it is seen in case of attenuated vaccines.

(ii) Secondly these are highly pure, specific and elicits strong immune response.

Chapter

09

Strategies for Enhancement in Food Production*

Multiple Choice Questions (MCQs)

Q.1 The chances of contacting bird flu from a properly cooked (above 100°C) chicken and egg are

(a) very high (b) high (c) moderate (d) None of these

Ans. *(d)* The chances of contacting bird flu from a properly cooked (above 100°C) chicken and egg are negligible. This is because, proper cooking at or above 70°C, prior to eating, will inactivate the virus in the egg as well as in the meat.

Q.2 A group of animals which are related by descent and share many similarities are referred to as

(a) breed (b) race (c) variety (d) species

Ans. *(a)* A group of animals that are related by descent and are similar in most characters like general appearance, features, size, configuration, etc., are said to belong to a breed.

Q.3 Inbreeding is carried out in animal husbandry because it

(a) increases vigour (b) improves the breed

(c) increases heterozygosity (d) increases homozygosity

Thinking Process Inbreeding refers to the mating of more closely related individuals within the same breed for 4-6 generations.

Ans. *(d)* Inbreeding increases homozygosity, *i.e.*, state of possessing two identical alleles, one inherited from each parent. It is necessary for development of a pureline in animals. It also helps in accumulation of superior genes and elimination of less desirable genes. However, inbreeding exposes harmful recessive genes that are eliminated by selective breeding.

Q.4 Sonalika and Kalyan Sona are varieties of

(a) wheat (b) rice (c) millet (d) tobacco

Ans. *(a)* Sonalika and Kalyan Sona are outstanding semi-dwarf varieties of wheat possessing amber grains and good yield potential. They were developed in 1963 at Indian Agriculture Research Institute, as a part of systematic programme for breeding semi-dwarf wheat varieties.

Note (*) *This Chapter has been deleted from latest NCERT.*

Q.5 Which one of the following is not a fungal disease?

(a) Rust of wheat (b) Smut of bajra
(c) Black rot of crucifers (d) Red rot of sugarcane

Ans. *(c)* Black rot of crucifers is not a fungal disease. It is caused by a bacteria, *Xanthomonas campestris*. Whereas Rust of wheat is caused by a fungus, *Puccinia*, red rot of sugarcane is caused by *Colletotrichum falcatum* and smut of bajra is caused by *Tolyposporium penicillariae*.

Q.6 In virus-infected plants the meristematic tissues in both apical and axillary buds are free of virus because

(a) the dividing cells are virus resistant
(b) meristems have anti viral compounds
(c) the cell division of meristems are faster than the rate of viral multiplication
(d) viruses cannot multiply within meristem cell(s)

Ans. *(c)* In virus infected plants the meristematic tissues in both apical and axillary buds are free of virus because the multiplication of meristematic cells is faster than replication of viruses.

Q.7 Several South Indian states raise 2-3 crops of rice annually. The agronomic feature that makes this possible is because of

(a) shorter rice plant
(b) better irrigation facilities
(c) early yielding rice variety
(d) disease resistant rice variety

Ans. *(c)* The agronomic feature that makes this possible is early yielding rice variety. These varieties are a group of crops created intentionally during the green revolution to increase global food production.

Q.8 Which one of the following combination would a sugarcane farmer look for in the sugarcane crop?

(a) Thick stem, long internodes, high sugar content and disease resistant
(b) Thick stem, high sugar content and profuse flowering
(c) Thick stem, short internodes, high sugar content, disease resistant
(d) Thick stem, low sugar content and disease resistant

Ans. *(a)* In the sugarcane crop, a sugarcane farmer looks for thick stem, long internodes, high sugar content and disease resistance. *Saccharum barberi* and *Saccharum officinarum* are being used to develop such combination

Q.9 Fungicides and antibiotics are chemicals that

(a) enhance yield and disease resistance
(b) kill pathogenic fungi and bacteria, respectively
(c) kill all pathogenic microbes
(d) kill pathogenic bacteria and fungi respectively

Ans. *(b)* Fungicides and antibiotics are the chemicals that kill pathogenic fungi and bacteria, respectively.

Q.10 Use of certain chemicals and radiation to change the base sequences of genes of crop plants is termed as

(a) recombinant DNA technology (b) transgenic mechanism
(c) mutation breeding (d) gene therapy

Thinking Process Mutation is a phenomenon by which genetic variation is achieved through changes in the base sequences within genes that creates a new character or trait absent in parental generation.

Ans. *(c)* Inducing mutations artificially in crop plants through the use of chemicals or radiations (like gamma radiations), and then selecting and using those plants that have the desirable character as a source in breeding. This is termed as mutation breeding.

Q.11 The scientific process by which crop plants are enriched with certain desirable nutrients is called

(a) crop protection (b) breeding
(c) bio-fortification (d) bio-remediation

Ans. *(c)* Biofortication is the proceses by which crop plants are enriched with higher levels of vitamins, proteins and minerlals etc. This is achieved through conventional breeding, genetic engineering or agronomic practices. It is the most practical means to improve public health.

While breeding involves artificial mating of two plants with desirable characteristics to produce a progeny with features of both the parents. Bioremediation is a waste management technique that involves the used of organisms to remove or neutralise pollutants from a contaminated site. Crop protection refers to the methods and practices used to protect crops from pests, diseases and environmental stresses.

Q.12 The term 'Totipotency' refers to the capacity of a

(a) cell to generate whole plant (b) bud to generate whole plant
(c) seed to germinate (d) cell to enlarge in size

Ans. *(a)* The capacity of a cell or an explant (any part of plant taken out and grown in test tube) to grow into a whole plant is called 'totipotency'.

Q.13 Given below are a few statements regarding somatic hybridisation. Choose the correct statements.

I. Protoplasts of different cells of the same plant are fused .
II. Protoplasts from cells of different species can be fused.
III. Treatment of cells with cellulase and pectinase is mandatory.
IV. The hybrid protoplast contains characters of only one parental protoplast.

(a) I and III (b) I and II (c) I and IV (d) II and III

Thinking Process The process of fusion of protoplast of somatic cells obtained from different varieties or species of plant and growing them on a suitable nutrient medium in vitro to develop a somatic hybrid is called somatic hybridisation.

Ans. *(d)* Statement II and III are correct as Protoplast from cells of different species can be fused to produce hybrid protoplast and treatment of cells with cellulose and pectinase is mandatory to obtain wall free or naked protoplast. While other options are incorrect and can be corrected as hybrid protoplast contains characters of both parental protoplast and cells of different species are fused to obtain somatic hybrid.

Q.14 An explant is

(a) dead plant
(b) part of the plant
(c) part of the plant used in tissue culture
(d) part of the plant that expresses a specific gene

Ans. *(c)* An explant is part of plant used in tissue culture. An explant is any part of a plant taken out and grown in a test tube under sterile conditions in a special nutrient media. A whole plant can be generated from an explant.

Q.15 The biggest constraint of plant breeding is

(a) availability of desirable gene in the crop and its wild relatives
(b) infrastructure
(c) trained manpower
(d) transfer of genes from unrelated sources

Ans. *(a)* Breeding (conventional) is often constrained by the limited availability of desirable gene in crop and its wild relations. This is because genes can only be transferred from wild type when they belongs to related species.

Q.16 Lysine and tryptophan are

(a) proteins
(b) non-essential amino acids
(c) essential amino acids
(d) aromatic amino acids

Ans. *(c)* Lysine and tryptophan are essential amino acids. Essential amino acids are the type of amino acids that the body does not makes and must obtain from outside sources.

Q.17 Micro-propagation is

(a) propagation of microbes *in vitro*
(b) propagation of plants *in vitro*
(c) propagation of cells *in vitro*
(d) growing plants on smaller scale

Ans. *(b)* Micropropagation is the method of producing plants *in vitro* to achieve a large number of plants in very short durations. This results in genetically identical plants and is widely used in forestry and floriculture. For *e.g.*, Banana, Apple, tomato are produced on commercial scale using this method.

Q.18 Protoplast is

(a) another name for protoplasm
(b) an animal cell
(c) a plant cell without a cell wall
(d) a plant cell

Ans. *(c)* A protoplast is a plant, bacterial or fungal cell whose cell wall is completely or partially removed using either mechanical or enzymatic means.

Q.19 To isolate protoplast, one needs

(a) pectinase (b) cellulase
(c) both pectinase and cellulase (d) chitinase

Ans. ***(c)*** The cell wall of plant cells consists of pectin and cellulose which can be removed by digestion with a combination of pectinase and cellulase to isolate the protoplast.

Q.20 Which one of the following is a marine fish?

(a) Rohu (b) *Hilsa* (c) *Catla* (d) Common carp

Ans. ***(b)*** *Hilsa,* sardines, mackerel and pomfrets are some of the marine fishes. wheras *Catla*, rohu and common carp are freshwater fishes.

Q.21 Which one of the following products of apiculture is used in cosmetics and polishes?

(a) Honey (b) Oil (c) Wax (d) Royal jelly

Ans. ***(c)*** Bees wax finds many uses in industry, such as in the preparation of cosmetics and polishes of various kinds.

- Honey, is a food of high nutritive value and also finds use in the indigenous systems of medicine.
- Royal jelly, is the queen bees extraordinary source of food. It is rich in nutrition values and is believed to be a potent antioxidant.

Q.22 More than 70% of livestock population is in

(a) Denmark (b) India (c) China (d) India and China

Ans. ***(d)*** It is estimated that more than 70% of the world livestock population is in India and China.

Q.23 The agriculture sector of India employs about

(a) 50% of the population (b) 70% of the population
(c) 30% of the population (d) 60% of the population

Ans. ***(d)*** India is mainly an agricultural country. Agriculture employs nearly 60% of the population.

Q 24 33% of India's Gross Domestic Product comes from

(a) industry (b) agriculture
(c) export (d) small-scale cottage industries

Ans. ***(b)*** Agriculture accounts for approximately 33% of India's GDP (Gross Domestic Products).

Q.25 A collection of all the alleles of all the genes of a crop plant is called

(a) germplasm collection (b) protoplasm collection
(c) herbarium (d) somaclonal collection

Ans. ***(a)*** Germplasm collection is the entire collection of plants/seeds having all the diverse alleles for all genes in a given crop. Whereas protoplasm collection deals mainly with collection of protoplast, *i.e.* cell without cell wall. Herbarium is a collection of Preserved plant specimens while somaclonal collection refers to plants collected through somaclonal variation.

Very Short Answer Types Questions

Q.1 Millions of chicken were killed in West Bengal, Assam, Odisha and Maharashtra recently. What was the reason?

Ans. Millions of chicken were killed or in West Bengal, Assam, Odisha and Maharashtra because they were found to be infected with H5N1 virus, which is the causal the organism of bird flu.

Q.2 Can gamma rays used for crop improvement programmes prove to be harmful for health? Discuss.

Ans. No, gamma rays used for crop improvement programme are not harmful to health because the mutated plant do not emit gamma radiations. Radiation treatment has been used to create thousands of new plant varieties. These varities are cultivated as food and feed.

Such radiation treatment of crop plants has caused no documented instances of ill-health among consumers despite having been used commercially for several decades.

For rice crops hundreds of different mutant varieties have been developed mostly made by using ionising radiations, like gamma rays.

Q.3 In animal husbandry, if two closely related animals are mated for a few generations, it results in loss of fertility and vigour. Why is this so?

Thinking Process The phenomenon being referred to is called 'Inbreeding Depression' and results in loss of fertility and vigour.

Ans. The loss in fertility and vigour occurs after successive inbreeding for few generations. It causes inbreeding depression in which the recessive alleles tend to get together and express harmful effects in the progeny.

Q.4 In the area of plant breeding, it is important not only to preserve the seeds of the variety being cultivated, but also to preserve all its wild relatives. Explain with a suitable example.

Ans. Collection and preservation of all the different wild varieties, species and relatives of the cultivated species is important for effective exploitation of natural genes available in the population. As many high yielding and disease resistant varieties of wheat, and maize have been produced by selective breeding which became possible due better germplasm collection.

Q.5 Name a man-made cereal. Trace how it was developed and where is it used?

Ans. *Triticale* is a man-made cereal. It was developed by crossing *Triticum aestivum* (common wheat) and *Secale cereale* (European rye).

Triticale seed grain is being used in some parts of the world as a substitute for wheat.

Q.6 Fill in the blanks.

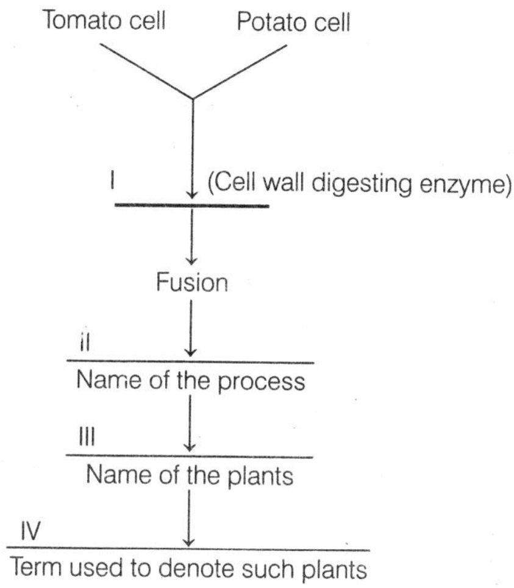

Ans. The correct answers are as follows.

(I) Cellulase

(II) Somatic hybridisation

(III) Pomato

(IV) Somatic hybrid

Q.7 A few statements are given below followed by a set of terms in a box. Pick the correct term and write it against the appropriate statement

(a)	Mating of closely related individuals within the same breed.	(i)	Cross breeding
(b)	Mating of animals of same breed but having no common ancestors on either side for 4-6 generations.	(ii)	Inter-specific hybridisation
(c)	Mating of animals of two different species.	(iii)	Outbreeding
(d)	Breeding of animals belonging to different breeds.	(iv)	Outcrossing
		(v)	Inbreeding

Ans. (a) Mating of closely related individuals within the same breed is called inbreeding.

(b) Mating of animals of same breed but having no common ancestors on either side for 4-6 generations is called outcrossing.

(c) Mating of animals of two different species is called inters-pecific hybridisation.

(d) Breeding of animals belonging to different breeds is called cross-breeding.

Q.8 What is meant by 'hidden hunger'?

Ans. Consumption of food deficient in nutrients particularly, micronutrients, proteins and vitamins is called 'hidden hunger'.

Q.9 Why are plants obtained by protoplast culture called somatic hybrids?

Ans. Plants obtained by protoplast culture are called somatic hybrids because they are a result of fusing protoplasts from the somatic cells of two different plants species.

Such plants inherit characteristics from both parental plants.

Q.10 What is protoplast fusion?

Ans. The ability of protoplasts, obtained from two different cells to fuse and form a hybrid protoplast is called protoplast fusion.

Q.11 Why is it easier to culture meristems compared to permanent tissues?

Ans. Meristems have the capacity to divide continuously throughout their life. Their walls are thin and elastic, to facilitate the division, hence are suitable for tissue culture.

Cells of permanent tissue lose their ability to divide and their walls are thick. They have to differentiate to divide, hence are not easier to culture.

Q.12 Why are proteins synthesised from *Spirulina* called single cell proteins?

Ans. Single cell proteins are proteins obtained from unicellular organisms/ microorganisms. *Spirulina* is one such unicellular microbe. Therefore, the proteins synthesised by *Spirulina* are called single cell proteins.

Q.13 A person who is allergic to pulses was advised to take a capsule of *Spirulina* daily. Give the reasons for the advise.

Ans. The person with allergies to pulses is advised to take *Spirulina* daily due to the following reasons

(i) It is rich in proteins and can serve as a which substitute for protein-rich pulses.

(ii) *Spirulina* is also rich in beta-carotene and anti-oxidants, which helps improve immunity and reduces allergic symptoms.

Q.14 What is aquaculture? Give example of an animal that can be multiplied by aquaculture.

Ans. Aquaculture is the practice of cultivating aquatic organisms such as fish, crustaceans and plants in controlled aquatic environment including both freshwater and marine systems.

Examples of animals that can be multiplied by aquaculture are

Finfish — Tilapia, Carp, Catfish, etc.

Shellfish — Shrimps, Oysters, etc.

Q.15 What are the duties of a veterinary doctor in management of a poultry farm?

Ans. A veterinary doctor has to ensure proper and safe farm conditions to keep the animals disease-free and treat them appropriately if diseased. In addition a farm lot has to ensure nutritious diet for the birds.

Q.16 Would it be wrong to call plants obtained through micro-propagation as 'clones'? Comment.

Ans. *No*, it is not wrong to call plants obtained through micro-propagation as clones because each of these plants will be genetically identical to each other and the parent plant.

Q.17 How is a somatic hybrid different from a hybrid?

Ans. Somatic hybrids are obtained by fusing protoplasts from two different varieties of plants and then further culturing to form a whole plant. Compatibility between two plants is not a limitation. Any two protoplasts can be united. It is a form of asexual hybridisation.

Whereas, hybrids are obtained by crossing two selected parent plants of opposite sex. Many times compatibility is a limitation for breeding. Sexual reproduction is necessary to produce hybrids

Q.18 What is emasculation? Why and when is it done?

Ans. Removal of anthers from the bisexual flower without affecting female reproductive part in plant hybridisation is called emasculation. This is done to avoid unwanted self-pollination. This has to be done in the bud condition before the anthers dehisce.

Q.19 Discuss the two main limitations of plant hybridisation programme.

Ans. The limitations of plant hybridisation programme include

(i) Availability of a limited number of identified disease resistant genes

(ii) Compatibility of parents.

(iii) Time consuming and tedious process.

Q.20 Interspecific crosses are rare in nature and intergeneric crosses almost unknown. Why?

Ans. In interspecific crosses, male and female animals of two different species are mated. These are rare in nature due to reproductive isolating mechanisms, such as behavioural, temporal and genetic barriers that prevent successful mating or hybrid viability. Intergeneric hybridisation is the crossing of two different animals/plants of different genus. It is almost unknown in nature. Intergeneric hybrids more or less never form complete zygotes/embryos. These are sterile/infertile.

Q.21 Differentiate between pisciculture and aquaculture.

Ans. Fish farming in isolated water bodies is called pisciculture.

Similarly, when culturing of aquatic plants and animals is done in freshwater bodies, it is called aquaculture.

Q.22 Give two important contribution of Dr. MS Swaminathan.

Thinking Process Green revolution which was responsible for not merely meeting the national requirement in food production but also helped us to export it. It was due to the initiative taken by **Dr. MS Swaminathan** in collaboration with **Dr. N. Borlaug**.

Ans. Contributions of Dr. MS Swaminathan are as follows

(i) Introduction of short, high yielding varieties of wheat in India.

(ii) Development of short duration, high yielding varieties of rice.

Q.23 The term 'desirable trait' can mean different things for different plants. Justify the statement with suitable examples.

Thinking Process Plant breeding is the purposeful manipulation of plant species in order to create plants with desirable traits.

Ans. The term desirable trait can vary for different plants because different plants have different needs and respond differently to environmental factors for example

(i) Thick and tall stems are preferred in sugarcane, dwarf stems are ideal in rice plants.

(ii) While more leaves are desired in spinach, this may not be the case for the mustard plant.

Short Answer Type Questions

Q.1 You are planning to set up a dairy farm. Describe the various aspects you would consider before you start the venture.

Ans. The following aspects are required to be considered

(i) Good breeds with high-yielding potenital should be kept.

(ii) Cattle should be fed with good quality and quantity of fodder.

(iii) Animal shed should be kept clean, away from dirt and pollution.

(iv) Cattle and handler should be kept in hygienic condition.

(v) Regular visit by veterinary doctors with proper record is needed.

(vi) Cattle should be housed well with adequate water and conditions should be disease-free.

Q.2 It is said, that diseases are spreading faster due to globalisation and increased movement of people. Justify the statement taking the example of H5 Nl virus.

Ans. The avian flu (bird flu) is a current and significant issue involving the global environment as well as the health of millions of people around the world. The H5N1 virus (influenza-A) occurs mainly in birds, is highly contagious among them and, can be deadly. The major global environmental issue that plays a large role in the advancement of the H5 Nl avian influenza virus is globalisaiton. *i.e.,* increasing integration of countries.

Globalisation will give the H5 Nl avian influenza virus an opportunity to travel to various parts of the world without impediment.

Once, it has developed the ability to spread easily from human to human, the major concern becomes the travel of individuals around the world, particularly air travel. Through air travel, an infected individual could infect dozens of people during their movement, those newly infected individuals would in turn, infect dozens more, and so on and so forth.

Q.3 Explain the concept of the blue revolution.

Ans. The term 'Blue Revolution' refers to the remarkable emergence of aquaculture as an important and highly productive agricultural activity.

Aquaculture refers to all forms of active culturing of aquatic animals (including fish) and plants, occuring in marine, brackish or freshwater.

Q.4 A farmer was facing the problem of low yield from his farm. He was advised to keep a beehive in the vicinity. Why? How would the beehive help in enhancing yield?

Ans. The low yeild can be due to absence of pollinators. As pollination is essential for seed production in most crop and insects are main pollinating agents. Therefore keeping a beehive near a farm will help in proper pollination crops. Thus improving group yeild.

The beehives when kept in the fields of sunflower, *Brassica*, apple and pear, increase the pollination efficiency of flowering plants and improve the yields.

Q.5 Life style diseases are increasing alarmingly in India. We are also dealing with large scale malnutrition in the population. Is there any method by which we can address both of these problems together?

Ans. To address both of these problems biofortification can be done. This area focuses at improving food quality with respect to protein, oil, vitamin, micronutrient and mineral content. The oils need to be rich in omega 3 fatty acids which are good for heart.

Similarly, proteins should have more of lysine and tryptophan (essential amino acids). Many varieties of maize, carrots and spinach have been released which fulfill the above criteria.

Q.6 How can we improve the success rate of fertilisation during artificial insemination in animal husbandry programmes?

Ans. To improve chances of successful production of hybrids during artificial insemination few methods are used. One such programme is called MOET or Multiple Ovulation Embryo Transfer. During this procedure, a cow is given hormonal treatment so that more than one ovule (6-8 eggs) is produced per cycle.

After mating or artificial insemination, the embryos at 8-32 celled state are transferred to different surrogate mothers. This method has been successfully used for cattle, sheep, buffalo, etc.

Q.7 What is meant by germplasm collection? What are its benefits?

Ans. The collection of all the diverse alleles of all the genes of a crop plant is called germplasm collection. It is of great benefits in plant breeding programmes as it offers, to the breeders, the entire of genes and alleles and the characteristics which a plant expresses.

The breeder selects the most favourable characters of a particular gene, manipulates it and transfers to a desirable parent.

Q.8 Name the improved characteristics of wheat that helped India to achieve green revolution.

Ans. Improved characteristics of wheat that helped India to achieve green revolution are as follows

(i) Semi-dwarf nature (ii) Quick yielding feature
(iii) High yielding feature (iv) Disease resistance

Q.9 Suggest some of the features of plants that will prevent insect and pest infestation.

Ans. Features of plants that will prevent insect and pest infestation are as follows

(i) Increasing hair growth on aerial parts of plants.
(ii) Rendering the flowers nectarless.
(iii) Enabling plants to secrete insect killing chemicals (toxins).

Q.10 It is easier to culture plant cells *in vitro* as compared to animal cells. Why?

Ans. It is easier to culture the plant cells *in vitro* as compared to animal cells because, the plant cells have the property to grow into a new plant. This property of plant cell is termed as totipotency. This ability is limited in animal cells. In addition plant cells undergo dedifferentiation and become meristematic while animal cells can not.

Q.11 The culture medium (nutrient medium) can be referred to as a 'highly enriched laboratory soil'. Justify the statement.

Ans. Culture medium can be a referred to as highly enriched laboratory soil as it provides all the necessary nutrients and supplements, *e.g.*, carbon source such as sucrose and inorganic salts, vitamins, amino acids and growth regulators like auxins and cytokinins, etc., to the growing plant.

Q.12 Is there any relationship between dedifferentiation and the higher degree of success achieved in plant tissue culture experiments?

Ans. *Yes,* when a cell dedifferentiation it reverts to undifferentiated state and then can again redifferentiate into various cell types. So, the plant tissue culture can be more successful as any kind of tissue can be produced even from differentiated cells.

Q.13 Give me a living cell of any plant and I will give you a thousand plants of the same type", Is this only a slogan or is it scientifically possible? Write your comments and justify them.

Ans. It is scientifically possible to grow thousand plants from a living cell of any plant and this process is called micropropagation. The property of plant cells that helped them to grow into a new plant is totipotency. Micropropagation is the use of plant cell culture to regenerate large number of plants. This results in genetically identical plants and is also called clonal propagation.

Hence, the desirable characters are kept constant for many generations. Micropropagation is widely used in forestry and in floriculture. Plants can be obtained throughout the year under controlled conditions.

Q.14 What is the difference between a breed and a species? Give an example for each category.

Ans. A breed is a specific group of animals or plants having homogenous appearance, behaviour and other characteristics that distinguish it from other animals or plants of the same species, *e.g.*, Afghan shepherd, American bulldog are breeds of dog. Species is one of the basic units of biological classification and a taxonomic rank. It can be defined as the group of organisms capable of interbreeding and producing fertile offspring. *e.g.*, lion, cow, dog are species.

Q.15 Plants raised through tissue cultures are clones of the 'parent' plant. Discuss the utility of these plants.

Ans. Utility of tissue cultured plants are as follows

(i) A large number of clones can be grown in a shorter amount of time

(ii) Cloned plants retain parent plant's genetic uniformity and desirable traits.

(iii) It can be used to create high yielding cultivars.

(iv) A diseased plant can be recovered into a healthy plant.

Q.16 Discuss the importance of testing of new plant varieties in a geographically vast country like India.

Ans. Testing new plant varieties in geographically vast country like India is important due to country's diverse agro-climatic zone, soil types and different farm practices across the regions. Here are some of the reason why such testing is essential

(i) Regional climatic variations - India has wide range of climates, from tropical to temperature with varying rainfall pattern and temperature.

(ii) Soil Diversity : India's soil types range from alluvial to saline in coastal areas and Lateritic soil in western Ghats and hence have varying nutrient profiles, water retention capacities etc. So, testing ensures that crops are optimixes for regional environmental conditions and other such diversity.

Q.17 Define the term 'stress' for plants. Discuss briefly the two types of stress encountered by plants.

Ans. Stress for plants can be defined as any external factor that negatively influences plant growth, productivity, reproductive capacity or survival. This includes a wide range of factors which can be broadly divided into abiotic or environmental stress factors like salinity, extreme temperatures, drought, etc., and biotic or biological stress factors.

Q.18 Discuss natural selection and artificial selection. What are the implications of the latter on the process of evolution?

Ans. Natural selection is a gradual, non-random process by which biological traits become either more or less common in a population as a function of differential reproduction of their bearers. It is a key mechanism to evolution. In natural selection the environment acts as a sieve through which only certain variations can pass.

Artificial selection is a process in which animals and plants with desirable traits are considered by human breeders and favoured for reproduction. It is an artificial mechanism by which evolution can occur. It is also called selective breeding as it promotes traits that suit human preferences. In contrast to natural selection, here the evolution is intentional or guided.

Q.19 Discuss briefly how pure lines are created in animal husbandry.

Thinking Process Inbreeding increases homozygosity.

Ans. The breeding is between animals of the same breed, it is called inbreeding. If a pureline in any animal, has to be evolved inbreeding (for 4-6 generation) is necessary. It also helps in accumulation of superior genes and elimination of less desirable genes by increasing homozygosity.

Q.20 What are the physical barriers of a cell in the protoplast fusion experiment? How are the barriers overcome?

Ans. Cell wall is the most important physical barrier in protoplast fusion experiments. This can be overcome by treatment with enzymes like cellulase which have the ability to digest the cell wall and liberate the naked protoplast surrounded only by the cell membrane.

Q.21 Give few examples of biofortified crops. What benefits do they offer to the society?

Ans. Maize, wheat, rice, bathua, spinach, pulses have biofortified varieties. Maize hybrids have twice the amount of amino acids, fortified wheat variety has high protein content, while fortified rice has high quantity of iron.

Consumption of such biofortified foods will enrich the nutritive value of our common foods and will vastly improve public health. Instead of consuming different food items for obtaining different nutrients, if 2 or 3 nutrients can be incorporated into a single crop, it would offer enormous benefits to human beings and may even help to overcome several nutrient deficiency disorders.

Long Answer Type Questions

Q.1 You are a Botanist working in the area of plant breeding. Describe the various steps that you will undertake to release a new variety.

Ans. Plant breeding programmes are carried out in a systematic way world wide in government institutions and commercial companies.

The main steps in breeding a new genetic variety of a crop are as follows

(i) **Collection of Variability** Genetic variability is the root of any breeding programme. In many crops pre-existing genetic variability is available from wild relatives of the crop.

Collection and preservation of all the different wild varieties, species and relatives of the cultivated species (followed by their evaluation for their characteristics) is a pre-requisite for effective exploitation of natural genes available in the populations.

The entire collection (of plants/seeds) having all the diverse alleles for all genes in a given crop is called germplasm collection.

(ii) **Evaluation and Selection of Parents** The germplasm is evaluated so as to identify plants with desirable combination of` characters. The selected plants are multiplied and used in the process of hybridisation. Purelines are created wherever desirable and possible.

(iii) **Cross Hybridisation Among the Selected Parents** The desired characters have to be combined from two different plants (parents), *e.g.*, high protein quality of one parent may need to be combined with disease resistance from another parent.

This is possible by cross hybridising the two parents to produce hybrids that genetically combine the desired characters in one plant. This is a very time-consuming and tedious process since the pollen grains from the desirable plant chosen as male parent have to be collected and placed on the stigma of the flowers selected as female parent. Also, it is not necessary that the hybrids do combine the desirable characters, usually only one in few hundred to a thousand crosses shows the desirable combination.

(iv) **Selection and Testing of Superior Recombinants** This step consists of selecting, among the progeny of the hybrids, those plants that have the desired character combination. The selection process is crucial to the success of the breeding objective and requires careful scientific evaluation of the progeny. This step yields plants that are superior to both of the parents (very often more than one superior progeny plant may become available). These are self-pollinated for several generations till they reach a state of uniformity (homozygosity), so that the characters will not segregate in the progeny.

(v) **Testing, Release and Commercialisation of New Cultivars** The newly selected lines are evaluated for their yield and other agronomic traits of quality, disease resistance, etc.

This evaluation is done by growing these in the research fields and recording their performance under ideal fertiliser application, irrigation and other crop management practices. The evaluation in research fields is followed by testing the materials in farmers' fields, for at least three growing seasons at several locations in the country, representing all the agroclimatic zones where the crop is usually grown. The material is evaluated in comparison to the best available local crop. After evaluation the variety can be relased for the farmers.

Q.2 (a) The shift from grain to meat diets creates more demands for cereals. Why?

(b) A 250 kg cow produces 200 g of protein per day but 250 g of *Methylophillus methylotrophus* can produce 25 tonnes of protein. Name this emerging area of research. Explain its benefits.

Ans. (a) The shift from grain to meat diets creates more demand for cereals as it takes 3-10 kg of grain to produce 1 kg of meat by animal farming.

(b) This research is related to single cell protein.

Microbes are being grown on an industrial scale as a source of good protein. Microbes like *Spirulina* can be grown easily on materials like wastewater from potato processing plants (containing starch), straw, molasses, animal manure and even sewage. These microbes can then be used to produce large quantities of food rich in protein, minerals, fats, carbohydrate and vitamins. Such utilisation also reduces the environmental pollution.

Q.3 What are the advantages of tissue culture methods over conventional method of plant breeding in crop improvement programmes?

Ans. As traditional (conventional) breeding methods failed to keep pace with growing demand and were sufficient in providing fast and efficient systems for crop improvement, another technology called tissue culture was developed.

The advantages of tissue culture over conventional breeding are as follows

(i) It can be used to produce large number of plantlets within a short period by micropropagation.

(ii) All cells in the culture are derived from a single explant by mitotic division, therefore all have the similar genotype and constitute a clone.

(iii) Tolerance to stress can be obtained by providing pollutants, toxins, salts, etc., in culture medium in increasing dosage. The surviving healthy cells are selected for raising resistant plants.

(iv) Virus free plantlets can be obtained by meristem culture.

(v) Embryos which do not survive inside seeds can be grown by tissue culture to form new plants.

Q.4 'Modern methods of breeding animals and plants can alleviate the global food shortage'. Comment on the statement and give suitable examples.

Ans. With ever increasing population of the world, enhancement of food production is a major necessity. Modern biological principles as applied to animal husbandry and plant breeding have a major role in our efforts to increase food production. These modern techniques include embryo transfer technology and tissue culture techniques. Multiple Ovulation Embryo Transfer Technology (MOET) is a programme for herd improvement in animals like cattle, sheep, rabbits, buffaloes, mares, etc.

High milk-yielding breeds of female are bred with high quality meat-yielding (meat with less lipid) bulls to increase herd size. It ensures good quality of progeny. It is also economic and time saving process to obtain the desirable progeny.

Modern methods in plant breeding involves following

(i) Tissue culture is an in *vitro* technique of regeneration of a whole plant from any part of a plant (explant) by growing it on culture medium under aseptic conditions.

(ii) Biofortification is the method for developing crops with higher levels of vitamins, minerals, proteins and healthier fats to improve public health.

(iii) Single cell protein is an alternative protein source for animal and human nutrition from certain beneficial microorganisms like *Spirulina*.

Q.5 Does apiculture offer multiple advantages to farmers? List its advantages if it is located near a place of commercial flower cultivation.

Ans. Yes, apiculture offers many advantages to farmers

It can offer multiple advantages to farmers, when it is located near a place of commercial flower cultivation. Some advantages are given on next page.

Following are the advantages

Pollination of crops Bees plays a crucial role in pollinating flowers, which is essential for production of many crops, so farmers can enchance pollination by keeping beehives near flower cultivation, which can improve yields.

Enhanced biodiversity Bee keeping can contribute to the overall biodiversity of the farm by encouraging a healthy ecosystem. Overall, proximity of apiculture to commercial flower cultivation can create a mutual beneficial relationship that enhances both agricultured production and environmental sustainability.

Q.6 (a) Mutations are beneficial for plant breeding. Taking an example, justify the statement.

(b) Discuss briefly the technology that made us self-sufficient in food production.

Thinking Process Mutation is the process by which genetic variations are created through changes in the base sequence within genes resulting in the creation of a new character or trait not found in the parental type.

Ans. (a) Mutations can be beneficial for plant breeding as they introduce genetic variations, which is crucial for developing new varieties with desirable traits. The process of inducing mutations artificially in plants through use of chemicals or radiations and then selecting and using those plants as a source of breeding is called mutational breeding. Ex : Resistance to yellow mosaic virus and powdery mildew in mung bean was induced by mutations.

(b) Traditional farming can only yield a limited biomass, as food for humans and animals. Better management practices and increase in agricultural land area can increase yield, but only to a limited extent. Plant breeding as a technology has helped increase production to a very large extent. Plant breeding is the purposeful manipulation of plant species in order to create desired plant types that are better suited for cultivation, give better yields and are disease resistant. This technology has given support to green revolution, which was responsible for not merely meeting the national requirements in food production, but also helped us to export it.

Q.7 Discuss how the property of plant cell totipotency has been utilised for plant propagation and improvement.

Thinking Process The property of plant cells that helped them to grow into a new plant is totipotency. The production of healthy plantlet by rapid vegetative multiplication is done under aseptic and controlled conditions.

Ans. Plant cell totipotency can be utilised for plant propagation and improvement

(i) By application of these methods it is possible to achieve propagation of a large number of plants in very short time. Plants like tomato, banana, apple, etc., have been produced on commercial scale.

(ii) Healthy plants can be recovered from diseased plants (by micropropagation). This is done by removing the meristem, (which is disease free) and growing it *in vitro*. This has been done in banana, sugarcane potato, etc.

Q.8 What are three options to increase food production? Discuss each giving the salient features, merits and demerits.

Ans. Traditional farming can only yield a limited biomass as food for humans and animals. Better management practices and increase in agricultural land can increase yield, but only to a limited extent.

Following are the three options to increase food production

(a) **Single Cell Protein** The biomass obtained from microorganisms can be treated or processed in industry to be used as food and is called single cell protein.

Merits of Single Cell Proteins

(i) Its production reduces pollution as it uses organic wastes and industrial effluents.
(ii) It provides a protein-rich diet.
(iii) It fulfills the demand of protein for human diet and takes off the pressure on agriculture system.

Demerits of Single Cell Protein

(i) Sometimes the microbial biomass when taken as diet supplement may lead to allergic reactions.
(ii) Many types of microorganisms produce substances which are toxic to the humans and also to the animals.

(b) **Conventional Breeding Methods**

It involves selective breeding, hybridisation and cross-pollination to enhances traits like yield, disease resistance and drought tolerance.

Merits of Conventional Breeding Methods

(i) It is natural and biodiversity-friendly.
(ii) It is cost-effective with proven results.

Demerits of Conventional Breeding Methods

(i) It is a time-consuming process.
(ii) It provides limited genetic variability increases vulnerability.

(c) **Tissue-Culture**

It is an *in vitro* technique for regeneration of a whole plant from any part of a plant by growing it on culture medium under aseptic conditions.

Merits of Tissue Culture

(i) A large number of plants can be grown in short time.
(ii) Disease-free plants can be multiplied.
(iii) Seedless plants can be multiplied
(iv) The plants where sexual reproduction is absent may undergo somatic hybridisation.

Demerits of Tissue Culture

(i) It requires great expense because it needs latest techniques in the laboratory.
(ii) It requires acclimatisation of plants grown by tissue culture to the external environment.
(iii) It requires special expertise.

Chapter

10 Microbes in Human Welfare

Multiple Choice Questions (MCQs)

Q.1 The vitamin whose content increases following the conversion of milk into curd by lactic acid bacteria is

(a) vitamin-C
(b) vitamin-D
(c) vitamin-B_{12}
(d) vitamin-E

Ans. *(c)* Vitamin B_{12} content increases following the conversion of milk into curd by lactic acid bacteria. Microorganisms such as *Lactobacillus* and others commonly called Lactic Acid Bacteria (LAB) grow in milk and convert it into curd. During growth, the LAB produce acids that coagulate and partially digest the milk proteins.

Q.2 Waste water treatment generates a large quantity of sludge, which can be treated by

(a) anaerobic digesters
(b) floc
(c) chemicals
(d) oxidation pond

Thinking Process The treatment of waste water is divided into three phases-pre treatment, primary treatment and secondary treatment.

Ans. *(a)* Sludge is treated by anaerobic digesters. These digesters are large heated tanks in which sludge's chemical decomposition is catalysed by microorganisms. This process is used for industrial and domestic waste purposes.

Q.3 Methanogenic bacteria are not found in

(a) rumen of cattle
(b) gobar gas plant
(c) bottom of water-logged paddy fields
(d) activated sludge

Ans. *(d)* Methanogenic bacteria (that produce methane) are not found in activated sludge. They are found in anaerobic conditions environments such as rumen of cattle, gobar gas plants and waterlogged paddy fields. Aerobic bacteria grow rapidly and form flocs.

Q.4 Match the following column of bacteria and their commercially important products.

Column I (Bacterium)	Column II (Products)
A. *Aspergillus niger*	1. Lactic acid
B. *Acetobacter aceti*	2. Butyric acid
C. *Clostridium butylicum*	3. Acetic acid
D. *Lactobacillus*	4. Citric acid

Codes

	A	B	C	D		A	B	C	D
(a)	2	3	4	1	(b)	2	4	3	1
(c)	4	3	2	1	(d)	4	1	3	2

Ans. ***(c)*** The correct sequence is A - 4, B - 3, C - 2 and D - 1.

Aspergillus niger is commonly used in industrial production of citric acid.

Acetobacter aceti is involved in the fermentation of alcohol to acetic acid, which produces vinegar.

Clostridium butylicum is known for the production of butyuic acid.

Lactobacillus is involved in fermentation of sugars, to produce lactic acid.

Q.5 Match the following column of bioactive substances and their roles.

Column I (Bioactive Substances)	Column II (Roles)
A. Statin	1. Removal of oil stains
B. Cyclosporin A	2. Removal of clots from blood vessels
C. Streptokinase	3. Lowering of blood cholesterol
D. Lipase	4. Immuno-suppressive agent

Choose the correct match

Codes

	A	B	C	D		A	B	C	D
(a)	2	3	1	4	(b)	4	2	1	3
(c)	4	1	3	2	(d)	3	4	2	1

Ans. ***(d)*** The correct sequence is A-3, B-4, C-2 and D-1

Statins, produced by the yeast *Monascus purpureus* have been commercialised as blood cholesterol lowering agents.

Cyclosporin A, produced by the fungus *Trichoderma polysporum* is used as an immuno-suppressive agent in organ transplant patients.

Streptokinase, produced by the bacterium *Streptococcus* and modified by genetic engineering is used as a 'clot buster' for removing clots from the blood vessels of patients who have undergone myocardial infarctions leading to heart attack.

Lipases are used in detergent formulations and are helpful in removing oily stains from the laundry.

Q.6 The primary treatment of waste water involves the removal of

(a) dissolved impurities (b) stable particles
(c) toxic substances (d) harmful bacteria

Ans. ***(b)*** The primary treatment of waste water involves physical removal of both larger and small particles (stable particles) from the sewage through filtration and sedimentation. These are removed in stages; initially, floating debris is removed by sequential filtration. Then the grit (soil and small pebbles) are removed by sedimentation. All solids that settle form the primary sludge and the supernatant forms the effluent. The effluent is taken for the secondary treatment.

The primary treatment does not remove the dissolved impurities, toxic substances and harmful bacteria.

Q.7 BOD of waste water is estimated by measuring the amount of

(a) total organic matter (b) biodegradable organic matter
(c) oxygen evolution (d) oxygen consumption

Ans. ***(d)*** BOD *i.e.,* Biochemical Oxygen Demand refers to the amount of the oxygen that would be consumed if all the organic matter in one litre of water were oxidised by bacteria. Hence, BOD of waste water is estimated by measuring amount of oxygen consumption by microbes. The higher the BOD, the more organic matter present in the water and it becomes more polluted.

Q.8 Which one of the following alcoholic drinks is produced without distillation?

(a) Wine (b) Whisky (c) Rum (d) Brandy

Ans. ***(a)*** Wine is produced without distillation. It is produced by fermentation of grapes. Whereas whisky, brandy and rum are produced by distillation of the fermented broth.

Q.9 The technology of biogas production from cow dung was developed in India largely due to the efforts of

(a) Gas Authority of India
(b) Oil and Natural Gas Commission
(c) Indian Agricultural Research Institute, Khadi and Village Industries Commission
(d) Indian Oil Corporation

Ans. ***(c)*** Cow dung is used for the production of biogas, commonly called gobar gas.

The technology of biogas production from cowdung was developed in India mainly due to the efforts of Indian Agricultural Research Institute (IARI) and Khadi and Village Industries Commission (KVIC).

Q. 10 The free-livings fungus *Trichoderma* can be used for

(a) killing insects (b) biological control of plant diseases
(c) controlling butterfly caterpillars (d) producing antibiotics

Ans. ***(b)*** *Trichoderma* species are free-living fungi that are very common in soil. They are effective biocontrol agents of several soil-borne plant pathogens and hence can be used as biological control agent of plant disease.

Q.11 What would happen if oxygen availability to activated sludge flocs is reduced?

(a) It will slow down the rate of degradation of organic matter

(b) The center of flocs will become anoxic, which would cause death of bacteria and eventually breakage of flocs

(c) Flocs would increase in size as anaerobic bacteria would grow around flocs

(d) Protozoa would grow in large numbers

Thinking Process During secondary treatment, the primary effluent is passed into large aeration tanks where it is constantly agitated mechanically and air is pumped into it. This allows vigorous growth of useful aerobic microbes into flocs (masses of bacteria associated with fungal filaments to form mesh like structures).

Ans. ***(b)*** Activated sludge microorganisms need oxygen as they oxidise wastes to obtain energy for growth. Insufficient oxygen will slow down or kill aerobic microorganisms, ultimately lead to the breakage of flocs.

It will also result in the production of the foul-smelling byproducts of anaerobic decomposition. Therefore, sufficient oxygen must always be maintained in the aeration tank to ensure complete waste stabilisation.

Q.12 Mycorrhiza does not help the host plant in

(a) enhancing its phosphorus uptake capacity

(b) increasing its tolerance to drought

(c) enhancing its resistance to root pathogens

(d) increasing its resistance to insects

Ans. ***(d)*** Mycorrhiza does not help the host plant in increasing its resistance to insects. As fungi form symbiotic association with the roots of higher plants called mycorrhiza *e.g., Glomus.* This symbiotic association help in absorption of phosphous from soil, tolerance to salinity, drought etc.

Q 13 Which one of the following is not a nitrogen-fixing organism?

(a) *Anabaena* (b) *Nostoc*

(c) *Azotobacter* (d) *Pseudomonas*

Ans. ***(d)*** *Pseudomonas* is a denitrifying bacteria, which convert ammonia and nitrates into free nitrogen. These denitrifying bacteria are responsible to liberate free nitrogen in the environment through nitrogen cycle.

Q.14 Big holes in Swiss cheese are made by a

(a) a machine

(b) a bacterium that produces methane gas

(c) a bacterium producing a large amount of carbon dioxide

(d) a fungus that releases a lot of gases during its metabolic activities

Thinking Process Different varieties of cheese are known by their characteristic texture, flavour and taste, the specificity coming from the microbes used.

Ans. ***(c)*** The large holes in 'Swiss cheese' are due to the production of a large amount of carbon dioxide by a bacterium named *Propionibacterium shermanii.*

Q.15 The residue left after methane production from cattle dung is

(a) burnt (b) burried in land fills

(c) used as manure (d) used in civil construction

Ans. ***(c)*** The residue left after methane production from cattle dung is used as manure. This is because the residues supply organic matter and minerals to the soil.

Q.16 Methanogens do not produce

(a) oxygen (b) methane

(c) hydrogen sulphide (d) carbon dioxide

Ans. ***(a)*** Methogens to not produce oxygen because they are found in anaerobic conditions. They produce other mixture of gases like methane, hydrogen sulphide and carbon dioxide which forms biogas.

Q 17 Activated sludge should have the ability to settle quickly so that it can

(a) be rapidly pumped back from sedimentation tank to aeration tank

(b) absorb pathogenic bacteria present in waste water while sinking to the bottom of the settling tank

(c) be discarded and anaerobically digested

(d) absorb colloidal organic matter

Ans. ***(a)*** Activated slude should have the ability to settle quickly so that it can be rapidly pumped back from sedimentation tank to aeration tank. This is done rapidly for the process of decomposition organic matter to start again.

Q.18 Match the following columns.

Column I	Column II
A. Lady bird	1. *Methanobacterium*
B. Mycorrhiza	2. *Trichoderma*
C. Biological control	3. *Aphids*
D. Biogas	4. *Glomus*

Codes

	A	B	C	D		A	B	C	D
(a)	2	4	3	1	(b)	3	4	2	1
(c)	4	1	2	3	(d)	3	2	1	4

Ans. ***(b)*** The correct sequence is A-3, B-4, C-2 and D-1.

Ladybird is beetle with red and black markings, used to get rid of *Aphids*.

Fungi form symbiotic association, with the roots of higher plants called mycorrhiza, *e.g., Glomus*.

A biological control being developed for the treatment of plant disease is the fungus *Trichoderma*.

Methanogens, particularly *Methanobacterium*, are found in cowdung. These bacteria grow anaerobically on cellulosic material and produce large amount of methane along with carbon dioxide and hydrogen.

Very Short Answer Type Questions

Q.1 Why does 'Swiss cheese' have big holes?

Thinking Process Different varieties of bakery like bread and cheese are known by their characteristic texture, flavour and taste, the specificity coming from the microbes used.

Ans. The large holes in 'Swiss cheese' are due to production of a large amount of carbon dioxide by a bacterium named *Propionibacterium shermanii*.

Q.2 What are fermentors?

Ans. For large scale production of biotechnological products, like antibiotics, beverages etc, microbes are provided with nutrient and are grown in very large vessels called fermentors or bioreactors.

Q.3 Name a microbe used for statin production. How do statins lower blood cholesterol level?

Ans. Statins are bioactive molecules, produced by the yeast *Monascus purpureus*. These bioactive molecules have been commercialised as blood-cholesterol lowering agents. It acts by competitively inhibiting the enzyme responsible for synthesis of cholesterol.

Q.4 Why do we prefer to call secondary waste water treatment as biological treatment?

Ans. Secondary waste water treatment is called biological treatment because microorganisms are involved in the breakdown of organic matter in this phase of waste water treatment.

The primary effluent is passed into large aeration tanks where the organic matter is consumed by aerobic microbes. These are later digested by anaerobic bacteria and fungi in anaerobic sludge digesters.

Q.5 What for nucleopolyhedro viruses are being used now a-days?

Ans. Nucleo polyhedro viruses are used as biological control pests. These viruses are excellent candidates for species-specific, narrow spectrum insecticidal applications. They have been shown to have no negative impacts on plants, mammals, birds, fish or even on non-target insects. These are used against cotton bollworm.

Q.6 How has the discovery of antibiotics helped mankind in the field of medicine?

Ans. Antibiotics produced by microbes are regarded as one of the most significant discoveries of the twentieth century and have greatly contributed towards the welfare of the human society. It helps mankind in overcoming most of the bacterial and fungal diseases.

Antibiotics have greatly improved the capacity to treat deadly diseases such as plague, whooping cough (Kali khansi), diphtheria (Gal ghotu) and leprosy (Kusht rog), which had killed millions of people. Today, we can not imagine a world without antibiotics.

Q.7 Why is distillation required for producing certain alcoholic drinks?

Ans. Distillation increases the alcohol content in alcoholic drinks. This is because distillation separates the components based on their differences in boiling points. That's why for production of certain alcoholic drinks, distillation is required. e.g., whiskey.

Q.8 Write the most important characteristic that *Aspergillus niger*, *Clostridium butylicum*, and *Lactobacillus* share.

Ans. Their common characteristic is that they produce organic acids as part of their metabolism and therefore, used for commercial and industrial production of the same. It can be seen as follows.

(i) *Aspergillus niger* (a fungus) for citric acid.

(ii) *Clostridium butylicum* (a bacterium) for butyric acid.

(iii) *Lactobacillus* (a bacterium) for lactic acid.

Q.9 What would happen if our intestine harbours microbial flora exactly similar to that found in the rumen of cattle?

Ans. If human intestine harbours microbial flora exactly similar to that found in the rumen of cattle, they would be able to digest the cellulose present in their food. This is because the microbes present in the rumen (a part of stomach) of cattle, collectively called methanogens, are capable of digesting cellulose as they have cellulase enzyme. Therefore, humans will be able to digest cellulose.

Q.10 Give any two microbes that are useful in biotechnology.

Ans. Two microbes that are useful in biotechnology are as follows

(i) *Bacillus thuringiensis*, when a gene is isolated from this bacterium is introduced in cotton plants, makes them pest-resistant.

(ii) *Escherichia coli* is a bacterium that is used in many biotechnological procedures. Their plasmid is used as vector to introduce foreign DNA segment in desired organisms.

Q.11 What is the source organism for *Eco*RI, restriction endonuclease?

Ans. *Escherichia coli* strain RY 13 is the source organism for *Eco* RI.

Q.12 Name any genetically modified crop.

Ans. *Bt* cotton is a genetically modified plant. It has been modified to resist attack by insect and pests *e.g.*, cotton ball worm. These are developed by introducing a gene from *Bacillus thuringiensis* which produces toxin in plants that is lethal to insects.

Q.13 Why are blue-green algae not popular as biofertilisers?

Ans. Blue-green algae add organic matter to the soil and increase its fertility still these are not popular as biofertilisers. This is due to several constraints that limit the application or implementation of the biofertiliser technology. It posses copious mucilage which makes fields slippery. This gives rise to algal bloom. Few other constraints are environmental, technological, infrastructural, financial, unawareness, quality, marketing etc.

Q.14 Which species of *Penicillium* produces Roquefort cheese?

Ans. Roquefort cheese is formed by ripening of cheese with the fungi *Penicillium roqueforti* for a particular flavour.

Q.15 Name the states involved in Ganga Action Plan.

Ans. Ganga runs from Gangotri in the Himalayas to Ganga Sagar in the Bay of Bengal. The Ganga Action Plan (GAP) was a program launched in April 1986 in order to reduce the pollution load on the River Ganga.

The states involved in Ganga Action Plan are— Uttarakhand, UP, Bihar, West Bengal and Jharkhand.

Q.16 Name any two industrially important enzymes.

Ans. Two industrially important enzymes are as follows

(i) Lipases are used in detergent formulations and are helpful in removing oily stains from the laundry.

(ii) Pectinases and proteases are used as clarifying agents in making commercial fruit and vegetable juices.

Q.17 Name an immuno-supressive agent?

Ans. Cyclosporin-A, produced by the fungus *Trichoderma polysporum* is used as an immuno-supressive agent in organ transplant patients.

Q.18 Given an example of a rod-shaped virus.

Ans. Tobacco mosaic virus is a rod-shaped virus. This was the first plant virus to be discovered.

Q.19 What is the group of bacteria found in both the rumen of cattle and sludge of sewage treatment?

Ans. Methanogens (*e.g., Methanobacterium*), are the group of bacteria that found in both the rumen of cattle and sludge of sewage treatment. They, anaerobically break down cellulosic material to produce carbon dioxide and hydrogen, which are part of biogas.

Q.20 Name a microbe used for the production of swiss cheese.

Ans. Swiss cheese is formed by the bacterium *Propionibacterium shermanii*. Its characteristic feature is formation of large holes due to production of large amount of Carbon di oxide.

Short Answer Type Questions

Q.1 Why are flocs important in biological treatment of waste water?

Ans. Flocs are masses of bacteria associated with fungal filaments that form mesh - like structures. These are important in biological treatment of waste water, as they help in digestion of organic matter, removing pathogens and release nutrients in the sewage effluent. Flocs helps in reducing the BOD of the effluent as well.

It can be used as inoculum and taken to anaerobic digester for generation of biogas. The resulting sludge can be used as manure and in landfills.

Q.2 How has the bacterium *Bacillus thuringiensis* helped us in controlling caterpillars of insect pests?

Ans. *Bacillus thuringiensis* produces an endotoxin which, when ingested and released in the gut of the insect pest especially bollowrms and corn borers.

Q.3 How do mycorrhizal fungi help the plants harbouring them?

Ans. The mycorrhizal fungi absorb phosphorus from the soil and transfer them to the host cells. They also impart resistance to host plants against root pathogens. They show tolerance to salinity and drought as well as increases overall growth and development of plant. Hence, fungal hyphae help in synthesising organic food and in turn receive or get shelter and nourishment from the host plant.

Q.4 Why are cyanobacteria considered useful in paddy fields?

Ans. Cyanobacteria like *Anabaena, Nostoc, Oscillatoria* serve as an important biofertiliser in paddy fields as they fix atmospheric nitrogen and add organic matter to the soil and increase its fertility.

Q.5 How was penicillin discovered?

Ans. Penicillin was the first antibiotic to be discovered and it was a chance discovery. Sir, Alexander Fleming observed that in unwashed culture plates of *Staphylococcus,* a mould Penicillium was growing. This mould inhibited the growth of *Staphylococcus*. Later the antibiotic was isolated from this fungus and named penicillin after the mould *Penicillium notatum.*

Q.6 Name the scientists who were credited for showing the role of penicillin as an antibiotic?

Ans. Penicillin was discovered by Sir Alexander Fleming while, working on *Staphylococcius* bacteria. However, its therapeutic value as an effective antibiotic was established much later by Ernst Chain and Howard Florey. This antibiotic was extensively used to treat American soldiers wounded in World War II. Fleming, Chain and Florey were awarded with Nobel Prize in 1945, for this discovery.

Q.7 How do bioactive molecules of fungal origin help in restoring good health of humans?

Ans. Some bioactive molecules of fungal origin have been reported for their role in restoring good health of humans. For example :

Cyclosporin-A, which is used as an immuno-suppressive agent in organ transplant patients is produced by the fungus *Trichoderma polysporum.*

Statins, produced by yeast *Monascus purpureus* have been commercialised as blood cholesterol lowering agents.

Q.8 What roles do enzymes play in detergents that we use for washing clothes? Are these enzymes produced from some unique microorganisms?

Ans. Enzymes like lipases are used in detergent formulations, which cause breakdown of oils and thus help in removing oily and greasy stains from the clothes in laundry. These are obtained from *Candida lipolytica* and *Geotrichum candidum.*

Another enzyme Amylase is used for removing starch based stains. It is produced from *Aspergillus oryzae.*

Q.9 What is the chemical nature of biogas. Name an organism which is involved in biogas production?

Ans. The chemical nature of biogas is carbon dioxide, water, methane and a trace amount of hydrogen sulphide. *Methanobacterium*, a type of methanogen is employed for biogas production.

Q.10 How do microbes reduces the environmental degradation causes by chemicals?

Ans. The process of reducing environmental degradation caused by chemicals with the help of microbes is called **bioremediation.**

Chemicals from fertilisers and pesticides are highly toxic to human beings and animals alike, and have been polluting environment. To reduce the environmental degradation caused by chemicals, microbes can be used both as fertilisers and pesticides and can be called biofertilisers and biopesticides, respectively.

Microbes are used as biofertilisers to enrich the soil nutrients, *e.g., Rhizobium, Azotobacter, Azospirillum,* etc., which can fix atmospheric nitrogen in the soil. *Bacillus thuringiensis* bacteria act as biopesticides to control the growth of insect pests.

Q.11 What is a broad spectrum antibiotic? Name one such antibiotic.

Ans. A broad spectrum antibiotic is one which can inhibit the growth of a wide range of bacteria like both Gram positive and Gram negative bacteria.

Examples are tetracyclines, phenicols, neomycin, fluoroquinolones, third-generation and fourth-generation antibiotics cephalosporins.

Q.12 What are viruses parasitising bacteria called? Draw a well labelled diagram of the same.

Thinking Process The word **phage** means 'to eat'.

Ans. Viruses parasitising bacteria are called **bacteriophages.** These viruses do not actually eat bacteria but they infect and replicate within the bacteria.

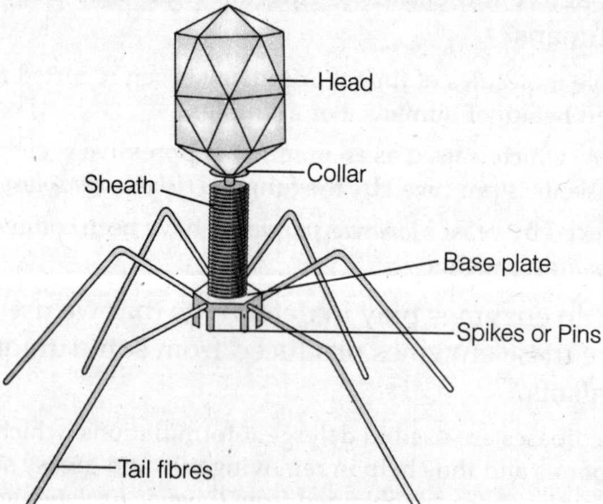

Bacteriophage

Q.13 Which bacterium has been used as a clot buster? What is its mode of action?

Ans. The bacterium *Streptococcus* that produces streptokinase is used as a 'clot buster'.

This enzyme has a **fibrinolytic** action that breaks down the clots formed in the blood vessels of patients who have undergone myocardial infarction. This prevents heart attack in these patients that can otherwise occur because of occlusion by the clots.

Q.14 What are biofertilisers? Give two examples.

Ans. Biofertilisers are organisms that enrich the nutrient quality of the soil. The main source of biofertilisers are bacteria, fungi and cyanobacteria.

e.g., Few examples are given below

(i) *Azospirillum, Rhizobium* and *Azotobacter* can fix atmospheric nitrogen in the soil.

(ii) Blue-green algae like *Anabaena, Nostoc, Oscillatoria* add organic matter to the soil and responsible for increasing its fertility.

Long Answer Type Questions

Q.1 Why is aerobic degradation more important than anaerobic degradation for the treatment of large volumes of wastewaters rich in organic matter. Discuss.

Ans. Aerobic degradation is more important than anaerobic degradation because naturally occurring aerobic and facultative microbes (bacteria, fungi, protozoa and others) in the waste water can rapidly oxidise the soluble organic and nitrogenous compounds.

Flocs and flocules settle down and clear supernatant water is obtained.

Mechanical addition of oxygen makes the process faster and most of the pathogenic content of the effluent is removed.

During aerobic degradation, BOD (Biological oxygen Demand) is lowered, and water becomes more favourable for aquatic species.

Q.2 (a) Discuss about the major programs that the Ministry of Environment and Forests, Government of India, has initiated for saving major Indian rivers from pollution.

(b) Ganga has recently been declared the national river. Discuss, the implication with respect to pollution of this river.

Ans. (a) Most of the sewage water of urban as well as rural areas was discharged directly into rivers, resulting in their pollution. Importance of microbial treatment of sewage was then realised and more sewage treatment plants were established.

Still, they are not sufficient due to increasing urbanisation and production of much larger quantities of sewage as compared to earlier days. Realising the importance of microbes in pollution control, the Ministry of Environment and Forests has initiated the development of sewage treatment plants under the National River Conservation Authority.

For example, **Ganga Action Plan** (GAP) and **Yamuna Action Plan** (YAP) to save these major rivers of our country from pollution.

(b) The declaration of the Ganga as the National River highlights its cultural and ecological importance while drawing urgent attention to its pollution problems.

The key implications with respect to pollution of Ganga include

- Greater government focus with stricter pollution control and better waste management.
- Launch of conservation projects like NGRBA and Namami Gange.
- Stricter enforcement of pollution laws for industries.
- Public awareness to reduce harmful rituals and promote cleanliness.
- Sustainable development through eco-friendly tourism and reduced plastic use.

Q.3 Draw a diagrammatic sketch of biogas plant and label its various components given below gas holder, sludge chamber, digester, dung, water chamber.

Ans. The raw material for biogas production is excreta (dung) of cattle. The biogas plant has a concrete tank (10-15 feet deep) in which bio-wastes and slurry of dung is collected.

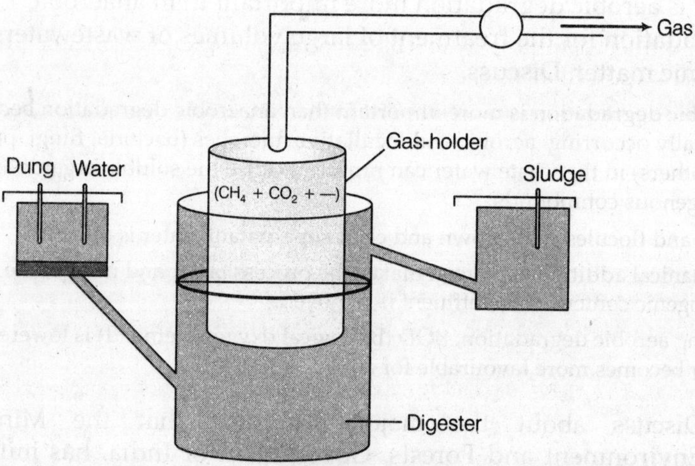

A typical biogas plant

The tank has a floating cover which rises on production of gas in the tank. *Methanobacterium* in the dung acts on the bio-wastes to produce biogas. The gas produced is supplied to nearby houses by an outlet. Through another outlet, the spent slurry is removed to be used as fertiliser. Biogas is also used as fuel for cooking and lighting.

Q.4 Describe the main ideas behind the biological control of pests and diseases.

Ans. It's a natural and eco-friendly concept. It employs the use of organisms to control the population of pathogens and pests in an ecosystem.

It does not eliminate harmful organisms but keeps its population in limit that it can not harm agricultural practices. Classical examples are *Trichoderma* which is antagonist, *i.e.*, against many soil-borne plant pathogens.

Similarly, *Penicillium* inhibits the growth of *Staphylococcus* and therefore has been successfully used in the production of penicillin antibiotic to control many human bacterial pathogens. *Bacillus thuringiensis* acts as biopesticide to control insect.

Baculovirus used as biological control agents in genus Nucleo polyhedrovirus are excellent for species-specific, narrow spectrum insecticidal application. Use of Ladybird Beetle for biocontrol of aphids and Dragonfly are used for mosquitoes. The overall biological control of pest is considered much more beneficial in an ecological sensitive area.

Q.5 (a) What would happen if a large volume of untreated sewage is discharged into a river?

(b) In what way anaerobic sludge digestion is important in sewage treatments?

Ans. (a) If untreated sewage is discharged directly into rivers it will lead to serious pollution of the waters with organic matter and pathogenic bacteria, protozoa and many other disease causing agents. There will be eutrophication. BOD will increase resulting in depletion of oxygen. This water, if used, will cause outbreaks of water-borne diseases.

(b) In anaerobic sludge digestion, anaerobic bacteria, digest the aerobic bacteria and the fungi in the sludge and the remaining organic matter. This reduces the BOD (Biological Oxygen Demand)

During this digestion, bacteria produce a mixture of gases such as methane, hydrogen sulphide and carbon dioxide. These gases (biogas) can be used as source of energy as it is inflammable. The remaining sludge can be used in the formation of manure.

Q.6 Which type of food would have lactic acid bacteria? Discuss their useful application.

Ans. The most common food item are curd and yoghurt which contain Lactic Acid Bacteria (LAB) of *Lactobacillus* species. Curd is formed by adding a small amount of curd to milk, which acts as a starter. Microbes present in starter multiply at suitable temperature and convert milk into curd.

Acids released by LAB during the growth coagulate and partially digest milk proteins. This increases the digestion of milk protein.

Application of LAB

(i) Improves nutritional quality of milk by increasing vitamin-B_{12} content.

(ii) Checks disease-causing microbes in stomach.

(iii) LAB (Lactic acid bacteria) are used for making probiotics which promote gut health.

Chapter 11

Biotechnology : Principles and Processes

Multiple Choice Questions (MCQs)

Q.1 Rising of dough is due to

(a) multiplication of yeast

(b) production of CO_2

(c) emulsification

(d) hydrolysis of wheat flour starch into sugars

Thinking Process Dough is formed by fermentation by bacteria.

Ans. ***(b)*** The rising of dough is due to production of carbon dioxide (CO_2). The Inoculation of kneaded flour with baker's yeast; *Saccharomyces cerevisiae* produce CO_2 during the process of fermentation, causes puffing up of the dough and make it soft and spongy. It is used to make foods like idli, dosa, bread, etc.

Q.2 Which of the following enzyme catalyse the removal of nucleotides from the ends of DNA?

(a) endonuclease (b) exonuclease (c) DNA ligase (d) *Hind* II

Ans. ***(b)*** Exonucleases catalyse the removal of nucleotides from the ends of DNA. Whereas endonucleases make cuts at specific positions within the DNA. DNA ligase is a sealing enzymes (also called as genetic gum), which is responsible for joining of two individual fragments of DNA and *Hind* II is a restriction endonuclease.

Q.3 The transfer of genetic material from one bacterium to another through the mediation of a vector like virus is termed as

(a) transduction (b) conjugation (c) transformation (d) translation

Ans. ***(a)*** **Transduction** is the process by which genetic material (DNA) is transferred from one bacterium to another through the mediation of a vector, like virus Whereas, **bacterial conjugation** is the transfer of genetic material (plasmid) between bacterial cells by direct cell-to-cell contact or by a bridge-like connection between two cells. Transformation is the genetic alteration of a cell resulting from the direct uptake and incorporation of exogenous genetic material (exogenous DNA) from its surroundings and taken up through the cell membranes. Translation is the process in which cellular ribosomes makes proteins. It is a part of the process of gene expression.

Q.4 Which of the given statement is correct in the context of observing DNA separated by agarose gel electrophoresis?

(a) DNA can be seen in visible light.
(b) DNA can be seen without staining in visible light.
(c) Ethidium bromide stained DNA can be seen in visible light.
(d) Ethidium bromide stained DNA can be seen under exposure to UV light.

Thinking Process Gel electrophoresis is a technique for separating DNA fragments based on their size.

Ans. *(d)* Statements (d) is correct as the separated DNA fragments (by the process of gel electrophoresis) are visualised after staining the DNA with ethidium bromide followed by exposure to UV-radiation. These fragments are seen as orange coloured bands.

Q.5 'Restriction' in restriction enzyme refers to

(a) cleaving of phosphodiester bond in DNA by the enzyme
(b) cutting of DNA at specific position only
(c) prevention of the multiplication of bacteriophage in bacteria
(d) All of the above

Ans. *(c)* The term 'restriction' in restriction enzyme refer to the ability of certain enzymes in bacterium to restrict the replication of bacteriophages by cutting their DNA.

These enzymes are present in bacteria to provide a type of defense mechanism called the 'restriction modification system'.

Q.6 Which of the following is not required in the preparation of a recombinant DNA molecules?

(a) Restriction endonucleases (b) DNA ligase
(c) DNA fragments (d) *E. coli*

Ans. *(d) E. coil* is not required in the preparation phase of recombinant DNA molecules. It may be required during the expression of recombinant DNA whereas restriction enzymes and DNA ligases are used to make a stable recombinant DNA molecule, with DNA fragments that has been spliced together from two different organisms.

Q.7 In agarose gel electrophoresis, DNA molecules are separated on the basis of their

(a) charge only (b) size only (c) charge to size ratio (d) All of these

Ans. *(b)* In agarose gel electrophoresis, the DNA fragments separate out (resolve) according to their size or length because of the sieving property of agarose gel. It means, the smaller the fragment size, the farther it will move.

Q.8 The most important feature in a plasmid to be used as a vector is

(a) Origin of replication (*Ori*)
(b) presence of a selectable marker
(c) presence of sites for restriction endonuclease
(d) its size

Ans. ***(a)*** All of the given features are important to facilitate cloning into a vector but out of them Origin of replication (*ori*) is the most important one.

This is due to the following reasons

(i) *Ori* is a DNA sequence that is responsible for initiating replication. Any piece of DNA when linked to this sequence can replicate within the host cells.

(ii) *Ori* also controls the copy numbers of the linked DNA. It is also essential for the replication of the inserted gene.

Q.9 While isolating DNA from bacteria, which of the following enzymes is not used?

(a) Lysozyme (b) Ribonuclease (c) Deoxyribonuclease (d) Protease

Ans. ***(c)*** While isolating DNA from bacteria, deoxyribonuclease is not used because it causes the lysis of DNA molecules. While, other enzymes like lysozyme is used for breaking down the bacterial cell wall, ribonuclease is used for digesting RNA and protease is used for protein digestion.

Q.10 Which of the following has popularised the PCR (Polymerase Chain Reaction)?

(a) Easy availability of DNA template

(b) Availability of synthetic primers

(c) Availability of cheap deoxyribonucleotides

(d) Availability of 'Thermostable' DNA polymerase

Ans. ***(d)*** The Polymerase Chain Reaction (PCR) is a reaction in which amplification of specific DNA sequences is carried out *in vitro*. Such repeated amplification is achieved by the use of a thermostable DNA polymerase (isolated from a bacterium, *Thermus aquaticus*), which remain active and stable during the high temperature and help in denaturation of double-standard DNA.

Q.11 An antibiotic resistance gene in a vector usually helps in the selection of

(a) competent cells (b) transformed cells (c) recombinant cells (d) None of these

Thinking Process The genes encoding resistance to antibiotics such as ampicillin, chloramphenicol, tetracycline or kanamycin, etc., are considered as useful selectable markers for *E. coli*.

Ans. ***(b)*** Antibiotic resistance gene are selectable markers that help in identifying and eliminating non-transformants and selectively permitting the growth of the transformants. It prevents non-transformants from growing because they die in the presence of antibiotic. The normal *E. coli* cells do not carry resistance against any of these antibiotics.

Note In process of transformation, a piece of DNA is introduced in a host bacterium.

Q.12 Significance of heat shock method in bacterial transformation is to facilitate.

(a) Binding of DNA to the cell wall

(b) Uptake of DNA through membrane transport proteins

(c) Uptake of DNA through transient pores in the bacterial cell wall

(d) Expression of antibiotic resistance gene

Thinking Process DNA being a hydrophilic molecule cannot pass through cell membranes. Therefore, the bacteria should be made competent to accept the DNA molecules by chemical and physical methods.

Ans. *(c)* Heat shock method is one of the method to make cells competent to take up DNA. This method facilitates the uptake of DNA by creating transient pores in bacterial cell wall.

Q.13 The role of DNA ligase in the construction of a recombinant DNA molecule is

(a) formation of phosphodiester bond between two DNA fragments
(b) formation of hydrogen bonds between sticky ends of DNA fragments
(c) ligation of all purine and pyrimidine bases
(d) None of the above

Ans. *(a)* DNA ligase (joining or sealing enzymes) are also called genetic gum. They join two individual fragments of double-stranded DNA by forming phosphodiester bonds between them. Thus, they help in sealing gaps in DNA fragments. Therefore, they act as a molecular glue.

Q. 14 Which of the following bacteria is not a source of restriction endonuclease?

(a) *Haemophilus influenzae* (b) *Escherichia coli*
(c) *Entamoeba coli* (d) *Bacilius amyloliquefaciens*

Ans. *(c)* *Entamoeba coli* is not a source of restriction endonucleas, present in the human gastrointestinal tract.

Q.15 Which of the following steps are catalysed by *Taq* polymerase in a PCR reaction?

(a) Denaturation of template DNA
(b) Annealing of primers to template DNA
(c) Extension of primer end on the template DNA
(d) All of the above

Ans. *(c)* In Polymerase Chain Reaction (PCR), polymerisation or extension step is catalysed by *Taq* polymerase enzyme. *PCR* is carried out in the following three steps

(i) **Denaturation** The double-stranded DNA is denatured by applying high temperature of 95°C for 15 seconds. Each separated single stranded DNA now acts as template for DNA synthesis.

(ii) **Annealing** Two sets of primers are added which anneal to the 3 end of each separated strand. Primers act as initiators of replication.

(iii) **Extension** DNA polymerase extends the primers by adding nucleotides complementary to the template provided in the reaction.

A thermostable DNA polymerase (*Taq* DNA polymerase) is used in the reaction which can tolerate the high temperature of the reaction.

All these steps are repeated multiple times to obtain several copies of desired DNA.

Q.16 **A bacterial cell was transformed with a recombinant DNA that was generated using a human gene. However, the transformed cells did not produce the desired protein. Reasons could be**

(a) human gene may have intron which bacteria cannot process
(b) amino acid codons for humans and bacteria are different
(c) human protein is formed but degraded by bacteria
(d) All of the above

Thinking Process Introns are parts of genes that do not directly code for proteins. There are commonly found in multicellular eukaryotes, such as humans and rare in bacteria.

Ans. *(a)* On transformation of bacterial cell with recombiant DNA it do not produced the desired protein because of presence of long non-coding introns in eukroyotic gene. As prokaryotes lacks intron splicing machinery it difficult to express eukaryotic genes in prokaryotes.

Q.17 **Which of the following should be choosen for best yield if one were to produce a recombinant protein in large amounts?**

(a) Laboratory flask of largest capacity
(b) A stirred-tank bioreactor without in-lets and out-lets
(c) A continuous culture system
(d) Any of the above

Ans. *(c)* For best yeild, continous culture is the preferred system. This is because the cells multiplied rapidly in a continuous culture system and high yields of the desired proteins were achieved. In this system the used medium is drained out from one side while fresh medium is added from the other to maintain the cells in their physiologically most active log or exponential phase. This type of culturing method produces a larger biomass leading to higher yields of desired protein.

Q.18 **Who among the following was awarded the Nobel Prize for the development of PCR technique?**

(a) Herbert Boyer
(b) Hargovind Khurana
(c) Kary Mullis
(d) Arthur Kornberg

Ans. *(c)* PCR (Polymerase Chain Reaction) technique was developed by **Kary Mullis** in 1985 and for this he received Nobel Prize for chemistry in 1993. While **HG Khurana** is known for cracking the genetic code.

While **Arthur kornberg** was awarded for his discovery of DNA polymerase and **Herbert Boyer** generated first recombinant DNA molecule.

Q.19 **Which of the following statement does not hold true for restriction enzyme?**

(a) It recognises a palindromic nucleotide sequence
(b) It is an endonuclease
(c) It is isolated from viruses
(d) It produces the same kind of sticky ends in different DNA molecules

Ans. ***(c)*** Statement (c) is not true and can be corrected as restriction enzymes are not isolated from viruses; they are obtained from bacteria as part of their defense mechanism against viruses.

Very Short Answer Type Questions

Q.1 How is copy number of the plasmid vector related to yield of recombinant protein?

Ans. The recombinant DNA can multiply as many times as the copy number of the vector plasmid thereby determining the yield of recombinant protein. So, higher the copy number of plasmid vector, higher the copy number of gene for coding and consequently, recombinant protein coded by the gene is produced in high amount.

Q.2 Would you choose an exonuclease, while producing a recombinant DNA molecule?

Ans. No, as exonuclease acts on the free ends of linear DNA molecule *i.e.*, it removes nucleotides only from the free ends.. Therefore, instead of producing DNA fragments with sticky ends, it will shorten or completely degrade the DNA fragment containing the gene of interest and the circular plasmid (vector) will not get cut as it lacks free ends.

Q.3 What does *H* in '*d*' and III refer to the enzyme *Hind* III?

Ans. (i) The first letter '*H*' indicates the genus of the organism from which the enzyme was isolated, *H* = Genus = *Haemophilus*.

(ii) 'in' refers to influenza.

(iii) The fourth letter d indicates the particular strain used to produce the enzyme, *d* = strain Rd.

(iv) The Roman numerals denoted the sequence in which the restriction endonuclease enzyme from that particular genus, species and strain of bacteria have been isolated-III, *i.e.*, third restriction endonuclease to be isolated from this species.

Q.4 Restriction enzymes should not have more than one site of action in the cloning site of a vector. Comment.

Ans. Yes, restriction enzymes should not have more than one site of action. If the restriction enzymes have more than one recognition site in a vector, then the vector itself will get fragmented upon treatment with the restriction enzymes.

Q.5 What does 'competent' refer to in competent cells used in transformation experiments?

Ans. Competent cells are those bacterial cells that can take foreign DNA from its surroundings.

DNA being a hydrophilic molecule it can not pass through cell membranes easily. Therefore, the bacteria should be made competent by treatment with chemicals like $CaCl_2$ which make them capable of taking up foreign DNA.

Q.6 What is the significance of adding proteases at the time of isolation of genetic material (DNA)?

Ans. Proteases degrade the proteins present inside a cell (from which DNA is being isolated). Since, proteins forms wrapping units for DNA. If the proteins are not removed from DNA preparation then they could interfere with downstream treatment of DNA.

Q.7 While doing a PCR, 'denaturation' step is missed. What will be its effect on the process?

Ans. If denaturation of double-stranded DNA does not take place then two DNA strands will not open and primers will not be able to anneal (joining) to the template. Hence, no extension will take place and as a result there will be no amplification.

Q.8 Name a recombinant vaccine that is currently being used in vaccination program.

Ans. Hepatitis-B recombinant vaccine is used for vaccination against the hepatitis-B virus.

Q.9 Do biomolecules (DNA and protein) exhibit biological activity in anhydrous conditions?

Thinking Process Water is critical not only for the correct folding of proteins but also for the maintenance of the structure of DNA and protein.

Ans. Biomolecules (DNA and protein) do not exhibit change in biological activity in anhydrous conditions, in non-aqueous condition the rigidity of protein and DNA increases due to the weakening of hydrogen bond strength.
It results into the change in overall free energy, which is responsible for the denaturation of biomolecules.

Q.10 What modification is done on the Ti-plasmid of *Agrobacterium tumefaciens* to convert it into a cloning vector?

Thinking Process T-DNA is the only essential part required to make Ti-plasmid a cloning vector.

Ans. The Ti-plasmid is disarmed by deleting the tumour inducing genes in the plasmid. So, it become an effective cloning vector. The modified tumour inducing (Ti) plasmid of *Agrobacterium tumefaciens* will no longer remain pathogenic to the plants but still deliver genes of interest into a variety of plants.

Short Answer Type Questions

Q.1 What is meant by gene cloning?

Ans. Gene cloning refers to a process of formation of multiple copies of a particular gene in which a gene of interest is ligated to a vector. The recombinant DNA thus produced is introduced in a host cell by transformation.

Each cell gets one DNA molecule and when the transformed cell grows to a bacterial colony, each cell in the colony has a copy of the gene. This is gene cloning.

Q.2 Both a wine maker and a molecular biologist who had developed a recombinant vaccine claim to be biotechnologists. Who in your opinion is correct?

Ans. In my opinion both of them are correct. As biotechnology is a very wide area which deals with techniques of using a 'natural' organism (or its parts) as well as genetically modified organism to produce products and processes useful for mankind.

A wine maker employs a strain of yeast to produce wine by fermentation (a natural phenomenon), while the molecular biologist has cloned gene for the antigen (that is used as vaccine) in an organism which allows the production of the antibodies in large amount.

Q.3 A recombinant DNA molecule was created by ligating a gene to a plasmid vector. By mistake, an exonuclease was added to the tube containing the recombinant DNA. How does this affect the next step in the experiment, *i.e.*, bacterial transformation?

Thinking Process Bacterial transformation is the process by which bacterial cells take up naked DNA molecules (exogenous or foreign DNA).

Ans. The experiment will not likely to be affected as recombinant DNA molecule is circular and closed, with no free ends. Hence, it will not be a substrate for exonuclease enzyme which removes nucleotides from the free ends of DNA.

Q.4 Restriction enzymes that are used in the construction of recombinant DNA are endonucleases which cut the DNA at 'specific'-recognition sequence? What would be the disadvantage if they do not cut the DNA at specific-recognition sequence?

Ans. If the restriction enzymes would cut DNA at random sites instead of at specific sites, then the DNA fragments obtained will not have 'sticky ends'. In the absence of sticky ends, construction of recombinant DNA molecule would not be possible.

Q.5 A plasmid DNA and a linear DNA (both are of the same size) have one site for a restriction endonuclease. When cut and separated on agarose gel electrophoresis, plasmid shows one DNA band, while linear DNA shows two fragments. Explain.

Ans. When a plasmid DNA and a linear DNA having one site for a restriction endonuclease are cut and separated, plasmid shows one DNA band, while linear DNA shows two band because of difference in their basic structure. Plasmid is a circular DNA molecule and when cut with these enzyme, it becomes linear but does not get fragmented due to presence of only one restriction site, whereas a linear DNA molecule gets cut into two fragment hence shows two bands on the gel.

Q.6 How does one visualise DNA on an agarose gel?

Ans. Visualisation of DNA fragments on agarose get can be done with **fluorescent compounds**. A compound called ethidium bromide **stains** DNA, which on exposure with ultra-violet (UV) radiation gives orange light band of DNA. Hence, DNA fragments appear as orange band in the presence of ethidium bromide and UV light.

Q.7 A plasmid without a selectable marker was choosen as vector for cloning a gene. How does this affect the experiment?

Ans. In a gene cloning experiment, first a recombinant DNA molecule is constructed, where the gene of interest is ligated to the vector (the step would not be affected) and introduced inside the host cell (transformation). Since, not all the cells get transformed with the recombinant or plasmid DNA, in the absence of selectable marker, it will be difficult to distinguish between transformants and non-transformant, because role of selectable marker is the selection of transformants.

Q.8 A mixture of fragmented DNA was electrophoresed in an agarose gel. After staining the gel with ethidium bromide, no DNA bands were observed. What could be the reason?

Ans. The reasons for no observations are as follows

(i) DNA sample that was loaded on the gel may have got contaminated with nuclease (exo or endo both) which completely degraded the DNA.

(ii) Electrodes were put in opposite orientation in the gel assembly *i.e.,* anode towards the wells where DNA sample is loaded). Since, DNA molecules are negatively charged, they move towards anode and hence, move out of the gel instead of moving into the matrix of gel.

(iii) Ethidium bromide was not added at all or was not added in sufficient concentration and so DNA was not visible.

Q.9 Describe the role of $CaCl_2$ in the preparation of competent cells?

Ans. $CaCl_2$ is known to increase the efficiency of DNA uptake to produce transformed bacterial cells. The divalent Ca^{+2} ions create **transient pores** on the bacterial cell wall by which the entry of foreign DNA is facilitated into the competent bacterial cells.

Q.10 What would happen when one grows a recombinant bacterium in the bioreactor but forget to add antibiotic to the medium in which the recombinant is growing?

Ans. In the absence of antibiotic, there will be no pressure on recombinants to retain the plasmid (containing the gene of our interest). Since, maintaining a high copy number of plasmids is a metabolic burden to the microbial cells, it will tend to loose the plasmid. Therefore, in absence of antibiotic the desired bacterium may not be able to grow to its optimum level.

Q.11 Identify and explain *A*, *B* and C in the PCR diagram given below.

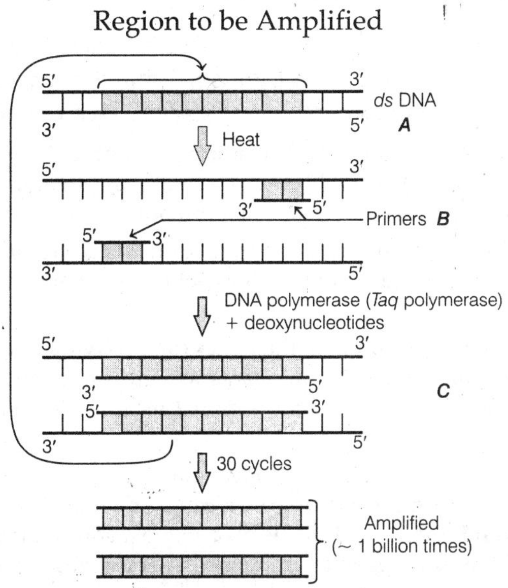

Ans. In the given figure

A - Denaturation B - Annealing and C - Extension

In PCR, each cycle has three steps

(i) **Denaturation of DNA Sample** Unwinding of two strand of DNA by heating the sample at 92-94°C.

(ii) **Primer Annealing** Primers get positioned on the exposed nucleotides as per base pairing rules.

(iii) **Extension of Primers** DNA polymerase recognises primers as 'start' tags and begins to extend the primers using the free nucleotides provided in the reaction and the genomic DNA as template. With each round of reactions, the DNA doubles.

Q.12 Name the regions marked *A*, *B* and *C*.

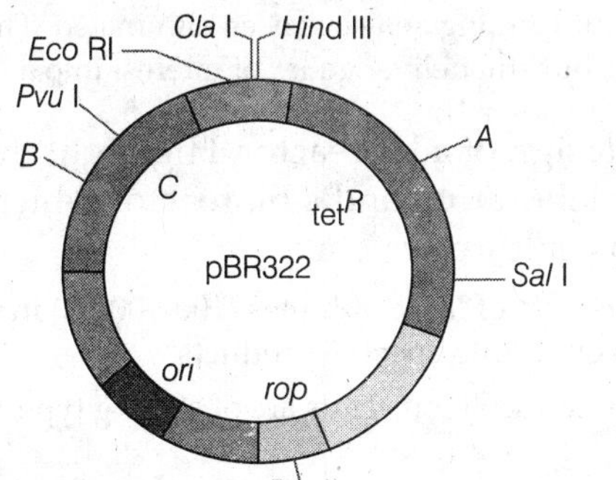

Ans. The regions are as follows

Region A-*Bam* HI **Region** *B*-*Pst* I **Region** C-amp^R.

Long Answer Type Questions

Q.1 For selection of recombinants, insertional inactivation of antibiotic marker has been superceded by insertional inactivation of a marker gene coding for a chromogenic substrate. Give reasons.

Ans. In selection of recombinants, the transformed cells are first plated on the antibiotic plate which has not been insertionally inactivated (*e.g.*, ampicillin) and incubated overnight for growth of transformants.

For selection of recombinants, these transformants are replica-plated on to second antibiotic plate (*e.g.*, tetracycline) which got inactivated due to insertion of gene.

Non-recombinants grow on both the plates (one carrying ampicillin and the other carrying tetracycline) while recombinants will grow only on ampicillin plate.This entire exercise is labourious and takes more time (two overnight incubation) as well.

However, the insertional inactivation of a marker that produces colour in the presence of a chromogenic compound, it can distinguish between the recombinants and non-recombinants on a single medium plate (containing one antibiotic and the chromogenic compound) after overnight growth.

Q.2 Describe the role of *Agrobacterium tumefaciens* in transforming a plant cell.

Ans. A soil-inhabiting, plant pathogenic bacterium, *Agrobacterium tumefaciens,* infects broad-leaved crops including tomato, soyabean, sunflower and cotton but not the cereals. It causes tumours called crown galls.

Tumour formation is induced by its plasmid, which is therefore called **Ti-plasmid** (Ti for tumour inducing). The Ti-plasmid integrates a segment of its DNA, termed T-DNA, into the chromosomal DNA of its host plant cells. The T-DNA causes tumours. As gene transfer occurs without human effort, the bacterium is known as **natural genetic engineer** of plants.

Plant molecular biologists have started using Ti-plasmids as vectors to transfer foreign genes of interest into the target plant cells. They use a version of the plasmid from which tumour forming gene has been eliminated. The transformed bacteria do not cause disease, but still deliver genes of interest into a variety of plants.

Q.3 Illustrate the design of a bioreactor. Highlight the difference between a flask in your laboratory and a bioreactor which allows cells to grow in a continuous culture system.

Ans. Bioreactors are vessels of large volumes (100-1000 L) in which raw materials are biologically converted into specific products.

The most commonly used bioreactors are of stirring type, which are shown in figure.

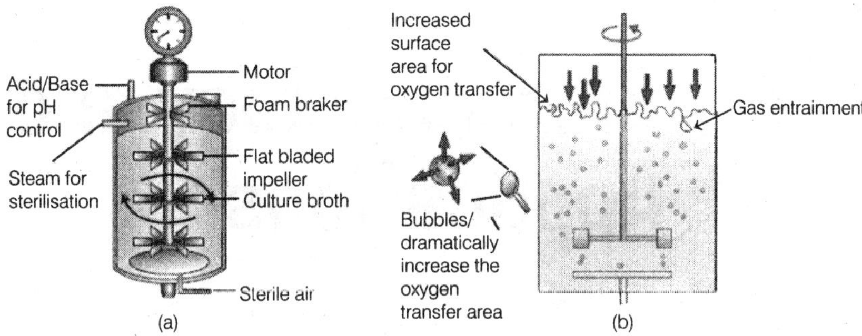

(a) Simple stirred-tank bioreactor
(b) Sparged stirred-tank bioreactor through which sterile air bubbles are sparged

A stirred-tank reactor is usually cylindrical or with a curved base to facilitate the mixing of the reactor contents. The stirrer facilitates even mixing and oxygen availability throughout the bioreactor. Alternatively air can be bubbled through the reactor.

The bioreactor has an agitator system, an oxygen delivery system and a foam control system, a temperature control system, pH control system and sampling ports so, that small volumes of the culture can be withdrawn periodically.

Small volume cultures are usually employed in laboratories in a flask for research and production of less quantities of products. However, large scale production of the products is carried out in bioreactors.

Flask	Bioreactor
1. It provides a batch type culture.	1. It provides continuous culture.
2. No gadget can be connected.	2. Gadgets are connected for optimum functioning.
3. It is a laboratory scale testing of a process.	3. It is a scaled up commercial process.

Chapter 12 Biotechnology and Its Applications

Multiple Choice Questions (MCQs)

Q.1 *Bt* cotton is not

(a) a GM plant
(b) insect resistant
(c) a bacterial gene expressing system
(d) resistant to all pesticides

Ans. ***(d)*** *Bt* cotton is not resistant to all pesticides. It is a genetically modified plant whose genes have been altered to make it insect resistant through the introduction of *Bt* toxin gene.

It produces proteins that kills certain insects like lepidopterans (tobacco budworm, armyworm), coleopterans (beetles) and dipterans (flies, mosquitoes).

Q.2 C-peptide of human insulin is

(a) a part of mature insulin molecule
(b) responsible for the formation of disulphide bridges
(c) removed during maturation of pro-insulin to insulin
(d) responsible for its biological activity

Thinking Process Mature functional insulin is obtained by the processing of pro-hormone, which contains extra peptide called C-peptide.

Ans. ***(c)*** C-peptide is a short connecting protein which connects the A and B chain of proinsulin molecule. After the processing of proinsulin molecule, C-peptide is removed leaving behind A and B chains which are bound together by disulphide bonds to constitute a insulin molecule.

Q.3 GEAC stands for

(a) Genome Engineering Action Committee
(b) Ground Environment Action Committee
(c) Genetic Engineering Approval Committee
(d) Genetic and Environment Approval Committee

Ans. ***(c)*** GEAC stands for Genetic Engineering Approval Committee. The Indian government has set up this organisation to make decisions regarding the validity of GM research and the safety of introducing GM organisms for public services.

Q.4 α-1 antitrypsin is

(a) an antacid
(b) an enzyme
(c) used to treat arthritis
(d) used to treat emphysema

Ans. ***(d)*** α-antitrypsin is a protease inhibitor that is produced by the introduction of specific sequence of DNA (or genes) which codes for a particular product in the transgenic animals. It is used to treat emphysema as it inhibits the enzymes of inflammatory cells that contributes to the respiratory complications.

Q.5 A probe which is a molecule used to locate homologus sequences in a mixture of DNA or RNA molecules could be

(a) a single stranded RNA
(b) a single stranded DNA
(c) either RNA or DNA
(d) can be *ss*DNA but not *ss*RNA

Ans. ***(c)*** A probe is a single stranded DNA or RNA molecule tagged with a radioactive or fluorescent molecule. It is used to detect the complementary sequences by hybridisation techniques.

Q.6 Choose the correct option regarding retrovirus.

(a) a RNA virus that synthesises DNA during infection
(b) a DNA virus that synthesises RNA during infection
(c) a *ss*DNA virus
(d) a *ds*RNA virus

Thinking Process HIV is the most common example of retrovirus.

Ans. ***(a)*** A retrovirus is a single-stranded RNA virus that stores its nucleic acid in the form of *m*RNA genome (5′cap and 3′poly A tail).

In most viruses, DNA is transcribed into RNA, and then RNA is translated into protein. However, in retroviruses their RNA is reverse-transcribed into complementary DNA, which is integrated into the host cell's genome (where it becomes a provirus) and then undergoes the transcription and translational process to express the genes carried by the virus,

i.e., RNA → *c*DNA → RNA → Polypeptide.

Q.7 The site of production of ADA in the body is

(a) erythrocytes
(b) lymphocytes
(c) blood plasma
(d) osteocytes

Ans. ***(b)*** ADA gene is responsible for producing the enzyme adenosine deaminase. It is primarily involved in the development and maintenance of immune system.

It is produced in lymphocytes, which develop in lymphoid tissues.

Q.8 A protoxin is

(a) a primitive toxin
(b) a denatured toxin
(c) toxin produced by Protozoa
(d) inactive toxin

Ans. ***(d)*** A protoxin is an inactive toxin. The word 'pro' in protoxin signifies 'inactive form'

For example *Bt* toxins are initially inactive protoxins but once ingested by insect, the inactive toxin, gets converted into an active form due to the alkaline pH of insect gut, which solubilises the crystals.

Q.9 Pathophysiology is the

(a) study of physiology of pathogen (b) study of normal physiology of host
(c) study of altered physiology of host (d) None of these

Thinking Process Causes and Effects of diseases (Pathology) + Study of body function (Physiology) = Pathophysiology

Ans. *(c)* Pathophysiology is the study of functional changes in the body of the host that occurs in response to any disease or injury. For examples, if someone ingests a toxin, it may result into a variety of physical changes, such as inflammation in the stomach lining.

Q.10 The trigger for activation of toxin of *Bacillus thuringiensis* is

(a) acidic pH of stomach
(b) high temperature
(c) alkaline pH of gut
(d) mechanical action in the insect gut

Ans. *(c)* *Bt* toxins are initially inactive protoxins. After ingestion by the insect these inactive toxins become active due to the alkaline pH of the gut which solublise the crystals. Hence, high pH value is required to make *Bt* toxins active. Under high temperature and acidic pH, *Bt* toxins remain insoluble and inactive.

Q.11 Golden rice is

(a) a variety of rice grown along the yellow river in China
(b) long stored rice having yellow colour tint
(c) a transgenic rice having gene for β - carotene
(d) wild variety of rice with yellow coloured grains

Ans. *(c)* Golden rice is a genetically modified crop with enhanced nutritional value. It is rich in vitamin-A (β-carotene). Golden rice prevents childhood blindness which is caused due to the deficiency of vitamin-A.

Q.12 In RNA*i*, genes are silenced using

(a) *ss* DNA (b) *ds* DNA (c) *ds* RNA (d) *ss* RNA

Thinking Process RNA interference (RNAi) process is used to produce pest resistant plants.

Ans. *(c)* In RNA*i*, genes are silenced using *ds* RNA. For instance, a nematode *Meloidogyne incognitia* infects the roots of tobacco plants which reduces the production of tobacco. It can be prevented by using RNA interference process, which is achieved by silencing of specific *m*RNA due to a complementary *ds*RNA. *ds*RNA binds and prevents the translation of *m*RNA (silencing).

Q.13 The first clinical gene therapy was done for the treatment of

(a) AIDS
(b) Cancer
(c) Cystic fibrosis
(d) SCID (Severe Combined Immuno Deficiency resulting from the deficiency of ADA)

Ans. *(d)* The first clinical gene therapy was done for the treatment of SCID (Severe Combined Immuno Deficiency) resulting from the deficiency of ADA.

The SCID patient has a defective gene for the enzyme Adenosine Deaminase (ADA) due to which he or she lacks functional T-lymphocytes and therefore, fails to fight against the infecting pathogen.

Q.14 ADA is an enzyme which is deficient in a genetic disorder SCID. What is the full form of ADA?

(a) Adenosine Deoxy Aminase
(b) Adenosine Deaminase
(c) Aspartate Deaminase
(d) Arginine Deaminase

Ans. *(b)* ADA is an enzyme which is deficient in a genetic disorder (Severe Combined Immuno Deficiency). ADA stands for adenosine deaminase. This enzyme is crucial for the immune system to function.

Q.15 Silencing of a gene could be achieved through the use of

(a) short interfering RNA (RNAi) only
(b) antisense RNA only
(c) Both RNA*i* and antisense RNA
(d) None of these

Thinking Process Gene silencing is a molecular process involved in the down regulation of specific genes and is used as a genetic defense system against viruses and other, organisms

Ans. *(c)* Gene silencing could be achieved through various routes including the use of RNA*i*, antisense RNA, ribozymes, etc. All these mechanisms interrupts or suppresses the expression of genes at transcriptional or translational level.

Very Short Answer Type Questions

Q.1 In view of the current food crisis, it is said, that we need another green revolution. Highlight the major limitations of the earlier green revolution.

Ans. Major limitations of the earlier green revolution are as follows (any two)

(i) Generally undesired characters also breed along with desired ones.
(ii) Regular use of fertilisers affected both soil fertility and quality.
(iii) Extensive use of pesticides, insecticides, and weedicides resulted in harmful effects on the natural components of the ecosystem.
(iv) Management practice which can improve food availability.

Therefore, another green revolution that can curb these problems and enhance the quality food production in limited land resources is certainly required.

Q.2 Expand GMO. How is it different from a hybrid?

Ans. GMO stands for Genetically Modified Organism. It contains one or more genes from an entirely different species and is genetically altered during molecular techniques such as gene cloning, protein engineering etc. It does not require crossing between organisms and completely new trait introduction.

On the other hand, hybrids contains the recombinant genome of different alleles present in the population of the same species, It is formed by crossing two different organisms. In this only the existing traits are improved.

Q.3 Differentiate between diagnostics and therapeutics. Give one example and for each category.

Ans.
- A diagnostic technique helps us to identify a disease. *e.g.*, ELISA for HIV. Therapeutics on the other hand helps in the treatment of a disease. *e.g.*, antibiotics for bacterial infections.
- Diagnosis is based on signs symptoms and history of tests while therapeutics is based on effectiveness of therapy for curing a disease.

Q.4 Give the full form of ELISA. Which disease can be detected using it? Discuss the principle underlying the test.

Ans. **ELISA** stands for Enzyme Linked Immunosorbent Assay. It is used for the detection of (HIV) AIDS disease.

ELISA is based on the principle of antigen-antibody interaction. Infection by pathogen can be detected by the presence of antigens (proteins, glycoproteins, etc.) or by detecting the antibodies synthesised by the host against the pathogen.

Q.5 Can a disease be detected before its symptoms appear? Explain the principle involved.

Ans. Detection of a disease before the appearance of symptoms is possible by the amplification of patients nucleic acid by PCR (*i.e.*, polymerase chain reaction).

The principle involved in PCR is that a single DNA molecule can be copied endlessly in a test tube using primers, DNA polymerase enzyme and free nucleotides. The desired DNA of the pathogen is amplified by PCR from a limited amount of DNA template.

Q.6 Write a short note on biopiracy highlighting the exploitation of developing countries by the developed countries.

Ans. **Biopiracy** is the term used to refer the use of bio-resources by the multinational companies and other organisations without proper authorisation and compensation from the countries and the people concerned.

Most of the developed nations are financially rich but poor in biodiversity and traditional knowledge. In contrast, the developing and the underdeveloped countries is rich in biodiversity and traditional knowledge related to bio-resources.

Therefore, sometimes industrialised nations tend to exploit the resources or biodiversity of developing nations, for their own advantages.

Q.7 Many proteins are secreted in their inactive form. This is also true to many toxic proteins produced by micro organisms. Explain how the mechanism is useful for the organism producing the toxin?

Ans. Many proteins including certain toxins are secreted in their inactive form. They get activated only when exposed to a specific trigger like pH, temperature etc. This mechanism is advantageous to the organism (*e.g.*, bacteria) producing the toxins, as the bacteria does not get killed by the action of proteins present in the toxin while they are in their inactive form.

Q.8 While creating genetically modified organisms, genetic barriers are not respected. How can this be dangerous in the long run?

Ans. Genetic modification of organisms can have unpredictable results when such organisms are introduced into the ecosystem. This is because the real effects of gene manipulation are visible only when such organisms interact with other components and organisms of the ecosystem.

Transgenes can be transferred from one plant to another and ruin the genetic setup giving rise to super weeds and super insecticides.

Q.9 Why has the Indian parliament cleared the second amendment of the country's patents bill?

Ans. The Indian parliament cleared the amendment to the patent bill as it empowered India to prevent unauthorised exploitation of our bio-resources and traditional knowledge by other countries. This bill also considers patent terms and initiated research development in this field.

Q.10 Give any two reasons why the patent on Basmati should not have gone to an American Company.

Ans. The patent on Basmati should not have gone to an American Company, because of the following reasons

(i) The Basmati rice variety has been grown in India since time immemorial. Traditionally, it belongs to India.

(ii) The new variety of Basmati that got patent rights to an American Company is actually derived from 'Indian farmers variety'.

Q.11 How was insulin obtained before the advent of *r*DNA technology? What were the problems encountered?

Ans. Before the rDNA technology, insulin was extracted from the pancreas of slaughtered cattle and pigs.

This insulin caused some patients to develop allergy and other types of reactions to the foreign protein.

It only gave small amount of insulin therefore making it a costly process.

Q.12 With respect to understanding diseases, discuss the importance of transgenic animal models.

Ans. Transgenic animals are important in the following fields (any two)

(i) They are being used in basic science research to elucidate the role of genes in the development of diseases like cancer, cystic fibrosis, rheumatoid arthritis and alzheimer's.

(ii) They are valuable tools in the drug development process itself.

(iii) They can produce medicines or human proteins (insulin, growth hormone, etc.) in large quantities.

(iv) Transgenics can be a source of transplant organs as well.

(v) The animals are also used to study various lines of treatment.

(vi) Vaccine safety is tested.

Q.13 Name the first transgenic cow. Which gene was introduced in this cow?

Ans. **Rosie** was the first transgenic cow. Gene for human **alpha lactalbumin** was introduced in her genes, which made the milk nutritionally more balanced than normal cow milk.

Q.14 PCR is a useful tool for early diagnosis of an infectious disease. Elaborate.

Ans. PCR is a very sensitive technique which enables the amplification of desired DNA from a limited amount of DNA template.

Hence, it can detect the presence of an infectious organism in the infected patient at an early stage of infection (even before the infectious organism has multiplied to large number).

Q.15 What is GEAC and what are its objectives?

Ans. GEAC (Genetic Engineering Approval Committee) is an Indian Government Organisation.

Its objectives include

(i) Examine the validity of Genetic Modification (GM) research on organism.

(ii) Inspect the safety of introducing GMO for public services.

Q.16 For which variety of Indian rice, the patent was filed by a USA company?

Ans. Indian Basmati rice was crossed with semi-dwarf variety and was claimed as a new variety for which the patent was field by a USA company.

Q.17 Discuss the advantages of GMO.

Ans. Advantages of GMO are (any two)

(i) GMO food crops have shorter growing cycles, greater resistance to both insects and diseases, higher yields and higher nutritional value.

(ii) GMO animals have increased production and nutritive values, *e.g.*,GM cows may produce more milk.

(iii) The World Health Organisation (WHO), claims that GMO plants and animals may allow food prices to drop as food sources become more abundant.

Short Answer Type Questions

Q.1 Gene expression can be controlled with the help of RNA. Explain the method with an example.

Ans. **RNA interference** (RNA*i*) technology is used to block the expression of certain genes and is also referred to as gene silencing. During this process, a specific *m*RNA is silenced to complementary *ds* RNA molecule (double stranded RNA)

e.g., a nematode *Meloidogyne incognita* infects the roots of tobacco plants which reduces the production of tobacco.

By using *Agrobacterium* vectors, nematode-specific genes were introduced into the host plants which produced both sense and anti-sense RNA in the host cells.

These two RNA*s* are complementary to each other and form a double-stranded RNA (*ds*RNA) that initiates RNAi and hence, silence the specific *m*RNA of the nematode. The parasite cannot survive in transgenic host and so prevents the plants from pests.

Q.2 Ignoring our traditional knowledge can be prove costly in the area of biological patenting. Justify.

Ans. Human communities have always generated, refined and passed on the knowledge from generation to generation. This has been developed by local communities, tribes etc. Such knowledge is called traditional knowledge and is often an important part of the cultural identities. A number of cases relating to traditional knowledge have attracted international attention.

As a result, the issue of traditional knowledge has been brought to the general debate surrounding intellectual property. These cases involve, what is often referred to as 'biopiracy'.

Examples like turmeric and neem (Indian traditional herbal medicine) illustrates the issues that can arise when patent protection is granted to inventions relating to traditional knowledge which is already in the public domain. In these cases, invalid patents were issued because the patent examiners were not aware of the relevant traditional knowledge.

Q.3 Highlight any four areas where genetic modification of plants has been useful.

Ans. Genetically Modified Plants (GMOs) are the plants whose genes have been altered by manipulation.

Genetic modification of plants is useful in different areas. Because of following reasons (any four)

(a) It increases tolerance against abiotic stresses (cold, drought, salt, heat).

(b) It reduces reliance on chemical pesticides (pest-resistant crops).

(c) It reduces post-harvest losses.

(d) It increases the efficiency of minerals used by plants (this prevents early exhaustion of fertility of soil).

(e) It enhances nutritional value of food, *e.g.*, vitamin-A enriched rice (golden rice).

(f) It creates tailor-made plants to supply alternative resources such as starch fuels and pharmaceuticals to industries.

Q.4 What is a recombinant DNA vaccine? Give two examples.

Ans. Recombinant DNA vaccines are produced by using genetically engineered plasmids that have gene inserts possessing the surface proteins of a pathogen. After the binding of pathogens to these surface proteins, a weak immune response is elicited but it does not results in infection. It contains only immunogenic protein which develops antibodies against the disease. These plasmids are inserted into bacteria or yeast cells that expresses the viral proteins, which are then injected into the human host as vaccine, where they are recognised as foreign and an immune response is elicited.

For example recombinant hepatitis-B vaccine and polio vaccine.

Q.5 Why is it that the line of treatment for a genetic disease is different from infectious diseases?

Ans. The line of treatment for a genetic disease is different from infectious diseases because genetic diseases, are caused by mutations in DNA which cannot be treated with any medication, only the signs and symptoms can be taken care of. The only way to treat them is by the correct manipulation of genes or replacement of the faulty genes. On the other hand, infectious diseases are caused by pathogens and therefore, can be treated by substances that kill the pathogen or hamper its growth.

Q.6 Discuss briefly how a probe is used in molecular diagnostics.

Thinking Process A single stranded DNA or RNA tagged with a radioactive molecule is called probe.

Ans. Early detection of a disease is not possible by conventional diagnostic methods. Therefore, some techniques have been implanted for early diagnosis like PCR, recombinant DNA technology and ELISA.
In recombinant DNA technology, a probe is used. Molecular probe can be radio labelled or non radio labelled DNA segment or RNA segment that is used to detect a specific disorder. It is allowed to hybridise to its complementary DNA in the clone of cells. The cells are then detected by autoradiography.

e.g., Western blotting.

Q.7 Who was the first patient to be treated with gene therapy? Why was the given treatment recurrent in nature?

Ans. The first clinical gene therapy was given in 1990 to a 4 yrs old girl named Ashanti Desilva with Adenosine Deaminase (ADA) deficiency.

ADA deficiency is caused due to the deletion of gene for Adenosine Deaminase. It can be cured by bone marrow transplantation or by enzyme replacement therapy. In both the approaches, it is not completley curable.
It may be recurrent in nature because in the process of gene therapy, lymphocytes used are found to be mortal in nature and the patient requires periodic infusion of such genetically engineered lymphocytes.

For permanent cure, gene isolated from the bone marrow cells producing ADA is introduced into the cells at early embryonic stages.

Q.8 Taking examples under each category, discuss upstream and downstream processing.

Ans. The upstream processing refers to the processes involved from isolation of DNA, cloning, culturing of the cells to obtain desired results.

Example of upstream processing included production of antibiotics (*e.g.*, Penicillin), recombinant proteins and fermentation processeses.

Downstream processing refers to the processes involved in purification, separation and concentration of bioproducts. After the product is produced it need to be purified and prepared for commercial used.

Examples of downstream processes are centrifugation, chromatography, filtration, purification of proteins or organic compounds.

Q.9 Define antigen and antibody. Name any two diagnostic kits based upon them.

Ans. An antigen is a foreign substance that elicits the immune response and results in the formation of an antibody.

Antibody is a glycoprotein that is synthesised by the body in response to an antigen.

Antigen and antibody shows high degree of specificity in binding to each other.

Two diagnostic kits based on antigen-antibody interaction are

(a) ELISA for HIV.

(b) Immunarray for Pregnancy test kits.

Q.10 ELISA technique is based on the principles of antigen-antibody interaction. Can this technique be used in the molecular diagnosis of a genetic disorder, such as phenylketonuria?

Thinking Process ELISA is based on the principle of antigen - antibody interaction. Any infection caused by a pathogen can be detected by the presence of antigens (proteins, glycoproteins, etc.) or by detecting the antibodies synthesised against the pathogen.

Ans. *Yes*, one can use antibody against the enzyme (that is responsible for the metabolism of phenylalanine to develop ELISA based diagnostic technique. The patient, in which the enzyme-protein complex is absent would give a negative result in ELISA when compared to the normal individual.

Q.11 How is a mature, functional insulin hormone different from its pro-hormone form?

Ans. Insulin is synthesised as pro-hormone, as it contains a chain of C-peptide (chain called the, connecting peptide c-peptide). It is processed to form mature functional insulin.

It connects the A and B chains in pro-insulin. This C-peptide is removed during the maturation of pro-insulin to insulin and A and B chains gets linked by disulphide linkage to form active insulin.

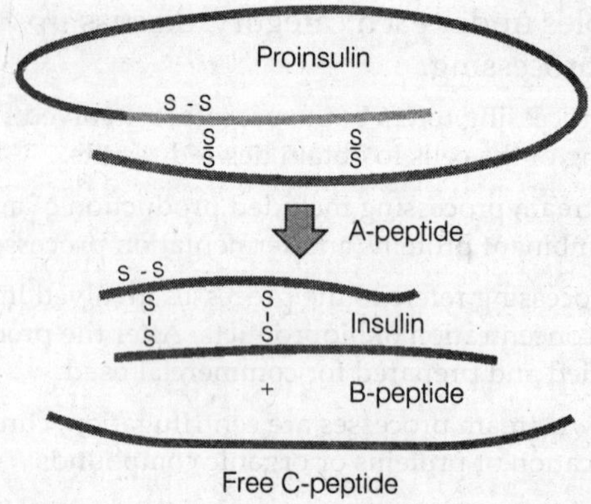

Maturation of pro-insulin into insulin after removal of C-peptide

Q.12 Gene therapy is an attempt to correct a genetic defect by providing a normal gene into the individual. By this the normal function can be restored. An alternate method would be to provide the gene product (protein/enzyme) known as enzyme replacement therapy, which would also restore the function. Which in your opinion is a better option? Give reason for your answer.

Ans. Gene therapy would be a better option because it has the potential to completely cure the patient. It is because once the correct gene is introduced in the patient, can continue to produce the correct protein or enzyme. Enzyme replacement therapy does not offer permanent cure as it needs to be given to the patient on regular basis. It is also more expensive and any disturbance can cause weakening effect.

Q.13 Transgenic animals are the animals in which a foreign gene is expressed. Such animals can be used to study the fundamental biological process, phenomenon as well as for producing products useful for mankind. Give one example for each type.

Ans. Transgenic animals are the animals in which a foreign genes are expressed. Such animals can be used to study the fundamental biological process or phenomenon.

By using model organisms like mouse we can determine how genes are regulated (gene regulation), how they affect the normal functions of the body and its development, etc. *e.g.*, a transgenic mouse model is used to study gene regualtion.

Transgenic animals are also used for producing products useful for mankind, *e.g.*, Transgenic cow (Rosie) which produced human protein enriched milk (2.4 g/L). The milk contained the human **alpha-lactalbumin** and was nutritionally a more balanced product for human babies than natural cow-milk.

Q.14 When a foreign DNA is introduced into an organism, how is it maintained in the host and how is it transferred to the progeny of the organism?

Ans. **Foreign gene** is usually ligated to a plasmid vector and introduced in the host. As plasmid replicates, and makes multiple copies of itself, the foreign gene gets replicated and several copies are made. When the host organism divides, its progeny also receives the plasmid. DNA containing the foreign gene.

The whole process can be visualised in the figure given below

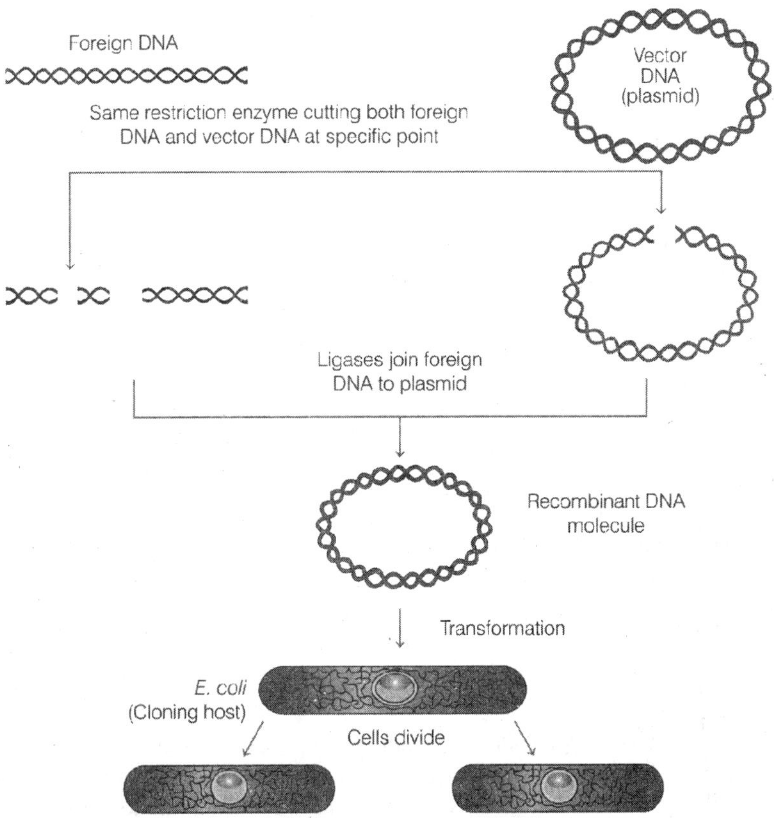

Recombinant DNA technology

Q.15 *Bt* cotton is resistant to pest, such as lepidopteran, dipterans and coleopterans. Is *Bt* cotton also resistant to other pests as well?

Ans. *Bt* cotton is made resistant to certain specific taxa of pests (lepidopteran, dipterans and coleopterans). The *Bt* gene produces a **toxin** that is effective only against specific insect groups. It does not protect against sap-sucking insect, such as aphids, white flies which can damage the crop. Therefore, additional pest management practices are required to control there non-target pests.

Long Answer Type Questions

Q.1 A patient is suffering from ADA deficiency. Can he be cured? How?

Ans. A patient suffering from ADA deficiency can be cured by using 'gene therapy'. Gene therapy is a collection of methods that allows the correction of a gene defect that has been diagnosed in a child or embryo. ADA enzyme is crucial for the immune system to function. Deletion of the gene for adenosine deaminase results into ADA deficiency. In some children, ADA deficiency can be cured by bone-marrow transplantation, while in others it can be treated by enzyme replacement therapy, in which functional ADA is given to the patient by injection. The only drawback with both of these approaches is that they are not completely curative.

It may recurrent in nature as in the process of gene therapy, lymphocytes used are found not immortal in nature and the patient requires a periodic infusion of such genetically engineered lymphocytes. For permanent cure, gene isolated from the bone-marrow cells producing ADA can be introduced into cells at early embryonic stages.

Q.2 Define transgenic animals. Explain in detail any four areas where they can be utilised.

Ans. Animals that have had their DNA manipulated to possess and express an extra (foreign) gene are known as transgenic animals.

Following are the four main areas where they can be utilised

(i) **To Study Normal Physiology and Development** These animals can be used to study that which factor or gene products are needed at specific time during development. By the expression of certain genes, they help scientists to understand the normal gene expression at various stages of growth and development.

(ii) **Study of Diseases** Transgenic animals can be created to serve as models for various human diseases. They also help us to understand the involvement of various genes in diseases like cancer, Parkinson' disease etc.

(iii) **Vaccine Safety** Transgenic animals can be used to test vaccines like polio vaccine. Transgenic mice have shown promising results in this area and would replace the vaccine testing on monkeys in the years to come.

(iv) **Chemical Safety Testing** Transgenic animals are created which are more sensitive to certain chemicals or drugs. These animals are used to study the toxicity or side effects of that chemical or drug. One major advantage of this method is that provides faster and max reliable results.

(v) **Biological products** The important and expensive biological products are harvested by this method. For example, protein like α-1 antitrypsin for treating emphysema etc.

Q.3 You have identified a useful gene in bacteria. Make a flow chart of the steps that you would follow to transfer this gene to a plant.

Ans. After identifying a useful gene in bacteria, following steps should be followed

(i) Isolation of useful gene using restriction endonucleases

↓

(ii) Making a cut in T-DNA with the same restriction endonuclease.

↓

(iii) Transferring the gene to a Ti-plasmid to create a recombinant DNA molecule.

↓

(iv) Transfer of these recombinant DNA molecules to the target plant cells using a suitable method (e.g., Agrobacterium-mediated transformation).

↓

(v) Screening of cells for transformation.

↓

(vi) Selection of transformed cells.

↓

(vi) Regeneration of whole plants from the transformed cells to get transgenic plants.

Q.4 Highlight five areas where biotechnology has influenced our lives.

Ans. Biotechnology has influenced our lives in the following ways

(i) It has provided us with genetically modified crops of better quality and high nutritive value.

(ii) It has made better and safer recombinant vaccines available to the human.

(iii) It has helped to develop transgenic animals that can produce human proteins.

(iv) It has enabled the cure of genetic diseases using gene therapy.

(v) Environment protection has also been taken care of with the help of genetically engineered microbes.

Q.5 What are the various advantages of using genetically modified plants to increase the overall yield of the crop?

Ans. Genetically modified plants have been useful in many ways as follows

(i) These plants are more tolerant to abiotic stresses (cold, drought, salt, heat).

(ii) They have reduced the reliance on chemical pesticides (pest-resistant crops).

(iii) They helped to reduce post-harvest losses.

(iv) They increase the efficiency of mineral usage by plants (this prevents early exhaustion of fertility of soil).

(v) Enhanced nutritional value of food, *e.g.*, vitamin-A enriched rice.

(vi) Resistance to viral diseases has been introduced in Tobacco and potato.

(vii) Transgenic plants can engineered to produce pharmaceuticals products like insulin.

In addition to these uses, GM plants have been used to create tailor-made plants to supply alternative resources to industries, in the form of starches, fuels and pharmaceuticals.

Q.6 Explain with the help of one example how genetically modified plants can

(a) Reduce usage of chemical pesticides.

(b) Enhance nutritional value of food crops.

Ans. (a) Genetically modified plants can reduce the usage of chemical pesticides by introducing pest resistant plants.

e.g., There are several nematodes that acts as a parasitie, to a wide variety of plants and animals including human beings. A nematode *Meloidegyne incognitia* infects the roots of tobacco plants and causes a great reduction in yield. A novel strategy was adopted to prevent this infestation which was based on the process of **RNA interference** (RNAi).

Using *Agrobacterium* vectors, nematode-specific genes were introduced into the host plant. The introduction of DNA was such that it produced both sense and antisense RNA in the host cells. These two RNA's being complementary to each other formed a double stranded *ds*RNA that initiated RNA*i* and thus, silenced the specific *m*RNA of the nematode. The consequence was that the parasite could not survive in a transgenic host expressing specific interfering RNA.

(b) Genetically modified plants can enhance nutritional value of food crops.

e.g., 'Golden rice' developed at Swiss Federal Institute of technology is an example of nutritionally modified crop. It is rich in vitamin-A (β-carotene). The rice grains are golden-yellow in colour. Golden rice can prevent child blindness which is caused due to the deficiency of vitamin-A.

Q.7 List the disadvantages of insulin obtained from the pancreas of slaughtered cows and pigs.

Ans. The disadvantages of insulin obtained from the pancreas of slaughtered cows and pigs are

(i) Insulin being a hormone is produced in very little amounts in the body. Hence, a large number of animals need to be sacrificed for obtaining small quantities of insulin. This makes the cost of insulin very high (demand being many fold higher than supply).

(ii) Slaughtering of animals is not ethical.

(iii) There is a potential chance of immune response in humans against the administered insulin which is derived from animals.

(iv) There is possibility of slaughtered animals being infested with some infectious microorganisms which may contaminate the insulin.

Q.8 List the advantages of recombinant insulin.

Ans. The advantages of recombinant insulin are as follows

(i) There is no need of animals to be sacrificed for the production of recombinant insulin.

(ii) Recombinant insulin was not found allergic to patients, while the insulin from an animal source caused some patients to develop allergy or other types of reactions to the foreign protein.

(iii) The cost of recombinant insulin is not very high.

(iv) There is minimal risk of immune response or any other side effects.

Q.9 What is meant by the term biopesticide? Name and explain the mode of action of a popular biopesticide.

Ans. *Biopesticide is a pesticide which is*

(i) not chemical in nature.

(ii) more specific in action against the pest.

(iii) safer for environment than chemical pesticides.

(iv) It does not enter the food chain and is highly specific.

A popularly known bio-pesticide is *Bt* toxin, which is produced by a bacterium called *Bacillus thuringiensis*. *Bt* toxin gene has been cloned from this bacterium and expressed in plants. *Bt* toxin protein when ingested by the insect, gets converted to its active form due to the alkaline pH of the gut.

The activated toxin binds to the surface of midgut epithelial cells and create pores that causes swelling and lysis of the cell eventually killing the insect.

Q.10 Name the five key tools for accomplishing the tasks of recombinant DNA technology. Also mention the functions of each tool.

Ans. The key tools for accomplishing the tasks of recombinant DNA technology with their functions are mentioned below

(i) **Restriction endonucleases** for cutting the desired DNA at desired places.

(ii) **Gel electrophoresis** for separating the desired DNA fragments.

(iii) **Ligase enzyme** for creating recombinant DNA molecule by joining DNA fragments.

(iv) **DNA delivery system** like electroporation, microinjection, gene gun method, etc. to introduce recombinant DNA into host cells.

(v) **Competant host** (usually bacteria/yeast) to take up and replicate the recombinant DNA.

Chapter 13

Organisms and Populations

Multiple Choice Questions (MCQs)

Q.1 Autecology is the

(a) relation of a population to its environment

(b) relation of an individual to its environment

(c) relation of a community to its environment

(d) relation of a biome to its environment

Thinking Process Ecology is study of the relationship of living organisms with their abiotic and biotic components. It consists of two branches.

(i) Autecology

(ii) Synecology

Ans. *(b)* Autecology is the study of relationship of an individual to its environment including biotic and abiotic factors. Whereas, the relation of a population or community to its environment is called synecology.

Q.2 Ecotone is

(a) a polluted area

(b) the bottom of a lake

(c) a zone of transition between two communities

(d) a zone of developing community

Ans. *(c)* Ecotone is a **zone of transition** between two communities as the adjacent biotic (natural) communities, generally do not posses a fine demarcation edge or line between them.

Q.3 Biosphere is

(a) a component in the ecosystem

(b) composed of the plants present in the soil

(c) life in the outer space

(d) composed of all living organisms present on earth which interact with the physical environment

Ans. *(d)* Biosphere is composed of all living organisms present on earth which interact with their physical environment. In other words a biosphere is cluster of all the ecosystems of world.

Q.4 Ecological niche is

(a) the surface area of the ocean
(b) an ecologically adapted zone
(c) the physical position and functional role of a species within the community
(d) formed of all plants and animals living at the bottom of a lake

Ans. *(c)* Ecological niche refers to **specific role** and **position** or species occupies in its ecosystem. It is determined by factors such as its range of tolerance. *i.e.,* the physical position and functional role of a species within the community. The environmental conditions it needs to survive and perform functions.

Q.5 According to Allen's rule, the mammals from colder climates have

(a) shorter ears and longer limbs
(b) longer ears and shorter limbs
(c) longer ears and longer limbs
(d) shorter ears and shorter limbs

Thinking Process Animals adapted to cold climate have **small appendages**.

Ans. *(d)* According to Allen's rule, the mammals (endothermal animals) from colder climates or areas have shorter extremities like ears and limbs as compared to the mammals of warm region. The shorter extermities of mammals in colder region help to minimise heat loss and maintain homeostatis.

Q.6 Salt concentration (salinity) of the sea measured in parts per thousand is

(a) 10-15
(b) 30-70
(c) 0-5
(d) 30-35

Ans. *(d)* The salt concentration (salinity) of sea measured in parts per thousand is 30-35. Salinity of water bodies is measured in parts per thousand, determining the type of organisms that survive in sea.

Q.7 Formation of tropical forests needs mean annual temperature and mean annual precipitation as

(a) 18 - 25°C and 150 - 400 cm
(b) 5 - 15°C and 50 - 100 cm
(c) 30 - 50°C and 100 - 150 cm
(d) 5 - 15°C and 100 - 200 cm

Ans. *(a)* Formation of tropical forests need annual temperature 18-25°C and annual rainfall (precipitation) above 140 cm, usually between 150-400 cm and reach upto 1000 cm/year.

Tropical forest or evergreen forest are mainly present in equatorial or subequatorial region like Amazon, Central America and Orinoco and Congo river basins of South America and Africa respectively.

Q.8 Which of the following forest plants controls the light conditions at the ground?

(a) Lianas and climbers
(b) Shrubs
(c) Tall trees
(d) Herbs

Ans. *(c)* In forest, light's intensity, duration and quality at ground is controlled by tall trees, which have higher productivity than shrubs and herbs growing underneath. While lianas and climbers are woody vines which make commensalism association with tall trees. Herbs and shrubs occupies lower strata of forest.

Q.9 **What will happen to a well growing herbaceous plant in the forest if it is transplanted outside the forest in a park?**

(a) It will grow normally

(b) It will grow well because it is planted in the same locality

(c) It may not survive because of change in its micro climate

(d) It grows very well because the plant gets more sunlight

Ans. ***(c)*** A well growing herbaceous plant in forest receive less intensity, duration and quality of light, but when it is transplanted in a parks outside its natural habitat, the light will be received uninterrupted. This is because

In a forest ecosystem tall trees of forest plants controls the light condition, *i.e.*, intensity, duration and quality of light at the ground.

So, due to change in its microclimate, it may not survive.

Q.10 **If a population of 50 *Paramecium* present in a pool increases to 150 after an hour, what would be the growth rate of population?**

(a) 50 per hour (b) 200 per hour (c) 5 per hour (d) 100 per hour

Thinking Process Population growth is the important characteristic of population, which is determined by addition and loss of individual. In case of higher addition of organisms/individual than lost, population show positive growth, *i.e.*, vital index is more than 100. But when vital index is less than 100, population show negative growth.

Ans. ***(d)*** Population of *Paramecium* at time $1(t_1) = 50$

Population of *Paramecium* after 1 hour $(t_2) = 150$

Growth rate of population $150 - 50$ per hour $= 100$ Per hour

Population of *Paramecium* show 100 per hour growth, *i.e.*, two individuals are produced by one.

Q.11 **What would be the per cent growth or birth rate per individual per hour for the same population mentioned in the previous question (Question 10)?**

(a) 100 (b) 200 (c) 50 (d) 150

Ans. ***(b)*** Birthrate is per capita (increase or decrease) with respect to members of population.

So, Intial number of *Paramecium* = 50

No. of *Paramecium* after 1 hour = 150

$$\text{Birth rate} = \frac{\text{Number of new } Paramecium}{\text{Number of intial } Paramecium} = \frac{100}{50} \times 100 = 200\%$$

Growth rate is 200% as one organism is producing two individuals at a time. (Refer to Question number-10).

Q.12 **A population has more young individuals compared to the older individuals. What would be the status of the population after some years?**

(a) It will decline (b) It will stabilise

(c) It will increase (d) It will first decline and then stabilise

Ans. ***(c)*** Variation in number of individuals in a population is expressed as population density and population size. A population of more young individual than older individuals, will show positive growth in future (after some years), *i.e.*, it will increase after some time.

Q.13 What parameters are used for tiger census in our country's national parks and sanctuaries?

(a) Pug marks only
(b) Pug marks and faecal pellets
(c) Faecal pellets only
(d) Actual head counts

Ans. ***(b)*** The parameters used for tiger census in our country's national park and sanctuaries are foot prints (pug marks) and faecal pellets.

Q.14 Which of the following would necessarily decrease the density of a population in a given habitat?

(a) Natality > mortality
(b) Immigration > emigration
(c) Mortality and emigration
(d) Natality and immigration

Ans. ***(c)*** Mortality and emigration would necessarily decrease the density of a population in a given habitat due to loss of individual result from mortality *i.e.*, death rate and emigration *i.e.*, act of leaving one's own habitat.

Q.15 A protozoan reproduces by binary fission. What will be the number of protozoans in its population after six generations?

(a) 128 (b) 24 (c) 64 (d) 32

Ans. ***(c)*** **Binary fission**, a mode of asexual reproduction in protozoan produce two offsprings from parent individual in generation

So, Single protozoan $\xrightarrow{\text{Multiplied}}$ Two (2 individual) $\rightarrow$
(Ist generation)

$4 \longrightarrow 8 \longrightarrow 16 \longrightarrow 32 \longrightarrow 64$ Numbers

Thus, the population of protozoan will be 64, after six generations.

Q.16 In 2005, for each of the 14 million people present in a country, 0.028 were born and 0.008 died during the year. Using exponential equation, the number of people present in 2015 is predicted as

(a) 25 millions (b) 17 millions (c) 20 millions (d) 18 millions

Ans. ***(b)*** Exponential equation gives population growth rate as

$dN/dt = (b-d) \times N$ or $dN/dt = rN$ where, $r = (b-d)$

Where, $\dfrac{dN}{dT}$ = Increase in population size per unit time

r = difference between birth and death rate

$r = 0\cdot 028 - 0\cdot 008 = 0\cdot 02$

$= 0\cdot 02 \times 14$ million

$= 0\cdot 28$ million

For rent 10 years the population will be 2.8 million

Expected population in 2015 $(14 + 2\cdot 8)$ million = 17 million (approximately)

So, the number of people present in 2015 is predicted as 17 millions.

Q.17 Amensalism is an association between two species where

(a) one species is harmed and other is benefitted
(b) one species is harmed and other is unaffected
(c) one species is benefitted and other is unaffected
(d) both the species are harmed.

Thinking Process Interspecific interactions in population arise from the interaction of populations of two different species. This could be beneficial, neutral or detrimental to one or both of the species.

Ans. *(b)* When one species is benefitted and other is harmed, in an association between two species, it is called **amensalism**. Whereas in **commensalism** one species is benefitted and other is unaffected.

Q.18 Lichens are the associations of

(a) bacteria and fungus
(b) algae and bacterium
(c) fungus and algae
(d) fungus and virus

Ans. *(c)* Lichens represent a positive (beneficial) interaction between two different species, one fungus and another algae.

Note Algal species is called as phycobiont while fungal species is referred to as mycobiont.

Q.19 Which of the following is a partial root parasite?

(a) Sandal wood (b) Mistletoe
(c) *Orobanche* (d) *Ganoderma*

Ans. *(a)* Sandal wood (*Santalum album*) is partial root parasite. It synthesis its own food but is dependent on host's roots for water and inorganic nutrients. Mistletoe (*Viscum*) is considered as hemiparasite which derive a part of its nourishment from host plant. While *orobanche* is a holo parasite which infects species from favciae *i.e.*, beans, loranthus, *Ganoderma* are parasites.

Q.20 Which one of the following organisms reproduces sexually only once in its life time?

(a) Banana plant (b) Mango
(c) Tomato (d) Eucalyptus

Thinking Process Reproductive phase in higher plants is characterised by appearance of flowers. There are two types of sexually reproducing flowering plants: monocarpic and polycarpic.

Ans. *(a)* Banana is a monocarpic perennial plant, so reproduces sexually once in its lifetime.

Very Short Answers Type Questions

Q.1 Species that can tolerate narrow range of temperature are called......

Ans. **Stenothermal Species** On the basis of temperature tolerance, organism can be classified as eurythermal and stenothermal.

(i) Eurythermal organisms can tolerate and thrive in a wide range of temperatures.

(ii) Stenothermal organisms tolerate only a narrow range of temperatures.

Q.2 What are eurythermic species?

Ans. Eurythermic species are those species which possess or show a wide range of temperature tolerance. e.g., green crabs

Q.3 Species that can tolerate wide range of salinity are called........

Ans. **Euryhaline species** Organisms or species that can tolerate wide range of salinity are regarded as **euryhaline Species.** *e.g.*, Bullshark, lamprey, etc.

Q.4 Define stenohaline species.

Ans. Stenohaline species are those species which show a narrow range of salinity tolerance. *e.g.*, Goldfish.

Q.5 What is the interaction between two species called?

Ans. Interaction between two species is called **interspecific** interaction. These could be beneficial, detrimental or neutral to one of the species or both.

Q.6 What is commensalism?

Ans. Commensalism is an interaction where one species is benefitted and the other remains unaffected. *e.g.*, An orchid plant growing as an epiphyte on a mango branch.

Q.7 Name the association in which one species produces poisonous substance or a change in environmental conditions that is harmful to another species.

Ans. The association where one species produces a poisonous substance or changes the environment in a way that harms another species is called Amensalism. Eg. Bread mould *Penicillium* and bacteria. *Penicillium* releases pencillin, which kills bacteria.

Q.8 What is mycorrhiza?

Ans. Mycorrhiza is a symbiotic association between a fungus and the root of higher plants like conifers *i.e., Pinus.*

Note Fungal hyphae gets protection and nourishment from its symbiont, which in turn helps in absorption of organic solutes to higher plants.

Q.9 Emergent land plants that can tolerate the salinities of the sea are called.

Ans. **Halophytes** are emergent land plants that can tolerate the salinities of sea and are even able to maintain their water supply from the sea.

Q.10 Why do high altitude areas have brighter sunlight and lower temperatures as compared to the plains?

Ans. At high altitude the sun light is brighter as compared to plains, it is because of reduced dust particles in the air. Similarly, lower temperatures conditions are achieved due of lower atmospheric pressure as compared to plains.

Q.11 What is homeostasis?

Ans. **Homeostasis** is the tendency of the organism to maintain a constant internal environment despite varying external environmental conditions like temperature.

Q.12 Define aestivation.

Ans. **Aestivation** is a behavioural adaptation to avoid extreme heat and dessication in summer season. During aestivation the organism slows down its metabolic activities and adapted a state of prolonged **darmancy** or **inactivity**. It is also known as **summer sleep**.

Q.13 What is diapause and its significance?

Ans. **Diapause** is a temporary dormant stage of suspended development seen in organisms like zooplanktons in lakes and ponds. It is adopt by organisms to survive under unfavourable conditions.

Q 14 What would be the growth rate pattern, when the resources are unlimited?

Ans. In case of unlimited resources, the pattern of growth rate is **exponential**.

Q.15 What are the organisms that feed on plant sap and other plant parts called?

Ans. The organism that feed on plant sap and other parts of plants are termed as **phytophagous**.

Q.16 What is high altitude sickness? Write its symptoms.

Ans. **High altitude sickness** or **mountain sickness** is experienced by the people going to high altitudes, where oxygen concentrations are low. The human body reacts by developing the symptoms like nausea, headache, heart palpitations, breathlessness, muscular weakness, mental fatigue. These symptoms subside after some time.

Q.17 Give a suitable example for commensalism.

Ans. The interaction between blue whale and the barnacles, growing on its back is an example of commensalism (interspecific relation) between them.

Q.18 Define ectoparasite and endoparasite and give suitable examples.

Ans. Ectoparasite feeds on the external surface of the host organism, *e.g.*, Lice on humans and ticks on dogs. Many marine fishes are infested with ectoparasitic, copepods. Whereas, endoparasites live inside the host body at different sites (liver, kidney, lungs, red blood cells, etc.). Such as malarial parasites, *P. vivax* and gut parasites, tapeworm.

Q.19 What is brood parasitism? Explain with the help of an example.

Ans. **Brood parasitism** is the phenomenon in which an organism (parasite) lays eggs in the nest of other organisms (host). *e.g.*, Cuckoo (koel) bird lays its eggs in the nest of its host and let the host incubate them. The eggs of the parasitic bird resemble the host's egg in size and colour to reduce the chances of the host bird detecting the foreign eggs and ejecting them from the nest.

Short Answer Type Questions

Q.1 Why are coral reefs not found in the regions from West Bengal to Andhra Pradesh but are found in Tamil Nadu and on the east coast of India?

Ans. Coral reefs are found in zones with high salt concentration (salinity), optimal temperature, no fresh water inflow and a less siltation condition. There conditions are not met in regions from West Bengal to Andhra Pradesh but are found in Tamil Nadu on the east coast of India.

Q.2 If a freshwater fish is placed in an aquarium containing sea water, will the fish be able to survive? Explain giving reasons.

Ans. No, a freshwater fish placed in the aquarium containing sea water, will not be able to survive. This is because, its body system is adapted to function in a narrow range of salinity *i.e.*, it is stenohaline thus it cannot survive in the high salinity of sea water.

Q.3 Why do all the freshwater organisms have contractile vacuoles whereas majority of marine organisms lack them?

Ans. Contractile vacuole helps in **osmoregulation**. Due to the cellular environment of a freshwater organism being hypertonic, the water constantly diffuses inside the cell and gets collected in the contractile vacuole, which squeezes the extra water out of the cell periodically. Thus, keeping the internal environment constant. While in case of marine organisms, this does not occur due to high salinity, therefore contractile vacuole is not required.

Q.4 Define heliophytes and sciophytes. Name a plant from your locality that is either heliophyte or sciophyte.

Thinking Process On the basis of light tolerance or adaptation, plants may be heliophytes and sciophytes.

Ans. Plants growing well in bright sunlight or plants that favour bright light are called **heliophytes** or sun plants. *e.g.*, sunflowers, roses. While those plants which require low intensity of light or partial shade for growing are termed as shade loving plants or **sciophytes** *e.g.*, ferns, mosses.

Q.5 Why do submerged plants receive weaker illumination than exposed floating plants in a lake?

Ans. Submerged plants receive weaker illumination than exposed floating plants in a lake because all colours of the visible components of the spectrum of light do not enter or penetrate in the depths of water.

Q.6 In a sea shore, the benthic animals live in sandy, muddy and rocky substrata and accordingly developed the following adaptations.

(a) Burrowing
(b) Building cubes
(c) Holdfasts/peduncle

Find the suitable substratum against each adaptation.

Ans. Burrowing, building cubes and holdfast or pendunde adaptations are found in sandy, muddy and rocky substratum respectively.

Q.7 Categorise the following plants into hydrophytes, halophytes, mesophytes and xerophytes. Give reasons for your answers.

(a) *Salvinia* (b) *Opuntia* (c) *Rhizophora* (d) *Mangifera*

Ans. (a) *Salvinia* is a hydrophyte – Partially or completly submerged in water.

(b) *Opuntia* is a xerophyte – Found in dry habitat and has succulent leaves. It stores mucilage and water with no functional leaves.

(c) *Rhizophora* is a halophyte – Found in saline habitat along seashore.

(d) *Mangifera* is a mesophyte – Found in terrestrial habitat, in rows growns in soil with good moisture content.

Q.8 In a pond, we see plants which are free-floating; rooted-submerged; rooted emergent; rooted with floating leaves. Write the type of plants against each of them.

	Plant Name	Type
(a)	*Hydrilla*	
(b)	*Typha*	
(c)	*Nymphaea*	
(d)	*Lemna*	
(e)	*Vallisneria*	

Ans. (a) *Hydrilla* is submerged hydrophyte

(b) *Typha* is rooted emergent aquatic plant

(c) *Nymphaea* is rooted plant with floating leaves

(d) *Lemna* is free floating hydrophyte

(e) *Vallisnaria* is rooted submerged hydrophytes.

Q.9 The density of a population in a habitat per unit area is measured in different units. Write the unit of measurement against the following

(a) Bacteria .... (b) Banyan .... (c) Deer .... (d) Fish ....

Ans. The density of population per unit area is measured in following units

(a) Volume/number unit. (b) Biomass/area/region

(c) Number/area (d) Weight/area

Q.10

(a) Label the three tiers 1, 2, 3 given in the above age pyramid.

(b) What type of population growth is represented by the above age pyramid?

Ans. (a) The three tiers are to be labelled as

(i) Pre-reproductive phase (ii) Reproductive phase
(iii) Post-reproductive phase

(b) The given age pyramid represents the **expanding type** of population growth.

Q.11 In an association of two animal species, one is a termite which feeds on wood and the other is a protozoan *Trichonympha* present in the gut of the termite. What type of association they establish?

Ans. The termite provides shelter and space for the protozoan *Trichonympha* to live. The Protozoa present in gut digests the wood, which termite feeds upon. In the absence of *Trichonympha* the termite is unable to digest wood and hence dies. Thus, the association of two given animal species represent mutualism.

Q.12 Lianas are vascular plants rooted in the ground and maintain erectness of their stem by making use of other trees for support. They do not maintain direct relation with those trees. Discuss the type of association the lianas have with the trees.

Ans. The type of association, the lianas have with the trees is **commensalism** because the plant gets the support of the tree without harming or providing any benefit to the tree.

Q.13 Give the scientific names of any two microorganisms inhabiting the human intestine.

Ans. The scientific names of two microorganisms inhabiting the human intestine are *Escherichia coli* and *Lactobacillus*.

Q.14 What is a tree line?

Ans. Tree line is the edge of the habitat where trees are capable of growing. Due to environmental conditions such as cold temperature, high altitude or lack of moisture the trees are not found beyond this line and if found they show stunted growth or form low and dense bushes. Only shrubs and herbs are found.

Q.15 Define 'zero population growth rate'. Draw a age pyramid for the same.

Ans. Zero population growth is shown by a **stable population** in which growth and decline of population is not visible.

An inverted bell shaped age pyramid is obtained for zero population growth rate.

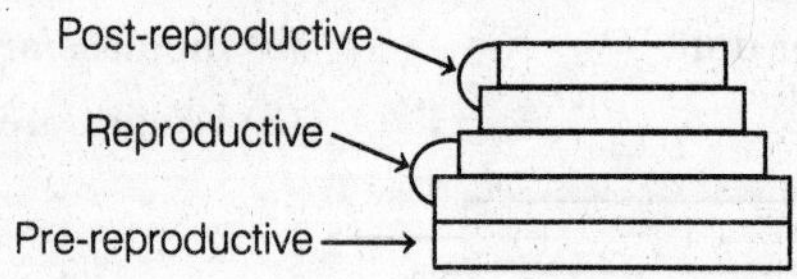

Q.16 List any four characters that are employed in human population census.

Ans. A population has the following characterstics that are employed in human population census.

(i) Natality and mortality
(ii) Sex ratio
(iii) Population density
(iv) Age distribution

Q.17 Give one example for each of the following types

(a) Migratory animal
(b) Camouflaged animal
(c) Predator animal
(d) Biological control agent
(e) Phytophagous animal
(f) Chemical defense agent

Ans. (a) Migratory animal-American buffalo and dolphins.
(b) Camouflaged animal-Grasshopper and chameleons..
(c) Predator animal-Lion.
(d) Biological control agent-*Myxoma* virus to kill European rabbit and *Gambusia* fish to check growth of mosquito larvae, Ladybird bettle against aphids.
(e) Phytophagous animal-Insects (beetle, butterfly, etc.).
(f) Chemical defense agent-Cardiac glycosides in calotropis.

Q.18 Fill in the blanks

Species A	Species B	Type of Interaction	Example
+	−	—	—
+	+	—	—
+	—	Commensalism	—

Ans.

Species A	Species B	Type of Interaction	Example
		Predation	Tiger eating deer
		Mutualism	Lichen, association between fungus and algae
	Zero		Cattle Egret and cattles

Q.19 Observe the set of 4 figures A, B, C and D and answer the following questions.

I. Which one of the figures shows mutualism?
II. What kind of association is shown in D?

III. Name the organisms and the association in C.
IV. What role is the insect performing in B?

Fig. (A)

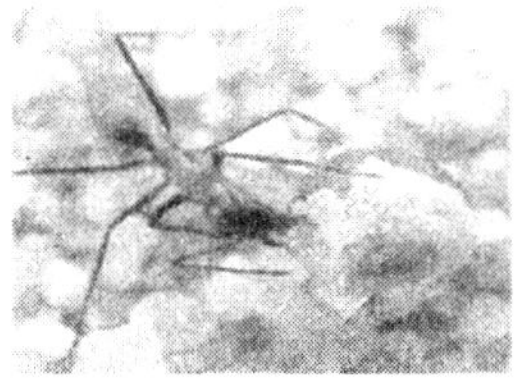

Fig. (B)

Fig. (C)

Fig. (D)

Ans. I. Figure *A* show a pollinator (bee) on a flower. The association between pollinator (insect) and plant is termed as mutualism.
II. Predation – Lion eating dear
III. Egrets and grazing cattle is good example of commensalism.
IV. Phytophagy – The insect is sucking plant sap.

Long Answer Type Questions

Q.1 Comment on the following figure: I, II and III, A, B, C, D, G, P, Q, R, S are species.

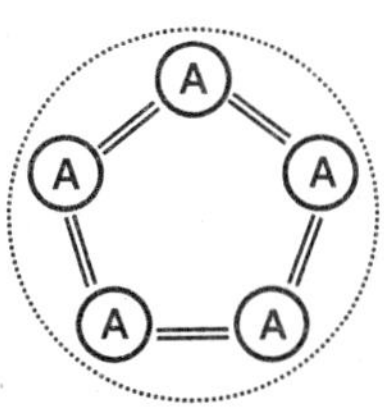

Fig. I

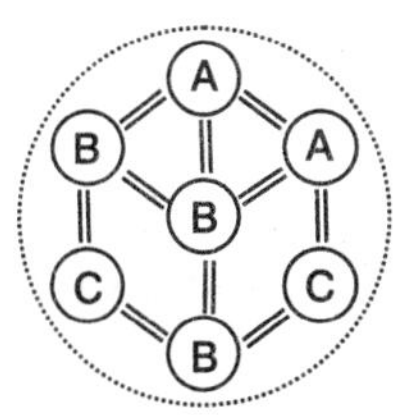

Fig. II

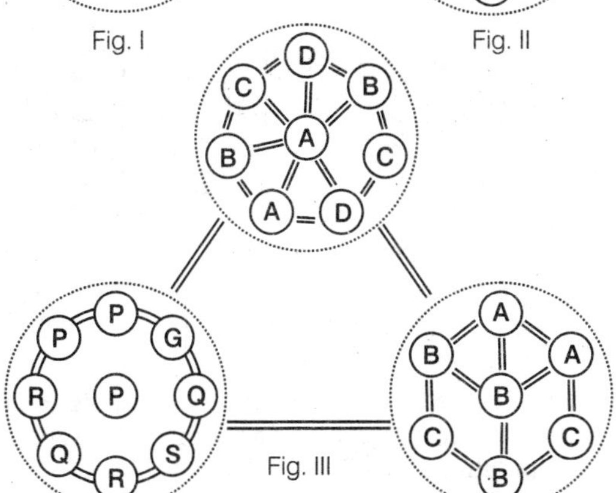

Fig. III

Ans. **Figure I** It is a single population and all individuals are of the same species, *i.e.*, individuals interact among themselves and their environment. This is called **intraspecific interaction**.

Figure II It is a community and it contains three populations of species A, B and C. They interact with each other and their environment and is called **interspecific interaction**.

Figure III It is a biome. It contains three communities containing different species, interacting witheach other. All three communities are in the same environment and they interact with each other and their environment.

Q.2 An individual and a population has certain characteristics. Name these attributes with definitions.

Ans. An individual and a population has certain attributes like pattern of distribution, dispersal, biotic potential and gene pool. Phenomenon of distribution of individual within geographical boundaries of the population is termed as intrapopulation dispersion or internal distribution patterns or dispersion.

Birth rate – Population has birth rate which tends to increase the number of individual.

Death rate – Population also has death rate that decrease the number of individual.

Age or Sex – An individual can be male/female and of particular age.

Dispersal – An individual is dispersed at one or another time during their life in a population which is revealed by immigration or emigration.

(i) Immigration is the number of individuals of the same species that have come into the habitat from elsewhere during a specified time period.

(ii) Emigration is the number of individuals of the population who exit or leave the habitat and go elsewhere during a specified time period.

Biotic Potential – It is the natural capacity of a population to increase its size under ideal environmental conditions.

Gene pool – All the genotypes of all individuals in a breeding population is referred to as gene pool.

Q.3 The following diagrams are the age pyramids of different populations. Comment on the status of these poulations.

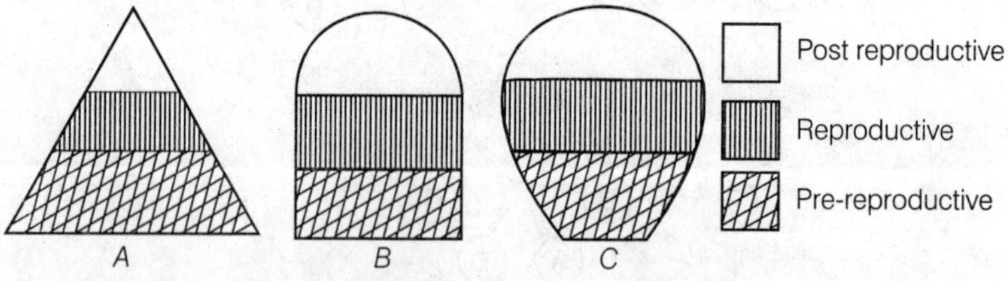

Ans. **Figure A** It is a 'pyramid' shaped age pyramid. In this figure, the base, *i.e.*, pre-reproductive stage is very large as compared with the reproductive and post-reproductive stages of the population. This type of age structure indicate that the population would increase rapidly.

Figure B It is an 'inverted bell' shaped pyramid. In this figure, the pre-reproductive and reproductive stages are same. This type of age structure indicates that the population is stable.

Figure C It is 'urn' shaped pyramid. In this figure, the pre-reproductive stage are less than the reproductive stages of this population. In this population, more older people are present. This type of age structure indicates that the population is declining.

Q.4 Comment on the growth curve given below.

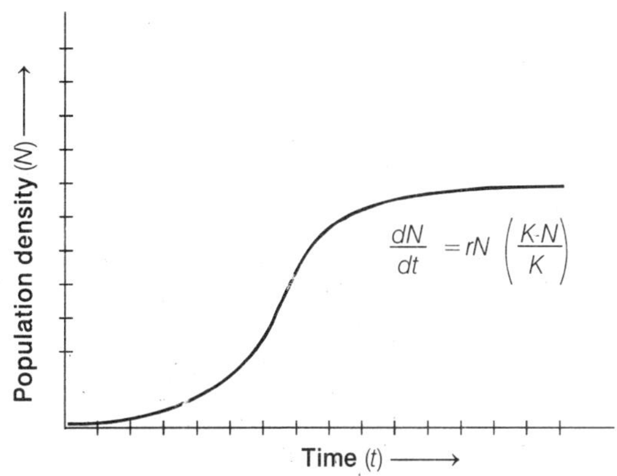

Ans. The growth curve shown above is **logistic growth curve** or **S-shaped curve**.

Logistic growth curve is considered more realistic because limited resources are available in an ecosystem or in a habitat, where, $\frac{dN}{dt} = rN\left(\frac{K-N}{K}\right)$

K–stands for carrying capacity.

N–indicates population density, which is the number of species of a population per unit area.

r–is for intrinsic rate of natural increase.

Q.5 A population of *Paramecium caudatum* was grown in a culture medium. After 5 days the culture medium became overcrowded with *Paramecium* and had depleted nutrients. What will happen to the population and what type of growth curve will the population attain? Draw the growth curve.

Ans. Initially, after a lag phase, the population will grow in an exponential manner as the nutrients and space will be abundant.

When the food sources get depleted, the population density starts decreasing and ends in an **asymptote phase**, then the population density reaches the carrying capacity (maximum number of individuals of a population or species that a given environment can sustain indefinitely).

The population shows a pattern of logistic growth giving an S-shaped curve. It is represented by the following equation.

$$\frac{dN}{dt} = rN\left(\frac{K-N}{K}\right)$$

Where K = carrying capacity

N= population density at time 't'

r = Intrinsic rate of natural increase

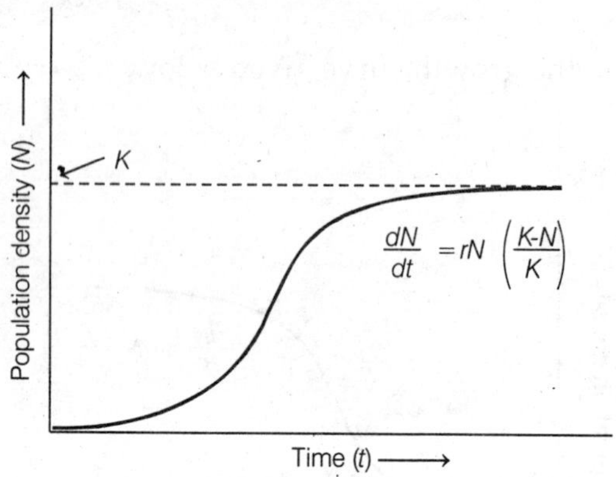

Logistic growth curve

Q.6 Discuss the various types of positive interactions between species.

Ans. The interspecific interaction are of three types positive or beneficial, negative or antagonistic and last neutral interaction.

Some positive interactions are commensalism, protocooperation and mutualism.

Mutualism This interaction confers benefits on both the interacting species. Some example are given below.

(i) Lichens represent an intimate mutualistic relationship between a fungus and photosynthesising algae or cyanobacteria.

(ii) The mycorrhizae are associations between fungi and the roots of higher plants. The fungi help the plant in the absorption of essential nutrients from the soil while the plant in turn provides the fungi with energy-yielding carbohydrates.

(iii) Plants offer nectar, juicy and nutritious fruits to animals that help pollinate their flowers and disperse their seeds.

Commensalism This is the interaction in which one species benefits without affecting the other, *e.g.,*

(i) An orchid growing as an epiphyte on a mango branch.

(ii) Barnacles growing on the back of a whale.

(iii) The cattle egret foraging close to the cattle that stir up and flush out insects from the vegetation.

(iv) Sea anemone that has stinging tentacles and the clown fish that lives among them to get protection from predators.

Protocooperation is the type of relationship in which both partners mutually obtain benefits. But they associate purely to benefit from each other and can live without each other.

Q.7 In an aquarium two herbivorous species of fish are living together and feeding on phytoplanktons. As per the Gause's principle, one of the species is to be eliminated in due course of time, but both are surviving well in the aquarium. Give possible reasons.

Ans. **Competition** is a rivalry relationship between two or more organisms. A competition between individuals of same species (intraspecific) is more intense than the competition between individual of different species as all the members in a intraspecific competition have same basic requirements like food, water, light, space, mating and shelter.

Few possible reasons for survival of both the species are as follows.

- Conditions favour abundant growth of phytoplanktons.
- There is no zooplankton.

But this is true only when resources are unlimited. According to Gause's principle, one of the species is to be eliminated in the presence of limited resources.

But studies recently have revealed that species facing intraspecific competition may evolve mechanism to **encourage co-existence** rather than exclusion. This can also be done by a method known as ' resource partitioning'.

Q.8 While living in and on the host species, the animal parasite has evolved certain adaptations. Describe these adaptations with examples.

Ans. Parasites have evolved special adaptations such as

(i) The loss of unnecessary sense organs as lice, mites and fleas don't have wings.

(ii) Presence of adhesive organs or suckers to cling on to the host like in tapeworms and leeches.

(iii) Loss of digestive system *i.e.*, tapeworm.

(iv) High reproductive capacity *i.e.*, roundworm produces large progeny.

Q.9 Do you agree that regional and local variations exist within each biome? Substantiate your answer with suitable example.

Ans. Yes, regional and local variatious exist within each biome. A biome can be defined as the large communities of the world and shows that area with similar climate have communities of same type.

Climate is the main factor that determine the type of soil which in turn determines the type of vegetation. The type of vegetation and climate together determine the kind of microorganisms and animals. Different ecosystems are joined by transitional forms. A same species occuring in different ecosystems of a biome has regional variations which are genetically based and are called **ecotypes**.

The other determining factors are latitude and altitude, intensity and duration of winter and summer days, water mass and topography. The main biome of the world does not show boundary of any country and regional and local variations exist in each biome.

For examples temperate deciduous forest receives an annual precipitation between 75-150 cm and tropical rain forest show a rainfall above 140 cm/yr which may reach upto 400 cm/yr.

Q.10 Which element is responsible for causing soil salinity? At what concentration does the soil become saline?

Ans. **Soil salinity** is the salt content in soil, which is caused by improper irrigation and by the accumulation of soluble salts and sodium (Na^+) ion. The process of increasing salt content is termed as salinisation.

The high salt concentration of soil is caused by improper irrigation method from a salt laden water table. When salt concentration in soil is increased, than it get accumulated due to evaporation. Human activities like fertilising crop is also responsible for salinity of soil.

As fertiliser contain potassium, which can form a naturally occuring salt-sylvite. Salinity of soil degrades soil quality and vegetation. Normally the pH value of soil comprises between 2.2-9.7, which increase due to high salt content thus degrading the soil.

Q.11 Does light factor affect the distribution of organisms? Write a brief note giving suitable examples of either plants or animals.

Ans. Plants require sunlight for photosynthesis. Plants show stratification both in forest and deep lake according to penetration of light. Therefore, light is an important factor that affects the distribution of plants. Some examples are given below,

(i) Many species of small plants (herbs and shrubs) growing in forests are adapted to photosynthesise optimally under very low light conditions as a result, they will be seen distributed in shady areas under tall, canopied trees.

(ii) Many plants in the shade will grow vertically to gain access to light. These plants will appear to have smaller leafs as compared to others of the same species and or same age found in conditions with better sunlight.

(iii) Large sized trees will be present in areas that get abundant sunlight.

(iv) Plants which are dependent on sunlight to meet their photoperiodic requirements for flowering, will try to get distributed in the area, where this requirement is being met for their reproductive success.

Q.12 Give one example for each of the following

I. Eurythermal plant species ....

II. A hot water spring organism ....

III. An organism seen in deep ocean trenches ....

IV. An organism seen in compost pit ....

V. A parasitic angiosperm ....

VI. A stenothermal plant species ....

VII. Soil organism ....

VIII. A benthic animal ....

IX. Antifreeze compound seen in antarctic fish...............

X. An organism which can conform...............

Ans. I. Pine trees (Any one)

II. *Thermus aquaticus*

III. An glerfish Jelly fishes, Euplectella (Any one)

IV. Earthworm

V. *Cuscuta*

VI. *Cocos nucifera,* Palm (Anyone)

VII. Actinomycetes

VIII. *Octopus,* starfish (Anyone)

IX. Antifreeze Glycoprotiens

X. Amphibians

Chapter 14

Ecosystem

Multiple Choice Questions (MCQs)

Q.1 Decomposers like fungi and bacteria are

(i) autotrophs
(ii) heterotrophs
(iii) saprotrophs
(iv) chemo-autotrophs

Choose the correct answer

(a) (i) and (iii)
(b) (i) and (iv)
(c) (ii) and (iii)
(d) (i) and (ii)

Thinking Process On the basis of mode of nutrition organism can be classified as autotrophs and heterotrophs.

Ans. *(c)* Decomposers like fungi and bacteria are both heterotrophs and saprotrophs. Heterotrophs are the organisms that cannot produce their own food and derive their nutrition from other organisms. Whereas, autotrophs and chemo-autotrophs are those organisms which synthesis their own food.

While **Saprotrophs** are the organisms which obtain their nourishment from dead organic matter or remains of both plant and animals. They are also known as decomposer as they play an important role in recycling of minerals by decomposing dead organic matter.

Q.2 The process of mineralisation by microorganisms helps in the release of

(a) inorganic nutrients from humus
(b) both organic and inorganic nutrients from detritus
(c) organic nutrients from humus
(d) inorganic nutrients from detritus and formation of humus.

Ans. *(a)* The process of mineralisation by micro-organisms helps in the release of inorganic nutrients from humus. Humus and mineral (inorganic nutrients) are obtained by the process of humification and mineralisaton.

Mineralisation is also responsible for release of inorganic substances, both minerals (K^+, Mg^{++}, Ca^{++} and NH_4^+) and non-minerals by products like H_2O and CO_2 from dead organic matter of plant's and animal's remains.

Q.3 Productivity is the rate of production of biomass expressed in terms of

(i) $(\text{kcal m}^{-3})\ \text{yr}^{-1}$ (ii) $\text{gm}^{-2}\text{yr}^{-1}$
(iii) $\text{g}^{-1}\text{yr}^{-1}$ (iv) $(\text{kcal m}^{-2})\ \text{yr}^{-1}$

(a) (ii) (b) (iii) (c) (ii) and (iv) (d) (i) and (iii)

Ans. *(c)* **Productivity** is the rate of production of biomass or organic matter by any trophic level per unit area over a time period. It is expressed/measured in term of weight (*e.g.*, $\text{gm}^{-2}\text{yr}^{-1}$) or energy (*e.g.*, $\text{kcal/m}^2\text{/yr}$).

Q.4 An inverted pyramid of biomass can be found in which ecosystem?

(a) Forest (b) Marine (c) Grass land (d) Tundra

Thinking Process Biomass is the amount of living organic matter in an ecosystem while its pyramid show relationship between producers and consumers in an ecosystem.

Ans. *(b)* In case of marine ecosystem the pyramid of biomass is inverted because the biomass of fishes exceeds the biomass of phytoplanktons which make the small standing crop of aquatic ecosystems.

Q.5 Which of the following is not a producer?

(a) *Spirogyra* (b) *Agaricus* (c) *Volvox* (d) *Nostoc*

Ans. *(b)* *Agaricus* belongs to basidiomycetes fungi which is, heterotrophs (saptrotrophs) class. It is popularly called as mushroom.

Whereas *Spirogyra*, and *volvox* are green algae and autotrophs, *i.e.*, producer. While *Nostoc* is blue-green algae (cyanobacteria) that is also a producer (autotroph).

Q.6 Which of the following ecosystems is most productive in terms of net primary production?

(a) Deserts (b) Tropical rain forests
(c) Oceans (d) Estuaries

Ans. *(b)* In terms of net primary productivity tropical rain forests are at the top followed by coral reef, esturies, desert and ocean.

Q. 7 Pyramid of numbers is

(a) always upright (b) always inverted
(c) either upright or inverted (d) neither upright nor inverted

Thinking Process Ecological pyramids are generally prepared on the basis of 3 ecological parameters, number of individuals, organic matter or biomass and amount of energy.

Ans. *(c)* Pyramid of number in ecosystems can be inverted or upright. For instance, in terrestrial ecosystem, pyramids of number is upright. Whereas in case of successive decrease in members of trophic level like a big tree as in parasitic food chains, it is inverted.

Q.8 Approximately how much of the solar energy that falls on the leaves of a plant is converted to chemical energy by photosynthesis?

(a) Less than 1% (b) 2-10%
(c) 30% (d) 50%

Ans. *(b)* Aproximately 2-10% of the solar energy that falls on the leaves of plants is converted to chemical energy by photosynthesis. This is because of all the incident solar radiation less than 50% is Photosynthetically Active Radiation (PAR) and about 2-10% or 1-5% of solar incident energy is captured by the autotrophs for conversion.

Q.9 Among the following where do you think the process of decomposition would be the fastest?

(a) Tropical rain forest (b) Antarctic
(c) Dry arid region (d) Alpine region

Thinking Process Tropical rain forest biome show well defined stratification, *i.e.,* grouping of plants in well defind layer of trees according to their heights. These layer of plant are called as **strata** or storeys.

Ans. *(a)* The lowest strata of the tropical rain forest recieves less solar radiation and the soil is rich in minerals and humus.

As high temperature and moisture (humidity) are favourable for high microbial activity, the process of decomposition is fastest in this type of biome.

Q.10 How much of the net primary productivity of a terrestrial ecosystem is eaten and digested by herbivores?

(a) 1% (b) 10% (c) 40% (d) 90%

Ans. *(b)* 10% of the Net Primary Productivity (NPP) of a terresterial ecosystem is eaten and digested by herbivores. This is due to the 10% law of energy transfer.

According to the 10% law, only 10% percent of the energy is tranferred to each trophic level from the lower trophic level.

Q.11 During the process of ecological succession the changes that take place in communities are

(a) orderly and sequential
(b) random
(b) very quick
(d) not influenced by the physical environment

Ans. *(a)* The **gradual** and **predictable** changes in the species composition of a given area is called ecological succession. These changes are **orderly** and **sequential**.

Q.12 Climax community is in a state of

(a) non-equilibrium (b) equilibrium
(c) disorder (d) constant change

Thinking Process A climax community is the final stage of ecological succession.

Ans. *(b)* During ecological or biotic succession, climax community is stable, self perpetuating and is the final biotic community. As it is developed at the end of succession. Therefore, it is in the state of equilibrium.

Q.13 Among the following bio-geo-chemical cycles which one does not have losses due to respiration?

(a) Phosphorus (b) Nitrogen
(c) Sulphur (d) All of these

Ans. *(d)* Phosphorus, nitrogen and sulphur biogeochemical cycle does not have any losses due to the process of respiration. This is because they are not involved in any gaseous exchanges. While cycles like carbon and oxygen are affected by the process of respiration.

Q.14 The sequence of communities of primary succession in water is

(a) Phytoplankton, sedges, free-floating hydrophytes, rooted hydrophytes, grasses and trees.
(b) Phytoplankton, free-floating hydrophytes, rooted hydrophytes, sedges, grasses and trees.
(c) Free-floating hydrophytes, sedges, phytoplankton, rooted hydrophytes, grasses and trees.
(d) Phytoplankton, rooted submerged hydrophytes, floating hydrophytes, reed swamp, sedges, meadow and trees.

Ans. *(d)* The sequence of communities of primary succession in water is phytoplankton (pioneer stage) → rooted submerged hydrophytes → floating hydrophyte (floating stage) → reed swamp → sedges → meadow and woodland (trees).

Q.15 The reservoir for the gaseous type of bio-geochemical cycle exists in

(a) stratosphere (b) atmosphere (c) ionosphere (d) lithosphere

Thinking Process Nutrient cycles are of two types, gaseous and sedimentry.

Ans. *(b)* The reservoir for the gaseous type of bio-geochemical cycle exists in the atmosphere. Whereas stratosphere, ionosphere and lithosphere are the parts of atmosphere.

For example, in carbon cycle, carbon is found in CO_2 (carbondioxide) form in the atmosphere. Similarly, in the nitrogen cycle, nitrogen exists as N_2 in the atmosphere

Q.16 If the carbon atoms fixed by producers already have passed through three species, the trophic level of the last species would be

(a) scavenger (b) tertiary producer
(c) tertiary consumer (d) secondary consumer

Ans. *(c)* If the carbon atoms fixed by producers already have passed through three species, it means that the carbon atoms already moved through producers *i.e* primary consumers and a secondary consumer. Therefore, the trophic level of the last species will be tertiary consumer.

Producer ⟶ Ist Trophic level (Primary consumer) ⟶ IInd Trophic level (Secondary consumer) ⟶ IIIrd Trophic level (Tertiary consumer)

Q.17 Which of the following type of ecosystem is expected in an area where evaporation exceeds precipitation, and mean annual rainfall is below 100mm?

(a) Grassland (b) Shrubby forest
(c) Desert (d) Mangrove

Ans. ***(c)*** In true desert biome, rainfall is less than 100mm/year, characterised by extremely hot days and cold nights. Evaporation from true desert always exceeds 7-50 times the precipitation (rainfall). Desert ecosystem of biomes are more in Northerm hemisphere than Southern hemisphere.

Whereas, Grassland ecosystem receives medium rain fall ranging from 25-75 cm/yr, but evaporation rate is not higher than precipitation rate.

Shrubby forest receives rainfall 90 – 150 cm/yr.

Mangrove forests receive annual rainfall ranging from 100 – 150 cm/yr.

Q.18 The zone at the edge of a lake or ocean which is alternatively exposed to air and immersed in water is called

(a) pelagic zone (b) benthic zone

(c) lentic zone (d) littoral zone

Thinking Process On the basis of light availability, an aquatic habitat can be categorised into littoral, limnetic, profundal and benthic zone.

Ans. ***(d)*** The **littoral zone** is the zone at the edge of a lake or ocean or in aquatic habitat which is alternatively exposed to air. Hence, light is also available and immersed in water.

Whereas, **pelagic zone** refers to any zone of water in a sea or lake that is neither close to bottom nor the shore.

Benthic zone refers to the bottom part of the water body where light is not available (aphotic zone) and it is dark. Microorganisms and benthic organisms are found in this zone.

Lentic zone refers to standing or relatively still water in an aquatic ecosystem.

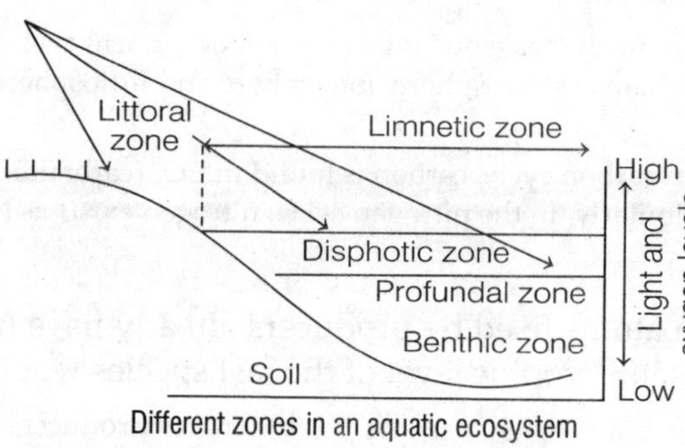

Different zones in an aquatic ecosystem

Q.19 Edaphic factor refers to

(a) water (b) soil

(c) relative humidity (d) altitude

Thinking Process Edaphic factor is a type of abiotic factor

Ans. ***(b)*** Edaphic factor refers to soil properties like soil texture, soil type, pH value, topography and nutrient availability.

Whereas water, relative humidity and altitude are the abiotic components of an ecosystem as well, but affects the climatic conditions hence are climatic factors.

Q.20 Which of the following is an ecosystem service provided by a natural ecosystem?

(a) Cycling of nutrients
(b) Prevention of soil erosion
(c) Pollutant absorption and reduction of the threat of global warming
(d) All of the above

Ans. ***(d)*** A natural ecosystem maintain its biotic and abiotic factors naturally. The products of ecosystem processes are called the ecosystem services. A healthy ecosystem provides a wide range of economic, environmental and aesthetic goods and services.

The various ecosystem services provided by a natural ecosystem includes

(i) Pur air and water
(ii) Nutrient cycling
(iii) Generation of fertile soil
(iv) Maintenance of biodiverstity
(v) Storage site for carbon
(vi) Pollination of crops

Very Short Answer Type Questions

Q.1 Name an organism found as secondary carnivore in an aquatic ecosystem.

Ans. Water birds like ducks and water fowls are the tertiary consumers in an aquatic ecosystem and occupy the secondary carnivore position in aquatic ecosystem. In an aquatic ecosystem, this can be understood as follows

Producer (Phytoplankton) → Primary consumer (Zooplankton) → Secondary consumer (small fish and water beetle) (Ist to carnivore) → Tertiary consumer (IInd carnivore like large fish, water birds like fowl and duck).

Q.2 What does the base tier of the ecological pyramid represent?

Ans. The base tier of the ecological pyramids represent the producers (first trophic level).

Q.3 Under what conditions would a particular stage in the process of succession revert back to an earlier stage?

Ans. Conditions due to which a particular stage in process of succession can revert back are as follows.

(i) Natural disturbances like fire, flood or any other natural disaster.
(ii) Anthropogenic activities like deforestation, pollution by humans.

Q.4 Arrange the following as observed in vertical stratification of a forest. Grass, Shrubby plants, Teak, *Amaranthus*.

Ans. Vertical stratification (dispersion) of species in a forest ecosystem is arranged as grass (floor of forest) → *Amaranthus* → Shrubby plants → Teak (tree).

Q.5 Name an omnivore which occurs in both grazing food chain and the decomposer food chain.

Ans. Cockroaches and crow are two omnivore, that are present in both grazing and decomposer food chain.

Q.6 Justify the pitcher plant as a producer.

Ans. Pitcher plant (*Napenthes*) is an insectivores plant, which posseses chlorophyll and is capable of capturing solar radiations for photosynthesis. These plants are present in the soil lacking nitrogen thus to make up their nitrogen deficiency they trap insects.

Q.7 Name any two organisms which can occupy more than one trophic level in an ecosystem.

Ans. Human being (man) and birds (sparrow) can be frequently seen in more than one trophic level, in an ecosystem.

Q.8 In the North East region of India, during the process of jhum cultivation, forests are cleared by burning and left for regrowth after a year of cultivation. How would you explain the regrowth of forest in ecological term?

Ans. Forests that are cleared by burning and left for regrowth will show secondary succession. Since, soil is already present, the buried seeds germinates. Due to wind dispersal and some other natural forces, new seeds will be brought into the area and new species will colonise the forest again.

Q.9 Climax stage is achieved quickly in secondary succession as compared to primary succession. Why?

Ans. The rate of ecological succession is quicker in secondary succession as compared to primary succession as the soil (substratum) is already available for further succession. While in primary succession, the succession starts from bare rocks, which take time for first colonisation by plants as there is no nutrient holding mechanisms.

Q.10 Among bryophytes, lichens and fern which one is a pioneer species in a xeric succession?

Ans. The species that invade a bare area are called pioneer species. In a xeric succession, the pioneer species are usually lichens followed by bryophytes which are succeeded by ferns and some other bigger plants.

Lichens produces chemical substances which corrodes rock surface and release minerals required for growth. The corroded rocks accumulate soil particles get accumulated by wind and provides substrate for the growth of bryophytes and ferns.

Q.11 What is the ultimate source of energy for the ecosystems?

Ans. **Solar radiation** is the ultimate source of energy for the ecosystem.

Q.12 Is the common edible mushroom an autotroph or a heterotroph?

Ans. Common edible mushroom (*Agaricus*) is **achlorophyllous** (does not possess chlorophyll) and therefore they are heterotroph.

Q.13 Why are oceans least p ductive?

Ans. Oceans are least productive ecause

(i) There is insufficient sol radiation as sunlight decreases with the increasing depth of the ocean.

(ii) Oceans are nitrogen defi nt which is an important nutrient for plants.

(iii) They have high salinity which is not favourable for all plants.

Q.14 Why is the rate of assimilation of energy at the herbivore level called secondary productivity?

Ans. The rate of assimilation of energy at herbivore level is called secondary **productivity**. This is because the biomass available to the organisms of next trophic level (consumer) for further consumption is a resultant of the primary productivity (energy captured by producers) which is formed by autotrophs (plants).

Q.15 Why are nutrient cycles in nature called biogeochemical cycles?

Ans. Nutrient cycles are called biogeochemical cycles because they are involved in the circulation of nutrients through biological, geological (abiotic components) and chemical processes.

Nutrients like carbon, phosphorus, nitrogen and sulphur are recycled through the, ecosystem.

Q.16 Give any two examples of xerarch succession.

Ans. Two example of xerach succession are succession on bare rocks (lithosere) and succession in desert sand dunes.

Q.17 Define self sustainability

Ans. Self sustainability is the maintenance of an ecosystem by itself or naturally. A self sustains ecosystem remains viable and functional indefinitely due to self regulations and inputs.

Q.18 Given below is a figure of an ecosystem. Answer the following questions?

(i) What type of ecosystem is shown in the figure?

(ii) Name any plant that is characteristic of such ecosystem.

Ans. (i) It is a tropical deciduous forest ecosystem.

(ii) In India this type of forest ecosystem is characterised by, *Dipterocarpus*, Jamun, Amla, Palas, mahua and Semul plants.

Q.19 What is common to earthworm, mushroom, soil mites and dung beetle in an ecosystem.

Ans. They all are designated as primary consumer in a detritus food chain and are termed as detritivores. All of them take part in decomposition.

Short Answer Type Questions

Q.1 Organisms at a higher trophic level have less energy available. Comment.

Ans. Energy flow in the ecosystem follows the 10% energy flow law, proposed by Lindeman. According to this law only 10% of the energy available at each trophic level, gets transferred to the next trophic level, the rest is lost in the environment as heat. There is 90% loss of energy at each trophic level.

At higher trophic levels, the energy available to organisms keeps on decreasing. Thus, the top carnivore gains least amount of energy in a food chain.

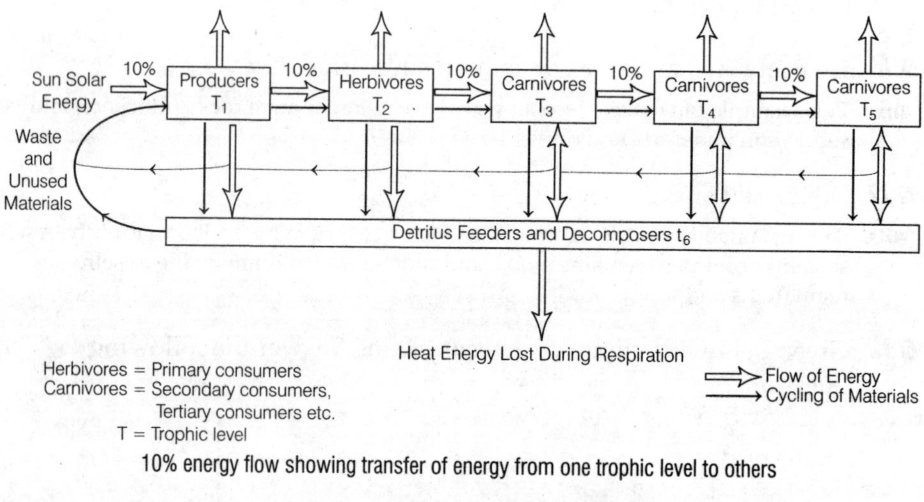

10% energy flow showing transfer of energy from one trophic level to others

Q.2 The number of trophic levels in an ecosystem are limited. Comment.

Ans. The number of trophic level in an ecosystem are each limited and are not more than 4-5. This is because the amount of energy decreases with successive trophic level, as only 10% of energy is transferred from one trophic level to the next successive level.

Therefore, rest of the energy is lost in the form of respiration and other vital activities to maintain life. In the case of more trophic levels the residual energy will be limited and decrease to such an extent that it cannot further support any trophic level by the flow of energy.

Given below is an example of food chain.

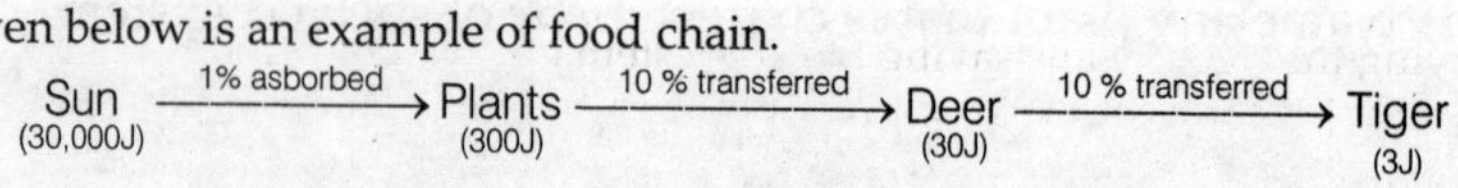

Q.3 Is an aquarium a complete ecosystem?

Ans. Yes, aquarium is a complete ecosystem. Aquarium is a man made ecosystem (artificial). It Possess all biotic (plants and fishes) and abiotic components (air, water) required for survival of fishes.

Q.4 What could be the reason for the faster rate of decomposition in the tropics?

Ans. Tropics are characterised by high temperature moisture and soil which is rich in humus and minerals. As the decomposition rate is regulated by climatic factors, thus optimum temperature (25°-30°C) and humidity enhance the activity of decomposers. While the dead remain is also available in large amount, which supports the faster rate of decomposition in the tropics.

Q.5 Human activities interfere with carbon cycle. List any two such activities.

Ans. Two human activities that interfere with carbon cycles are

(i) Rapid deforestation

(ii) Massive burning of fossil fuel for energy and transport.

Both these activities increase the carbon dioxide concentration in the atmosphere.

Q.6 Flow of energy through various trophic levels in an ecosystem is unidirectional and non-cyclic. Explain.

Ans. Flow of energy in an ecosystem is always unidirectional, *i.e.*, energy flows in one way. It is is non-cyclic as energy is not recycled. Once energy is used or lost as heat, it cannot be reused within a system.

Q.7 Apart from plants and animals, microbes form a permanent biotic component in an ecosystem. While plants have been referred to as autotrophs and animals as heterotrophs. What are microbes referred to as? How do the microbes fulfill their energy requirements?

Ans. On the basis of nutrition, organisms are classified as autotrophs and heterotrophs.

Microbes are **saprotrophs** and derive nourishment from dead organic remains of plants and animals. They are also responsible for decomposition of organic remains.

Q.8 Poaching of tiger is a burning issue in today's world. What implication would this activity have on the functioning of the ecosystem of which the tigers are an integral part?

Ans. Tiger represents an important part of the food web and helps in maintaining the ecological stability. As a carnivore, it keeps a check on the unlimited growth of herbivores and also removes sick or old animals from the population. It also acts as an indicator of the forest's health. Decrease in the number of tigers will increase the number of herbivores, large numbers of herbivore will result in destruction of vegetation and desertification of an area.

Saving the tiger means saving the ecosystem.

Q.9 In relation to energy transfer in ecosystem, explain the statement "10kg of deer's meat is equivalent to 1 kg of lion's flesh".

Ans. In an ecosystem, flow (transfer) of energy is unidirectional. As per 10% law of lindeman, energy and biomass transfer from one trophic level to the next trophic is only 10%.

Deer (Biomass 10 kg) ⟶ Lion (1 kg)
Energy lost in the process of respiration and other vital activities, 90% i.e., 9kg

Q.10 Primary productivity varies from ecosystem to ecosystem. Explain?

Ans. Primary productivity is the rate at which primary producers (plants) capture and store solar radiation to form chemical energy. Primary production depends upon number of producers (green plant) which are available in different ecosystem.

So, primary productivity varies from ecosystem to ecosystem as no two ecosystem are similar.

Q.11 Sometimes due to biotic/abiotic factor the climax remain in a particular seral stage (pre climax) without reaching climax. Do you agree with this statement. If yes give a suitable example.

Ans. Sometimes climax remains in a particular seral stage without reaching to the climax because during ecological succession any change in abiotic and biotic component may affect the particular seral stage, leading to preclimax stage before the climax is achieved.

This type of condition occurs due to presence of seeds and other agents. Secondarily, the base area may be invaded by moss or exotic weeds thus exhibiting succession and the climax community is never regenerated. This may also occur due to overgrazing, excessive human exploitation, natural calamities like-fire landslide, floods, change in soil texture.

Q.12 What is an incomplete ecosystem? Explain with the help of suitable example.

Ans. An ecosystem that is devoid of certain biotic and abiotic factors is know as incomplete ecosystem.

An incomplete ecosystem is characterised by the absence of an essential component of ecosystem.

For example, aquariums, as they contain producers and consumers but do not have decomposers.

Q.13 What are the shortcomings of ecological pyramids in the study of ecosystem?

Ans. **Ecological pyramids** are the graphical representation of ecological parameters. These are characterised by pyramid of number, pyramid of mass and pyramid of energy in an ecosystem.

Shortcoming of ecological pyrmids are

1. It does not take acount of same species that belongs two or more trophic levels.
2. It is based on assumption of simple food chains, which do not exist in nature.
3. It does not in clude decomposers.

Q.14 How do you distinguish between humification and mineralisation?

Ans. **Humification** is the process of decomposition of soil that leads to accumulation of a dark-coloured amorphous substance called **humus**. Humus is highly resistant to microbial action and undergoes decomposition at a very slow rate. This process is essential for disposal of organic remains.

Mineralisation is the process by which the humus is further degraded by microbes and inorganic nutrients or minerals and are released back into the substratum. This process is essential for biogeochemical cycles.

Q.15 Fill in the trophic levels (1, 2, 3 and 4) in the boxes provided in the figure.

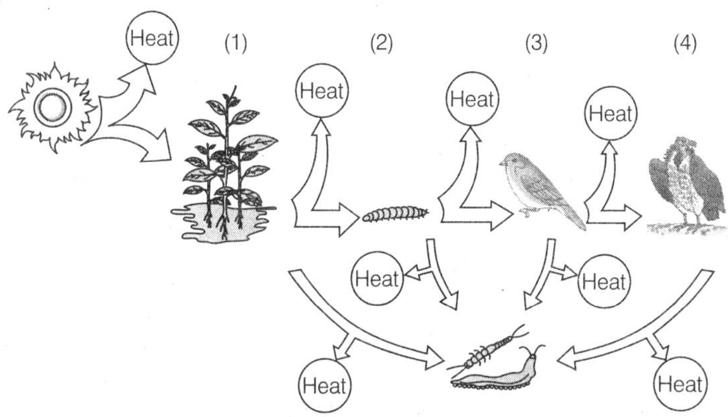

Ans.
1. First trophic level (producers) - Plants
2. Second trophic level (primary consumers) - Herbivores
3. Third trophic level (secondary consumers) - Carnivores
4. Fourth trophic level (tertiary consumers) - Top carnivores

Q.16 The rate of decomposition of detritus is affected by the abiotic factors like availability of oxygen, pH of the soil substratum, temperature etc. Discuss.

Ans. **Decomposition** of dead remain or matter of animal and plant is carried out by microorganisms like bacteria, fungi etc. The growth rate of these decomposers is affected by abiotic factors like temperature, humidity, pH of soil and light etc.

The soil pH affect acidophilic, neutrophilic and basophilic microorganisms. The aerobic and anaerobic processes depend on the availability of oxygen.

In presence of oxygen, complete degradation while in absence of oxygen, there will be an incomplete degradation. Similarly, at extreme temperatures microbes can not grow optimally but moderate temperature favours the growth of microorganisms.

Long Answer Type Questions

Q.1 A farmer harvests his crop and expresses his harvest in three different ways.

(a) I have harvested 10 quintals of wheat.

(b) I have harvested 10 quintals of wheat today in one acre of land.

(c) I have harvested 10 quintals of wheat in one acre of land, 6 months after sowing.

Do the above statements mean one and the same thing. If your answer is '**yes**', give reasons. And if your answer is '**no**' explain the meaning of each expression.

Ans. No, as the different statement mean different outcomes.

(a) This statements shows the quantity of biomass produced, but does not show the duration or area of production.

(b) This statement show quantity as well as area but duration of production is not mentioned.

(c) This statement shows quantity, area and duration of production. Therefore, this can be used to calculate productivity of the farm.

Q.2 Justify the following statement in terms of ecosystem dynamics. "Nature tends to increase the gross primary productivity, while man tends to increase the net primary productivity".

Ans. In term of ecsosystem dynamics, flow of energy takes place from one trophic level to the next trophic level and occurs in **unidirectional way**. About 50% of solar energy incident over earth is present in **Photosynthetic Active Radiation** (PAR) and only 2-10% of this PAR is utilised by green plants to form chemical energy through photosynthesis. This total rate of energy capture is known as Gross Primary Productivity (GPP).

GPP utilised by plants minus respiration losses is the net primary productivity and is available to the organism of next trophic level (herbivore and decomposers) for consumption.

Gross primary productivity of an ecosystem is the rate of production of organic matter during photosynthesis. So nature tend to increase gross primary productivity through supporting the large number of plant (producers) in an ecosystem. Net primary productivity is the available biomass for the consumption to heterotrophs (human and animals). Man tries to increase net primary productivity by cultivating food and other crops.

Formula to generate NPP is GPP – R = NPP

Q.3 Which of the following ecosystems will be more productive in terms of primary productivity? Justify your answer. A young forest, a natural old forest, a shallow polluted lake, alpine meadow.

Ans. **Primary Productivity** can be defind as the rate at which primary producers (Green plants) captures and store solar radiation in form of biomass. This is measured in terms of weight (g^{-2}) and energy (Kcal m^{-2}) per year in given time.

So, primary productivity varies from ecosystem to ecosystem. The ecosystem which possess more producers will be more productive in term of primary productivity.

Therefore, young forest grows quicker than older and are more productive. While the shallow polluted lake and alpine meadow will be less productive because of less number of producers and high amount of dead and decaying matter.

Q.4 What are the three types of ecological pyramids. What information is conveyed by each pyramid with regard to structure, function and energy in the ecosystem.

Ans. An ecological pyramid is a **graphical representation** of an ecological parameters as the number of individual present various trophic level of food chain.

Properties of ecological pyramid

(i) The trophic structure of an ecosystem is represented in the form of ecological pyramids.

(ii) The base of each pyramid represents the producers or the first trophic level, while the apex represents tertiary or top level consumer.

The three types of ecological pyramids are

(a) **Pyramid of number** shows relationship between producers and consumers in an ecosystem in terms of numbers. It may be inverted or upright pyramid.

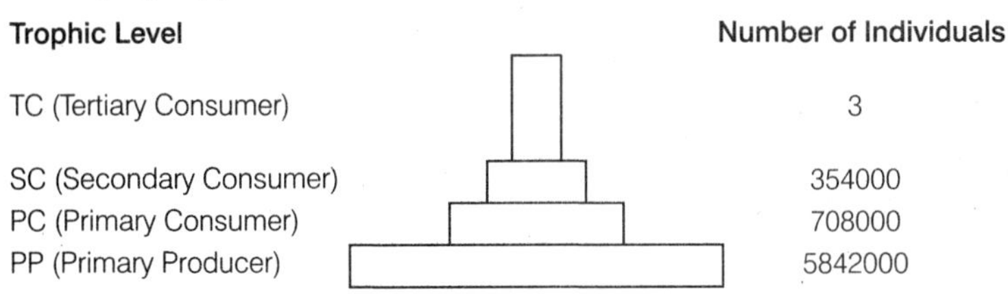

Pyramid of numbers in a grassland ecosystem

(b) **Pyramid of biomass** shows relationship between producers and consumers in an ecosystem terms of biomass. It can be

- Upright, *e.g.*, in case of grass land ecosystem.
- Inverted, *e.g.*, in case of pond ecosystem.

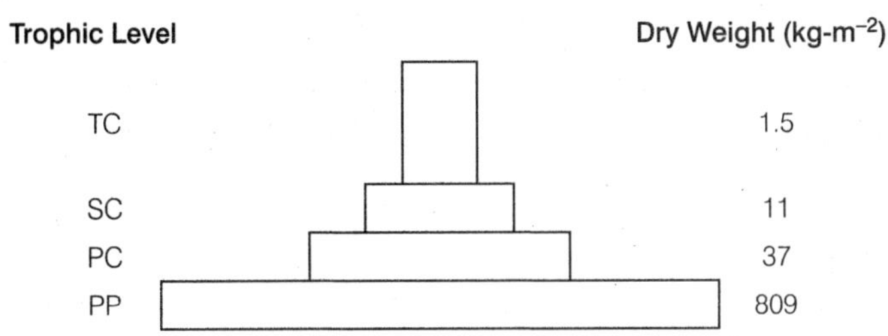

Upright pyramid of biomass shows a sharp decrease in biomass at higher trophic levels

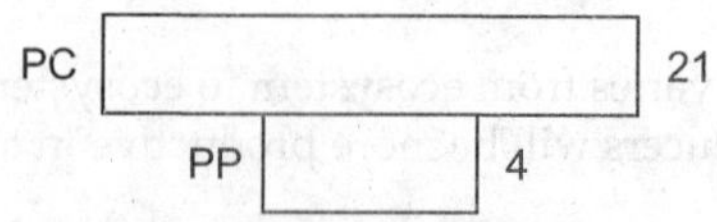

Inverted pyramid of biomass

Small standing crop of phytoplankton supports large standing crop of zooplankton.

(c) **Pyramid of energy** is the relationship between producers and consumers in an ecosystem in terms of flow of energy. It is always upright because energy is lost as heat at each step. The energy level is maximum at the producer level.

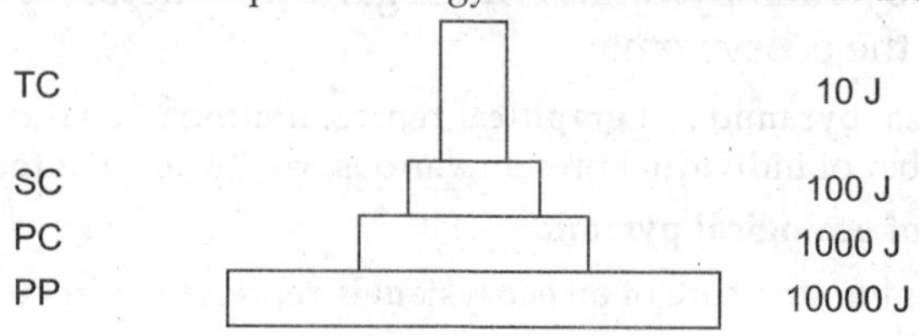

1000000 J of sunlight

Q.5 Write a short note on pyramid of numbers and pyramid of biomass.

Ans. Ecological pyramids are graphical representations of the relationship between organisms of different trophic levels that can be expressed in terms of number, biomass or energy. In most ecosystems, the pyramid of number is **upright**, *i.e.*, producers are more in number than the herbivores and herbivores are more in number than the carnivores. But, the pyramid of number may be **inverted** as in a forest ecosystem, where the number of insects (primary consumers) are greater than the number of trees (producers). The pyramid of biomass is **upright**, generally, as the biomass of producers is more than biomass of herbivores and that of herbivores is more than biomass of carnivores. But, it is **inverted** in ecosystems like sea ecosystem, where the biomass of fishes (primary consumers) exceeds than phytoplankton (producers).

Q.6 Given below is a list of autotrophs and heterotrophs. With your knowledge about food chain, establish various linkages between the organisms on the principle of 'eating and being eaten'. What is this inter-linkage established known as?
Algae, *hydrilla*, grasshopper, rat, squirrel, crow, maize plant, deer, rabbit, lizard, wolf, snake, peacock, phytoplankton, crustaceans, whale, tiger, lion, sparrow, duck, crane, cockroach, spider, toad, fish, leopard, elephant, goat, *Nymphaea, Spirogyra*.

Ans. A straight line sequence of 'who eats whom' or eating and being eaten in an ecosystem is called a **food chain**. A network of cross connecting food chains involving producers, consumers and decomposers is termed as a **food web**.

Leopard, Lion, Tiger—**Top carnivore** (Top tropic level)

Spider, cockroach, lizard, wolf, snake, toad, fish, crane, Crow — **Secondry Consumer** (IIIrd trophic level).

Crustaceans, grasshopper, deer, rat, squirrel, rabbit, elephant, goat — **Primary Consumer** (IInd trophic level).

Phytoplankton, algae, *Hydrilla,* maize plant, *Nymphaea, Spirogyra*—**Producers** (Ist trophic level).

Q.7 "The energy flow in the ecosystem follows the second law of thermodynamics." Explain.

Ans. According to second law of thermodynamics every activity involving energy transformation is accompanied by dissipation of energy as heat and only a part of it is used in building up tissues in an organisms.

This trapped energy as biomass is transferred to next trophic level. It also stands true for lindemans 10% law, according to which, only 10% of the stored energy is passed from one trophic level to successive trophic level.

Q.8 What will happen to an ecosystem if

(a) All producers are removed

(b) All organisms of herbivore level are eliminated and

(c) All top carnivore population is removed

Ans. (a) Removal of all producer will leads to the collapse of an entire ecosystem. As no biomass will be available to the successive or higher trophic level or heterotrophic organisms.

(b) Elimination of all organisms of herbivore level results into an increase in primary productivity and biomass of producer. As well as carnivores will not be able to survive due to inavailability of food.

(c) Removal of top carnivores also disturb the ecosystem as it will result in huge increase in number of herbivores which will consume all the plants (producers), creating desertification.

Q.9 Give two examples of artificial or man made ecosystems. List the salient features by which they differ from natural ecosystems.

Ans. **Aquarium** and **farm house**, are artificial or man made ecosystem. In artificial ecosystem biotic and abiotic component are maintained artificially like cleaning, feeding and supply of oxygen to fishes in aquarium and irrigation of crop or farm house. Artificial ecosystems are mostly incomplete and they are based on high net productivity. While abiotic and biotic component of natural ecosystem are maintained naturally like nutrient cycle, self sutainability, prevention of soil erosion, pollutant absorption and reduction of threat to global warming (ecological servicer), etc. Natural ecosystems are usually complete and are based on gross productivity.

Q.10 The biodiversity increases when one moves from the pioneer to the climax stage. What could be the explanation?

Ans. During ecological succession biodiversity increase from pioneer to climax stages, due to following reasons.

(a) As succession progresses, the environment becomes **more complex** with the development of various plant species, trees and shrubs. This creates diverse **habitats** and **niches** for different species of animals, plants and microorganisms.

(b) In the early stages (pioneer stage), the environment often has limited resources such as nutrients, space and food. As succession continues, the **soil quality** improves and resources like **water, nutrients**, and **light** become more abundant. With better resource availability, more species are able to establish themselves in the ecosystem. This leads to an **increase in species diversity.**

(c) The **climax community** represents a stable, mature ecosystem, where conditions like temperature, moisture and nutrient cycling are balanced and predictable. This stability supports a **wider variety of organisms** that can adapt to specific conditions of the ecosystem. In contrast, the **pioneer stage** tends to be harsher, with fluctuating environmental conditions, making it difficult for many species to survive.

(d) In the pioneer stage, ecosystems are often more **disturbed** (*e.g.*, by wind, water, or fire). Over time, as succession progresses, the ecosystem becomes more resilient to disturbances, allowing more species to thrive and persist. **Climax** communities are less prone to disturbances allowing the organisms present to **co-exist** over longer periods and increasing **species richness.**

Q.11 What is a biogeochemical cycle. What is the role of the reservoir in a biogeochemical cycle? Give an example of a sedimentary cycle with reservoir located in earth's crust.

Ans. The movement of nutrient elements through the various components of an ecosystem is called nutrient cycling or biogeochemical cycles (Bio–living; geo–including air, water and rocks). Nutrient cycles are of two types

(a) Gaseous (b) Sedimentary

Atmosphere is the reservoir for gaseous type of nutrient cycle (*e.g.*, nitrogen and carbon cycle). Earth's crust is the reservoir of **sedimentary cycle** (*e.g.*, sulphur and phosphorus cycle). The function of the reservoir is to meet with the deficit, which occurs due to **imbalance** in the rate of influx and efflux.

Phosphorus cycle is an example of sedimentary nutrient cycle since, it moves from land and sedimented at the bottom of the seas, then back to land again. The natural reservoir of phosphorus is earth's crust. Rock contains phosphorus in the form of phosphates. By weathering and soil erosion, phosphates enter streams, rivers and then to oceans. With great movements of the crustal plates, sea floor is uplifted and phosphates become exposed on the drained land surfaces. From here, weathering over long periods of time releases phosphates.

From rocks, minute amount of these phosphates dissolve in soil and are absorbed by the roots of the plants. Herbivores and other animals obtain this element from plants when they consume plants as their food.

The waste products and the dead organisms are decomposed by **phosphate-solubilising bacteria**, thus releasing phosphorus.

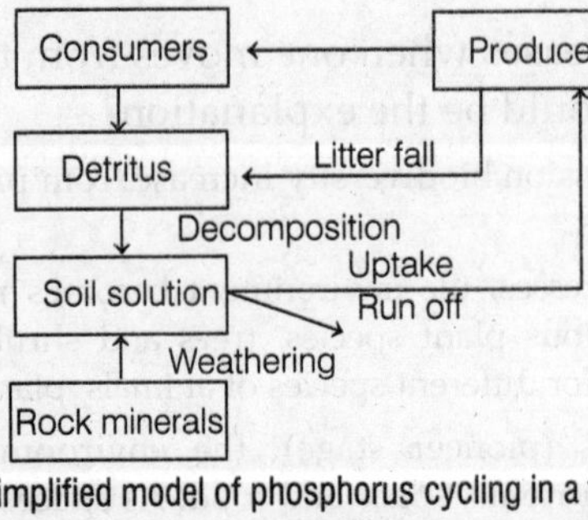

A simplified model of phosphorus cycling in a terrestrial ecosystem

Q.12 What will be the P/R ratio of a climax community and a pioneer community? What explanation could you offer for the changes seen in P/R ratio of a pioneer community and the climax community?

Ans. **Production/Respiration ratio** (P/R) ratio shows the relationship between gross production and total community respiration. If P/R=1 a steady state community results in stability in climax community.

If productivity of community is more than respiration in pioneer community it helps in building of biomass.

This result may be instantaneously or over a period of time. If P/R is persistantly greater or less then the organic matter either accumulates or is depleted respectively.

Pioneer Community	Climax Community
The species that invade a bare area are called pioneer species e.g., lichens on bare rockes.	It is a final biotic community that develops in an area.
In aquatic ecosystem there are phytoplanktons.	It occurs over an area previously occupied by several intermediate communities.
In pioneer community the P/R ratio will be more than one.	In climax community the P/R ratio will be 1.

Chapter 15

Biodiversity and Conservation

Multiple Choice Questions (MCQs)

Q.1 Which of the following countries has the highest biodiversity?

(a) South America (b) South Africa
(c) Russia (d) India

Thinking Process Tropical regions (23.5° N – 23.5° S) show the highest biodiversity as climatic conditions, temperature and moisture favour variety of flora and fauna.

Ans. ***(a)*** South America has the highest biodiversity. This is because climate in tropical countries like south America remain relatively undisturbed, constant and predictable. This Provides a sustainable environment for diversification, which favours rich biodiversity. It is known for its vast rainforest (Amazon Rainforest).

Q.2 Which of the following is not a cause for loss of biodiversity?

(a) Destruction of habitat
(b) Invasion by alien species
(c) Keeping animals in zoological parks
(d) Over-exploitation of natural resources

Ans. ***(c)*** Keeping animals in zoological parks is not a cause for loss of biodiversity.

Some of the major causes of biodiversity loss are as follows

(i) Destruction of natural habitat (primary cause).
(ii) Introduction of invasive (alien species) species.
(iii) Over exploitation of natural resources.
(iv) Habitat loss
(v) Pollution

Q.3 Which of the following is not an invasive alien species in the Indian context?

(a) *Lantana* (b) *Cynodon*
(c) *Parthenium* (d) *Eichhornia*

Ans. ***(b)*** *Cynodon* (doob grass) is not an invasive alien species. The other three *Parthenium* (congress or carrot grass), *Eichhornia* (water hyacinth) and *Lantana* are alien species which pose threat to native species.

Q.4 Where among the following will you find pitcher plant?

(a) Rain forest of North-East India (b) Sunderbans
(c) Thar desert (d) Western ghats

Ans. ***(a)*** Pitcher plant (*Nepenthes*) an insectivorous plant is found in rain forest of North-East India. These type of plants generally grow in nitrogen deficient soil, areas with high rainfall and acidic soil.

Q.5 Which one of the following is not a feature of biodiversity hotspots?

(a) Large number of species (b) Abundance of endemic species
(c) Mostly located in the tropics (d) Mostly located in the polar regions

Thinking Process A biodiversity hotspot is a biogeographic region with a significant reservoir of biodiversity which is under threat from humans.

Ans. ***(d)*** There are no biodiversity hotspots in polar regions. Biodiversity hotspots are characterised by large number of flora and fauna and abundance of endemic species. They are mostly found in tropical and temperate regions.

Q.6 Match the following columns.

Column I	Column II
A. Dodo	1. Africa
B. Quagga	2. Russia
C. Thylacine	3. *Mauritius*
D. Stellar's sea cow	4. Australia

Choose the correct match form the following

	A	B	C	D
(a)	1	2	3	4
(b)	4	3	1	2
(c)	3	1	2	4
(d)	3	1	4	2

Ans. ***(d)*** Dodo – *Mauritius*

Quagga – Africa

Thylacine – Australia

Stellar's sea cow – Russia

All these species are extinct.

Q.7 What is common to the following plants *Nepenthes, Psilotum, Rauwolfia* and *Aconitum*?

(a) All are ornamental plants
(b) All are phylogenic link species
(c) All are prone to over exploitation
(d) All are exclusively present in the Eastern Himalayas

Ans. ***(c)*** All of these are prone to over exploitation due to their respective properties listed below.

Nepenthes (pitcher plant) is an insectivorous plant used for its carnivorous and ornamental values.

Rauwofia is used for its medicinal properties, the treatment of high BP.

Psilotum is a pteridophyte over exploited for its wound healing properties. *Aconitum* is a medicinal plan which is used in traditional medicine as well.

Q.8 The one-horned rhinoceros is specific to which of the following sanctuary?

(a) Bhitar Kanika (b) Bandipur
(c) Kaziranga (d) Corbett Park

Ans. ***(c)*** Kaziranga National Park is situated in Golaghat and Nagaon district of Assam. One horned rhinoceros are specific to this park.

While Corbett National Park is situated in district Nainital (Uttarakhand) and is specific for tiger. It is the first National Park of India, which is famous for tigers. The Bandipur National Park (Mysore) is specific for tigers as well. Bhitar Kanika National Park is located in odisha and is specific for salt water crocodile.

Q.9 Amongst the animal groups given below, which one appears to be more vulnerable to extinction?

(a) Insects (b) Mammals (c) Amphibians (d) Reptiles

Ans. ***(c)*** Amphibians have the highest endangerment percentage *i.e.,* 32% of all amphibian species in the world face the threat of extinction. whereas, 23% of all mammal species, 21% of reptile species and 12% of all bird species also facing the risk.

Q.10 Which one of the following is an endangered plant species of India?

(a) *Rauwolfia serpentina* (b) *Santalum album* (sandal wood)
(c) *Cycas beddonei* (d) All of these

Ans. ***(d)*** All of the above mentioned plants are endangered plant species of India. *Rauwolfia serpentina* (sarpgandha), *Santalum album* (sandal wood) and *Cycas beddonei* are facing the threat of extinction due to their medicinal and commercial importance.

Q.11 What is common to *Lantana, Eichhornia* and African catfish?

(a) All are endangered species of India
(b) All are key stone species
(c) All are mammals found in India
(d) All the species are neither threatened nor indigenous species of India.

Ans. ***(d)*** All the three above mentioned species are neither threatened nor indigenous species of India. *Lantana, Eichhornia* (water hyacinth) and African catfish (*Clarias gariepinus*) all are alien (exotic species) which are invasive and have an harmful impact, resulting in extinction of the indigenous species.

Q.12 The extinction of passenger pigeon was due to

(a) Increased number of predatory birds (b) Over-exploitation by humans
(c) Non-availability of the food (d) Bird flu virus infection

Ans. *(b)* Extinction of passenger pigeon (*Ectopistes migratorius*) was due to over exploitation activities like overhunting and habitat destruction by human beings. Factors like increase in number of predatory birds, non-availability of food and bird flu virus infection did not contribute to the extinction of passenger pigeon.

Q.13 Which of the following statements is correct?

(a) *Parthenium* is an endemic species of our country.
(b) African catfish is not a threat to indigenous catfishes.
(c) Steller's sea cow is an extinct animal.
(d) *Lantana* is popularly known as carrot grass.

Ans. *(c)* Statement (c) is correct as Stellar's sea cow (from Russia) is an extinct animal. Factors like overhunting etc. were the major reasons for its extinction.

While *Parthenium* (carrot grass) is an exotic weed, which grows rapidly and adversly affects the native species.

African catfish is also an alien species which adversly affects the growth of indigenous (*Clarias batrachus*) species.

Lantana camara, another alien species, is also strongly competing with native species.

Q.14 Among the ecosystem mentioned below, where can one find maximum biodiversity?

(a) Mangroves (b) Desert (c) Coral reefs (d) Alpine meadows

Thinking Process Formation of coral reef takes place in favourable climatic conditions in costal regions.

Ans. *(c)* Coral reefs are the most productive ecosystem. They form the most diverse parts of only coastal regions, providing a home to fishes, molluscs, crustaceans sponges, cnidarians, etc.

While mangroves, found in coastal regions usually have plants growing in swampy and saline water, deserts have mostly xerophytic species and alpine meadows are related to high altitudes and do not show much tree growth.

Q.15 Which of the following forests is known as the **"Lungs of the planet Earth'**?

(a) Taiga forest (b) Tundra forest
(c) Amazon rain forest (d) Rainforests of North-East India

Thinking Process Tropics possess maximum biological diversity due to undisturbed climatic conditions.

Ans. *(c)* Amazon is a rain forest that covers most of the Amazon basin of South America and teritory including nine nations. It represents over half of the planet's rain forests and exhibits the largest and the most diversified tropical rainforest.

While taiga forest, present in broad belt of Northern hemisphere, represents the largest terrestrial biome. Rain forests of North-East India are tropical forests with a natural reservoir of genetic diversity. Where as tundra forest is a biome where tree growth is hindered by low temperature and short growing season.

Q.16 The active chemical drug reserpine is obtained form

(a) *Datura* (b) *Rauwolfia* (c) *Atropa* (d) *Papaver*

Ans. **(b)** *Rauwolfia vomitoria* roots are the source of the active chemical drugs, reserpine, which is prescribed in hypertension and can also act as tranquiliser. It was also used to treat snake bites and insomnia. While *datura* is a plant with hallucinogenic properties. Drug *belladonna* is obtained from *Atropa belladonna* and drug Opium is obtained from *Papaver somniferum.*

Q.17 Which of the following group exhibit more species diversity?

(a) Gymnosperms (b) Algae (c) Bryophytes (d) Fungi

Ans. **(d)** Fungi are group of eukaryotic heteromorphic organisms with diverse forms, sizes, physiology and mode of reproduction. It has nearly 1.5 lakh recognised species including yeasts, molds, mushrooms etc. They exhibits more specific diversity whereas algae (blue-green algae etc.) have relatively fewer species diversity, followed by bryophytes (mosses etc.) and then gymnosperms (conifers).

Q.18 Which of the below mentioned regions exhibit less seasonal variations?

(a) Tropics (b) Temperates
(c) Alpines (d) Both (a) and (b)

Ans. **(a)** Maximum biodiversity is observed in tropics because the tropical regions exhibit less seasonal variations, *i.e.*, they remain undisturbed.

Whereas temperate region are more seasonal, less constant and exhibit less species diversity. Alpines with low temperature and high altitudes show less diversity as well.

Q.19 The historic convention on biological diversity held in Rio de Janeiro in 1992 is known as

(a) CITES Convention (b) The Earth Summit
(c) G-16 Summit (d) MAB Programme

Ans. **(b)** The historic convention on biological diversity held in Rio de Janeiro (Brazil) in 1992 is known as the Earth Summit (Ist). While CITES (Convention on International Trade in Endangered Species of wild flora and fauna) has helped in restricting poaching and loss of rare species.

MAB stands for Man and Biosphere Programme which undertakes the establishment and maintenance of biosphere reserves.

G-16 summit was held in Rome (2021) and its them was people, planet and prosperity.

Q.20 What is common to the techniques

(i) *in vitro* fertilisation
(ii) cryopreservation
(iii) tissue culture?

(a) All are *in situ* conservation methods.
(b) All are *ex situ* conservation methods.
(c) All require ultra modern equipment and large space.
(d) All are methods of conservation of extinct organisms.

Ans. ***(b)*** All the three above mentioned techniques are *ex-situ* conservation methods i.e., they are used to protect endangered species outside of their natural habitat. At present, gametes of threatened species can be preserved in viable conditions for longer duration by cryopreservation method (at very low temperature *i.e.,* – 196°C).

Fertilisation can be achieved in laboratory *in vitro,* and species can be improved or propagated by tissue culture method, a plant breeding principle.

Very Short Answer Type Questions

Q.1 What characteristics make a community stable?

Ans. The characteristics that make a community stable are as follows

(i) Less variation in productivity from year to year.

(ii) Resistance or resilience to occasional disturbances (natural or man-made).

(iii) Resistance to invasions by alien species.

(iv) Occurence of large number of niches.

Q.2 What could have triggered mass extinctions of species in the past?

Ans. The main reason for mass extinctions of species, are given below

(i) Fall of sea levels.

(ii) Change in temperature (freezing or warming).

(iii) Asteroid/meteorite hitting the planet.

(vi) Tectonics plate disruptions, leading to eathquakes.

(vii) Eruption of volcanoes.

Q.3 What accounts for the greater ecological diversity of India?

Ans. The greater ecological diversity of India is because of the geographical diversity in terms of varying topography. For example, deserts, rain forests, mangroves, coral reefs, wetlands, estuaries, deciduous, temperate forests as well as alpine meadows all are present in India. This gives rise to various ecosystems with greater ecological diversity.

Q.4 According to David Tilman, greater the diversity, greater is the primary productivity. Can you think of a very low diversity man-made ecosystem that has high productivity?

Thinking Process Artificial or anthropogenic ecosystems are man-made terrestrial or aquatic ecosystems. The most important are agriculture field, generally called as agro-ecosystems.

Ans. Yes, man-made ecosystems like agricultural fields (paddy or wheat) show very low diversity, but possess high productivity. This is an example of **monoculture** farming.

Q.5 What does 'Red' indicate in the IUCN Red list (2004)?

Ans. Red in the IUCN Red list (2004) refers to the **threatened** species or the taxa with the highest risk of extinction.

Q.6 Explain as to how protection of biodiversity hot Spots alone can reduce up to 30% of the current rate of species extinction.

Ans. The biodiversity hot spots are regions with very high level of species richness, especially those under threat from humans. They contain major part of endemic species, thus their protection can reduce the current rate of extinction. These regions can be protected as biological reserves, national parks and sanctuaries.

Q.7 What is the difference between endemic and exotic species?

Ans. **Endemic species** are native or indigenous species, which are restricted to a particular geographical region. These have limited distribution due to biotic and abiotic factors. **Exotic** or alien species are those species which are introduced from one geographical region to another geographical area. Exotic species may even lead to disappearance of native species.

Q.8 How does species diversity differ from ecological diversity?

Ans. Species diversity refers to the number and distribution of species in an area. It is expressed in terms of number of species per unit area and also as number of individuals of different species in an area. For *e.g.*, Tropical rain forests have extremely high species diversity.

Whereas, Ecological diversity refers to the diversity at ecosystem level. It is related to different types of ecosystem habitats *e.g.*, terrestrial (forests, grasslands, etc.) and aquatic (freshwater and marine) ecosystems. It is the occurence of different ecosystem in a geographical area.

Q.9 Why is genetic variation important in the plant *Rauwolfia vomitoria*?

Ans. Plant *Rauwolfia vomitoria* is a source of drug **reserpine** which acts as tranquiliser. Genetic variation shown by this medicinal plant might be in terms of the potency and concentration of active chemical (resperine), that plant produces.

Q.10 What is Red Data Book?

Ans. Red Data Book is a compilation of data or records of species threatened with risk of extinction (which are known to be endangered). The book is maintained by IUCN (headquarter at Gland in Switzerland).

Q.11 Define gene pool.

Ans. Gene pool refers to the sum total of all genes and their alleles of every individual in an population.

Q.12 What does the term 'Frugivorous' mean?

Ans. Frugivorous term is used for those animals which eat only fruits or eat fruit as their staple diet.

Q.13 What is the expanded form of IUCN?

Ans. IUCN stands for 'International Union for Conservation of Nature. It is headquartered in Switzerland.

Q.14 Define the terms (i) Bioprospecting (ii) Endemism

Ans. (i) **Bioprospecting** is a term that describes the process of discovery and commercialisation of new products based on biological resources like plants, microbes or animal.

(ii) **Endemism** refers to presence of some species in a particular regions only and nowhere else. It is uniqueness of flora and fauna of an area.

Q.15 What is common to the species shown in figures *A* and *B*?

A

B

Ans. Both Species in figure (*A*) and (*B*) are invasive alien species in India.

Q.16 What is common to the species shown in figures A and B?

A

B

Ans. Both the species in figure (A) and (B) are conserved in their natural habitats.

Short Answer Type Questions

Q.1 How is the presently occurring species extinction different from the earlier mass extinctions ?

Ans. In earlier time extinction of species occurred due to natural causes or calamities like flood, volcanic eruption, prolonged drought and landslides, etc. While at present human activities like overexpolitation, industrilisation, pollution, climate change, etc are the major cause of species extinction.

Q.2 Of the four major causes for the loss of biodiversity (Alien species invasion, habitat loss and fragmentation, over-exploitation and co-extinctions) which according to you is the major cause for the loss of biodiversity ? Give reasons in support.

Ans. Out of the four major causes for the loss of biodiversity, loss of habitat and fragmentation is the major cause, explained as follows

Habitat loss and fragmentation caused by clearing and over-exploitation of forest areas for agriculture, urbanisation and industrialisation, results in destruction of natural habitats. In addition, large habitats are broken up into small fragments, due of which mammals and birds requiring large territories are badly affected, leading to decline in population.

Q.3 Discuss one example, based on your day-to-day observations, showing how loss of one species may lead to the extinction of another.

Ans. **Co-extinction** is the extinction of two mutually related or interelated species for instance a host fish extinction leads to the extinction of all those parasites exclusively found on it. In case of a plant pollinator mutualism, extinction of one leads to the extinction of other. For example Insect like aphids are polyphagous (feed on more than one plant species) or monophagous (feed on a particular species of plant). Monophagous insects may become extinct, if the plant species upon which they feed becomes extinct.

Q.4 A species area curve is drawn by plotting the number of species against the area. How is it that when a very large area is considered the slope is steeper than that for smaller areas ?

Ans. In very large areas, like continent the number of species are abundant as compared to smaller areas. Therefore, the curve is much **steeper**. This is because the larger area has more food availability and other resources, so more species can easily thrive.

Q.5 Is it possible that productivity and diversity of a natural community remain constant over a time period of, say one hundred years?

Ans. No, it is not possible that productivity and diversity of a natural community remain constant over a certain time period.

There can be many reasons few are mentioned as follows

(i) The natural habitat can never maintained in real time.

(ii) Abundant resources are never available, they are always in short supply or just enough.

(ii) Environmental conditions for survival and reproduction are continuously changing.

Q.6 There is greater biodiversity in tropical/subtropical regions than in temperate region. Explain.

Ans. The tropical or subtropical region exhibit maximum biological diversity because these region remain **undisturbed** due to less variable climatic conditions. Tropics have non-seasonal and nearly uniform environment. More solar energy is available in tropics which enhances productivity. So, tropics had a longer evolutionary time for species diversification. Whereas, the temperate environment is more seasonal, less constant and unpredictable, therefore less niche specialisation and lesser species diversity are observed.

Q.7 Why are the conventional methods not suitable for the assessment of biodiversity of bacteria?

Ans. Many bacteria cannot be cultured under normal conditions *in vitro,* which creates a problem in studying their morphological and biochemical characteristics. Morphology and biochemistry along with few other characteristics are used for the assessment of biodiversity of bacteria. Bacteria exhibit similar morphology despite being genetically diverse. Thus, conventional methods are not suitable for the assessment of biodiversity of bacteria.

Q.8 What criteria should one use in categorising a species as threatened?

Ans. The criteria that should be used in categorising a species as threatened are as follows

(i) Number of the members of the species are declining at an alarming rate.
(ii) Their habitat is being modified or destroyed.
(iii) Predator or poacher activities are increasing.

Q.9 What could be the possible explanation for greater vulnerability of amphibians to extinction as compared to other animal groups?

Ans. Amphibians are more vulnerable to extinction as follows

(i) **Habitat Modification or Destruction** Amphibians generally need aquatic and terrestrial habitats to survive; If these wetlands are filled for land creation it can affect populations.

Hence, amphibians may be more vulnerable to habitat modification than organisms that require only one habitat type.

(ii) **Habitat Fragmentation** This means isolation of a few areas by habitat modification. Small populations that survive within such fragments are often susceptible to inbreeding, genetic drift or extinction due to small fluctuations in the environment.

(iii) **Large Scale Climate Changes** These changes can further modify aquatic habitats, preventing amphibians from spawning.

Q.10 How do scientists extrapolate the total number of species on earth ?

Ans. There are two methods to estimate and extrapolate the total number of species on earth they are follows

(i) The primary method used by the scientists to extrapolate the number of species on earth is the estimation rate of discovery of new species.
(ii) The secondary method is that the total number of species can also be extrapolated by the statistical comparison of the tropical and temperate species richness of exhaustively studied groups of insects. This ratio is then extrapolated with existing species of plants and animals to predict the gross estimate of the number of species on earth.

Q.11 Humans benefit from diversity of life. Give two examples.

Ans. Humans derive numerous economic benefits directly from diversity of organisms. Some of them are listed below

(a) Food products (cereals, pulses and fruits).
(b) Firewood.
(c) Fibre (cotton, jute from plants and silk, wool from animals).
(d) Construction material (timber for making furniture, houses and sports goods).
(e) Industrial products (tannins, lubricants, dyes, resins and perfumes).
(f) Products of medicinal importance (about 25000 plants are used in traditional medicine).

Q.12 List any two major causes other than anthropogenic causes of the loss of biodiversity.

Ans. The two major causes other than anthropogenic causes of the loss of biodiversity are as follows

(i) **Alien Species Invasions** When alien species are introduced unintentionally or deliberately in a habitat, some of them can cause decline or extinction of indigenous species.

(ii) **Co-extinctions** When a species becomes extinct, the plant and animal species associated with it in an obligatory way, also become extinct.

(iii) **Mass extinction** Extinction of large number of species from an area due to volcano eruption, drought, heavy rains, etc.

Q.13 What is an endangered species? Give an example of an endangered plant and animal species each?

Ans. An endangered species is a population of organisms, which are facing a high risk of becoming extinct because

(i) They have lower frequency of species (decreasing numbers).

(ii) They are threatened by changing environment.

(iii) They are facing predator threat.

Example of endangered plant species-Venus fly trap

Example of endangered animal species-Siberian tiger

Q.14 What are sacred groves and their role in biodiversity conservation?

Ans. Sacred groves are sacred tracts, which are held in high esteem by local communities.

The sacred groves are dedicated to local ancestral spirits and are protected by local communities through social traditions and taboos that incorporate spiritual and ecological values.

Sacred groves represent native vegetation in a natural or near natural state and are thus, rich in biodiversity and harbour many rare species of plants and animals.

Such sacred groves are found in Meghalaya (Khasi and Jaintia hills), Aravalli hills of Rajasthan, Western Ghats, regions of Karnataka and Maharashtra and Madhya Pradesh (Bastar, Chanda and Sarguja region).

Q.15 Suggest a place where one can go to study coral reefs, mangrove vegetation and estuaries.

Ans. Places for studying coral reefs are Andaman and Nicobar Islands. For mangrove vegetation-Sunderban, and for estuaries-Coastal areas of Karnataka.

Q.16 Is it true that there is more solar energy available in the tropics? Explain briefly.

Ans. Yes, there is more solar energy available in the tropics because of the following reasons

(i) The sun's rays are more concentrated.

(ii) The sun's rays have less atmosphere to pass through, so less energy is lost in absorption and reflection by the atmosphere.

(iii) Tropical rainforest areas absorbs radiations due to presence of dense vegetation. Availability of more solar energy in tropics contribute higher productivity which in turn might contribute greater biodiversity.

Q.17 What is co-extinction? Explain with a suitable example?

Ans. When a species becomes extinct, the plant and animal species associated with it, in an obligatory way, also become extinct. This is called **co-extinction**, for example, when a host fish species becomes extinct, its parasites also vanish.

Some other examples of co-extinction are; plant-pollinator (mutualism) where extinction of one leads to the extinction of other. Monophagous insect that feeds on particular plant species becomes extinct due to extinction of that plant species.

Long Answer Type Questions

Q.1 Elaborate how invasion by an alien species reduces the species diversity of an area.

Ans. When alien species are introduced unintentionally or deliberately in a habitat, some of them can cause decline or extinction of indigenous species. For example, invasive weed species like carrot grass (*Parthenium*), *Lantana* and water hyacinth (*Eichhornia*) caused environmental damage and posed threat to native species. Another example of exotic species invasion is Nile perch, a large predator fish. When this alien species was introduced into lake of Victoria in East Africa, it started feeding on native, cichlid fish. As a result indigenous cichlid fish became extinct and due to scarcity of food, predator Nile perch died too.

Q.2 How can you, as an individual, prevent the loss of biodiversity?

Ans. **Biodiversity** is the occurrence of different type of species, habitat, ecosystem, gene, genepool in a particular place and various parts of earth.

As an individual, biodiversity can be conserved with conservation strategies and management of both biotic and abiotic resources.

Some of the conservation strategies are as follows

(i) Protection of useful animals and plants in their natural habitat (*in situ* conservation).

(ii) Making posters to provide information about biodiversity.

(iii) setting up bird and but houses where everpossible

(iv) Using the three R's i.e reduce, reuse and recycle wherever possible.

(v) Using enviornmental friendly products.

(vi) Obeying all or any rules under the biodiversity act.

Q.3 Can you think of a scientific explanation, besides analogy used by Paul Ehrlich, for the direct relationship between diversity and stability of an ecosystem?

Ans. Scientific explanation for the direct relationship between diversity and stability of an ecosystem could be as follows

Imagine a forest area, where diverse species of plants are growing. Plants harbour a variety of insects on which a lot of bird species would depend for their food.

If a specific plant species dies, the related insect population will be affected that would lead to food unavailability for the birds. In addition, if the plant species was a nitrogen fixer, the death of these plants would mean no replenishment of soil with nitrogen. This will obviously affect the other plants as well. So, if the cycle continues, the whole habitat or ecosystem will be negatively affected. Increased biodiversity provides resilience to the ecosystem which in turn increases productivity. Both this actions results in stability.

Q.4 Though the conflict between humans and wildlife started with the evolution of man, the intensity of conflict has increased due to the activities of modern man. Justify your answer with suitable examples.

Ans. The humans first evolved around 2.5 million years ago and agriculture began about 11 thousand years ago. It is since then that humans have started to exploit the forest land for agriculture.

Development in medical technology has increased the lifespan of humans, decreased the mortality rate of mother and child, further aggravating the problem of human population.

Along with this, the industrial revolution caused enormous consumption of earth's resources but giving back nothing. The monumental amount of waste is destroying the natural habitat of other species, be it aquatic or terrestrial, endangering and later causing extinction thereof.

This is how human activities have led to the increase in conflict between humans and wildlife.

Q.5 What is an ecosystem service? List any four important ecosystem services provided by the natural ecosystems. Are you in favour or against levying a charge on the service provided by the ecosystem?

Ans. The products of ecosystem processes are termed as **ecosystem services**. Forests are the major sources of ecological services. Some of the ecosystem services they provide are

(i) Purification of air and water.
(ii) Mitigating droughts and floods.
(iii) Cycling nutrients.
(iv) Generating fertile soils.
(v) Providing wildlife habitat.
(vi) Maintenance of biodiversity.
(vii) Pollination of crops.
(vii) Providing storage site for carbon.
(ix) Providing aesthetic, cultural and spiritual values.

No, I am not in favour of levying a charge on ecological services but it is very important, to understand how much nature is providing us for free and if we overuse or misuse its resources, we'll have to pay a heavy price for it.

Q.6 Describe the consumptive use value of biodiversity as food, drugs and medicines, fuel and fibre with suitable examples.

Ans. Biological resources are the basis of life forms on this planet. The countries with maximum biodiversity possess better potential to compete with the rest of the world. Biodiversity has great economic importance to mankind due to its many uses, some of, which with consumptive value are following

Food is obtained from biodiversity sources like livestock, forestry and fish. Biodiversity in modern agriculture is beneficial due as a source of new crops. *e.g.*, just three cereals crop like wheat, rice and maize account for about 55% of protein and 60% of calories in humans.

Drugs such as morphine (*Papaver somniferum*), quinine (*Cinchona ledgeriana*), reserpine (*Rauwolfia vomitaria*), *belladonna* (*Atropa belladonna*), aconite (*Aconitum napellus*).

About 70-80% of entire population is dependent on plants or its extract for medicine. Penicillin (*Penicillium notatum*), tetracycline (bacteria), digitalin (*Digitalis*) are some examples of medicinal plants.

Fuels plant like *Chorchorus, Gossypium* are sources of fibre while *Jatropha* is a source of biofuels. Fossils fuels (*e.g.*, petroleum) are obtained from fossils of organisms.

Fats and Oils There are number of plants providing fats and oils like groundnut, cotton seed, sunflower, etc.

Biopesticides Chemical pesticides are generally persistant and degrade the ecosystem. Biopesticides, such as **thuringin** and **azadiractin** can overcome this defect.

Q.7 Species diversity decreases as we move away from the equator towards the poles. What could be the possible reasons?

Ans. Species diversity decreases as we move towards the poles, because

(i) Temperature decreases and conditions become harsh.

(ii) Both the amount and intensity of solar radiation decreases.

(iii) Vegetation decreases.

(iv) Less resources available to support species.

Speciation is generally a function of time and environmental stability, so if the conditions are too harsh, it is difficult for the species to survive and adapt. This results in decrease in biodiversity towards the poles.

Q.8 Explain briefly the 'rivet popper hypothesis' of Paul Ehrlich.

Ans. Ecologist **Paul Ehrlich** gave rivet popper hypothesis to understand the contribution of species richness. He compared each species with rivet in the body of an airplane.

(i) This hypothesis explains that ecosystem to be an airplane and the species to be the rivets joining all parts together.

(ii) If every passenger travelling in the aeroplane start taking rivets home (causing a species to become extinct), initially it may not affect flight safety (proper functioning of ecosystem), but over a period of time the plane becomes weak and dangerous *i.e.*, species become endangered and then extinct.

Q.9 The relation between species richness and area for a wide variety of taxa turns out to be a rectangular hyperbola. Give a brief explanation.

Ans. According to **AV Humboldt**, within a region, species richness increased with increasing explored area (only upto a limit). Accordingly the relation between species richness and area for a wide variety of taxa (birds, bat, angiosperms, aquatic fishes) turns out to be a rectangular hyperbola.

The relationship depicts a straight line on a logarithmic scale described by the following equation

$$\log S = \log C + Z \log A$$

Where, 'S stands for species richness, 'A' is area and 'Z' and 'C' are slope of line (regression coefficient) and y intercept respectively.

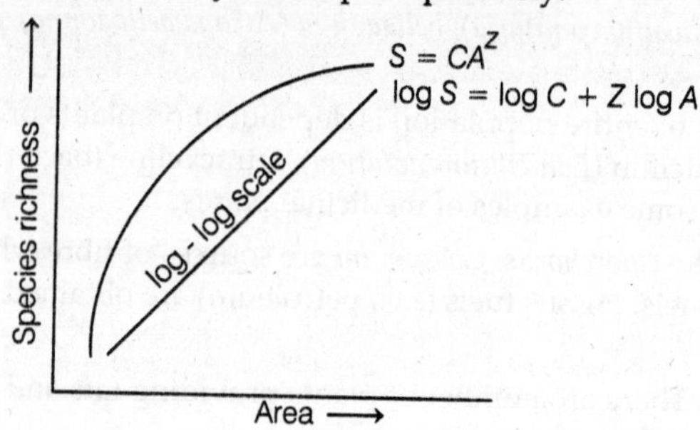

Chapter

16

Environmental Issues*

Multiple Choice Questions (MCQs)

Q.1 Non-biodegradable pollutants are created by

(a) nature (b) excessive use of resources

(c) humans (d) natural disasters

Thinking Process On the basis of degradation or natural disposal, pollutants may be classified as biodegradable and non-biodegradable. Nature and natural disasters don't generate non-biodegradable waste.

Ans. *(c)* Non-biodegradable pollutants are created by humans and have a slow or zero rate of degradation by general biological processes. They include plastics, tin containers, heavy metals, radioactive substances, etc. These are created by human activities like industrialisation etc. Whereas biodegradable pollutants are degraded or disposed of quickly by biological processes. Some biodegradable pollutant created by humans are paper, house hold waste (like peel of vegetables , fruits) and sewage.

Q.2 According to the Central Pollution Control Board, particles that are responsible for causing great harm to human health are of diameter

(a) 2.50 micrometers (b) 5.00 micrometers

(c) 10.00 micrometers (d) 7.5 micrometers

Thinking Process Air pollutants are gaseous material, radioactive substances and particulate matter.

Ans. *(a)* According to CPCB, particulate matter of 2.5 μ m or less in diameter are responsible for causing harm to human health. The particulate matter of 2.5 μm or in size get deeply embedded into the respiratory tract (upto lungs), causing respiratory problems and may even lead to death.

Q.3 The material generally used for sound proofing of rooms like a recording studio and auditorium etc., is

(a) cotton (b) coir (c) wood (d) styrofoam

Ans. *(d)* The material generally used for sound proofing of rooms like recording studio, cinema hall, auditorium which absorb sound and facilitate in sound proofing is styrofoam. It is lightweight and has excellent sound absorbing qualities.

te (*) *This Chapter has been deleted from latest NCERT.*

Q.4 Compressed Natural Gas (CNG) is

(a) propane (b) methane (c) ethane (d) butane

Ans. ***(b)*** CNG consists of around 90% methane, by compressing it to less than 1% of volume it occupies at standard atmospheric pressure. Whereas, propane and butane together form LPG or liquefied petroleum gas and ethane is used in chemical industry to produce ethene.

Q.5 World's most problematic aquatic weed is

(a) *Azolla* (b) *Wolffia* (c) *Eichhornia* (d) *Trapa*

Ans. ***(c)*** *Eichhornia* (water hyacinth) is considered as worlds most problematic equatic weed as it is an invasive species. If not controlled, water hyacinth covers the entire pond or lake and impacts water flow. It blocks sunlight, acts as prime habitat for mosquito (vector), host for snails and flatworm and starves water of oxygen.

Q.6 Which of the following causes biomagnification?

(a) SO_2 (b) Mercury (c) DDT (d) Both (b) and (c)

Ans. ***(d)*** Biomagnification, also called as bioaccumulation is the accumulation of non-biodegradable toxic material like Hg, DDT, etc, at different trophic levels.

In the process of bioaccumulation, the concentration of non- biodegradable pollutants increases at each successive trophic level of the food chain, thus harming the environment or ecosystem at an alarming rate, whereas SO_2 (sulphur dioxide) is an air pollutant and acts as precursor of acid rain, but it dos not cause biomagnification.

Q.7 The expanded form of DDT is

(a) dichloro diphenyl trichloroethane (b) dichloro diethyl trichloroethane
(c) dichloro dipyrydyl trichloroethane (d) dichloro diphenyl tetrachloroacetate

Ans. ***(a)*** The expanded form of DDT is dichloro diphenyl trichloroethane.

It is an insecticide which was first synthesised in 1874. It acts on insects and opens the sodium ion channels in their neurons which leads to spasms and eventually death.

Q.8 Which of the following material takes the longest time for biodegradation?

(a) Cotton (b) Paper (c) Bone (d) Jute

Ans. ***(c)*** Out of the given options, bone takes the longest time for biodegradation as bone is made up of a protein fraction, mineral fraction and organic compounds. Whereas cotton, paper and jute can be easily degraded by the action of microbes.

Q.9 Choose the incorrect statement.

(a) The Montreal protocol is associated with the control of emission of ozone depleting substances
(b) Methane and carbon dioxide are green house gases
(c) Dobson units are used to measure oxygen content
(d) Use of incinerators is crucial to disposal of hospital wastes

Ans. *(c)* Statement (c) is incorrect and can be corrected as **Dobson unit is** used to express the concentration or thickness of ozone. It quantifies the total amount of ozone in a vertical column of air above the earth's surface.

On the other hand, oxygen sensors are used to measure the exhaust gas concentration of oxygen.

Q.10 Among the following which one causes more indoor chemical pollution?

(a) Burning coal (b) Burning cooking gas
(c) Burning mosquito coil (d) Room spray

Ans. *(a)* Burning coal is the major cause of indoor chemical pollution. It releases carbon content in the atmosphere which combines with oxygen to form carbon dioxide, a threat to environment or may result in the formation of carbon monoxide which is a threat to human health.

Burning of coal also releases toxic substances like nitrogen oxides, sulphur dioxides, metal and silicates. Although, mosquito coil and room spray causes indoor chemical pollution but their effects are not for long term.

Q.11 The green scum seen in the freshwater bodies is

(a) blue green algae (b) red algae
(c) green algae (d) Both (a) and (c)

Ans. *(d)* The green scum seen in the freshwater bodies mainly consists of green algae and blue-green algae, while the red algae is mostly marine.

Q.12 The loudness of a sound that a person can withstand without discomfort is about

(a) 150 dB (b) 215 dB
(c) 30 dB (d) 80 dB

Ans. *(d)* Relative loudness of sound ranges from 30 dB-60 dB and is generally not hazardous. The loudness above 60-80 dB, is not uncomfortable but prolonged exposure to noise level above 80 dB is painful and gradually leads to permanent loss of hearing ability or deafness.

Q.13 The major source of noise pollution, worldwide is due to

(a) office equipment
(b) transport system
(c) sugar, textile and paper industries
(d) oil refineries and thermal power plants

Ans. *(b)* The major source of noise pollution worldwide is the transport system *i.e.,* transport vehicles (both public and private).

While all machines (noise producing) whether, agricultural or engine of motor machinery employed in various industries like textile, printing, sugar, engineering and agricultural implements are also sources of noise pollution.

Q.14 Match correctly the following and choose the correct option

A. Environment Protection Act	1.	1974
B. Air Prevention and Control of Pollution Act	2.	1987
C. Water Act	3.	1986
D. Amendment of Air Act to include noise	4.	1981

The correct matches are

	A	B	C	D		A	B	C	D
(a)	3	4	1	2	(b)	1	3	2	4
(c)	4	1	2	3	(d)	3	4	2	1

Ans. ***(a)*** The correct match is A-3, B-4, C-1 and D-2.

They can be explained as

Environment Protection Act came into force on November 1986, at the birth anniversary of late Prime Minister of India Smt. Indira Gandhi.

Air prevention and control of pollution Act came into force in 1981 which is meant for the preservation of quality air.

Water Act 1974 is meant for restoration of quality of surface and ground water.

In **1987**, the Air Act was amended to include noise pollution under its scope.

Q.15 Catalytic converters are fitted into automobiles to reduce emission of harmful gases. Catalytic converters change unburnt hydrocarbons into

(a) carbon dioxide and water

(b) carbon monoxide

(c) methane

(d) carbon dioxide and methane

Ans. ***(a)*** Catalytic converters contain costly metals like rhodium. Platinum and palladium as catalysts. When exhaust gases pass through fitted catalytic converter, the unburnt hydrocarbons (cause of cancer) are oxidised into water and carbon dioxide, thereby reducing harmful emissions.

Q.16 Why is it necessary to remove sulphur from petroleum products?

(a) To reduce the emission of sulphur dioxide in exhaust fumes

(b) To increase efficiency of automobiles engines

(c) To use sulphur removed from petroleum for commercial purposes

(d) To increase the life span of engine silencers

Ans. ***(a)*** Removal of sulphur from petroleum products (diesel) reduces the emission of harmful air pollutants like oxides of sulphur (SO_2 and SO_3) in the exhaust fumes.

Q.17 Which one of the following impurities is easiest to remove from waste water?

(a) Bacteria (b) Colloids
(c) Dissolved solids (d) Suspended solids

Thinking Process Domestic sewage (household waste water) consists of everything which are transferred from residential blocks to sewer.

Ans. *(d)* Sand is the easiest impurity to remove from waste water as it is a suspended impurity.

Three type of impurities found in waste water *i.e.,* suspended particles (solids), colloidal impurities and dissolved material (inorganic and organic) like calcium, ammonia, toxic material, phosphate, sodium, calcium and nitrate.

Q.18 Which one of the following diseases is not due to contamination of water?

(a) Hepatitis-B (b) Jaundice
(c) Cholera (d) Typhoid

Ans. *(a)* **Hepatitis-B** is not caused by contamination of water, but it is transmitted through exposure to infectious body fluids such as blood and semen. While jaundice, cholera and typhoid are water and food borne diseases which are caused by contaminated food and water.

Q.19 Nuisance growth of aquatic plants and bloom-forming algae in natural water is generally due to high concentrations of

(a) carbon (b) sulphur
(c) calcium (d) phosphorus

Ans. *(d)* Nuisance growth of aquatic plants and bloom forming algae in natural water bodies is generally due to high concentration of dissolved organic and inorganic materials especially phosphorus. Phosphorus favours the growth of aquatic weed plants like *Eichhornia* (water hyacinth) and certain blue-green algae.

Q.20 Algal blooms impart a distinct colour to water due to

(a) their pigments
(b) excretion of coloured substances
(c) formation of coloured chemicals in water facilitated by physiological degradation of algae
(d) absorption of light by algal cell wall

Ans. *(a)* Algal bloom impart distinct colour to water due to their pigments.

Q.21 Match the items in column I and column II and choose the correct option.

Column I	Column II
A. UV	1. Biomagnificatron
B. Biodegradable organic matter	2. Eutrophication
C. DDT	3. Snow blindness
D. Phosphates	4. BOD

The correct matches is

	A	B	C	D		A	B	C	D
(a)	2	1	4	3	(b)	3	2	4	1
(c)	3	4	1	2	(d)	3	1	4	2

Ans. ***(c)*** The correct match is A-3, B-4, C-1 and D-2. They can be explained as

Snow blindness is a temporary eye condition due to exposure of UV rays (UV-B).

Biochemical oxygen demand refers to the amount of oxygen consumed by bacteria and other microbes during decomposition of organic matter.

Biomagnification is the increase in accumulation of toxic substances within organisms at every successive trophic level (due to decreased excretion and metabolism). It is caused by insecticides like DDT.

Eutrophication is a process in which water bodies get enriched with dissolved nutrients like nitrogen and phosphorus. This results in excessive growth of algal bloom.

Q.22 In the textbook you Same across Three Mile Island and Chernobyl disasters associated with accidental leakage of radioactive wastes. In India we had Bhopal gas tragedy. It is associated with which of the following?

(a) CO_2 (b) Methyl isocyanate (c) CFC's (d) Methyl cyanate

Ans. ***(b)*** MIC (Methyl Isocynate) was leaked from insecticide producing unit of Union Carbide pesticide plant at Bhopal, which lead to Bhopal Gas Tragedy. This chemical tragedy occured on December 2nd 1984 at Bhopal, the capital of Madhya Pradesh in which around 2000-3000 people died on that same night.

Very Short Answer Type Questions

Q.1 Use of lead-free petrol or diesel is recommended to reduce the pollutants emitted by automobiles. What role does lead play?

Ans. Use of lead free petrol or diesels is necessary for the proper functioning of catalytic converters.

Motor vehicles equipped with catalytic converter need to use unleaded petrol because lead in the petrol, inactivates the catalyst and increases the hydrocarbon emission, there by harming the environment. Lead is added to petrol in form of $Pb(C_2H_5)_4$ as **antiknock** agent.

Q.2 In which year was the Air (Prevention and Control of Pollution) Act amended to include noise as air pollution.

Ans. In 1987, the Air (Prevention and Control of Pollution) Act was amended to include noise as a source of air pollution.

Q.3 Name the city in our country where the entire public road transport runs on CNG.

Ans. In Delhi, the entire public road transport runs on Compressed Natural Gas (CNG).

Q.4 It is a common practice to undertake desilting of the overhead water tanks. What is the possible source of silt that gets deposited in the water tanks?

Ans. The source of silt that get deposited in overhead water tank are soil particles, which are carried out with water from the source of supply like deep borewell, rivers, etc.

Q.5 What is cultural eutrophication?

Ans. The phenomenon wherein effluents from the industries and homes like sewage waste and run off of fertilizers from fields accelerate the natural ageing process of lakes and other water bodies that normally may take thousands of years is called accelerated or cultural eutrophication.

Q.6 List any two adverse effects of particulate matter on human health.

Ans. The fine particulate matter (PM of size 2.5 μm or less) can cause problems such as

(i) Breathing and respiratory problems
(ii) Irritation
(iii) Inflammations
(iv) Damage to the lungs and premature death

e.g., Asthma, bronchitis, emphysema, etc.

Q.7 What is the raw material for polyblend?

Ans. Polyblends are man made fibres, made by the mixture of two or more polymers especially plastic waste products.

Q.8 Blends of polyblend and bitumen, when used, help to increase road life by a factor of three. What is the reason?

Ans. **Polyblend** is a fine powder of recycled modified plastic. The binding property of plastic makes the road last longer besides giving added strength to withstand more loads. This is because

(i) Plastic increases the melting point of the bitumen which would prevent it from melting in India's hot and extremely humid climate, where temperature frequently cross 50°C.
(ii) Rainwater will not seep through because of the plastic in the tar.

Q.9 Mention any two examples of plants used as wind breakers in the agricultural fields.

Ans. Wind breakers or shelter belts provide shelter from wind and protect soil from erosion. Jamun and imli and some other trees like Babul, Lawsonia, Thevetia and Calotropis acts as wind breakers in the agricultural field.

Q.10 Name an industry which can cause both air and thermal pollution and as well as eutrophication.

Ans. Chemical fertiliser unit, thermal power plant, refineries, smelting and metallurgical processing units steel mills and the industries using steam or water as coolant causes both air and thermal pollution. The chemical release form these industries (if rich in nitrogen and phosphorus) may result in eutrophication.

Q.11 What is an algal bloom?

Ans. The extensive growth of planktonic (free-floating) algae in water bodies due to the presence of organic matter in water (nitrogen and phosphorus) that acts as a food source is called an algal bloom. This also imparts a distinct colour to the water bodies.

Q.12 What do you understand by biomagnification?

Ans. **Biomagnification** refers to the increase in the concentration of the toxic substances at successive trophic level in the food chain. This happens because a toxic substance accumulated by an organism cannot be metabolised or excreted and when this organism is eaten up by another animal of higher trophic level, the substance moves up the food chain, accumulating at each level.

Q.13 What are the three major kinds of impurities in domestic wastewater?

Ans. The three major kinds of impurities in domestic waste water are

(i) Dissolved salts such as nitrates, phosphates, other nutrients, toxic metal ions and organic compounds.

(ii) Bio-degradable organic matter.

(iii) Pathogenic microorganisms.

Q.14 What is reforestation?

Ans. **Reforestation** is the process of restoring a forest that once existed but was removed at some point of time in the past. Though, it can occur naturally in a deforested area but can be restored by planting trees, with due consideration to biodiversity that earlier existed in that area.

Q.15 What is the best solution for the treatment of electronic wastes?

Ans. The best solution for the treatment of electronic wastes is to recycle it. Electronic waste can be recycled 95-98% by weight.

Recycling has two fold benefits

(i) It prevents the toxic components of computers from entering the delicate environment and ground water *via* landfill.

(ii) It also slows the use and mining of primary raw materials.

Short Answer Type Questions

Q.1 Is it true that carpets and curtains/drapes placed on the floor or wall surfaces can reduce noise level. Explain briefly?

Ans. Yes, it is true, that the placing of carpets on floor and curtains on wall surface, windows reduces noise level. This is because that the curtains and carpets on wall surface acts as sound-muffling device and absorb sounds of moderate level.

Q.2 What is hybrid vehicle technology? Explain its advantages with a suitable example?

Ans. The technology used to run vehicles on dual mode like petrol or compressed natural gas is said to be hybrid vehicle technology. These vehicles runs on either petrol or CNG. As CNG is a clean and green fuel so it is helpful to reduce environmental pollution and conserve petrol which is a fossil fuel.

Q.3 Is it true that if the dissolved oxygen level drops to zero, the water will become septic. Give an example which could lower the dissolved oxygen content of an aquatic body.

Ans. Yes, it is true, in case of zero level of dissolved oxygen (DO), the water becomes septic.

For example, nutrient pollution like fertiliser in aquatic bodies is responsible for lowering (upto zero) the level of dissolved oxygen.

Q.4 Name any one green house gas and its possible source of production on a large scale. What are the harmful effects of it?

Ans. The common green house gases are carbon dioxide, hydro carbons, chlorofloro carbons, oxides of nitrogen (NO_2), water vapour and ozone. The level of CO_2 (green house gas) is increasing due to large scale deforestation, change in land use and unlimited burning of fossils fuel and is leading to global warming.

The source of methane and other main green house gases are garbage dump, incomplete decomposition by anaerobic methanogens, flooded paddy field and marshy land.

Q.5 It is a common practice to plant trees and shrubs near the boundary walls of buildings. What purpose do they serve?

Ans. A common practice to grow and maintain trees and shrub near the boundary wall of residential, official building acts as a barrier for sound and check noise pollution. This green belt of tree and shrub also acts as an effective measure to check primary air pollutants like dust, fly ash, etc.

Q.6 Why has the National Forest Commission of India recommended a relatively larger forest cover for hills than for plains?

Ans. Recommendation of a large forest area for hills is due to its properties like checking soil erosion, percolation and recharging ground water, checking landslide and other natural calamities and to maintain the original flora and fauna of hills. Forests on hills moderate the climate and rainfall.

It is our moral duty to protect, restore and conserve or preserve forest as they are highly beneficial for mankind. In India, around 30% of land was covered by forest in early 20th century, which has been reduced to 18-19% by the year 2000. National Forest Commission of India (1988) recommended a relatively large forest cover (67%) for the hills and 33% for the plains.

Q.7 How can slash and burn agriculture become environment friendly?

Ans. Slash and burn agriculture is a primitive type of agro forestry. It allows growth of forest after clearing land for few years. It can be environment friendly if

(i) Small and widely scattered plots are used for cultivation as the forest ecosystem will not suffer damage.

(ii) Crop rotation is used so that soil does not loose fertility entirely.

(iii) Keeping cropping period small and **fallow** (unplanted) period

Q.8 What is the main idea behind "Joint Forest Management Concept" introduced by the Government of India?

Ans. The main idea behind Joint Forest Management (JFM) concept introduced by the Government of India was involving the local communities in the forest conservation. This concept was adopted considering the extraordinary courage and dedication of the local people, showed in protecting the wildlife through the movements like Bishnoi's is movement in Jodhpur and Chipko Movement in Garhwal, Himalayas. Under JFM, locals are given the responsibility of taking care of the planted trees in return some honorarium and plant products.

Q.9 What do you understand by Snow-blindness?

Ans. The inflammation of cornea caused due to the excessive absorption of ultravoilet-B radiations is called snow-blindness. Continued exposure to these radiations causes permanent damage to cornea.

Q.10 How has DDT caused decline in bird population?

Ans. The concentration of DDT rises with every trophic level *i.e.,* **biomagnification**.

DDT was used as insecticide in agriculture and released in water bodies. It was accumulated in fishes and the birds feed on these fishes. This accumulation disturbed the calcium metabolism in birds, which caused thinning of egg shell and their premature breaking, eventually causing decline in bird populations.

High DDT levels also brings death of adult birds due to liver cirrhosis is, softening of brain and cerebral hemmorrhage.

Q.11 Observe the figure *A* and *B* given below and answer the following questions

A

B

(i) The power generation by the above two methods is non-polluting, True/False.

(ii) List any two applications of solar energy

(iii) What is a photovoltaic cell?

Ans. (i) True, Figure *A* is solar energy panel and figure *B* is windmill. Both methods produce power without polluting the environment.

(ii) Solar lamp made up of a LED lamp, a photo-voltaic solar panel and rechargeable battery and solar hot water system (geyser) are the two application of solar energy.

(iii) A solar cell is also called as photovoltaic cell. It is a form of photoelectric cell which converts the light energy into electrical energy by photovoltaic cell.

Long Answer Type Questions

Q.1 Write a short note on electronic waste. List the various sources of e-wastes and the problems associated with its disposal.

Ans. Solid waste can be biodegradable, recyclable, non-biodegradable, and can be categorised as municipal wastes (sewage), industrial waste, hospitals and nursing wastes and electronic waste.

Irrepairable computers, mobiles and other electronic goods are often known as 'e' waste or electronic waste.

Source of e-waste Majority of the developing countries like China, Pakistan and India import irrepairable electronic goods for their valuable metals like copper, nickel and gold.

Disposal of e-waste Such waste should be burried in landfills or incinerated. In developing countries, metal from e-waste is extracted manually. So, during working with e-waste, one can get exposed with toxic substances present in it, and may get affected leading to skin diseases in future. However, recycling is the only solution for the treatment of electronic waste.

Q.2 What is organic farming? Discuss the benefits of organic farming as a viable practise in the context of developing nations like India.

Ans. Organic farming system primarily aims at sustainable production in an eco-friendly and pollution free environment. The land is cultivated by using techniques such as crop rotation, green manure, composting and biological pesticides alongwith beneficial microbes (biofertilisers) instead of chemical fertilisers and pesticides, etc.

Benefits of organic farming are

(i) Maintains long-term soil fertility.

(ii) Controls pests and diseases without harming the environment.

(iii) Ensures that water stays clean and safe.

(iv) It make use of resources that the farmer already has, making the practice economically viable.

(*v*) Helps produce nutritious food and high quality crops.

Organic farming in India

Using organic farming techniques makes much more sense for developing nations like India.

It is know that modern, intensive agriculture makes the use of expensive chemical fertilisers and herbicides, which leach out from the soil and pollute rivers, lakes and water bodies and also damage the soil fertility in the long run. Organic farming offers a sustainable alternative for long-term agricultural health.

Q.3 Water logging and soil salinity are some of the problems that have come in the wake of the Green Revolution. Discuss their causes and adverse effects to the environment.

Ans. **Water logging** and **soil salinity** is caused by extensive irrigation without proper drainage of water. Continuous presence of water draws salt to the surface of the soil, which gets deposited as a thin crust on the land surface or start collecting at the roots of the plants.

Adverse effects

(i) Increased salt content stunts the growth of crop plants.

(ii) Root cells saturated with saline water gets damaged.

(iii) Death of plants

(iv) Crop yield gets affected.

(v) Financial loss to the farmers.

Although, By properly managing the soil-water system can correct the salination and water logging, but their economic costs are very high.

Q.4 What are multipurpose trees? Give the botanical and local names of any two multipurpose trees known to you and list their uses.

Ans. **Multipurpose trees** are those tree which on plantation fulfills a number of purpose, like shade soil improvement, provide wood, fruit and food etc. In other words, multipurpose trees serve a wide variety of function and services for human needs.

Neem (*Azadirachta indica*) is known for its medicinal properties. Its fruit, leaves, wood and oil extracted from wood is used in most of the ayurvedic medicines. Its wood is pest resistant.

Another most important tree is coconut palm. Its botanical name is *Cocos nucifera,* and belongs to the family-Palmae, it serves a variety of function such as. Oil, wood, food and fibre, are extracted from this plant. This plant has fibre, medicinal and commercial importance.

Some other multipurpose trees are *Moringa oleifera* and *Gliricidia sepium,* which are widely used for fences in central America and provide fire wood, fooder and fix atmospheric N_2. While *M.oleifera* is commonly used for animal forage and shade, its leaves are edible.

Q.5 What are the basic characteristics of a modern landfill site. List any three and also mention the reasons for their use.

Ans. Characteristics of a modern landfill includes

(i) Methods to contain leachate such as lining clay or plastic liners to prevent leaching.

(ii) Compaction and covering of the waste to prevent it from being blown by wind.

(iii) Installation of a landfill gas extraction system to extract the gas for use in generation of power.

The use of modern landfill sites must be promoted due to the following reasons

(i) They stimulate the waste prevention *via* recycling and recovery of waste.

(ii) They create a uniform cost for the disposal of waste which consequently will prevent the unecessary transport of waste.

(iii) They prevent or reduce the negative effects on the environment, as well as the risks to human health arising from the landfilling of the waste.

Q.6 How does an electrostatic precipitator work?

Ans. Electrostatic precipitator can remove over 99% particulate matter present in the exhaust from a thermal power plant by the following mechanism

(i) It has electrode wires that are maintained at several thousand volts, which produce a corona that releases electrons.

(ii) These electrons attach to dust particles giving them a net negative charge.

(iii) The collecting plates are grounded and attract the charged dust particles.

(iv) The velocity of air between the plates is kept low enough to allow the dust to fall.

Q.7 Observe figure and answer the following questions.

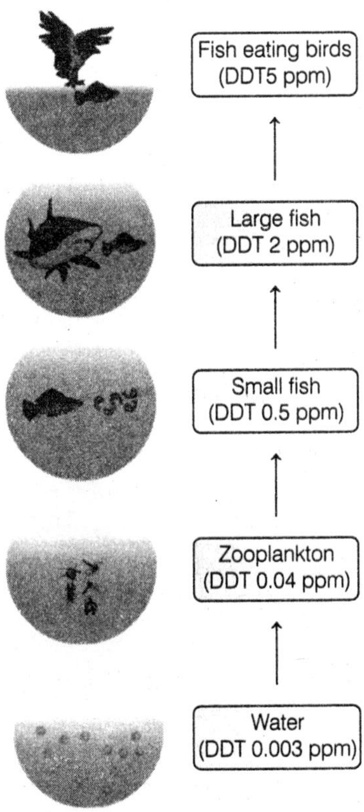

(i) What ecological term is used to describe the DDT accumulation at different trophic levels?

(ii) List any one effect of DDT accumulation on birds.

(iii) Will DDT accumulation lead to eutrophication?

(iv) Does it affect the BOD?

(v) Name disease caused by accumulation of any heavy metal.

Ans. (i) The ecological term used to describe the DDT accumulation at different trophic levels is called **biomagnification**.

(ii) High concentrations of DDT disturb calcium metabolism in birds, which causes thinning of egg shell and their premature breaking, eventually causing decline in bird populations.

(iii) No, DDT accumulation does not lead to eutrophication.

(iv) No, it does not affect BOD.

(v) Eating fish that has accumulated mercury, a heavy metal causes a disease called Minamata. It is characterised by diarrhoea, haemolysis, numbness, deafness, mental derangement, meningitis and death.